America Now

Short Essays on Current Issues

THIRTEENTH EDITION

EDITED BY

Robert Atwan

Series Editor, *The Best American Essays*

EXERCISES PREPARED WITH THE ASSISTANCE OF

Valerie Duff-Strautmann

Gregory Atwan

bedford/st.martin's
Macmillan Learning
Boston | New York

For Bedford/St. Martin's

Vice President, Editorial, Macmillan Learning Humanities: Edwin Hill
Executive Program Director for English: Leasa Burton
Program Manager: John E. Sullivan III
Executive Marketing Manager: Joy Fisher Williams
Director of Content Development, Humanities: Jane Knetzger
Executive Developmental Editor: Christina Gerogiannis
Assistant Editor: Cari Goldfine
Senior Digital Content Project Manager: Ryan Sullivan
Senior Workflow Project Manager: Lisa McDowell
Production Supervisor: Robin Besofsky
Advanced Media Product Manager: Rand Thomas
Project Management: Lumina Datamatics, Inc.
Editorial Services: Lumina Datamatics, Inc.
Composition: Lumina Datamatics, Inc.
Text Permissions Manager: Kalina Ingham
Text Permissions Researcher: Mark Schaefer, Lumina Datamatics, Inc.
Photo Permissions Editor: Angela Boehler
Photo Researcher: Krystyna Borgen, Lumina Datamatics, Inc.
Director of Design, Content Management: Diana Blume
Text Design: Lumina Datamatics, Inc.
Cover Design: William Boardman
Cover Image: Darren Hopes/Ikon Images/Getty Images
Printing and Binding: LSC Communications

Manufactured in the United States of America.

1 2 3 4 5 6 24 23 22 21 20 19

For information, write: Bedford/St. Martin's, 75 Arlington Street, Boston, MA 02116

ISBN 978-1-319-05657-5 (paperback)
ISBN 978-1-319-26844-2 (hardcover)

Acknowledgments

Destry Adams. "Why Students Should Care about Affirmative Action." *Technician,* January 22, 2019. Reprinted by permission of Technician, NC State Student Media.

American Civil Liberties Union (ACLU). "Speech on Campus." https://www.aclu.org/other/speech-campus. Reprinted by permission.

American Dialect Society. "2015 Word of the Year Is Singular 'They.'" americandialect.org, January 8, 2016. Copyright © 2016. Reprinted by permission.

American Dialect Society (press release). *Word of the Year: Fake News.* January 6, 2018. Reprinted by permission.

Text acknowledgments and copyrights continue at the back of the book on pages 405–7, which constitute an extension of the copyright page. Art acknowledgments and copyrights appear on the same page as the art selections they cover.

Preface for Instructors

People write for many reasons, but one of the most compelling is to express their views on matters of current public interest. Browse any website, social media, newsstand, or library magazine rack, and you'll find an abundance of articles and opinion pieces responding to current issues and events. Too frequently, students see the writing they do in a composition class as having little connection with real-world problems and issues. *America Now*, with its provocative professional and student writing — all very current opinion essays drawn from a range of sources — shows students that by writing on the important issues of today, they can influence campus and public discourse and truly make a difference.

The thirteenth edition of *America Now* offers a generous sampling of timely material. *America Now* is designed to immerse introductory writing students in the give-and-take of public dialogue and to stimulate thought, discussion, and composition. Its overriding instructional principle — which guides everything from the choice of readings and topics to the design of questions — is that participation in informed discussion will help generate and enrich student writing.

America Now encourages its users to view reading, thinking, discussing, and writing as closely interrelated activities. It assumes that (1) attentive reading and reflection will lead to informed discussion; (2) participation in open and informed discussion will result in a broadening of viewpoints; (3) an awareness of different viewpoints will stimulate further reflection and renewed discussion; and (4) this process in turn will lead to thoughtful papers.

The book's general introduction, "Expressing Opinions with Clarity, Confidence, and Civility," takes the student through these interrelated processes and offers some useful guidelines for engaging in productive discussion that will lead to effective essays. Two annotated student essays serve as models of persuasive writing. Instructors may also find helpful my essay "Writing and the Art of Discussion," which can be found in the instructor's manual.

New to This Edition

Following is a brief overview of the thirteenth edition of *America Now*. For a more in-depth description of the book, see "Using *America Now*" below.

Over half of the readings are new and were written since 2018, making *America Now* the most current short-essay reader available. These selections, while current, have been chosen because they will remain timely and relevant past the book's publication, and past any given semester — saving instructors time and providing students with a high-quality collection at a value. And as always, the readings are supported by the practical, trustworthy support for students for which *America Now* is known.

Two new chapter themes of high student interest, including "Immigration: Is It Our Most Serious Issue?" and "The News Media: How Well Does It Serve the Public?" offer multiple perspectives that students will want to read on issues they'll want to respond to.

New "connect" questions throughout the book offer opportunities for students to do more with their reading and writing — including developing their short responses into well-considered essays.

Using *America Now*

Professional and Student Writing from a Wide Variety of Sources

The book's selections by professional writers are drawn from a wide range of publications. As would be expected in a collection that focuses heavily on social trends and current events, *America Now* features several newspapers and news-oriented magazines, including the *Philadelphia Inquirer*, the *Chicago Tribune*, the *Atlanta Journal-Constitution*, the *New York Times*, and the *Washington Post Magazine*. With its additional emphasis on public discourse, this collection also draws on some of America's leading political magazines, including *The Nation*, *The Texas Observer*, *Pacific Standard*, and *The New Republic*. Also represented are magazines that appeal primarily to specialized audiences, such as *World Literature Today*, *Foreign Affairs*, and the newsletter of the

American Dialect Society. In general, the selections illustrate the variety of personal, informative, and persuasive writing encountered daily by millions of Americans. The readings are kept short (many under three pages, and some no longer than a page) to hold student interest and to serve as models for the student's own writing. To introduce a more in-depth approach to various topics, the book includes a few longer essays.

America Now also features student selections from both college newspapers and professional publications. These recent works reveal student writers confronting in a public forum the same topics and issues that challenge some of our leading social critics and commentators, and they show how student writers can enter into and influence public discussion. In this way, the student selections in *America Now* — many complemented by "Student Writer at Work" interviews — encourage students to see writing as a form of personal and public empowerment. This edition includes eight brief, inspiring interviews in which student authors in the book explain how — and why — they express their opinions in writing. In addition, the book contains two examples of student writing for a classroom assignment.

To highlight models of persuasive writing, each chapter contains an annotated section of a student paper labeled "Looking Closely." The comments point out some of the most effective strategies of the student writers in the book and offer advice for stating a main point, shaping arguments, presenting examples and evidence, using quotations, recommending a course of action, and more.

Timely Topics for Discussion and Debate

Student essays not only make up a large percentage of the readings in this book, but also shape the volume's contents. As we explored the broad spectrum of college publications — and reviewed several hundred student essays — we gradually found the most commonly discussed campus issues and topics. Issues such as those mentioned on page iv of this preface have provoked so much recent student response that they could have resulted in several single-topic collections. Many college publications do not restrict themselves to news items and editorial opinion but make room for personal essays as well. Some popular student topics are free speech, gender, racial and ethnic identity, and political polarization, all of which are reflected in the book's table of contents.

To facilitate group discussion and in-class work, *America Now* features twelve bite-sized units. These focused chapters permit instructors to cover a broad range of themes and issues in a single semester. Each can be conveniently handled in one or two class periods. In general, the chapters move from accessible, personal topics (language, for example) to more public and controversial issues (the Second Amendment, immigration, and the role of the news media), thus accommodating instructors who prefer to start with personal writing and gradually progress to exposition, analysis, and argument.

Since composition courses naturally emphasize issues revolving around language and the construction of meaning, *America Now* also includes a number of selections designed to encourage students to examine the powerful influence of words and symbols.

The Visual Expression of Opinion

Reflecting the growing presence of advertising in public discussion, among the book's images are opinion advertisements (or "op-ads"). These pieces, which focus on financial responsibility, encourage students to uncover the visual and verbal strategies of an advocacy group trying to influence the consciousness and ideology of a large audience.

Because we live in an increasingly visual culture, the book's introduction offers a section on expressing opinions visually — with striking examples from photojournalism, cartoons, and opinion advertisements.

The Instructional Apparatus: Before, During, and After Reading

To help promote reflection and discussion, the book includes a prereading assignment for each main selection. The questions in "Before You Read" provide students with the opportunity to explore a few of the avenues that lead to fruitful discussion and interesting papers. A full description of the advantages gained by linking reading, writing, and classroom discussion can be found in my introduction to the instructor's manual.

The apparatus of *America Now* supports both discussion-based instruction and more individualized approaches to reading and writing. Taking into account the increasing diversity of students (especially the growing number of speakers for whom English is not their first language) in today's writing programs, the apparatus offers extensive help with college-level vocabulary and features a "Words to Learn" list preceding each selection. This vocabulary list with brief definitions will allow students to spot ahead of time some of the words they may find difficult; encountering the word later in context will help lock it in memory. It's unrealistic, however, to think students will acquire a fluent knowledge of new words by memorizing a list. Therefore, the apparatus following each selection includes additional exercises under the headings "Vocabulary/Using a Dictionary" and "Responding to Words in

Context." These sets of questions introduce students to prefixes, suffixes, connotations, denotations, tone, and etymology.

Along with the discussion of vocabulary, other incrementally structured questions follow individual selections. "Discussing Main Point and Meaning" and "Examining Sentences, Paragraphs, and Organization" questions help guide students step-by-step through the reading process, culminating in the set of "Thinking Critically" questions. As instructors well know, beginning students can sometimes be too trusting of what they see in print, especially in textbooks. Therefore, the "Thinking Critically" questions invite students to take a more skeptical attitude toward their reading and to form the habit of challenging a selection from both analytical and experiential points of view. The selection apparatus concludes with "Writing Activities," which emphasize freewriting exercises and collaborative projects.

In addition to the selection apparatus, *America Now* contains end-of-chapter questions designed to stimulate further discussion and writing. The chapter apparatus approaches the reading material from topical and thematic angles, with an emphasis on group discussion. The introductory comments to each chapter highlight the main discussion points and the way selections are linked together. These points and linkages are then reintroduced at the end of the chapter through three sets of interlocking study questions and tasks: (1) a suggested topic for discussion, (2) questions and ideas to help students prepare for class discussion, and (3) several writing assignments that ask students to move from discussion to composition — that is, to develop papers out of the ideas and opinions expressed in class discussion and debate. Instructors with highly diverse writing classes may find "Topics for Cross-Cultural Discussion" a convenient way to encourage an exchange of perspectives and experiences that could also generate ideas for writing.

Acknowledgments

While putting together the thirteenth edition of *America Now*, I was fortunate to receive the assistance of many talented individuals. I am enormously grateful to Valerie Duff-Strautmann and Gregory Atwan, who contributed to the book's instructional apparatus and instructor's manual. Liz deBeer of Rutgers University contributed a helpful essay in the instructor's manual on designing student panels ("Forming Forums"), along with advice on using the book's apparatus in both developmental and mainstream composition classes.

To revise a text is to entertain numerous questions: What kind of selections work best in class? What types of questions are most helpful?

How can reading, writing, and discussion be most effectively intertwined? This edition profited immensely from the following instructors who generously took the time to respond to my revision plan for the thirteenth edition: Lysbeth Benkert, Northern State University; Lana Bogdanich, St. Augustine College; Kendra Bryant, Florida International University; Satwik Dasgupta, Spokane Falls Community College; Adam Floridia, Middlesex Community College; Kajsa Henry, Florida Agricultural and Mechanical University; Laura Jeffries, Florida State College at Jacksonville; Larisa Kradinova, Middlesex Community College; Kate McDonald, Mitchell College; Terry McNulty, Middlesex Community College; John Robertson, University of California, Santa Barbara; Guy Shebat, Youngstown State University; and Alexis Terrell, Oregon State University.

Other people helped in various ways. I'm indebted to Barbara Gross of Rutgers University, Newark, for her excellent work in helping to design the instructor's manual for the first edition. Two good friends, Charles O'Neill and the late Jack Roberts, both of St. Thomas Aquinas College, went over my early plans for the book and offered many useful suggestions.

As always, it was a pleasure to work with the superb staff at Bedford/St. Martin's. I thank Jane Knetzger, Leasa Burton, John Sullivan, Maura Shea, and Joy Fisher Williams for their continued support. I also am indebted to my developmental editor, Christina Gerogiannis. As usual, Christina provided excellent guidance and numerous suggestions, while doing her utmost best to keep a book that depends on so many moving parts and timely material on its remarkably tight schedule. Cari Goldfine, assistant editor, took care of many crucial details with grace and skill. Cari is also responsible for the student interviews that are such an important feature of this edition. Kalina Ingham, Mark Schaefer, Angela Boehler, and Krystyna Borgen expertly managed text and art permissions. Ryan Sullivan and Murugesh Rajkumar guided the book through production with patience and care, staying on top of many details. Finally, I especially want to thank cofounders of Bedford/St. Martin's, Charles H. Christensen and Joan E. Feinberg, for their deep and abiding interest in college composition. It has been a great pleasure and privilege to work with them.

Robert Atwan

Bedford/St. Martin's puts you first

From day one, our goal has been simple: to provide inspiring resources that are grounded in best practices for teaching reading and writing. For more than 35 years, Bedford/St. Martin's has partnered with the field, listening to teachers, scholars, and students about the support writers need. We are committed to helping every writing instructor make the most of our resources.

How can we help you?

- Our editors can align our resources to your outcomes through correlation and transition guides for your syllabus. Just ask us.
- Our sales representatives specialize in helping you find the right materials to support your course goals.
- Our *Bits* blog on the Bedford/St. Martin's English Community (**community.macmillan.com**) publishes fresh teaching ideas weekly. You'll also find easily downloadable professional resources and links to author webinars on our community site.

Contact your Bedford/St. Martin's sales representative or visit **macmillanlearning.com** to learn more.

Print and Digital Options for America Now

Choose the format that works best for your course, and ask about our packaging options that offer savings for students.

Print:

- **Hardcover or paperback.** To order the hardcover edition, use ISBN 978-1-319-26844-2. To order the paperback edition, use ISBN 978-1-319-05657-5.

Digital:

- **Innovative digital learning space.** Bedford/St. Martin's suite of digital tools makes it easy to get everyone on the same page by putting student writers at the center. For further details, visit **macmillanlearning.com/college/us/englishdigital**.
- **Popular e-book formats.** For details about our e-book partners, visit **macmillanlearning.com/ebooks**.
- **Inclusive Access.** Enable every student to receive their course materials through your LMS on the first day of class. Macmillan Learning's Inclusive Access program is the easiest, most affordable way to ensure all students have access to quality educational resources. Find out more at **macmillanlearning.com/inclusiveaccess**.

Your Course, Your Way

No two writing programs or classrooms are exactly alike. Our Curriculum Solutions team works with you to design custom options that provide the resources your students need. (Options below require enrollment minimums.)

- **ForeWords for English.** Customize any print resource to fit the focus of your course or program by choosing from a range of prepared topics, such as Sentence Guides for Academic Writers.
- **Macmillan Author Program (MAP).** Add excerpts or package acclaimed works from Macmillan's trade imprints to connect students with prominent authors and public conversations. A list of popular examples or academic themes is available upon request.
- **Bedford Select.** Build your own print handbook or anthology from a database of more than 800 selections, and add your own materials to create your ideal text. Package with any Bedford/St. Martin's text for additional savings. Visit **macmillanlearning.com/bedfordselect**.

Instructor Resources

You have a lot to do in your course. We want to make it easy for you to find the support you need — and to get it quickly.

From Discussion to Writing: Instructional Resources for Teaching America Now is available as a PDF that can be downloaded from **macmillanlearning.com**. In addition to chapter overviews and teaching tips, the instructor's manual includes sample syllabi and classroom activities.

How *America Now* Supports WPA Outcomes for First-Year Composition

This chart aligns with the latest WPA Outcomes Statement, ratified in July 2014.

2014 Desired Outcomes	Relevant Features of *America Now*
Rhetorical Knowledge	
Learn and use key rhetorical concepts through analyzing and composing a variety of texts.	• *America Now* is a collection of readings on many of today's most widely discussed topics. Students will learn and use key rhetorical concepts by analyzing and composing texts that are relevant to them and that inspire sincere debate and consideration. • The readings in *America Now* are diverse and topical. For example, Chapter 2, "Free Speech: Is It Endangered On Campus?" is timely and of high interest to students. In Chapter 5, "Identity: How Does It Shape Our Sense of Self?" students will learn and use key rhetorical concepts to analyze a variety of texts about identity. • Included in every chapter are exercises, such as "Vocabulary/Using a Dictionary" and "Discussing Main Point and Meaning," for learning and using key rhetorical concepts.
Gain experience reading and composing in several genres to understand how genre conventions shape and are shaped by readers' and writers' practices and purposes.	• *America Now* centers itself on understanding readers' and writers' practices and purposes. For example, throughout the book "Thinking Critically" questions present students with reflective, thoughtful prompts that help them realize how genre conventions inform the outcome of an essay. • The "Student Writer at Work" sections, popular with both instructors and students, throughout the book allow students to identify with and explore the purposes of other student writers. The essays featured represent several genres of student writing and provide in-depth analysis of composing strategies that work.

2014 Desired Outcomes	Relevant Features of *America Now*
Develop facility in responding to a variety of situations and contexts, calling for purposeful shifts in voice, tone, level of formality, design, medium, and/or structure.	• The introduction to *America Now* offers students six rules for participating in class discussion. This text encourages students to engage with and respond to a variety of situations and contexts by listening, speaking, and examining all sides of a discussion. • The introduction also defines opinion as a central theme of the book. With sections entitled "How Do We Form Opinions?" and "How to Support Opinions," *America Now* encourages students to consider shifts in voice, tone, and structure in reading and responding to a variety of situations. • Though the entire book focuses on opinions, Chapter 9, "Gender: What Are the Issues Today?" is particularly useful in instructing students on how best to respond to different rhetorical situations and contexts. In discussing gender, students will clearly see how writing calls for shifts in tone, structure, level of formality, or design. See the "Responding to Words in Context" questions following each essay.
Understand and use a variety of technologies to address a range of audiences.	*America Now* can be packaged with Bedford/St. Martin's digital learning tools to help students understand and use a variety of technologies in thinking and writing about topics covered in the book. Students can participate in interactive tutorials, take quizzes, and more.
Match the capacities of different environments (e.g., print and electronic) to varying rhetorical situations.	• See above (Bedford/St. Martin's digital learning tools). • Chapter 1 covers language and prompts students to consider how language has changed over time and how time has influenced the way we communicate.
Critical Thinking, Reading, and Composing	
Use composing and reading for inquiry, learning, thinking, and communicating in various rhetorical contexts.	• As previously discussed, "Expressing Opinions with Clarity, Confidence, and Civility," the introductory chapter in *America Now*, provides a framework for students to communicate in various rhetorical contexts. "The American Political Spectrum: A Brief Survey"

2014 Desired Outcomes	Relevant Features of *America Now*
	encourages reading for inquiry, learning, and thinking when confronted with the highly opinionated modern political landscape. • Another example is Chapter 3, "U.S. History: How Do We Remember Our Past?" which guides students through various rhetorical contexts and encourages them to grapple with questions around our history and our present. • The "America Then" essays at the end of each chapter offer students context for composing and reading essays on modern American topics. This reflection guides students toward learning and thinking about how these issues have shifted over time. For an example, see Langston Hughes's 1951 piece "That Word *Black*" in Chapter 1, "Language: Do Words Matter?"
Read a diverse range of texts, attending especially to relationships between assertion and evidence, to patterns of organization, to interplay between verbal and nonverbal elements, and to how these features function for different audiences and situations.	Before each of the readings in *America Now*, students will be prompted to consider the topic, attending to relationships between assertion and evidence and the interplay between verbal and nonverbal elements. Chapter 1, "Language: Do Words Matter?" among others, invites students to examine the interplay between verbal and nonverbal elements in writing. This chapter emphasizes the importance of word choice and how different words function for different audiences and situations. For another example, see Francie Diep's "Why Did We Ever Call Undocumented Immigrants 'Aliens'?" in Chapter 4.
Locate and evaluate primary and secondary research materials, including journal articles, essays, books, databases, and informal Internet sources.	*America Now* demonstrates to students that source material can come from anywhere, particularly in relation to writing about current topics. This book offers students a wide variety of such material to analyze, from journal articles and student essays to articles on the Internet and relevant historical documents.
Use strategies — such as interpretation, synthesis, response, critique, and design/redesign — to compose texts that integrate the writer's ideas with those from appropriate sources.	• *America Now* teaches students to compose texts that integrate their ideas with their understanding of differing opinions on American issues. Part of this is interpreting and synthesizing information from appropriate sources. For example, see

2014 Desired Outcomes	Relevant Features of *America Now*
	"Looking Closely: Supporting Opinions with Specific Examples" in Chapter 10. • Following each article, students will encounter a series of critical thinking questions that demonstrate key reading strategies like response, critique, and design/redesign.
Processes	
Develop a writing project through multiple drafts.	In Chapter 7's "Looking Closely: Effective Openings: Establishing a Clear Context for an Argument," students will learn how to lay the groundwork for developing their writing project. Prior to drafting an essay, students will learn the importance of summarizing the context of a given situation.
Develop flexible strategies for reading, drafting, reviewing, collaborating, revising, rewriting, rereading, and editing.	• *America Now* provides students with ample "Writing Activities," which appear in each chapter after the readings. Students will develop flexible strategies for reading and drafting thoughtful essays, building on the material they've just read. • In Chapter 1's student essay feature, "Looking Closely: Establishing Your Main Point," students will be asked to consider the simple yet important question of thesis clarity. Students will develop strategies for reading and drafting main points by looking at examples from other readings in this chapter. • The "Writing Activities" throughout the book get students thinking and reading about the strategies employed to persuade an audience. Students will develop their own strategies for collaborating and drafting writing.
Use composing processes and tools as a means to discover and reconsider ideas.	• The "Looking Closely" section in Chapter 8 covers persuasion. Understanding the audience as a composing process allows students to write more effective essays. Students will learn to discover and reconsider ideas by utilizing persuasion in college writing. • The "Student Writer at Work" feature in each chapter gives students insight into their peers' composing processes and enables them to develop, discover, and reconsider ideas.

2014 Desired Outcomes	Relevant Features of *America Now*
Experience the collaborative and social aspects of writing processes.	Each chapter of *America Now* features both professional and student essays so that students can experience the social nature of the writing process. In presenting students with various perspectives, *America Now* demonstrates the collaborative aspects of opinion writing.
Learn to give and act on productive feedback to works in progress.	The readings selected for *America Now* aim to get students to read about current events with a critical eye and apply the feedback they give to each reading (through discussion questions) to their own works in progress.
Adapt composing processes for a variety of technologies and modalities.	See section on Bedford/St. Martin's digital learning tools (p. xii).
Reflect on the development of composing practices and how those practices influence their work.	• Following the readings and preliminary questions in each chapter, students will move to "Discussing the Unit" exercises. This section allows students to reflect on the development of composing processes by considering the authors' intent, comparing various perspectives, and eventually writing an essay of their own. • The "Looking Closely" feature in Chapter 6 offers guidelines for reflecting on the development of composing processes in oppositional writing and considering how those differences influence the student's work.
Knowledge of Conventions	
Develop knowledge of linguistic structures, including grammar, punctuation, and spelling, through practice in composing and revising.	• Students will develop their knowledge of linguistic structures throughout *America Now* as they go. Often, instruction appears alongside activities for composing essays. • At the beginning of each reading selection in *America Now*, students will find an easy-to-navigate list of "Words to Learn," which includes the location of the word, the definition, and the part of speech that key word represents to help them develop their knowledge of spelling, grammar, and context.

2014 Desired Outcomes	Relevant Features of *America Now*
Understand why genre conventions for structure, paragraphing, tone, and mechanics vary.	In *America Now*, the genre conventions of structure, paragraphing, and tone, among others, are presented organically throughout each chapter. Often, these elements are posed as reading response questions, simultaneously encouraging students to consider the context and learn to recognize the mechanics.
Gain experience negotiating variations in genre conventions.	• See first section (p. xi). • The introduction includes information on the importance of photography. The "Visual Expression of Opinion" section offers students an overview of negotiating genre conventions in different kinds of texts. This section covers iconography, political cartoons, and symbolic photographs.
Learn common formats and/or design features for different kinds of texts.	• More than ever, it is important for students to explore a variety of design features and formats in analyzing and composing texts. *America Now* includes photographs and other visual material alongside written text so that students can make connections between the material in the book and the material they encounter on a daily basis. • *America Now* is divided by topic and theme, with an emphasis on public discourse. Students will learn common formats for different kinds of texts by reading a variety of texts. The selections in *America Now* range in length and design, to offer a more rounded reading experience.
Explore the concepts of intellectual property (such as fair use and copyright) that motivate documentation conventions.	Digital material offers further instruction on concepts of intellectual property and documentation conventions.
Practice applying citation conventions systematically in their own work.	Digital tutorials offer students practice in learning and applying citation conventions.

Brief Contents

Contents

2

Free Speech: Is It Endangered on Campus? 75

Should a university serve as a forum for robust, unflinching dialogue on public issues? Or is the old liberal ideal of free and open discussion a thing of the past? Do colleges today need to worry about what content is appropriate and what isn't?

3

U.S. History: How Do We Remember Our Past? 103

Can we hold figures from the past accountable for behavior considered acceptable in their time but not today? For example, should statues of famous people who owned slaves be toppled, even though the practice was legal in their day and even if their national contributions were outstanding? These are difficult questions in any era, but in today's society, with its ideals of diversity and inclusiveness, the debates can grow heated.

4

Immigration: Is It Our Most Serious Issue? 135

The U.S. has long been considered a land of immigrants, a country that not only welcomed the foreign-born but offered them the opportunities to thrive. Yet that ideal often falls short, and from time to time — especially during economic downturns and global conflicts — the welcome mat appears to be removed from the nation's doorstep. Is the system broken? Is immigration the nation's most urgent problem?

5

Identity: How Does It Shape Our Sense of Self? 167

If you ever saw TV commercials for Ancestry.com, you will notice how obsessed Americans seem to be with ethnic and national identities. Why is this? Why do so many people get excited when their DNA indicates they are part Irish, Scandinavian, or Native American? Does such identity truly define someone? Can our identity be both a blessing and a burden? And does today's notion of "identity politics" help us mutually understand each other or divide us further?

6

Race: Why Does It Still Matter? 199

With the groundbreaking election of the first African American president in 2008 and with his reelection in 2012, it appeared that the U.S. had finally set its disturbing racial history aside and entered, as many called it, a "postracial society." And yet recent years have witnessed anything but, as spontaneous protests and organized movements — largely provoked by police shootings — constantly called attention to the nation's ongoing racial strife. How deeply has the issue of race affected America's consciousness?

8 Feminism Today: What Are the Challenges? 273

Recent events have made it clear to many that — despite the enormous successes of the feminist movement over the years — women have still not achieved full equality. In the workplace, in the home, and in society women persistently face disadvantages. How can all the playing fields be leveled? Are men and women necessarily enemies? Does the commercial exploitation of feminism actually damage the cause? What have women gained from the #MeToo movement?

9

Gender: What Are the Issues Today? 299

With the rise of the feminist movement in the 1970s, the term *gender* took on increasing importance as a way to distinguish between one's biological sex and the sociopolitical construction of that sex. And with the rise of the LGBTQ+ movement, the word has taken on greater significance as society grows more accustomed to a more fluid and less stereotypical way of characterizing people.

10

The News Media: How Well Does It Serve the Public? 327

A healthy democracy depends upon an informed citizenry. But where does reliable information come from? Since we can't always depend on people in government — who usually have their own special interests to pursue — we tend to depend on the news media, trusting that they will be a source of accurate and unbiased information. That is why the First Amendment protects the rights to "freedom of speech, or of the press." Yet, how much trust can we put in the press? How politically biased are today's media? Are we drowning in "fake news"? Or is "fake news" itself another way to discredit news organizations that are doing their best to inform the public?

11

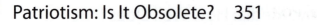

Patriotism: Is It Obsolete? 351

Opinion polls regularly show that most Americans believe their country is either the greatest or ranks among the greatest nations on earth. But that belief is shared more among older than younger Americans. In a 2017 Pew poll, only 12 percent of those between 18 and 29 thought the "U.S. stands above all other countries in the world," whereas close to half of Americans over the age of 65 agreed that we represent the best nation on earth. But does this mean that younger Americans are less patriotic? Is old-fashioned patriotism becoming obsolete? Do dissenting sports figures like Colin Kaepernick represent a growing trend? How is patriotism different from nationalism? And what does patriotism mean to those who don't fully share in the American Dream?

12

Political Polarization: How Disunited Is the United States? 377

Why is the nation so divided between left and right, blue and red, Democrat and Republican? Some commentators and pollsters even believe we are on the verge of another civil war. Would a return to civility help — or would it be futile? Is there anything that can be done to remedy the polarization? Or has our political divide been exaggerated?

A Rhetorical Table of Contents

America Now includes numerous examples of rhetorical strategies that aid us in expressing ourselves clearly, cogently, and convincingly. Listed below are eight of the most common rhetorical categories, with a brief account of how they are generally used in both verbal and visual texts. Nearly every selection in the book relies on more than one category, so you will find that several selections appear multiple times. The selections listed are those that most effectively demonstrate — either in whole or in their various segments — a particular strategy.

R.A.

1 Narration

Some uses: telling a story; reporting or summarizing a sequence of events; constructing a historical chronology; recounting a biography or autobiography; detailing how something is done or comes about; breaking down a process into a sequence of events.

2 Description

Some uses: creating a picture in word or image; making information more clear or vivid; reporting objective details.

3 Exemplification

Some uses: providing a "for instance" or "for example"; illustrating ideas; making something abstract more concrete; representing a larger concept or event by a single incident or image.

4 Definition

Some uses: clarifying key terms; reflecting on the significance of a word; enlarging or restricting a term's meaning; eliminating confusion or ambiguity; challenging conventional meanings and euphemisms.

5 Division and Classification

Some uses: dividing a subject into several key parts; organizing material into categories; making distinctions; constructing outlines; arranging ideas in the most appropriate order; viewing an issue from its various sides.

6 Comparison and Contrast

Some uses: finding similarities among different things or ideas; finding differences among similar things or ideas; organizing material through point-by-point resemblance or disparity; forming analogies; expressing a preference for one thing or position over another.

7 Cause and Effect

Some uses: identifying the cause of an event or trend; examining how one thing has influenced another; looking at the consequences of an action or idea; assigning credit, blame, or responsibility.

8 Argument and Persuasion

Some uses: convincing someone that an opinion is correct; defending or refuting a position; gaining support for a course of action; making proposals; resolving conflicts to reach consent or consensus.

About the Editor

Robert Atwan is the series editor of the annual *The Best American Essays,* which he founded in 1985. His essays, reviews, and critical articles have appeared in the *New York Times,* the *Los Angeles Times,* the *Atlantic, Iowa Review, Denver Quarterly, Kenyon Review, River Teeth,* and many other publications. For Bedford/St. Martin's, he has also edited *Ten on Ten: Major Essayists on Recurring Themes* (1992), *Our Times* (1998), and *Convergences* (2009). He has coedited (with Jon Roberts) *Left, Right, and Center: Voices from Across the Political Spectrum* (1996), and is coeditor with Donald McQuade of *The Writer's Presence.* He lives in California.

Introduction

Expressing Opinions with Clarity, Confidence, and Civility

It is not possible to extricate yourself from the questions in which your age is involved.

—Ralph Waldo Emerson, "The Fortune of the Republic" (1878)

What Is *America Now*?

America Now is a collection of very recent essays and articles that have been carefully selected to encourage reading, provoke discussion, and stimulate writing. The philosophy behind the book is that interesting, effective writing originates in public dialogue. The book's primary purpose is to help students proceed from class discussions of reading assignments to the production of complete essays that reflect an engaged participation in those discussions.

The selections in *America Now* come from two main sources: from popular, mainstream periodicals and from college newspapers. Written by journalists and columnists, by public figures and activists, as well as by professors and students from all over the country, the selections illustrate the types of material read by millions of Americans every day. In addition to magazine and newspaper writing, the book features a number of recent opinion advertisements (what I call "op-ads" for short). These familiar forms of "social marketing" are often sponsored by corporations or nonprofit organizations and advocacy groups to promote policies; programs; and ideas such as gun control, family planning, literacy, civil rights, and conservation. Such advertising texts allow the reader to pinpoint and discuss specific techniques of verbal and visual persuasion that are critical in the formation of public opinion.

I have gathered the selections into twelve chapters that cover today's most widely discussed issues and topics: gun control, racial identity, gender, free speech, feminism, immigration, and so on. As you respond to the readings in your discussion and writing, you will be actively taking part in some of the major controversies of our time. Although I have tried in this new edition of *America Now* to represent as many viewpoints as possible on a variety of controversial topics, it's not possible in a collection of this scope to include under each topic either a full spectrum of opinion or a universally satisfying balance of opposing opinions. For some featured topics, such as immigration or free expression, an entire book would be required to represent the full range of opinion; for others, a rigid pro-con, either-or format could distort the issue and perhaps overly polarize students' responses to it. Selections within a chapter usually illustrate the most commonly held opinions on a topic so that readers will get a reasonably good sense of how the issue has been framed and of the public discourse and debate it has generated. But if a single opinion isn't immediately or explicitly balanced by an opposite opinion or if a view seems unusually idiosyncratic, that in no way implies that the opinion or view presented is somehow editorially favored or endorsed. Be assured that questions following *every* selection will encourage you to analyze and critically challenge whatever opinion or perspective is expressed in that selection.

Participation is the key to this collection. I encourage you to view reading and writing as a form of participation. I hope you will read the selections attentively, think about them carefully, be willing to discuss them in class, and use what you've learned from your reading and discussion as the basis for your papers. If you do these things, you will develop three skills necessary for successful work in college and beyond: the ability to read critically, to discuss topics intelligently, and to write persuasively. These skills are also sorely needed in our daily lives as citizens. A vital democracy depends on them. The reason democracy is hard, said the Czech author and statesman Václav Havel, is that it requires the participation of everyone.

America Now invites you to see reading, discussion, and writing as closely related activities. As you read a selection, imagine that you have entered into a discussion with the author. Take notes as you read. Question the selection. Challenge its point of view or its evidence. Compare your experience with the author's. Consider how different economic classes or other groups are likely to respond. Remember, just because something appears in a newspaper or book — in print or online — doesn't make it true or accurate. Form the habit of challenging what you read. Don't be persuaded by an opinion simply because you believe you should accept it. Trust your own observations and experiences. Though logicians never say so, personal experiences and keen observations often form the basis of our most convincing arguments.

Participating in Class Discussion: Six Basic Rules

Discussion is a learned activity. It requires a variety of essential skills, including speaking, listening, thinking, and preparing. The following six basic rules are vital to healthy and productive discussion.

1. **Take an active speaking role.** Good discussion demands that everyone participates, not (as so often happens) just a vocal few. Many students remain detached from discussion because they are afraid to speak in a group. This fear is quite common — psychological surveys show that speaking in front of a group is one of our worst fears. It helps to remember that most people will be more interested in *what* you say than in how you say it. Once you get over the initial fear of speaking in public, your confidence will improve with practice.

2. **Listen attentively.** No one who doesn't listen attentively can participate in group discussion. Just think of how many senseless arguments you've had because either you or the person with whom you were talking completely misunderstood what was said. A good listener not only hears what someone is saying but also understands *why* he or she is saying it. Listening carefully also leads to good questions, and when interesting questions begin to emerge, you know good discussion has truly begun.

3. **Examine all sides of an issue.** Good discussion requires that we be patient with complexity. Difficult problems rarely have obvious and simple solutions, nor can they be easily summarized in popular slogans. Complex issues demand to be turned over in our minds so that we can see them from a variety of angles. Group discussion broadens our perspective and deepens our insight into difficult issues and ideas.

4. **Suspend judgment.** To fully explore ideas and issues, you need to be open-minded and tolerant of other opinions, even when they contradict your own. Remember, a discussion is not a debate. Its primary purpose is communication, not competition. The goal of group discussion should be to open up a topic so that everyone is exposed to a spectrum of attitudes. Suspending judgment does not mean you shouldn't hold a strong belief or opinion about an issue; it means that you should be receptive to rival beliefs or opinions. An opinion formed without an awareness of other points of view — one

continued

that has not been tested against contrary ideas — is not a strong opinion; it is merely a stubborn one.

5. **Avoid abusive or insulting language.** Free and open discussion occurs only when we respect the beliefs and opinions of others. If we speak in ways that fail to show respect for differing viewpoints — if we resort to name-calling or use demeaning and malicious expressions, for example — not only do we embarrass ourselves, but also we close off the possibility for an intelligent and productive exchange of ideas. Some popular radio and television talk shows are poor models of discussion: Shouting insults and engaging in hate speech are usually the last resort of those who have little to say.
6. **Be prepared.** Discussion is not merely random conversation. It demands a certain degree of preparation and focus. To participate in class discussion, you must consider assigned topics beforehand and read whatever is required. Develop the habit of reading with pen in hand, underlining key points, and jotting down questions, impressions, and ideas in your notes. The notes you bring to class will be an invaluable aid.

When your class discusses a selection, be especially attentive to what others think of it. It's always surprising how two people can read the same article and reach two entirely different interpretations. Observe the range of opinion. Try to understand why and how people arrive at different conclusions. Do some seem to miss the point? Do some distort the author's ideas? Have someone's comments forced you to rethink the selection? Keep a record of the discussion in your class notes. Then, when you begin to draft your paper, consider your essay as an extension of both your imaginary conversation with the author and the actual class discussion. If you've taken detailed notes of your own and the class's opinions about the selection, you should have more than enough information to get started.

What Are Opinions?

One of the primary aims of *America Now* is to help you learn through models and instructional material how to express your opinions in a persuasive, reasonable, civil, and productive fashion. But before we look at effective ways of expressing opinion, let's first consider opinions in general: What are they? Where do they come from?

When we say we have an opinion about something, we usually mean that we have come to a conclusion that something appears true or seems to be valid. But when we express an opinion about something, we are not claiming we are 100 percent certain that something is so. Opinion does not imply certainty and, in fact, it can be accompanied by some degree of doubt and skepticism. As a result, opinions are most likely to be found in those areas of thought and discussion where our judgments are uncertain. Because human beings know so few things for certain, much of what we believe, or discuss and debate, falls into various realms of probability or possibility. These we call opinions.

Journalists often make a distinction between fact and opinion. Facts can be confirmed and verified and therefore do not involve opinions. We ordinarily don't have opinions about facts, but we can and often do have opinions about the interpretation of facts. For example, it makes no sense to argue whether Washington, D.C., is the capital of the United States since this fact is a matter of record and can be established with certainty. Thus, we don't say we have an opinion that Washington, D.C., is the nation's capital; we know for a fact that it is. But it would be legitimate to form an opinion about whether that city is the best location for the U.S. capital and whether it should permanently remain the capital. For example:

- *Washington, D.C., is the capital of the United States of America* is a statement of fact.
- *Washington, D.C., is too poorly located to be the capital of a vast nation* is a statement of opinion.

Further, simply not knowing whether something is a fact does not necessarily make it a matter of opinion. For example, if we don't know the capital of Brazil, that doesn't mean we are then free to form an opinion about what Brazilian city it might be. The capital of Brazil is a verifiable fact and can be identified with absolute certainty. There is no conflicting public opinion about which city is Brazil's capital. The answer is not up for grabs. These examples, however, present relatively simple, readily agreed-upon facts. In real-life disputes, a fact is not always so readily distinguished from an opinion; people argue all the time about whether something is a fact. It's therefore a good idea at the outset of any discussion or argument to try to arrive at a mutual agreement of the facts that are known or knowable and those that could be called into question. Debates over gun control, for example, often hinge on the Second Amendment to the Constitution; that amendment is a fact, but the disputes arise from interpretations of that amendment (see Chapter 7).

An opinion almost always exists in the climate of other, conflicting opinions. In discourse, we refer to this overall context of competing opinions as public controversy. Every age has its controversies. At any given time, the public is divided on a great number of topics about which it holds a variety of different opinions. Often the controversy is reduced to two opposing positions — for example, we are asked whether we are pro-life or pro-choice, for or against government health care, in favor of or opposed to open borders, and so on. This book includes many such controversies and covers multiple opinions. One sure way of knowing that something is a matter of opinion is that the public is divided on the topic. We often experience these divisions firsthand as we mature and increasingly come into contact with those who disagree with our opinions.

Some opinions are deeply held — so deeply, in fact, that those who hold them refuse to see them as opinions. For some people, on certain issues there can be no difference of opinion; they possess the truth, and all who differ hold erroneous opinions. This frequently happens in controversies where one side in a dispute is so confident of the truth of its position that it cannot see its own point of view as one of several possible points of view. For example, someone may feel so certain that immigrants to this country should assimilate that he or she cannot acknowledge the possibility of another position. If one side cannot recognize the existence of a different opinion, cannot entertain or tolerate it, argues not with the correctness of another's perspective but denies the possibility that there can legitimately be another perspective, then discussion and debate become all but impossible.

To be open and productive, public discussion depends on the capacity of all involved to view their own positions, no matter how cherished, as opinions that can be subject to opposition. There is nothing wrong with possessing a strong conviction, with believing our position is the better one, or with attempting to convince others of our point of view. What is argumentatively wrong and what prevents or restricts free and open discussion is twofold: (1) the failure to recognize our own belief or position as an opinion that could be mistaken and (2) the refusal to acknowledge the possibility that another's opinion could be correct.

Is one person's opinion as good as another's? Of course not. Although we may believe that everyone has a right to an opinion, we certainly wouldn't ask our mail carrier to diagnose the cause of persistent heartburn or determine whether a swollen gland could be a serious medical problem. In such instances, we respect the opinion of a trained physician. And even when we consult a physician, in serious matters we often seek second and even third opinions just to be sure. An auto mechanic is in a better position to evaluate a used car than someone who's never repaired a car; a lawyer's opinion on whether a contract is valid is more reliable than that of someone who doesn't understand the legal nature of contracts. If an airline manufacturer wants to test a new cockpit instrument design, it solicits opinions from experienced pilots, not from passengers. This seems obvious, and yet people continually are persuaded by those who can claim little expert knowledge on a subject or an issue: For example, how valuable or trustworthy is the opinion of a celebrity who is paid to endorse a product?

When expressing or evaluating an opinion, we need to consider the extent of our or another person's knowledge about a particular subject. Will anyone take our opinion seriously? On what authority do we base our position? Why do we take someone else's opinion as valuable or trustworthy? What is the source of the opinion? How reliable is it? How biased? One of the first Americans to study the effects of public opinion, Walter Lippmann, wrote in 1925, "It is often very illuminating, therefore, to ask yourself how you get at the facts on which you base your opinion. Who actually saw, heard, felt, counted, named the thing, about which you have an opinion?" Is your opinion, he went on to ask, based on something you heard from someone who heard it from someone else, who in turn heard it from someone else?

How Do We Form Opinions?

How can we possibly have reasonable opinions on all the issues of the day? One of the strains of living in a democracy that encourages a diversity of perspectives is that every responsible citizen is expected to have informed opinions on practically every public question. What do you think about the death penalty? About the national debt? About the way the media cover the news? About the electoral college? Certainly no one person possesses inside information or has access to reliable data on every topic that becomes part of public controversy. Still, many people, by the time they are able to vote, have formed numerous opinions. Where do these opinions come from?

Although social scientists and psychologists have been studying opinion formation for decades, the sources of opinion are multiple and constantly shifting, and individuals differ so widely in experience, cultural background, and temperament that efforts to identify and classify the various ways opinion is formed are bound to be tentative and incomplete. What follows is a brief, though realistic, attempt to list some of the practical ways that Americans come by the opinions they hold.

1. *Inherited opinions.* These are opinions we derive from earliest childhood — transmitted through family, culture, traditions, customs, regions, social institutions, or religion. For example, young people may identify themselves as either Democrats or Republicans because of their family affiliations. Although these opinions may change as we mature, they are often ingrained. The more traditional the culture or society, the more likely the opinions that grow out of early childhood will be retained and passed on to the next generation.

2. *Involuntary opinions.* These are opinions that we have not culturally and socially inherited or consciously adopted but that come to us through direct or indirect forms of indoctrination. They could be the customs of a cult or the propaganda of an ideology. Brainwashing is an extreme example of how one acquires opinions involuntarily. A more familiar example is the constant reiteration of advertising messages: We come to possess a favorable opinion of a product not because we have ever used it or know anything about it but because we have been "bombarded" by marketing to think positively about it.

3. *Adaptive opinions.* Many opinions grow out of our willingness — or even eagerness — to adapt to the prevailing views of particular groups, subgroups, or institutions to which we belong or desire to belong. As many learn, it's easier to follow the path of least resistance than to run counter to it. Moreover, acting out of self-interest, people often adapt their opinions to conform to the views of bosses or authority figures, or they prefer to succumb to peer pressure rather than oppose it. An employee finds himself accepting or agreeing with an opinion because a job or career depends on it; a student may adapt her opinions to suit those of a professor in the hope of receiving a better grade; a professor may tailor his opinions in conformity to the prevailing beliefs of colleagues. Adaptive opinions are often weakly held and readily changed, depending on circumstances. But over time they can become habitual and turn into convictions.

4. *Concealed opinions.* In some groups in which particular opinions dominate, certain individuals may not share the prevailing attitudes, but, rather than adapt or "rock the boat," they keep their opinions to themselves. They may do this merely to avoid conflict or out of much more serious concerns, such as a fear of ostracism, ridicule, retaliation, or job loss. A common example is seen in the person who by day quietly goes along with the opinions of a group of colleagues but at night freely exchanges "honest" opinions with a group of friends. Some individuals find diaries and journals to be an effective way to express concealed opinions, and many today find online forums a space where they can anonymously "be themselves."

5. *Linked opinions.* Many opinions are closely linked to other opinions. Unlike adaptive opinions, which are usually stimulated by convenience and an incentive to conform, these are opinions we derive from an enthusiastic and dedicated affiliation with certain groups, institutions, or parties. For example, it's not uncommon for someone to agree with every position his or her political party endorses — this phenomenon is usually called "following a party line." Linked opinions may not be well thought out on every narrow issue: Someone may decide to be a Republican or a Democrat or a Green or a Libertarian for a few specific reasons — a position on war, cultural values, the environment, civil liberties, and so forth — and then go along with, even to the point of strenuously defending, all of the other positions the party espouses because they are all part of its political platform or system of beliefs. In other words, once we accept opinions A and B, we are more likely to accept C and D, and so on down the chain. As Ralph Waldo Emerson succinctly put it, "If I know your sect, I anticipate your argument."

6. *Considered opinions.* These are opinions we have formed as a result of firsthand experience, reading, discussion and debate, or independent thinking and reasoning. These opinions are formed from direct knowledge and often from exposure and consideration of other opinions. Wide reading on a subject and exposure to diverse views help ensure that our opinions are based on solid information and tested against competing opinions. One simple way to judge whether your opinion is carefully thought out is to list your reasons for holding it. Some people who express opinions on a topic are not able to offer a single reason for why they have those opinions. Of course, reasons don't necessarily make an opinion correct, but people who can support their opinions with one or more reasons are more persuasive than those who cannot provide any reasons for their beliefs (see "How to Support Opinions," p. 15).

This list is not exhaustive. Nor are the sources and types above mutually exclusive; the opinions of any individual may derive from all six sources or represent a mixture of several. As you learn to express your opinions effectively, you will find it useful to question yourself about the origins and development of those opinions. By tracing the process that led to the formation of our present opinions, we can better understand ourselves — our convictions, our inconsistencies, our biases, and our blind spots.

From Discussion to Writing

As this book amply demonstrates, we live in a world of conflicting opinions. Each of us over time has inherited, adopted, and gradually formed many opinions on a variety of topics. Of course, there are also a good number of public issues or questions about which we have not formed opinions or have undecided attitudes. In many public debates, members have unequal shares at stake. Eighteen-year-olds, for example, are much more likely to become impassioned over the government's reviving a military draft or a state's raising the legal age for driving than they would over Medicare cuts or Social Security issues. Some public questions personally affect us more than others.

Thus, not all the issues covered in this book will at first make an equal impact on everyone. But regardless of whether you take a particular interest in a given topic, this book invites you to share in the spirit of public controversy. Many students, once introduced to the opposing sides of a debate or the multiple positions taken on a public issue, will begin to take a closer look at the merits of different opinions. Once we start evaluating these opinions, once we begin stepping into the shoes of others and learning what's at stake in certain positions, we often find ourselves becoming involved with the issue and may even come to see ourselves as participants. After all, we are all part of the public, and to a certain extent all questions affect us: Ask the eighteen-year-old if he or she will be equipped to deal with the medical and financial needs of elderly parents, and an issue that appears to affect only those near retirement will seem much closer to home.

As mentioned earlier, *America Now* is designed to stimulate discussion and writing grounded in response to a variety of public issues. A key to using this book is to think about discussion and writing not as separate activities but as interrelated processes. In discussion, we hear other opinions and formulate our own; in writing, we express our opinions within the context of other opinions. Both discussion and writing require articulation and deliberation. Both require an aptitude for listening carefully to others. Discussion stimulates writing, and writing in turn stimulates further discussion.

Group discussion can stimulate and enhance your writing. For one thing, it can supply you with ideas. Let's say that you are participating in a discussion on the importance of ethnic identity. One of your classmates mentions some of the problems a mixed ethnic background can cause. But suppose you also come from a mixed background, and, when you think about it, you believe that your mixed heritage has given you more advantages than disadvantages. Hearing her viewpoint may inspire you to express your differing perspective on the issue. Your perspective could lead to an interesting personal essay.

Suppose you now start writing that essay. You don't need to start from scratch and stare at a blank page or computer screen for hours. Discussion has already given you a few good leads. You have your classmate's opinions and attitudes to quote or summarize. You can begin your paper by explaining that some people view a divided ethnic identity as a psychological burden. You might expand on your classmate's opinion by bringing in additional information from other student comments or from your reading to show how people often focus on only the negative side of mixed ethnic identities. You can then explain your own perspective on this topic. Of course, you will need to give several examples showing *why* a mixed background has been an advantage for you. The end result can be a first-rate essay, one that takes other opinions into account and demonstrates a clearly established point of view. It is personal, and yet it takes a position that goes beyond one individual's experiences.

Whatever the topic, your writing will benefit from reading and discussion, activities that will give your essays a clear purpose or goal. In that way, your papers will resemble the selections found in this book: They will be a *response* to the opinions, attitudes, experiences, issues, ideas, and proposals that inform current public discourse. This is why most writers write; this is what most newspapers and magazines publish; this is what most people read. *America Now* consists entirely of such writing. I hope you will read the selections with enjoyment, discuss the issues with an open mind, and write about the topics with purpose and enthusiasm.

The Practice of Writing

Suppose you wanted to learn to play the guitar. What would you do first? Would you search Google for articles on music theory? Would you then read some instructional books or watch some how-to videos on guitar playing? Might you try to memorize all the chord positions? Then would you get sheet music for songs you liked and memorize them? After all that, if someone handed you an electric guitar, would you immediately be able to play like Jimi Hendrix or Eric Clapton?

I don't think you would begin that way. You probably would start out by strumming the guitar, getting the feel of it, trying to pick out something familiar. You probably would want to take lessons from someone who knows how to play. And you would practice, practice, practice. Every now and then your instruction book or videos would come in handy. It would give you basic information on frets, notes, and chord positions, for example. You might need to refer to that information constantly in the beginning. But knowing the chords is not the same as knowing how to manipulate your fingers correctly to produce the right sounds. You need to be able to *play* the chords, not just know them.

Learning to read and write well is not that much different. Even though instructional books can give you a great deal of advice and information, the only way anyone really learns to read and write is through constant practice. The only problem, of course, is that nobody likes practice. If we did, we would all be good at just about everything. Most of us, however, want to acquire a skill quickly and easily. We don't want to take lesson after lesson. We want to pick up the instrument and sound like a professional in ten minutes.

Wouldn't it be a wonderful world if that could happen? Wouldn't it be great to be born with a gigantic vocabulary so that we instantly knew the meaning of every word we saw or heard? We would never have to go through the slow process of consulting a dictionary whenever we stumbled across an unfamiliar word. But, unfortunately, life is not so easy. To succeed at anything worthwhile requires patience and dedication. Watch a young figure skater trying to perfect her skills and you will see patience and dedication at work; or watch an accident victim learning how to maneuver a wheelchair so that he can begin again an independent existence; or observe a new American struggling to learn English. None of these skills are quickly or easily acquired. Like building a vocabulary, they all take time and effort. They all require practice. And they require something even more important: the willingness to make mistakes. Can someone learn to skate without taking a spill? Or learn a new language without mispronouncing a word?

What Is "Correct English"?

One part of the writing process may seem more difficult than others — correct English. Yes, nearly all of what you read will be written in relatively correct English. Or it's probably more accurate to say "corrected" English, because most published writing is revised or "corrected" several times before it appears in print. Even skilled professional writers make mistakes that require correction.

Most native speakers don't actually *talk* in "correct" English. There are numerous regional patterns and dialects. As the Chinese American novelist Amy Tan says, there are "many Englishes." What we usually consider correct English is a set of guidelines developed over time to help standardize written expression. This standardization — like any agreed-upon standards, such as weights and measures — is a matter of use and convenience. Suppose you went to a vegetable stand and asked for a pound of peppers and the storekeeper gave you a half pound but charged you for a full one. When you complained, he said, "But that's what *I* call a pound." Life would be very frustrating if everyone had a different set of standards: Imagine what would happen if some states used a red light to signal "go" and a green one for "stop." Languages are not that different. In all cultures, languages — especially written languages — have gradually developed certain general rules and principles to make communication as clear and efficient as possible.

You probably already have a guidebook or handbook that systematically sets out certain rules of English grammar, punctuation, and spelling. Like our guitar instruction book, these handbooks serve a very practical purpose. Most writers — even experienced authors — need to consult them periodically. Beginning writers may need to rely on them far more regularly. But just as we don't learn how to play chords by merely memorizing finger positions, we don't learn how to write by memorizing the rules of grammar or punctuation.

Writing is an activity, a process. Learning how to do it — like learning to ride a bike or prepare a tasty stew — requires *doing* it. Correct English is not something that comes first. We don't need to know the rules perfectly before we can begin to write. As in any activity, corrections are part of the learning process. You fall off the bike and get on again, trying to "correct" your balance this time. You sample the stew and "correct" the seasoning. You draft a paper about the neighborhood you live in, and as you (or a classmate or an instructor) read it over, you notice that certain words and expressions could stand some improvement. And step by step, sentence by sentence, you begin to write better.

Writing as a Public Activity

Many people have the wrong idea about writing. They view writing as a very private act. They picture the writer sitting alone and staring into space waiting for ideas to come. They think that ideas come from "deep" within and reach expression only after they have been fully articulated inside the writer's head.

These images are part of a myth about creative writing and, like most myths, are sometimes true. A few poets, novelists, and essayists do write in total isolation and search deep inside themselves for thoughts and stories. But most writers have far more contact with public life. This is especially true of people who write regularly for magazines, blogs, newspapers, and professional journals. These writers work within a lively social atmosphere in which issues and ideas are often intensely discussed and debated. Nearly all the selections in this book illustrate this type of writing.

As you work on your own papers, remember that writing is very much a public activity. It is rarely performed alone in an "ivory tower." Writers don't always have the time, the desire, the opportunity, or the luxury to be all alone. They may be writing in a newsroom with clacking keyboards and noise all around them; they may be writing at a kitchen table, trying to feed several children at the same time; they may be texting on subways or buses. The great English novelist D. H. Lawrence (1885–1930) grew up in a small impoverished coal miner's cottage with no place for privacy. It proved to be an enabling experience. Throughout his life, he could write wherever he happened to be; it didn't matter how many people or how much commotion surrounded him.

There are more important ways in which writing is a public activity. Writing is often a response to public events. Most of the articles you encounter every day in newspapers and magazines respond directly to timely or important issues and ideas, topics that people are currently talking about. Writers report on these topics, supply information about them, and discuss and debate the differing viewpoints. The chapters in this book all represent topics now regularly discussed on college campuses and in the national media. In fact, all the topics were chosen because they emerged so frequently in college newspapers.

When a columnist decides to write on a topic like the removal of Confederate statues or monuments on campus, she willingly enters an ongoing public discussion about the issue. She hasn't just made up the topic. She knows that it is a serious issue, and she is aware that a wide variety of opinions have been expressed about it. She has not read everything on the subject but usually knows enough about the different arguments to state her own position or attitude persuasively. In fact, what helps make her writing persuasive is that she takes into account the opinions of others. Her own essay, then, becomes a part of the continuing debate and discussion, one that you in turn may want to join.

Such issues not only are matters for formal and impersonal debate but also invite us to share our *personal* experiences. Many selections in this book show how writers participate in the discussion of issues by drawing on their experiences. For example, the essay by Dasia Moore, "When Does Renaming a Building Make Sense?" (see p. 113), is based largely on the author's personal observations and experience, though the topic — what to do about honoring historical figures with a racist past — is one widely discussed and debated by countless Americans. You will find that nearly every chapter in *America Now* contains a selection that illustrates how you can use your personal experiences to discuss and debate a public issue.

Writing is public in yet another way. Practically all published writing is reviewed, edited, and re-edited by different people before it goes to press. The author of a magazine article has most likely discussed the topic at length with colleagues and publishing professionals and may have asked friends or experts in the field to look over his or her piece. By the time you see the article in a magazine, it has gone through numerous readings and probably quite a few revisions. Although the article is credited to a particular author, it was no doubt read and worked on by others who helped with suggestions and improvements. As a beginning writer, you need to remember that most of what you read in newspapers, magazines, and books has gone through a writing process that involves the collective efforts of several people in addition to the author. Students usually don't have that advantage and should not feel discouraged when their own writing doesn't measure up to the professionally edited materials they are reading for a course.

How to Support Opinions

In everyday life, we express many opinions, ranging from weighty issues such as race relations or the environment to personal matters such as our Facebook profile. In conversation, we often express our opinions as assertions. An assertion is merely an opinionated claim — usually of our likes or dislikes, agreements or disagreements — that is not supported by evidence or reasons. For example, "Amnesty for illegal immigrants is a poor idea" is merely an assertion about public policy — it states an opinion, but it offers no reason or reasons why anyone should accept it.

When entering public discussion and debate, we have an obligation to support our opinions. Simple assertions — "Men are better at math than women" — may be provocative and stimulate heated debate, but the discussion will go nowhere unless reasons and evidence are offered to support the claim. The following methods are among the most common ways you can support your opinions.

1. **Experts and authority.** You support your claim that the earth is growing warmer by citing one of the world's leading climatologists; you support your opinion that a regular diet of certain vegetables can drastically reduce the risk of colon cancer by citing medical authorities.
2. **Statistics.** You support the view that your state needs tougher drunk driving laws by citing statistics that show that fatalities from drunk driving have increased 20 percent in the past two years; you support the claim that Americans now prefer smaller, more fuel-efficient cars by citing surveys that reveal a 30 percent drop in SUV and truck sales over the past six months.
3. **Examples.** You support your opinion that magazine advertising is becoming increasingly pornographic by describing several recent instances from different periodicals; you defend your claim that women can be top-ranked chess players by identifying several women who are. Note that when using examples to prove your point, you will almost always require several; one example will seldom convince anyone.
4. **Personal experience.** Although you may not be an expert or authority in any area, your personal experience can count as evidence in

continued

support of an opinion. Suppose you claim that the campus parking facilities are inadequate for commuting students, and, a commuter yourself, you document the difficulties you have every day with parking. Such personal knowledge, assuming it is not false or exaggerated, would plausibly support your position. Many reporters back up their coverage with their eyewitness testimony.

5. **Possible consequences.** You defend an opinion that space exploration is necessary by arguing that it could lead to the discovery of much-needed new energy resources; you support an opinion that expanding the rights of gun ownership is a mistake by arguing that it will result in more crime and more gun-related deaths.

These are only a few of the ways that opinions can be supported, but they are among the most significant. Note that providing support for an opinion does not automatically make it true or valid; someone will invariably counter your expert with an opposing expert, discover conflicting statistical data, produce counterexamples, or offer personal testimony that contradicts your own. Still, once you've offered legitimate reasons for what you think, you have made a big leap from "mere opinion" to "informed opinion." In each chapter of *America Now,* you will find a "Spotlight on Data and Research" feature that demonstrates how opinions can be supported by statistical data, surveys, polls, scientific studies, and laboratory experiments.

The American Political Spectrum: A Brief Survey

It's almost impossible to engage in public discourse today without immediately encountering terms like *liberal* and *conservative, right wing* and *left wing, libertarian* and *progressive.* Our discussion on public issues is largely framed by these affiliations, as well as by the big political parties (Republicans and Democrats) and the smaller ones (Tea Party, Green, and others) that are formed to advance the causes of those affiliations in government.

These terms don't necessarily account for how complex the spectrum of public opinion actually is. For the most part, however, the distinctions revolve around two key questions: What role should government play in regulating our behavior? and What role should government play in controlling the economy and our economic lives? Most Americans agree on having a representative government that is elected (and can be removed) and is responsible to the people. Commentators and op-ed columnists on all stretches of the spectrum more or less take this for granted. We also pretty much agree that the government should intervene in our lives at times, and should be restrained at other times.

Our debates are nearly always about exactly how much the state should intervene *socially* and *economically*.

In general, American liberals believe the government has a major role in regulating the economy, providing services that are available to everyone, and promoting economic equality among citizens. Conservatives often quote President Ronald Reagan's remark that "government is not the solution to our problem; government is the problem." Most conservatives believe that government mismanages money, that taxes should be lower, and that liberal social programs are wasteful and should be reduced or eliminated. Liberals gravitate toward government as the economic engine of a society, while conservatives believe that engine is the private sector.

Socially, conservatives tend to believe that individuals should be held to a standard of conduct consistent with past tradition. Many mainstream conservatives disapprove of same-sex marriage and abortion, think criminals should be punished harshly, and want religion to be a part of public life to some degree. Liberals mistrust government in the social sphere, and they tend to promote extended liberties, such as legalized protections for transgender people, and consider bans on abortion or severe penalties for drug use an invasion of personal privacy.

Of course, that's only the beginning of the story. Other points of view hover between these ideological pillars. Libertarians dislike the power of government in both the economic and social spheres. They argue that government should stay out of both the bedroom and the boardroom, advocating for much less intervention in the economy but often maintaining traditionally liberal positions on social issues. Many libertarians go further than both mainstream liberals and conservatives, arguing, for instance, that drugs should be legalized and the government should not deliberately manipulate the money supply or use taxes to reduce inequality. Opposite the libertarians are statists, believers in big government, who are economically liberal but socially conservative — this ideology is rather rare in the recent American political climate and the term is rarely used with positive connotations.

Centrists, however, are common but difficult to analyze. They either hold to a variety of positions too inconsistent with any one group to affiliate with it or take positions that fall between those of liberals and conservatives or libertarians and statists. For instance, a centrist position on gun control might be that government should be allowed to ban assault and automatic weapons, but individuals should have the right to keep handguns. Many centrists feel that the economy should shift to be more equitable, but gradually. Centrists are not, of course, automatically apathetic or dispassionate in their beliefs — their beliefs are simply in the middle. Politicians who are called moderate Democrats or moderate Republicans tend to be centrists.

There are quite a few other political positions in addition to these five groups. Progressives, for instance, believe that it's government's task to advance the human condition in a substantial way. Progressives are a great deal like liberals, but they focus more on using the levers of government to check the power that large institutions like corporations have in the public sphere. They often believe that society should aspire to something like total economic parity between people, a goal of which many mainstream liberals feel wary. Progressives have recently gravitated to the ideology of Democratic Socialism, popular in Europe, which calls for an aggressive approach to reducing modern wealth and income inequality, mostly involving much higher taxes for the wealthy and corporations. Progressives have often attacked mainstream liberal positions, and a number of politicians now call themselves progressives instead of liberals.

Populists, meanwhile, believe in the power of the people collectively, and desire the outcome that provides the most benefit to the most people. However, populists are typically antagonistic to government itself, which they believe to be part of a privileged elite.

Despite the many ideologies across the American political landscape, conversation is most often framed by the division between the two major political parties. It is oversimplified to say that Democrats are liberals and Republicans are conservatives, but it is a convenient place to start. You'll often hear references to "conservative Republicans" and "liberal Democrats," who take more extreme stances on some issues. Recently, the parties have faced pressure from various directions by factions within them — for instance, Democrats from the increasingly popular Democratic Socialists of America, and Republicans by both the Tea Party (a conservative libertarian faction) and populists, who helped elect Donald Trump. Trump is a Republican populist whose views are hard to pin down, but whose supporters are usually conservative. These supporters are bound more by mistrust of political elites, and sometimes by the political process itself.

Some issues, moreover, throw the Republican-conservative-Democratic-liberal equation off entirely. Consider military action, such as America's invasion of Iraq and Afghanistan. Not knowing any better, one might imagine Democrats would approve more of foreign wars, which cost money, create government jobs, and enhance the power of the government. However, those wars have, until recently, found more support from Republicans. Gun control is another issue in which conservatively aligned people tend to take the more socially liberal position: Government shouldn't make laws against guns in the name of maintaining law and order.

In response to these complications, many sociologists have developed a more geographical approach to the origin of American opinion. They point out that most American conservatives statistically live and vote more in rural and suburban areas. Their conservative opinions, these theorists argue, are a result of the landscape in which they live, where people are more isolated from each other, need and use government services less, and see fewer changes occurring around them. In these areas, religion, gun culture, and the military are traditional forces of social cohesion, perhaps explaining some of the anomalies listed above.

Liberals, however, are far more heavily concentrated in cities, where they are close to their neighbors, rely more heavily on government services like police and sanitation, and have more contact with people on all parts of the economic ladder. Tea Party member and former congresswoman Michele Bachmann once lampooned liberal Democrats by saying that their vision was for all Americans to "move to the urban core, live in tenements, [and] take light rail to their government jobs." Her joke contains a truth — many liberal positions seem concordant with urban life. Of course, in an age of unprecedented geographical mobility, it's an open question whether the places liberals and conservatives tend to live are the cause or the *result* of their opinions.

Free, Open, and Civil Discussion: The Challenges Today

As should be clear by now, *America Now* is intended to advance the ideal of free, open, and civil discussion as a way to both express our opinions and evaluate those of others in our conversation and writing. This ideal of discussion has been honored for centuries and is considered one of the foundations for the practice of democratic governments such as our own. It has not been a worldwide ideal, however, as many dictatorships and authoritarian regimes throughout the world remain in existence even today by suppressing the free discussion of ideas and punishing — at times by death — attempts to participate in such dialogue.

Yet how free and open can discussion be? Are there — even in free societies — limits and justifiable challenges to what someone can express? As many students are well aware, we are daily exposed to speech and opinions that are considered objectionable, unacceptable, offensive, inappropriate, insensitive, or inexcusable. Not a news cycle goes by where someone isn't vehemently attacking someone else's opinions with these very words, and you have only to read the comments section on any article to find opinions someone would object to. In a cover story, "Free Speech under Attack" (June 4, 2016), the *Economist* magazine observed "the swelling range of opinion deemed to fall outside civilized discourse." If free and open discussion has long been an ideal of modern democracy, why is so much expression now attacked and considered worthy of censorship? In summarizing eighteenth-century French philosopher Voltaire's passionate defense of free speech, British author Evelyn Beatrice Hall famously wrote: "I wholly disapprove of what you say, but I will defend to the death your right to say it." Have we reached an opposite position ("I wholly disagree with what you say and therefore you have no right to say it")? Has the once-lofty ideal of free expression been abandoned? Did it ever truly exist?

Democracies can often be tempestuous, and America has had its share of bitter conflicts, but many commentators believe that in the past twenty-five years the situation has worsened. For one thing, the nation has become increasingly polarized and fragmented (see "The American Political Spectrum: A Brief Survey," p. 16). This state of affairs has largely been blamed on the lack of a collegial and cooperative spirit in government and a determination of elected officials to defend their party's beliefs with no willingness to take into account opposing views. In other words, party becomes more important to politicians than the nation's welfare (though, of course, each party claims to be on the side of the people). Compromise — long considered the glue of representative democracy — is too often regarded as capitulation. So an overall turbulent political climate, in which opposing views are frequently demonized, has undeniably affected the ideals of free and open discourse.

Yet other factors are also at play. At the end of the twentieth century and the turn of the twenty-first, social media as we now know it barely existed. Today, politicians and political candidates tweet messages routinely, and everyone who cares to can voice opinions, no matter how crudely or offensively worded. More political opinion comes across the Internet unsupervised or un-curated than anyone living in 1993 (when the first edition of this book appeared) would ever have imagined. The number of news sites and political opinion blogs is hard to keep up with, while platforms like Twitter and Facebook allow anyone and everyone to share political opinions. Researchers have shown that when news sources become so fragmented, opinion becomes less diverse, not more, as audiences prefer to look at only the sources they agree with and have little patience or tolerance to see the other side's perspective or view all aspects of an issue. A 2018 Pew study showed that 68 percent of Americans say they sometimes get their news from social media, a format that rarely strives for balance of viewpoints and that tends to isolate readers in echo chambers of opinion.

So free, open, and civil discussion today meets more challenges than it did, say, a quarter of a century ago. To complicate matters, social media also introduced concepts that over the past few years have played a large role in affecting discussion on the campus and in the classroom. Two of these concepts — "trigger warnings" and "safe spaces" — have been widely publicized in the news media and are covered in the chapters that follow. They are concepts designed to protect students from potentially traumatizing material and hostile environments, but they can be easily caricatured as methods of coddling an overprotected younger generation incapable of confronting disagreeable ideas. Analysis and appraisal of these concepts will be taken up more fully in various selections throughout the book.

Perhaps the greatest advocate of free and open discussion was nineteenth-century British philosopher John Stuart Mill (1806–1873). In his once-classic but now little-read book, *On Liberty*, Mill took what could be called an extreme view of free discussion, which he considered a moral imperative. For example, in one famous statement he argues that "if all mankind minus one were of one opinion, and only one person were of the contrary opinion, mankind would be no more justified in silencing that one person, than he, if he had the power, would be justified in silencing mankind." Another statement demonstrates how seriously he took the stifling of opinion as a moral issue: "We can never be sure," he maintains, "that the opinion we are attempting to stifle is a false opinion; and, if we were sure, stifling it would be an evil still." Though it had its opponents, Mill's view of discussion was highly influential and helped form the groundwork of what used to be called classic liberalism.

We can wonder how a philosopher like John Stuart Mill might respond to the way issues are handled today, when certain topics are considered off limits, inappropriate, or simply problematic. His views have been challenged by some contemporary philosophers and social activists as examples of an elite reinforcement of power. Free and open discussion means nothing to people who aren't invited to the discussion or to those who are, through various means, eliminated from the discussion or to those who had no role in framing the terms or boundaries of the discussion. Whose voices get heard? The ideals of free and open discussion may be, some argue, an insidious way of making sure the public discussion of ideas is actually confined and restricted. And promoting the ideal of civility may be a way of preventing more urgent and less mannerly voices from being heard.

Mill's radical view of open discussion poses another problem, one highly relevant today. As can be easily inferred from the two quotations above, Mill regarded no issue or problem as "settled." For him, an opinion must be constantly and vigilantly tested, even though we are positive it is wrong. Should we then spend hour upon hour debating whether the earth is truly flat? It's unclear what Mill would have thought of those who, despite all hard evidence and testimony, deny that the Holocaust occurred. A large part of the climate-change debate is not about the facts that confirm or disconfirm that global warming was caused by humans; rather, it is about whether the matter is so "settled" scientifically that it is unethical to debate it at all. Thus, Mill's moral obligation that we must examine and weigh all opinions on a subject becomes in some cases an *immoral* imperative. For many, the patient sifting through of dubious opinion after dubious opinion just to be fair and open-minded may be a luxury our society can no longer afford.

The ideal of free and open discussion — as well as the many contemporary challenges to it — will play a large role in nearly all the chapters that make up this new edition of *America Now.*

Writing for the Classroom: Two Annotated Student Essays

The following student essays perfectly characterize the kind of writing that *America Now* features and examines. Written by Kati Mather, a student at Wheaton College in Massachusetts, and Erika Gallion, a student at Ashland University in Ohio, the essays will provide you with a convenient and an effective model of how to express an opinion on a public issue in a concise and convincing manner.

The essays also embody the principles of productive discussion outlined throughout this introduction. In fact, each essay was especially commissioned to perform a double service: to show a writer clearly expressing opinions on a timely topic that personally matters to her and, at the same time, to demonstrate how arguments can be shaped to advance the possibility of further discussion instead of ending it.

The two essays demonstrate two different ways of handling a topic — in this case, the value of a college education. In the first essay, Kati Mather's "The Many Paths to Success — with or without a College Education," a student expresses an opinion based on personal experience alone. In the second, Erika Gallion's "What's in a Major?," a student expresses an opinion by responding to an opposing opinion. In addition, the second example shows how opinions can be expressed with references to reading and research.

Although there are many other approaches to classroom writing (too many to be fully represented here), these two should provide you with accessible and effective models of the types of writing you will most likely be required to do in connection with the assignments in *America Now*.

Each essay is annotated to help you focus on some of the most effective means of expressing an opinion. First, read through each essay and consider the points the writer is making. Then, return to the essays and analyze more closely the key parts highlighted for examination. This process is designed to help you see how writers construct arguments to support their opinions. It is an analytical process you should begin to put into practice on your own as you read and explore the many issues in this collection. A detailed explanation of the highlighted passages follows each selection.

Expressing an Opinion Based on Personal Experience Alone

The first essay, Kati Mather's "The Many Paths to Success — with or without a College Education," expresses an opinion that is based almost entirely on personal experience and reflection. In her argument that Americans have grown so predisposed to a college education that they dismiss other forms of education as inferior, Mather shows how this common attitude can lead to unfair stereotypes. Her essay cites no formal evidence or outside sources — no studies, quotations, other opinions, or assigned readings. Instead, she relies on her own educational experience and the conclusions she draws from it to support her position.

Kati Mather wrote "The Many Paths to Success — with or without a College Education" when she was a senior at Wheaton College in Massachusetts, majoring in English and Italian Studies.

Kati Mather

The Many Paths to Success — with or without a College Education

1 Opens with personal perspective

(1) I always knew I would go to college. When I was 1
younger, higher education was not a particular dream of mine, but I understood that it was the expected path. Even as children, many of us are so thoroughly groomed for college that declining the opportunity is unacceptable. Although I speak as someone who could afford such an assumption, even my peers without the same economic advantages went to college. Education is important, but I believe our common expectations — that everyone can and should go to college, and that a college education is necessary to succeed — and the stigmas attached to those who forgo higher education, are false and unfair.

2 Establishes main point early

(2) In the past, only certain fortunate people could attain 2
a college education. But over time, America modernized its approach to education, beginning with compulsory high

school attendance in most states, and then evolving into a system with numerous options for higher learning. Choices for postsecondary education today are overwhelming, and — with full- and part-time programs offered by community colleges, state universities, and private institutions — accessibility is not the issue it once was. In our frenzy to adhere to the American dream, which means, among other things, that everyone is entitled to an education, the schooling system has become too focused on the social expectations that come with a college education. It is normally considered to be the gateway to higher income and an upwardly mobile career. But we would all be better served if the system were instead focused on learning, and on what learning means to the individual.

3
Supports main point

(3) It is admirable that we are committed to education 3
in this country, but not everyone should be expected to take the college track. Vocational education, for instance, seems to be increasingly a thing of the past, which is regrettable because careers that do not require a college degree are as vital as those that do. If vocational schooling were more widely presented as an option — and one that everyone should take the time to consider — we would not be so quick to stereotype those who do not attend traditional academic institutions. Specialized labor such as construction, plumbing, and automobile repair are crucial to a healthy, functioning society. While a college education can be a wonderful thing to possess, we need people to aspire to other forms of education, which include both vocational schooling and learning skills on the job. Those careers (and there are many others) are as important as teaching, accounting, and medicine.

Despite the developments in our educational system 4
that make college more accessible, financial constraints exist for many — as do family pressures and expectations, intellectual limitations, and a host of other obstacles. Those obstacles warrant neither individual criticism nor far-reaching stereotypes. For example, a handful of students from my high school took an extra year or two to graduate, and I sadly assumed that they would not be as successful as those who graduated on time. I did not stop to consider their situations, or that they might simply be on a different path in life than I was. Looking back, it was unfair to stereotype others in this way. Many of them are hardworking and fulfilled individuals today. (4) There is no law that says everyone has to finish high school and go

4
Provides examples of alternatives to college

to college to be successful. Many famous actors, musicians, artists, and professional athletes will freely admit that they never finished high school or college, and these are people we admire, who could very well be making more money in a year than an entire graduating class combined. Plus, we applaud their talent and the fact that they chose their own paths. But banking on a paying career in the arts or sports is not a safe bet, which is why it is so important to open all practical avenues to young people and to respect the choices they make.

We should focus on this diversity instead of perpetu- 5
ating the belief that everyone should pursue a formal college education and that those who do not are somehow inadequate. There are, of course, essential skills learned in college that remain useful throughout life, even for those who do not pursue high-powered careers. As a student myself, I will readily admit that a college education plays an important role in a successful life. (5) The skills we have the opportunity to learn in college are important in "real" life, and some of these can be used no matter what our career path. Among other things, I've learned how to interact with different people, how to live on my own, how to accept rejection, how to articulate what I want to say, and how to write. Writing is one of the most useful skills taught in college because written communication is necessary in so many different aspects of life.

5
Offers balanced view of alternatives

I hope that my college education will lead to success and 6
upward mobility in my career. But I can also allow that, once out of college, most students want to find a job that relates to their studies. In these hard times, however, that may not always be the case. I know from my own experience that other jobs — including those that do not require a college education — can be meaningful to anyone with the will to work and contribute. I'm grateful for the opportunities I've had that led to my college education, and though I do think we have grown too rigid in our thinking about the role of education, I also think we have the chance to change our attitudes and approaches for everyone's benefit.

6
Closes by summarizing position

(6) The widespread belief that everyone must go to 7
college to be a success, and that everyone *can* go to college, is not wholly true. Of course, many people will benefit greatly from a quality education, and a quality education is more accessible today than ever before. But college is not the only option. Hardworking people who do not take that path can still be enormously successful, and we should not

think otherwise. We can all disprove stereotypes. There are countless accomplished people who are not formally educated.

This country offers many roads to success, but we must remember that embracing diversity is essential to all of us. While I will not deny that my education has helped me along my chosen path, I firmly believe that, had I taken a different one, it too would have enabled me to make a valuable contribution to our society. 8

Comments

The following comments correspond to the numbered annotations that appear in the margins of Kati Mather's essay.

1. Opens with personal perspective. Mather begins her essay with an effective opening sentence that at once identifies her background and establishes the personal tone and perspective she will take throughout. The word *always* suggests that she personally had no doubts about attending college and knew it was expected of her since childhood. Thus, she is not someone who opted to skip college, and she is writing from that perspective. As a reader, you may want to consider how this perspective affects your response to arguments against attending college; for example, would you be more persuaded if the same argument had been advanced by someone who decided against a college education?

2. Establishes main point early. Mather states the main point of her essay at the end of paragraph 1. She clearly says that the "common expectations" that everyone should attend college and that only those who do so will succeed are "false and unfair." She points out that those who don't attend college are stigmatized. These general statements allow her to introduce the issue of stereotyping in the body of her essay.

3. Supports main point. Although Mather does not offer statistical evidence supporting her assumption that a college education is today considered a necessity, she backs up that belief with a brief history of how the increasing accessibility of higher education in the United States has evolved to the point that a college degree now appears to be a universal entitlement.

4. Provides examples of alternatives to college. In paragraph 3, Mather introduces the subject of vocational education as an alternative to college. She believes that vocational training is not sufficiently presented to students as an option, even though such skills are as "vital" to society as are traditional college degrees. If more students carefully considered vocational schooling, she maintains, we would in general be less inclined to "stereotype" those who decide not to attend college. In paragraph 4, she acknowledges how she personally failed to consider the different situations and options faced by other students from her high school class.

5. Offers balanced view of alternatives. In paragraph 5, Mather shows that she is attempting to take a balanced view of various educational options. She thus avoids a common tendency when forming a comparison — to make one thing either superior or inferior to the other. At this point in the argument, some writers might have decided to put down or criticize a college education, arguing that vocational training is even better than a college degree. By stating how important college can be to those who choose to attend, Mather resists that simplistic tactic and strengthens her contention that we need to assess all of our educational options fairly, without overvaluing some and undervaluing others.

6. Closes by summarizing position. In her concluding paragraphs, Mather summarizes her position, claiming that "college is not the only option" and reminding readers that many successful careers were forged without a college degree. Her essay returns to a personal note: Had she decided not to attend college, she would still be a valuable member of society.

Expressing an Opinion in Response to an Opposing Opinion

As mentioned earlier in this introduction, most of our opinions develop as a response to the opinions of others. It is difficult to imagine having an opinion in a complete vacuum. Much of the writing we encounter takes the form of a response to opinions that currently circulate in the media. In this case, the student essay is a response to a specific opinion piece that the *Washington Post* published in 2012: Michelle Singletary's "Not All College Majors Are Created Equal." The general topic — the value of a college education — has been covered frequently in the news ever since the economic downturn combined with a student loan crisis stimulated a broad discussion about the financial advantages of attending college. Singletary herself was responding to the general issue by arguing that college was worthwhile but only if one selected a major that paid off with high employment and competitive salaries.

We asked Erika Gallion to read Singletary's essay carefully and take notes on her responses, to note points she agreed with and others she didn't, to research other relevant material, and then to shape those responses and additional information into a short essay that presented her considered opinion on the issue. Note that Gallion, an English major, doesn't respond by recounting her own experiences and defending her career choice. Instead, she follows two of the most effective methods of composing an opinion essay: (1) she forms her opinion as a response to an opposing opinion and (2) she supports her response with additional reading and research that she discovered independently. These represent two common methods of learning to write for the classroom.

Erika Gallion (student essay)

What's in a Major?

1 *Cites opposing view concisely*

2 *Establishes main point early*

In January of 2012, columnist Michelle Singletary wrote a piece for the *Washington Post* titled "Not All College Majors Are Created Equal." (1) In it, Singletary discusses the importance of choosing a major that leads to a career after graduation — with the view that job preparation is the greatest benefit of a college education and, without it, the other benefits aren't worth the price. In fact, her essay implies that if a student selects a major that does *not* lead to a well-paying career right away, then attending college may not have been worth it. Although Singletary makes a good case for the importance of career planning, her essay fails to describe fully the meaning of a college education. (2) Colleges exist as more than preparatory schools for the job market and, despite the major students choose, we all generally benefit from attending college. 1

Singletary begins her argument by explaining a "game" she plays with college students in which she asks them their majors. She suggests that an English major, for example, without an internship will have no job after graduation, whereas an engineering major with three internships will find a job. Her argument that these majors are unequal is weakened because her example proves only that having one or more internships will benefit a student in a job search, regardless of the major. Of course an engineering major with three internships will find a job, but what about an English major who also took advantage of internships? Would she also have an equal chance of finding a job? (3) Singletary's scenario privileges engineering majors 2

3 *Challenges opponent's claim*

because it does not give students in the humanities, arts, and social sciences equal credentials.

Despite Singletary's argument that college is best taken 3
advantage of by students who enroll in a highly paid major, (4) there are many students today who simply want to pursue a certain subject because they love it. Singletary makes it seem as if students who choose to study the arts, humanities, or social sciences do not consider the worth of their major. But college is a serious investment, and it's safe to say that most of these students are completely aware of the extra schooling or work it will take to succeed in their area of interest. (5) Academic courses are more than simply strategy-sessions for a future career. As *Reason* editor Nick Gillespie writes in his article "Humanities Under Siege," "You should be going to college to have your mind blown by new ideas." If students feel truly passionate about their majors, their academic experiences will be much more interesting and desirable. The majors that Singletary views as unimportant because of the job market "will give you the tools to figure out who you are and what you want to be" (Gillespie). Career options represent only one aspect of a college education. And it's worth considering that if every prospective student were to major in engineering merely because of a more easily attainable career after graduation, those jobs would soon be all taken.

> 4
> *Offers an alternative argument*

> 5
> *Supports alternative view with apt quotations*

Most importantly, Singletary overlooks how much stu- 4
dents learn and grow outside of the academic curriculum. (6) As a result of a survey, the U.K.'s *Daily Mail* published a list of the top fifty lessons students actually learn during their time in college. The top three results are: budgeting and prioritizing, living with others, and doing a weekly food shop. Interestingly enough, only ten of these top fifty lessons have anything to do with academics at all. Most of these lessons involve cleaning, socializing, and making time for relaxation. The college years are a prime time for learning important and practical life lessons. College teaches more than just academics: In this sense, college majors *are* created equal.

> 6
> *Offers another view with support*

Although Singletary's concerns are understandable and 5
make perfect sense in this day and age, her desire for prospective students to major in only those areas that guarantee an immediate high-paying career is disappointing. (7) College benefits any student with an academic passion, whether it's English or engineering. As long as a student remains dedicated and determined, a major in any subject can be rewarding and worthwhile.

> 7
> *Summarizes her position*

8
Demonstrates sources

(8) Works Cited

Gillespie, Nick. "Where Higher Education Went Wrong." *Reason*, Apr. 2013, www.reason.com/archives/2013/03/19/where-higher-education-went-wrong/3.

Singletary, Michelle. "Not All College Majors Are Created Equal." *Washington Post*, 14 Jan. 2012, www.washingtonpost.com/business/not-all-college-majors-are-created-equal/2012/01/12/gIQAfz4XzP_story.html.

Smith, Jennifer. "Making Spaghetti Bolognese, Building Flat Pack Furniture and Going Three Nights without Sleep: What Students REALLY Learn at University." *Mail Online*, 12 Nov. 2013, www.dailymail.co.uk/news/article-2502847/What-students-REALLY-learn-university.html.

Comments

The following comments correspond to the numbered annotations that appear in the margins of Erika Gallion's essay.

1. Cites opposing view concisely. Because her readers may be unfamiliar with Singletary's position, Gallion needs to offer a brief summary. With little space for a detailed summary, she provides the gist of Singletary's argument in two sentences. Gallion's concision allows her to move straight into her own argument. But note that she will refer to various other points made by Singletary throughout the essay. Had she started with a full summary of Singletary's argument, including long quotations, the reader might feel burdened with too much extraneous information.

2. Establishes main point early. With little space to waste, Gallion clearly establishes her main point at the end of her first paragraph. As opposed to Singletary's view, she sees colleges to be "more than preparatory schools for the job market." One doesn't attend college simply for the purpose of finding a job. No matter what major students select, they will "all generally benefit from attending college." These comments show her dominant point of view, and the body of her essay will support and reinforce it.

3. Challenges opponent's claim. In crafting an opinion essay that takes an opposing view of another opinion, the writer should examine weaknesses in the opposing argument. Here, Gallion objects to an argument Singletary makes to support her point that all majors are not created equal. She points out that Singletary creates an unfair scenario in which an engineering major with multiple internships easily finds a job, and she contrasts this with an English major without internships who finds no job. Gallion argues that this argument is unfair because it "privileges" one major over another.

4. Offers an alternative argument. In effective arguments, it is usually not enough to discredit or refute an opponent's reasoning or claims. The writer ought to offer alternative arguments, other ways of viewing an issue. Note how Gallion accomplishes this by suggesting that many students attend college to study something they "love," and that this is sufficient motivation outside of selecting a major simply because it would make one more employable.

5. Supports alternative view with apt quotations. Gallion enhances her own point that students often select certain majors because they "love" them by citing remarks written by the political writer Nick Gillespie, who offers reasons for attending college that have nothing to do with the job market. Note that such quotations do not "prove" one's point, but they have the important effect of showing readers that other people, sometimes significant writers and experts, agree with your position and disagree with your opponent's. It is also important to note that the author she cites did not appear in Singletary's essay but that Gallion found the quotation independently, thus broadening the range of opinion.

6. Offers another view with support. Gallion develops her argument in opposition to Singletary's view by citing another source she found independently. Note that this source offers more objective data in the form of a survey that examined what students actually learn in college. As Gallion reports, these lessons have little to do with academics and more to do with practical skills. This information allows her to directly reverse Singletary's central claim. Since the lessons learned in college have little to do with the classroom and course work, majors are irrelevant. Or as Gallion points out: "In this sense, college majors *are* created equal."

7. Summarizes her position. In her concluding paragraph, Gallion summarizes her position. She concedes Singletary's concern about jobs, especially in today's world, but ends by saying she finds that point of view disappointing. Her final sentences restate the opinion she has expressed throughout her essay: that the benefits of a college education can apply to all majors.

8. Demonstrates sources. Gallion provides a "Works Cited" list to indicate the precise sources of her quotations. This list, arranged in alphabetical order by the authors' last names (not in the order that the citations appear in the essay), allows readers to find the works she cites.

STUDENT WRITER AT WORK

Erika Gallion

Courtesy of Erika Gallion

R.A. What inspired you to write this essay?

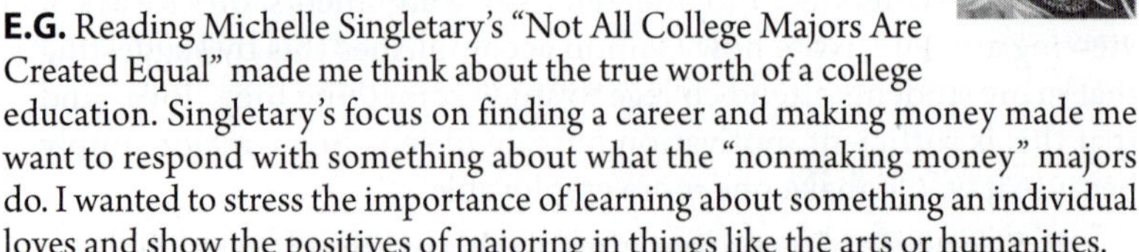

E.G. Reading Michelle Singletary's "Not All College Majors Are Created Equal" made me think about the true worth of a college education. Singletary's focus on finding a career and making money made me want to respond with something about what the "nonmaking money" majors do. I wanted to stress the importance of learning about something an individual loves and show the positives of majoring in things like the arts or humanities.

R.A. Are your opinions unusual or fairly mainstream given the general climate of discourse on campus?

E.G. I think there are a few who would agree with me, especially since I'm living on a liberal arts campus. But in the world of research, I think there's been much discourse about Singletary's view. More and more parents are stressing career-driven majors instead of valuing the education classes within the humanities (for example). And that worries me.

R.A. Who was your prime audience?

E.G. I wanted to specifically write this for potential students thinking or worrying about what to major in. I think it is important to advocate for things like true education and/or true passion. I also wanted to write to the current students majoring within the majors that Singletary views as unnecessary. I think it is empowering and comforting to see someone advocate for the opinions you have.

R.A. How long did it take for you to write this piece? Did you revise your work? What were your goals as you revised?

E.G. I drafted this about three times. It took me about two and a half weeks to completely finish it. The revision process included using more action verbs instead of using *is* a lot. I also focused on cutting things out that were unnecessary to the piece as a whole.

R.A. What do you like to read?

E.G. I love reading novels, short stories, essay collections, memoirs, poetry. Anything, really. As far as magazines go, I love reading *Time* and *National Geographic*. There are multiple blogs on tumblr that I frequently read. My heart lies in the literature realm.

R.A. What topics most interest you as a writer?

E.G. Issues surrounding multiculturalism and diversity. I love reading about different cultures and/or religions and the issues that surround them. As a writer, I like to attempt to tackle these issues because of how important they are in today's connected world.

R.A. Are you pursuing a career in which writing will be a component?

E.G. Yes. I'm going to graduate school for higher education administration, and afterward I hope to pursue a career at the university level helping with international student services. Being able to write well is essential in any career.

R.A. What advice do you have for other student writers?

E.G. Make time for it! I know how busy being a student is, but in order to develop writing skills, you have to sit down and spend time writing.

The Visual Expression of Opinion

Public opinions are expressed in a variety of ways, not only in familiar verbal forms such as persuasive essays, magazine articles, or newspaper columns. In newspapers and magazines, as well as in blogs and on social media, opinions are often expressed through photography, political cartoons, and paid opinion advertisements (or op-ads). Let's briefly look at these three main sources of visual opinion.

Photography

At first glance, a photograph may not seem to express an opinion. Photography is often considered an "objective" medium: Isn't the photographer simply taking a picture of what is actually there? But on reflection and careful examination, we can see that photographs can express subjective views or editorial opinions in many different ways.

1. A photograph can be deliberately set up, or "staged," to support a position, point of view, or cause. For example, though not exactly staged, the renowned World War II photograph of U.S. combat troops triumphantly raising the American flag at Iwo Jima on the morning of February 23, 1945, was in fact a reenactment. After a first flag raising was photographed, the military command considered the flag too small to be symbolically effective (though other reasons are also cited), so it was replaced with a much larger one and the event was reshot. The 2006 Clint Eastwood film *Flags of Our Fathers* depicts the reenactment and the photograph's immediate reviving effect on a war-weary public's patriotism. The picture's meaning was also more symbolic than actual, as the fighting on the island went on for many days after the flag was raised. Three of the six Americans who helped raise the famed second flag were killed before the fighting ended. The photograph, which was also cropped, is considered the most reproduced image in photographic history.

Joe Rosenthal/AP Images

"Flag Raising at Iwo Jima," taken by combat photographer Joe Rosenthal on February 23, 1945

2. A photographer can deliberately echo or visually refer to a well-known image to produce a political or an emotional effect. Observe how the now-famous photograph of firefighters raising a tattered American flag in the wreckage of 9/11 instantly calls to mind the heroism of the Iwo Jima marines. (See photograph on p. 35.)

3. A photographer can shoot a picture at such an angle or from a particular perspective to dramatize a situation, to make someone look less or more important, or to suggest imminent danger. A memorable photograph taken in 2000 of Cuban refugee Elián González, for example, made it appear that the boy, who was actually in no danger whatsoever, was about to be shot. (See photograph on p. 36.)

4. A photographer can catch a prominent figure in an unflattering position or an embarrassing moment, or in a flattering and lofty fashion. Newspaper or magazine editors can then decide based on their political or cultural attitudes whether to show a political figure in an awkward or a commanding light.

5. A photograph can be cropped, doctored, or digitally altered to show something that did not happen. For example, a photo of a young John Kerry was inserted into a 1972 Jane Fonda rally to misleadingly show Kerry's association with Fonda's anti–Vietnam War activism.

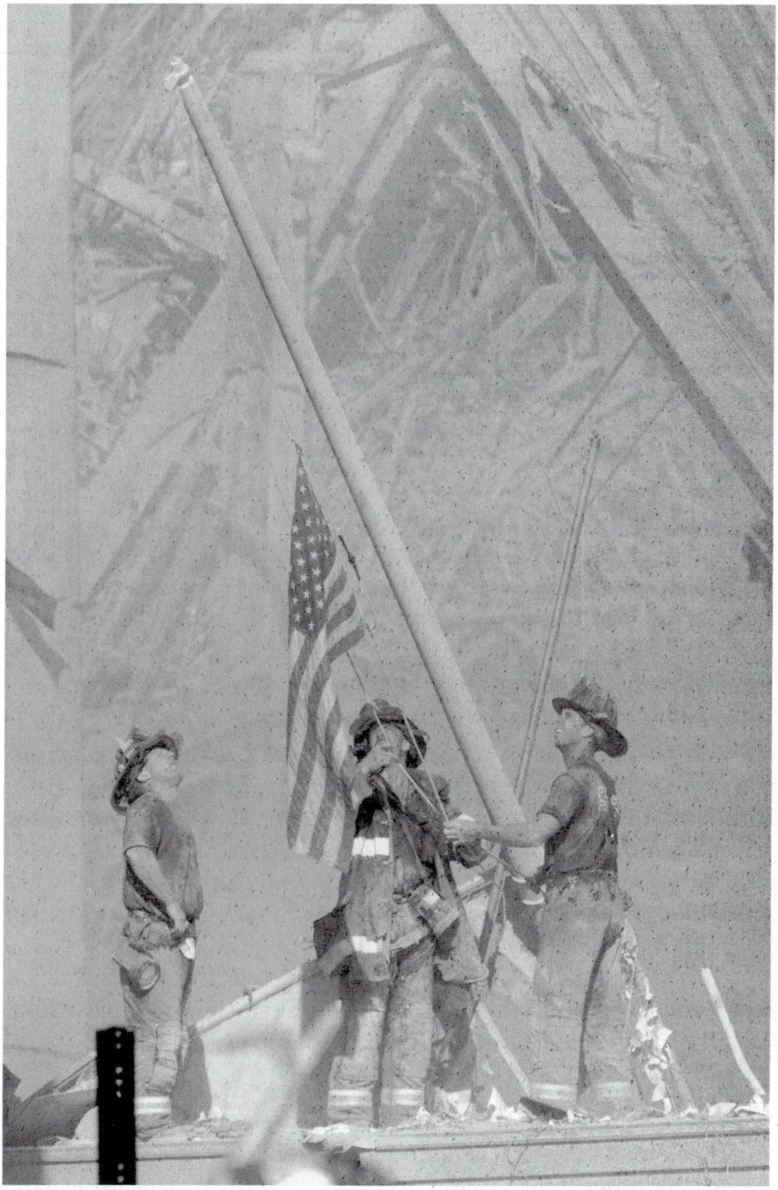

"Three Firefighters Raising the Flag," taken by Thomas E. Franklin, staff photographer for the *Record* (Bergen County, NJ), on September 11, 2001

ALAN DIAZ/AP Images

Federal agents seize Elián González from his Miami relatives to return him to his father in Cuba. Alan Díaz of the Associated Press won the Pulitzer Prize for this photo.

6. A photograph can be taken out of context or captioned in a way that is misleading.

These are only some of the ways that print and online media can use photographs for editorial purposes. Although most reputable news sources go to great lengths to verify the authenticity of photographs, especially those that come from outside sources, and enforce stiff penalties on photographers who manipulate their pictures, some experts in the field maintain that doctoring is far more common in the media than the public believes.

"We can no longer afford to accept news photography as factual data," claims Adrian E. Hanft III, a graphic designer, in an August 2006 photography blog. "If we are realistic," he continues,

> we will come to the conclusion that much of the photography in the news is fake — or at least touched up to better tell the story. It is relatively simple to doctor a photo and everybody knows it. . . . As photo manipulation becomes easier and easier . . . there is an increase in the demand for photographs that confirm what people want to believe. The market responds by flooding the world with "fake" photography. Today people can believe almost anything they want and point to photography that "proves" their beliefs.

Political Cartoons

The art of American political cartoons goes back to the eighteenth century; Benjamin Franklin was allegedly responsible for one of the nation's earliest cartoons. Almost from the start, political cartoonists developed what would become their favored techniques and conventions. Because cartoonists hoped to achieve an immediate intellectual and emotional impact, usually with imagery and a brief written message, they soon realized that exaggeration worked better than subtlety and that readily identified symbols were more quickly comprehended than nuanced or unusual imagery. The political cartoon is rarely ambiguous — it takes a decided position that frequently displays enemies negatively and friends positively. Rarely does a political cartoonist muddy the waters by introducing a mixed message or entertaining an opposing view. A cartoonist, unlike a columnist, cannot construct a detailed argument to support a position, so the strokes applied are often broad and obvious.

The humorous impact of most political cartoons depends on a combination of elements. Let's look at two relatively recent cartoons and examine the role of *context, iconography, exaggeration, irony, caption,* and *symbol.* Please note that the following cartoons are included for illustrative purposes only. They were selected not for their political and social opinions or for their artistic skill but primarily because they conveniently demonstrate the major elements and techniques of the political cartoon. Many other recent cartoons could just as easily have been selected.

First, a note about *context.* Chances are that if you don't know the political situation the cartoonist refers to, you won't "get" the cartoon's intended message. So it's important to remember that the cartoon's meaning depends on previously received information, usually from standard news sources. Most cartoonists expect their audience to know a little something about the news story to which the cartoon refers. Unlike the essayist, the cartoonist works in a tightly compressed verbal and visual medium in which it is unusually difficult to summarize the political context or the background the audience requires for full comprehension. This is one reason that cartoonists often work with material from headlining stories that readers are likely to be familiar with. In many cases, the audience needs to supply its own information to grasp the cartoon's full meaning.

Let's examine the context of the cartoon "Government Listens to Its Citizens" (see p. 39). The cartoonist expects his audience to be familiar with an ongoing news story: Documents leaked in the summer of 2013 showed that the National Security Administration (NSA) conducts extensive telephonic surveillance of people, including U.S. citizens, to an extent that made many Americans uncomfortable. The cartoon also plays on another, more perennial, complaint about the U.S. government — namely, that it is unresponsive to the needs and demands of its public. The cartoonist depicts the Capitol dome, seat and symbol of the U.S. legislature, literally flipped over to reveal a giant surveillance satellite dish. The message is clear — government *is*, in fact, listening to you, but maybe not in the ways you'd choose to have it do so. Notice how much the cartoonist expects the audience to bring to his cartoon, however. If you hadn't heard of the NSA spying scandal, the cartoon would be far more confusing. Imagine how you'd interpret the imagery if you didn't know the context of the cartoon.

Note the elements of *iconography*. Iconography is the use of shorthand images that immediately suggest an incident, idea, era, institution, and so on. Such images are intended to reflect immediately and clearly what they stand for. For example, a teenager with a pack of cigarettes rolled up inside the sleeve of his T-shirt is iconographic of the 1950s, a cap and gown indicate an academic, a briefcase represents a businessperson or a public official, horns and a pitchfork traditionally represent a devil. In this cartoon, the Capitol dome immediately suggests not only Washington but also all that American government is supposed to stand for: democracy, inclusiveness, openness, and justice for everyone. In the cartoon, this symbol of a people's government is turned on its head. On the other side is another icon — the parabolic dish that immediately conjures up thoughts of espionage, secrecy, and invasion of privacy.

Note, too, the cartoon's use of *exaggeration* and unrealistic depiction: We are not meant to think that the Capitol dome actually conceals a spy satellite, or — what would be equally ridiculous — that the controversial phone monitoring is going on in the Capitol building itself. The image is an extreme, hyperbolic representation of the frustrations its cartoonist wants to express. In expressing it as a cartoon, of course, he takes obvious liberties for the sake of demonstrating how big a problem he thinks the alleged spying is.

To "get" the cartoon's full meaning is to understand its clever use of *visual irony*. Although it's a large literary subject, irony can be understood simply as a contrast between what appears to be expressed and what is actually being expressed. The contrast is often humorous and could be sarcastic, as when someone says after you've done something especially dumb, "Nice work!" What appears to be expressed (verbally) in the cartoon is that the government is finally "listening" to its citizens, something many of those citizens have claimed it has failed to

ROLL CALL © MATSON
NSA
WHO SAYS GOVERNMENT DOESN'T LISTEN TO WHAT ITS CITIZENS HAVE TO SAY?

"Government Listens to Its Citizens," by *Roll Call* cartoonist R. J. Matson, published on June 17, 2013

do. What is actually expressed (visually) is that this statement is literally true, because it is "listening" to those citizens in a questionably legal way. Note also that this cartoon's irony is almost entirely dependent on its *caption* — without the apparently ordinary citizen delivering the line, with its telling double meaning of the word *listens,* the cartoon would have far less impact and meaning.

However, cartoons can be equally effective without a caption, and with few words to push their messages. Let's look at another cartoon from 2013, Nate Beeler's "Gay Marriage" (see p. 40). This cartoon comes on the heels of a decision by the U.S. Supreme Court striking down key aspects of the Defense of Marriage Act (DOMA), a 1996 law that refused gay and lesbian couples federal recognition for their marriages, even when states recognized them. The DOMA decision was seen as a major victory for gay rights, especially prior to the 2015 Supreme Court decision that made same-sex marriage legal in all states. In the cartoon, a gay couple celebrates the decision with a warm embrace, but it's an unexpected couple: Lady Justice, the personification of blind justice familiar from courthouses, and the Statue of Liberty.

"Gay Marriage" by *Columbus Dispatch* cartoonist Nate Beeler, published on June 26, 2013

Notice how the cartoonist tells a story with only one static image, rich in *symbol.* Justice appears to have dropped her iconic sword and scales as she's rushed into Liberty's arms, though she's still in her traditional blindfold. She carries the DOMA ruling with her, as if it's coming straight from the Supreme Court. Both characters look far more relaxed and joyous than they do in the well-known poses of the statues, signaling that this is a moment of jubilation for both. The image makes a conventional case for same-sex marriage to those who oppose it: These two women appear to be in love in the sense of the love that marriage exists to acknowledge. It's their symbolism, however, that makes this cartoon complete: The Supreme Court ruling not only has made the path for same-sex marriage easier but also is itself a kind of "marriage" between liberty and justice — a pair of words that immediately makes us think "for all."

Opinion Ads

Most of the ads we see and hear daily try to persuade us to buy consumer goods like cars, cosmetics, and cereal. Yet advertising does more than promote consumer products. Every day we also encounter numerous ads that promote not things but opinions. These opinion advertisements (op-ads) may take a variety of forms: political commercials, direct mail from advocacy groups seeking contributions, posters and billboards, or paid newspaper and magazine announcements. Sometimes the ads are released by political parties and affiliated organizations, sometimes by large corporations hoping to influence policy, and sometimes by public advocacy groups such as Amnesty International, the National Association for the Advancement of Colored People, the National Rifle Association, or — as we see on page 42 — the Ad Council, a nonprofit organization that distributes and promotes public service campaigns on a wide variety of important issues.

One of the Ad Council's recent campaigns attempted to promote financial literacy — that is, to advise people on how to think about the ways they waste money and to encourage them to save. These ads were prompted by the economic woes facing the nation over the past several years. Teaming up with the American Institute of Certified Public Accountants (AICPA), the Ad Council began targeting messages to those younger Americans who were feeling the financial pinch most severely. The ads used an image and text to persuade people to pay closer attention to the way they spend and directed them to an interactive site called "Feed the Pig," which offered practical tips on how to develop better spending habits and save money over time.

These three ads, which first appeared in magazines and newspapers, represent only a tiny sample of the hundreds of such ads readers come across daily. Carefully examining their verbal and visual techniques — regardless of whether you agree with the message — will help you become better acquainted with the essentials of rhetorical persuasion.

In print advertising, an ad's central argument is known as body copy, body text, or simply copy to distinguish it from the headline, illustrations, and other visuals. Note that all three ads reproduced here consist of three main elements: a visual image, a headline, and a body text in smaller type. This is typical of all kinds of advertising campaigns — whether print or digital — which try for a uniformity of design and message, though each particular ad may appear different. Let's look at these three elements — image, headline, and copy — more closely.

1. Image. Each advertisement features an arresting image that reinforces the ad's overall message. The creators of the ads clearly expect that readers will look first at the images, and therefore the creators want these images to be intriguing: A common french fry container stuffed not with fries but with rolled-up ten- and twenty-dollar bills visually makes the point that the food you may order for lunch is equivalent to money; familiar takeout containers strikingly packed into a safe like gold

Takeout can eat up your savings.
Pack your own lunch instead of going out. $6 saved a day x 5 days a week x 10 years x 6% interest = $19,592. That could be money in your pocket. Small changes today. Big bucks tomorrow. Go to feedthepig.org for free savings tips.
Ad Council
AICPA

Until this happens, start a savings plan.
Having money isn't about dumb luck. It's about a smart plan. Brew your own coffee, brown bag it to work, pay down that high-interest credit card. Saving just a few dollars a day can translate to literally thousands a year. And that's a much more reliable pile of gold. Small changes today. Big bucks tomorrow. Go to feedthepig.org for more free savings tips.
feedthepig.org

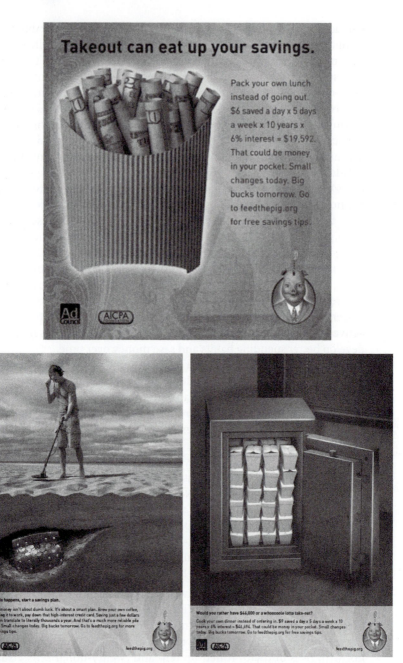

Would you rather have $44,000 or a whoooole lotta take-out?
Cook your own dinner instead of ordering in. $9 saved a day x 5 days a week x 10 years x 6% interest = $46,694. That could be money in your pocket. Small changes today. Big bucks tomorrow. Go to feedthepig.org for free savings tips.
feedthepig.org

bars also visually make the connection between food and money; and a young man searching a beach with a metal detector that is hovering over a buried pirate's chest drives home the notion of unrealistic financial dreams.

Ads are usually addressed to a particular audience, known in the advertising profession as the "target audience." This audience may be defined by sex, income, age, race, educational level, hobbies, or other characteristics. When an individual or a group is featured in an ad, it often signals that a particular audience is being targeted. Note that the only character that appears in these three ads is someone young. This suggests that the ad's creators are hoping to appeal to those in a younger age bracket, those who are still in a financial planning stage.

2. Headline. An effective headline needs to capture the audience's attention in a few words.

Though brief, headlines can be difficult to write since writers need to compress large amounts of content while still engaging the audience's interest. Each of the headlines reprinted here demonstrates some common feature of an effective headline:

Puns: When appropriate, headline writers like to use puns, such as "Takeout can *eat up* your savings." Puns are words or expressions that have two different meanings in the same context. "Eat up" can mean, literally, to devour food as well as to rapidly devour any commodity ("SUVs eat up a lot of gas").

Questions: Effective ads often use questions in their headlines. The questions are usually known as "rhetorical questions," meaning that the answer is obvious: "Would you rather have $46,000 or a whoooole lotta take-out?"

Image references: Some headlines like to refer the reader directly to the image. Images can only do so much persuasive work. Imagine how you would respond to the image of the young man with a metal detector if you had no verbal copy whatsoever. You would have no clue about what the image is intended to mean. The headline tells us how to "read" the image: "Until this happens, start a savings plan." Note that the key word in the headline is "this." The ad invites you to verbalize the image. We may all come up with different ways of saying it, but "this" will invariably refer to "luckily finding buried treasure."

3. Copy. Those writing and designing ads usually place the central argument in the body copy, which, as we can see from the financial literacy ads, constitutes the main text. Ads differ significantly in the amount of text used. Sometimes the persuasive elements can be simply an image and a headline. But often some verbal argument is employed to support the ad's message. The body copy will usually pick up details from the image and headline but will also supply new information. Two of the three ads encourage their audience to save money by packing their own lunch or cooking their own dinner and avoiding expensive takeout. The third ad encourages broader changes in habits.

Do the math: The first and last ads argue their point with simple arithmetic. If you pack your own lunch or cook your own dinner five times a week, then over a ten-year period you will be ahead $19,592 in lunches and $46,694 in dinners. Yes, that's an impressive $66,286 total. But where, an attentive reader might ask, are these numbers coming from? If we pack our own lunches and cook our own dinners, won't that cost something as well? We can't make lunch or dinner for nothing. Food may cost less at the supermarket than at a restaurant, but it still costs something. The ads claim that we will save $6 by packing our lunch and $9 by cooking dinner, but they don't say (a) how those costs are arrived at or (b) whether those amounts take into account what it costs to buy the food we prepare ourselves.

There's another bit of mystery in the math: Where does 6 percent interest come from? Most savings and checking accounts today offer interest rates that barely reach 1 percent. Are the ads suggesting that readers invest the money they are saving in other ways (the stock market?) and that this would be the average gain over ten years? And that there is no risk? This figure also remains unexplained.

Taglines: In advertising and marketing, a tagline is a memorable phrase closely associated with the brand or message that is repeated often in a campaign. Note that all three ads repeat (in addition to other language) the phrase "Small changes today. Big bucks tomorrow." The pun on "changes" is of course intentional. Small change now can accumulate into big bucks in the future. But, in this case, the word *changes* suggests not just coins but also a change in one's lifestyle.

Taking action: Most opinion ads often conclude with a call to take some direct action — vote, write, call, redeem a coupon, register a complaint, and so on. The financial literacy ads not only suggest that readers act to change their sloppy and wasteful economic habits but also invite them to visit a Web site called feedthepig.org for more savings tips. The pig stands for an old-fashioned piggy bank (and "feeding" again reinforces the connection between money and eating). Because of the Internet, an ad today is able to continue and expand its message in ways that could never have been done in earlier times.

Writing as Empowerment

Writing is one of the most powerful means of producing social and political change. Through their four widely disseminated gospels, the first-century evangelists helped propagate Christianity throughout the world; the writings of Adam Smith and Karl Marx determined the economic systems of many nations for well over a century; Thomas Jefferson's Declaration of Independence became a model for countless colonial liberationists; and the carefully crafted speeches of Martin Luther King Jr. and the books and essays of numerous feminists altered twentieth-century consciousness. In the long run, many believe, "The pen is mightier than the sword."

Empowerment does not mean instant success. It does not mean that your opinion or point of view will suddenly prevail. It does mean, however, that you have made your voice heard, that you have given your opinions wider circulation, and that you have made yourself and your position a little more visible. And sometimes you get results: a newspaper prints your letter, a university committee adopts your suggestion, you gain followers on social media, people visit your Web site or blog. Throughout this collection, you will encounter writing specifically intended to inform and influence a wide community.

Such influence is not restricted to professional authors and political experts. This collection features a large number of student writers who are actively involved with the same current topics and issues that engage the attention of professionals: gun control, feminism, racial and ethnic identity, gender differences, and so on. The student selections, all of them previously published and written for a variety of reasons, are meant to be an integral part of each chapter, to be read in conjunction with the professional essays, and to be criticized and analyzed on an equal footing.

America Now urges you to voice your ideas and opinions — in your notes, in your papers, in your classrooms, and, most important, on your campus and in your communities. Reading, discussing, and writing will force you to clarify your observations, attitudes, and values, and, as you do, you will discover more about yourself and the world. These are exciting times. Don't sit on the sidelines of controversy. Don't retreat into invisibility and silence. Jump in and confront the ideas and issues currently shaping America.

1

Language: Do Words Matter?

How do the words we use in ordinary conversation matter? Does it make any difference if we say *girl* instead of *woman* or *colored people* instead of *people of color*? Do some words indicate a hostile attitude? Do some words inflict harm? Can language — or words in themselves — be considered a form of violence?

In this opening chapter we will take a close look at some current words and phrases that have been considered offensive, inappropriate, or demeaning to many Americans. A good example to start with is the name of the Washington, D.C., football team, which has been the topic of a long-standing controversy, as many people feel the term *Redskins* disrespects and disparages Native Americans. Should fans and sportscasters continue to use this term even though there appears to be sufficient reason to consider it offensive? And what about other common words and expressions: should women be more careful about using the word *sorry*? Is the clichéd expression *thoughts and prayers* an easy way to avoid a serious matter? What does it really mean to call someone a Nazi or say someone is like Hitler? When we casually do so, are we trivializing the real victims of the Third Reich?

What's in a Name?

Our "In Brief" feature introduces a number of "sound bites" that focus on a controversy that has been in the news for decades: the name of the Washington football team. *Redskins* is a word that many Americans, both native and nonnative, find hostile, insulting, and racist. Is the term an ethnic slur from the past that is no longer appropriate, or is it simply a part of American sports tradition that was never intended to cause offense? A series of brief quotations demonstrates the range of opinion about this ongoing and often-heated controversy.

Native American images and logos have long been a part of the cultural history of the United States: A profile of an American Indian began appearing on the U.S. penny in 1859, and tobacco stores often featured a carved wooden statue of what became known as a "cigar store Indian" to attract customers. In 1912, the Boston baseball team (now in Atlanta) named itself the Braves, and three years later the Cleveland team began calling itself the Indians. The current Washington football team, which dates back to 1932, was soon after its founding renamed the Boston Redskins.

The controversy over the Redskins' name is not new but rather has been alive for decades, and every now and then it is reignited by a comment, demonstration, or newsworthy event. The main spark for the current heated controversy was the Washington team owner's categorical statement that he would never change the name. This prompted many media outlets to weigh in, and that led to a national debate on whether the word *Redskins* is a racial slur or an innocent label. Much of the debate was fueled by leading sports personalities. In October 2013, during a nationally televised game between the Redskins and the Dallas Cowboys (one of the biggest rivalries in sports, as their names indicate), NBC commentator Bob Costas called the word "an insult, a slur, no matter how benign the present-day intent." On the other side of the issue, former player, coach, and now ESPN commentator Mike Ditka had defended the name a few months earlier, calling the debate over it "so stupid it's appalling." His position was backed up by former vice presidential candidate and news personality Sarah Palin.

As you'll see in the following assorted sound bites, a number of people — despite what the team's owner declares — think the change of name is inevitable, that eventually enough political, economic, and social pressure will be put on the franchise so that a new name will be found. A large number of media outlets have stated that they will no longer use the word in print and on their broadcasts. The team also faces legal pressure from the government's trademark office, which decided the word was "disparaging" to Native Americans and therefore no longer eligible for trademark registration and protection. But in June 2017, the U.S. Supreme Court, hearing a similar case (*Matal v. Tam*), decided that the First Amendment protected disparaging speech and many accepted this as a victory for the Washington football team, though others — as the final sound bite shows — still believe the word is offensive and will continue to be challenged.

As you read the following comments, consider your position: Do you think the Redskins' name should be changed? If not, why not? And if you do, what name would you change it to?

Off in the distance the wheels of change are grinding. You may not be able to hear them yet. But it's only a matter of time until "Redskins" is gone.

— Sports columnist Tony Kornheiser
(*The Washington Post,* March 5, 1992)

The owners of professional sports franchises like the Cleveland Indians, the Atlanta Braves and the Washington Redskins continue to disrespect the heritage of Native American people with mascots and logos that insultingly portray aspects of our culture as a cheap cartoon — and nothing more.

— Ray Halbritter, Oneida Nation Representative
(*Daily News,* February 22, 2013)

We'll never change the name. It's that simple. NEVER — you can use caps.

— Dan Snyder, owner of the Washington
football team since 1999, to reporters in May 2013
(*USA Today,* May 10, 2013)

If I were the owner of the team and I knew that there was a name of my team — even if it had a storied history — that was offending a sizeable group of people, I'd think about changing it.

— President Barack Obama
(in an interview published by the Associated Press,
October 5, 2013)

The Redskins name will change sooner than you think — two or three years, tops.

— Sports columnist Chris Chase (*USA Today*, October 8, 2013)

No one picks a team name as a means of disparagement. San Francisco didn't choose the name "49ers" because it wanted to mock the foolish desperation of people panning for gold in the mid-19th century.

— Rich Lowry (*National Review Online*, October 8, 2013)

It is not that big a deal as long as you find a good name to replace the old one. I'd even prefer that you keep the Native American reference since this area of the country was home to several tribes. So here are my suggestions . . . : "Tribe"; "Nation"; "Rebels"; "Potomacs" and "Native Americans."

— Author and news commentator Juan Williams (*FoxNews.com*, October 13, 2013)

This page has for many years urged the local football team to change its name. . . . But the matter seems clearer to us now than ever, and while we wait for the National Football League to catch up with thoughtful opinion and common decency, we have decided that, except when it is essential for clarity or effect, we will no longer use the slur ourselves. That's the standard we apply to all offensive vocabulary.

— *The Washington Post* Editorial Board (May 22, 2014)

In the case of the Washington football team and the newly Supreme-Court-approved commercial protection of its racist name, please be advised, Mr. Snyder: your backdoor-victory doesn't mean the battle is over. The law says the word "redskin" remains, without question, a derogatory and racist term.

— Kevin Gover, Citizen of the Pawnee Nation of Oklahoma and director of the Smithsonian Institution's National Museum of the American Indian (si.edu, July 12, 2017)

POINTS TO CONSIDER

1. After reading the various sound bites, do you think the change of the Redskins' name is inevitable, despite the recent Supreme Court decision? Explain why or why not.

2. What do you think of Juan Williams's suggestions of alternative team names? Assuming you find the name Redskins inappropriate, what names would you suggest? Would you approve of "Washington Tomahawks"?
3. How do you respond to Rich Lowry's point that teams select names that indicate positive traits within the context of sports? In other words, is the name Redskins meant to honor Native Americans? If it is, is that a sufficient reason to keep the name?

Gene Weingarten

Thoughts and Prayers

[*The Washington Post*, October 29, 2017]

Sometimes when words or phrases are overused they do the opposite of what they were intended to express. In "Thoughts and Prayers," the popular columnist Gene Weingarten describes his reaction to hearing this "go-to banality" every time there is a national tragedy. Words intended to show sympathy and compassion become, by sounding routine and automatic, inauthentic and "knee-jerk." As Weingarten puts it, the phrase "suggests you have neither thought nor prayed, and have no intention of doing either. You are not only trite, but also a liar."

A two-time Pulitzer Prize–winning journalist, Gene Weingarten writes a weekly humor column for the Washington Post Magazine. *An excellent storyteller, he is the author of several books, including* The Fiddler in the Subway *(2010).*

BEFORE YOU READ

When do you hear the phrase "thoughts and prayers"? Do those words have meaning to you?

WORDS TO LEARN

withering (para. 1): devastating; scorching (adjective)
tragedies (para. 2): events causing destruction and distress (noun)
violate (para. 2): to fail to comply (verb)
consensus (para. 2): agreement (noun)
syntactic (para. 2): having to do with syntax (adjective)
sedition (para. 2): incitement to rebellion (noun)
vicinity (para. 5): area nearby (noun)
acerbic (para. 6): sharp; sarcastic (adjective)
authenticity (para. 9): genuineness (noun)
trite (para. 9): overused; stale (adjective)
template (para. 11) an example or model (noun)

Nothing can kill it. It has outlasted maniacs with machine guns. 1
It has withstood the fury of hurricanes and earthquakes. It has even endured withering satire — public ridicule of the sort that costs government officials their jobs — and each time it has come back in full force, unbowed and unashamed.

I am talking about "thoughts and prayers," the three-word hiccup of 2
a phrase uttered after tragedies by politicians, celebrities and ordinary folk. One's thoughts and prayers usually "go out to," or, less frequently, "are with" the victims and their families. Oddly, it is seldom "prayers and thoughts," as though that formulation so violates the consensus cliché, the go-to banality, that it approaches syntactic sedition.

The point is compassion and connection and a belief in something mightier than ourselves. So what's the problem?

As a fan of the Enlightenment, I think 3
"thoughts" are precious commodities. As a secular humanist I think "prayers" tend to reflect the better angels of our nature. Whether or not a deity is listening is beside the point: The point is compassion and connection and a belief in something mightier than ourselves.

So what's the problem? 4

The problem is that "thoughts and prayers" so often seems like a 5
reflex issued with all the forethought and sincerity of a "bless you" after a sneeze. ("Bless you" actually might be more sincere, at its self-involved core: In medieval Europe it was a prayer to ward off the Black Death, whose presenting symptom was often a blast into a hankie, dismayingly in your vicinity.) Particularly galling is when thoughts and prayers are issued by politicians after massacres whose underlying causes they have no courage to legislatively address.

Yes, I'm grumpy about this, and have been for a long time, 6
but I'm not alone. The splendidly acerbic political folk singer Roy Zimmerman has a viciously punny song about it. *"The congressperson semi-automatically declares / 'To the victims of this tragedy we send our thoughts and prayers.'"*

A YouTube video, already viewed a million times, advertises a 7
supposed app named TP that automatically posts your thoughts and prayers every time a new tragedy occurs. (A satisfied user giddily declares: "I feel like a better person, and I didn't have to do *anything*.")

You'd think that by now people would have re-crafted their sympa- 8
thies in a way that does not echo so hollowly. But no. The knee-jerk response is now just jerk. The numbers are startling. There were more

than 1,000 "thoughts and prayers" published on American news sites during the three days after the Las Vegas massacre.

To offer your thoughts and prayers is so instantly reactive and so lacking in authenticity that it suggests you have neither thought nor prayed, and have no intention of doing either. You are not only trite, but also a liar. Sorry. 9

How can we combat this scourge? The United States is about free speech. You can't legislate against a phrase any more than you can restrict people's access to weaponry with the ability to explode people's heads from great distances at enormous speed using military-issue firearms legally modified to exact maximum damage. 10

Or possibly we can. Possibly we can build upon a feeble template given to us by our state legislatures, which are trying to look as if they care. I propose a three-day "waiting period," between the time that you decide to issue your "thoughts and prayers" and the time you actually do. 11

Maybe given three days, 72 whole hours, we'll all think of something more productive to do. 12

Nice dream. But I don't think it has a prayer. 13

VOCABULARY/USING A DICTIONARY

1. What is a *satire* (para. 1)? Can you think of examples of *satire* that you have seen or read?
2. What is a *commodity* (para. 3)? What does the word usually refer to?
3. What is the root word of *dismayingly* (para. 5)? What part of speech is it?

RESPONDING TO WORDS IN CONTEXT

1. Why does Weingarten refer to "thoughts and prayers" as a *hiccup* (para. 2) of a phrase?
2. What *cliché* (para. 2) is Weingarten identifying in this article? What is a *cliché*?
3. What is a *pun*, and what does Weingarten mean when he says the song in paragraph 6 is *punny*?

DISCUSSING MAIN POINT AND MEANING

1. Though Weingarten takes a humorous stance, what serious national issue underlies the essay?
2. Aside from the fact that he thinks the phrase is a cliché, what else does Weingarten dislike about "thoughts and prayers"?
3. What does Weingarten say we should do about the phrase "thoughts and prayers"? What does he really think we should do?

EXAMINING SENTENCES, PARAGRAPHS, AND ORGANIZATION

1. What is the effect of Weingarten's use of the pronoun "it" in the first paragraph? Would the paragraph be different if he had used a more specific word or phrase?
2. What is the tone of this article? What examples can you find that support your description?
3. Why do you think Weingarten doesn't refer to the underlying issue of gun control more explicitly? If he had written about it explicitly, how would the focus of the essay change? Would the organization change?

THINKING CRITICALLY

1. From this essay, what can you tell about Weingarten's stance on gun control? Where do you see his position articulated in the writing?
2. How would Weingarten characterize politicians and legislators? What makes you think so?
3. When Weingarten says of the phrase "thoughts and prayers" that "nothing can kill it" (para. 1), do you think this is an exaggeration? How is it an exaggeration? How is it not?

WRITING ACTIVITIES

1. **Connect.** Both Fields ("Submerged in a Din of Identity Politics," p. 187) and Weingarten refer to what Abraham Lincoln called the "better angels of our nature" (Weingarten para. 3). Do you think either author is convinced that such a thing exists? How would these authors describe such angels (for example, are they weak or strong, active or passive)? Write an essay that explains how both authors perceive the "better angels of our nature," and compare their perceptions using examples from the texts.
2. Words can be a call to action or they can be an excuse to do nothing. Write a paper that argues, as Weingarten does, that words have effect or are ineffective. Choose a particular phrase or word (as Weingarten does, with "thoughts and prayers") that you will carefully examine in order to make your argument.
3. Try writing an article on a weighty topic (political issue or current event) in a humorous way. Think about tone, examples, organization. After you write it, take turns, in class, sharing your article and receiving feedback. Discuss where the writing succeeded and where it failed, and consider the same questions in the light of Weingarten's article.

Sarah Elliott (student essay)

Women: Stop Apologizing; Be Confident

[*Graphic*, Pepperdine University, October 28, 2015]

Is there anything wrong with saying the simple words "I'm sorry"? There could be if you are female, argues Pepperdine University student Sarah Elliott. In "Women: Stop Apologizing; Be Confident," Elliott argues that women are too inclined to apologize needlessly, a habit that hurts their chances at success. "Every day," she writes, "I sit in my classes and listen to girls apologize for speaking, for taking up too much time in discussion, for having an opinion."

Sarah Elliott wrote this essay when she was a student at Pepperdine University.

BEFORE YOU READ

Do women "cloak . . . thoughts" in ways that make them seem less powerful and educated than they are? Would women and men say the same things differently?

WORDS TO LEARN

insurmountable (para. 1): incapable of being overcome (adjective)
proficient (para. 1): skilled (adjective)
aspiration (para. 2): goal (noun)
linguistic (para. 4): belonging to language (adjective)
iconic (para. 5): relating to someone who is idolized (adjective)
audacity (para. 9): daring (adjective)
barrage (para. 9): an overwhelming quantity (noun)
simultaneously (para. 10): happening at the same time (adverb)
superfluous (para. 12): excessive; needless (adjective)

I was four years old during the 2000 presidential election, and quite fascinated with the concept of becoming a U.S. president. At four, it doesn't seem like such an insurmountable task to run a country, as I was perfectly proficient running the country of Beanie Babies in my bedroom. 1

It wasn't more than two seconds after I told my kindergarten teacher my new career aspiration when some boy sitting next to me piped up to say, "You can't be the president — you're a girl!" 2

If I had a dollar for every time I've heard those words, I could graduate debt-free. Too bad my dollar would only be worth 79 cents, 3 according to a 2014 report on the current pay gap from the Association of American University Women.

As a communication major and a woman, it's become apparent to me that social expectations set by a male-dominated society have driven women to code their communication to mask expressions of power or opinions. There's a reason why even a boy in a kindergarten class knew that girls aren't "allowed" to be president. Alexandra Petri illustrated this careful act of linguistic acrobatics perfectly in her October 13, 2015, opinion piece in the *Washington Post*, "Famous Quotes, the Way a Woman Would Have to Say Them during a Meeting." 4

"Give me liberty or give me death," Patrick Henry's iconic phrase from the American Revolution, becomes "Dave, if I could, I could just — I just really feel like if we had liberty it would be terrific, and the alternative would just be awful, you know? That's just how it strikes me. I don't know." 5

Try a more modern quote, such as FDR's "The only thing we have to fear is fear itself." Our friendly woman-in-meeting's version: "I have to say — I'm sorry — I have to say this. I don't think we should be as scared of non-fear things as maybe we are? If that makes sense? Sorry, I feel like I'm rambling." 6

If these translations sound familiar, it's because they are. You don't have to be in a meeting to hear a girl spin a turn of phrase like this; you could simply walk into a college classroom and wait. 7

Every day I sit in my classes and listen to girls apologize for speaking, for taking up too much time in discussion, for having an opinion.

Every day I sit in my classes and listen to girls apologize for speaking, for taking up too much time in discussion, for having an opinion. And if an opinion is expressed, half the time it comes with a disclaimer, mentioning how it's "probably not right" or finishing off with an "I don't know." 8

In the academic setting, much like the workplace, women are conditioned to say "I'm sorry" for everything: taking up their professors' time, asking questions, offering help — even reporting sexual harassment has become somewhat of an apologetic practice. We can never be too careful, because dropping the meek, gentle facade leaves us vulnerable to labels such as "bossy" or "feisty" or everyone's favorite b-word. Just look at Hillary Clinton, a woman who has the audacity to run for the presidency — like hundreds of men before her — only to be stoned by the media with a barrage of these misogynistic words. 9

Because our female role models are treated like this in the public eye, it follows quite logically that women shy away from creating spaces for themselves in powerful roles. According to statistics from 10 the *Washington Post* and the Pew Research Center, respectively, only 4.6 percent of Fortune 500 CEOs are women, and only 19 percent of our current Congress is female (which is, sadly, the largest number we've ever had). Those who do manage to break gender barriers suffer from criticisms in areas men don't receive: We are simultaneously too fat and too skinny, too ugly and too pretty, too smart and too stupid.

There's no middle ground for a powerful woman. The higher 11
women get on the totem pole of accomplishment, the more they suffer from the sinking realization that the patriarchy of their own society does not want them there.

So here's the challenge for all my Pepperdine ladies: Let's stop 12
cloaking our thoughts in superfluous disclaimers and start speaking like we deserve to be where we are, because we do. Our aspirations do not have to be limited to future first ladies, so we shouldn't have to be afraid of speaking like the educated, powerful, and influential women we are.

During a discussion at Georgetown University in February, 13
Supreme Court Justice Ruth Bader Ginsburg was asked when she thinks there will be enough women on the Supreme Court. She said, "My answer is when there are nine."

When do I think there will be enough women in the White House? 14
When kindergarten boys stop telling four-year-old girls who gets to run the country.

VOCABULARY/USING A DICTIONARY

1. What does it mean if one is *debt-free* (para. 3)?
2. What happens when one performs *acrobatics* (para. 4)?
3. What part of speech is *misogynistic* (para. 9)? What is its root word?

RESPONDING TO WORDS IN CONTEXT

1. If "it's probably not right" or "I don't know" is a *disclaimer* (para. 8), how would you define the word?
2. If someone is *conditioned* (para. 9) to do something, what is controlling his or her choices?
3. What is a *facade* (para. 9)? What does it mean in this context?

DISCUSSING MAIN POINT AND MEANING

1. Why, according to Elliott, do women tend to apologize?
2. Elliott brings Hillary Clinton in as an example of what happens to women when they present themselves as strong and unapologetic. What has happened to Clinton, according to Elliott?
3. Elliott offers a challenge at the end of her essay. What is it? Why does she offer it?

EXAMINING SENTENCES, PARAGRAPHS, AND ORGANIZATION

1. Why do you think Elliott introduces information about her college major in the fourth paragraph? Is there a benefit to knowing her major?
2. Explain the differences between the famous phrases Elliott introduces and the women's versions she imagines. Choose an aspect of the examples to focus on, such as the sound or the length of the statement.
3. Elliott begins one of her sentences with "If I had a dollar for every time I've heard those words." How does she turn that trite phrase into something meaningful and to the point?

THINKING CRITICALLY

1. Why would a boy in kindergarten think a girl couldn't be president in 2000?
2. What are the differences between the famous quotations (by men) and the reworkings of these statements by women? Based on what you see, what else could Elliott ask women to stop saying, besides "sorry"?
3. Elliott writes, "The higher women get on the totem pole of accomplishment, the more they suffer from the sinking realization that the patriarchy of their own society does not want them there" (para. 11). What gains have women made in terms of the totem pole of accomplishment, given what you learn in this article?

WRITING ACTIVITIES

1. Do you notice differences in the way men and women speak in the classroom, workplace, or public places? Try to identify a difference in words, tone, or style, and write about how men and women communicate differently.
2. With whom does Elliott begin the essay? With whom does she end it? Describe the arc of the essay, with an eye on the women mentioned throughout. How do her examples of women at the beginning and the end underscore her point?
3. Think about the labels Elliott mentions in the essay ("bossy," "feisty," "b-word"). What sort of labels do all of us — men and women — encounter every day? Are these based on stereotypes? Describe, in a short freewriting exercise, labels you've encountered (for yourself or others), what they are based on, and your reaction to them.

LOOKING CLOSELY

Establishing Your Main Point

As you learn to express opinions clearly and effectively in writing, you need to ask yourself a relatively simple question: What is my main point? In composition, a main point is sometimes called a thesis or a thesis statement. It is often a sentence or two that summarizes your central idea or position. It need not include any factual proof or supporting evidence — that can be supplied in the body of your essay — but it should represent a general statement that clearly shows where you stand on an issue, what you are attacking or defending, and what exactly your essay is about. Although main points are often found in opening paragraphs, they can also appear later on in an essay, especially when the writer wants to set the stage for his or her opinion by opening with a topical reference, an emotional appeal, a personal experience, or a general observation.

For instance, Pepperdine University student Sarah Elliott begins her essay on the ways women are conditioned to apologize for expressing opinions by recounting a relevant childhood experience. But in her fourth paragraph she states the main point of her essay explicitly. Note that she then immediately refers to her opening paragraphs to show their significance.

1
States the main point of her essay

2
Ties her opening to the main point

As a communication major and a woman, (1) it's become apparent to me that social expectations set by a male-dominated society have driven women to code their communication to mask expressions of power or opinions. (2) There's a reason why even a boy in a kindergarten class knew that girls aren't "allowed" to be president.

STUDENT WRITER AT WORK

Sarah Elliott

Photo by Lydia Kiros

R.A. What inspired you to write this essay? And publish it?

S.E. I read a piece in the *Washington Post* by Alexandra Petri that touched on the way professional settings limit the communication of women by enforcing socially constructed speech barriers. That piece resonated deeply with me because, as a young woman in college, I see examples of these barriers used nearly every day in my classes. I felt that it would be interesting to explore this subject at the classroom level instead of just at the professional level.

R.A. What response have you received to this piece?

S.E. The response to this piece has been very positive for me. I have had both faculty and students talk with me about the message and how it caused them to rethink the way they communicate or encourage others to communicate.

R.A. What do you like to read?

S.E. I love to read, and the first thing I do every morning is spend a couple minutes in bed catching up on current events with my news app or *theSkimm,* an e-mail newsletter I subscribe to. I tend to read a lot of online publications like the *Huffington Post* or *BuzzFeed,* but I also subscribe to the *New Yorker* (student discount!), so I have my physical publications, too. Honestly, I think I get most of my news from Twitter, which is a very millennial thing to say, but it's a great source of live updates on the world around me, and I love the bite-sized humor.

R.A. What topics most interest you as a writer?

S.E. I am very passionate about women's issues, feminism, and youth-focused topics. I also like to write about religion, specifically Christianity, and politics. I know those are the two topics you're never supposed to bring up (oops), so I try to balance it out with humor and fiction, which are some of my favorite things to write.

R.A. Do you plan to continue writing for publication?

S.E. I would love to publish a novel someday; it's been my dream ever since I learned how to talk, so I know that I will always keep pursuing publication in that regard. Once I graduate, I'm not sure how much opportunity I'll have to publish pieces like this, but I'm certainly going to go out of my way to try.

R.A. What advice do you have for other student writers?

S.E. I think the best thing any writer can do is just write consistently, whether it be for class, in a journal, for a student publication, for a blog, or even just for yourself. Sometimes it can be hard to think of something to write about, so I'd encourage you to try blogging or journaling about your life as a way to at least get pen to paper (or hand to keyboard) and start practicing. And then once you've written, share it. There are so many ways to engage with an audience through the Internet, and that kind of feedback and exposure is so valuable to us young writers, especially when there are so many communities that are specifically geared for people our age.

SPOTLIGHT ON DATA AND RESEARCH

Jonah Engel Bromwich

Tell Us What to Call the Generation after Millennials (Please)

[*The New York Times*, January 23, 2018]

For many years, the media, along with many historians and sociologists, have liked to think of particular generations as distinct entities that also possess a cultural identity. One of the earliest generations to be named was is the "Baby Boomers," a name intended to describe a spike in the birthrate immediately after World War II and that included people born between 1946 and 1964. Although such designations include many millions of people and are therefore generalities, particular generations are thought to share certain traits and values. Given the growth in America's postwar economy, Baby Boomers, for example, would inherit a more affluent world than any generation before them and would permanently alter the consumer society.

Understanding the dynamics and demographics of generations is important for marketing experts who want to be able to identify dominant trends and characteristics of large groups and subgroups and find ways to match products to collective tastes. As America's latest named generation (those born between approximately 1978 and 1995), usually termed Millennials, has grown older, with many reaching their early thirties, some of the attention has shifted to the next generation, the oldest of which will be in their early twenties by 2020. Demographers are now publishing research characterizing the traits and habits of this generation, which has not yet received a convenient name or label, though Generation Z is commonly used. You may want to see if you can come up with a name of your own as you read the following item on this new generation from the New York Times.

Jonah Engel Bromwich contributes breaking news to the New York Times *and* Pitchfork. *A Millennial himself, he specializes in arts, entertainment, and cultural trends.*

Feel free to skip this article and scroll all the way down to answer the question we asked in the headline because who has the time, really? 1

Millennials are getting older. 2

Not that much older, of course. We're a roughly defined generational cohort, but arguably the oldest members of our demographic set are just beginning to reach the age of 40. 3

Meanwhile, the American generation behind millennials has started to move into the workplace. And while some have proposed names for this group born in 1995 and after — Generation Z, Post-Millennials, The Homeland Generation, iGeneration — all of these names are bad. The first two don't even strive for originality! Come on. 4

Then again, it's hard to know what makes a generational name stick. 5

"Millennial" was coined in the late 1980s by the consultants Neil Howe and William Strauss, both baby boomers, before the term Generation X was even popularized. (They wanted to call them "13th Gen," but that didn't stick, and neither did "slackers.") 6

But their term "millennial" did not become the dominant name for the huge generation after those two until much later. 7

"In retrospect, it's easy to see that names that people gravitate to say something," Mr. Howe said in a recent interview. "Either the name itself or the way in which it was adapted." 8

But Malcolm Harris, the millennial author of "Kids These Days: Human Capital and the Making of Millennials," argues that those most interested in naming generations are those trying to sell things to that cohort. 9

"Generations are really only understood in retrospect," Mr. Harris said. 10

"Some people have a financial interest in naming them as soon as possible, people trying to sell stuff. 11

"That's the first perspective we get on any cohort, and I don't think it's necessarily a very good one." 12

One stumbling block is a lack of agreement about the birth years for each generation. People on the fringes can feel as if they've got almost nothing in common with the rest of the group. A few years' difference can determine if you could have been drafted for Vietnam, watched the first MTV videos, or were born into a world of instant messaging. 13

In 2015, the Census Bureau said that there were 83.1 million American millennials (born between 1982 and 2000), exceeding the 75.4 million baby boomers (between 1946 and 1964), and the 65 million that Pew Research said belong in Generation X (between 1965 and 1980). 14

But the generation after millennials is still so ill-defined (probably 15
because of the whole name issue) that an accurate count has not yet been established.

And a good name? Nope. 16

So in order to spare the new youngs years of enduring a bad label, 17
we've decided to offer a forum for you to name your own generation.

If you're 22 or younger, please do us a favor and tell us what to 18
call you and why. Or what NOT to call you and why. We'll collect your responses and publish a selection of them in a follow-up article.

UPDATE: Well, we heard from thousands of you. Here's what you 19
told us.

Editor's Note: The author did not seem overwhelmed by some of the 20
suggestions — iGeneration, iGen, Meme Generation, Memennials, Final or Last Generation. His favorite was Delta Generation or Deltas, the term denoting "change and uncertainty" in math and science. He quotes a young person who suggested Deltas: "We were kids when our parents lost their jobs in the recession. We also are a generation of demographic shift — we are more diverse than any in American history. We generally see it as something to embrace, and welcome changes that could make for a more inclusive and just America."

POINTS TO CONSIDER

1. What is your response to some of the names suggested for the new generation? Do you agree with the author that the "Delta Generation" might be the best name? Can you think of a better one?
2. What appear to be the most dominant characteristics of the next generation? How do you think this generation will help define future American culture?
3. Why are marketers and academics so interested in the next generation? What motives might they have to study it?

Sylvia Taschka

What's Wrong with Hitler Comparisons?

[*theconversation.com*, March 12, 2018]

In the early days of the Internet, the American author and lawyer Mike Godwin coined what is now known as Godwin's Law. Basically, the law claims that the longer an online discussion (or thread) continues the greater the possibility that Hitler or Nazis will be invoked. This is essentially a way of saying that as a discussion or an argument persists, people will often resort to extremes. In "What's Wrong with Hitler Comparisons?" historian Sylvia Taschka, citing Godwin's Law, examines this linguistic and intellectual phenomenon. As many have noted, Hitler comparisons often trivialize the horrors of the Nazi movement and the Holocaust. But, as Taschka notes, such comparisons shed little light on anything; rather, "they do more to confuse than clarify the urgent issues at stake."

Sylvia Taschka grew up in Germany and is an expert on the history of the Nazi movement. The author of several books on German history, she is a senior lecturer at Wayne State University.

BEFORE YOU READ

Do you think a public figure can be compared to someone like Hitler? Do you take such comparisons seriously, or do you think any such juxtapositions inevitably fall flat?

WORDS TO LEARN

trivial (para. 2): insignificant (adjective)
ill-fated (para. 3): destined for an unhappy end (adjective)
unbridled (para. 3): uncontrolled (adjective)
facile (para. 4): easily done (adjective)
skeptical (para. 5): unbelieving (adjective)
inflationary (para. 5): puffed up (adjective)
seamlessly (para. 7): smoothly (adverb)
fascist (para. 9): someone dictatorial (noun)
authoritarianism (para. 11): having to do with a political system that promotes obedience to authority over any individual freedom (noun)
empirical (para. 12): verifiable through evidence (adjective)
cudgel (para. 15): stick used as a weapon; a club (noun)
futile (para. 22): useless (adjective)

Everyone seems to have become Hitler." 1

Historian Gavriel D. Rosenfeld wrote these words in his study 2 of how the Nazi past has become a recurring theme in contemporary culture — to the point of almost becoming trivial. What is especially interesting is that he had already reached that conclusion a year before Donald Trump was elected to be the 45th president of the United States.

Since then, comparisons between Trump and Hitler — and even 3 between current developments in the United States and the waning days of Germany's ill-fated Weimar Republic — have become almost daily fare. This is perhaps no surprise, given his unbridled attacks against his political opponents and the mainstream press, his singling out of minority groups as scapegoats for the challenges that American society faces, and his populist, demagogic style more generally.

As a historian of modern Germany, I have spent many years explor- 4 ing the crimes that Hitler and his followers committed. When people make facile comparisons to Hitler and the Nazis, they are trying, usually in good faith, to warn us about the dangers of ignoring history and its supposed lessons.

But it is my very familiarity with that history that makes me highly 5 skeptical about the inflationary use of such comparisons. They do more to confuse than clarify the urgent issues at stake.

LONG HISTORY OF NAZI COMPARISONS

Godwin's Law holds that the longer an online discussion progresses, 6 the likelier someone will eventually be compared to Hitler. By now, this seems to apply not just to the virtual world of chat rooms, but also to living rooms across America.

Comparing politicians to Hitler is nothing new, of course. We live in 7 an age where George W. Bush, Saddam Hussein, Recep Tayyip Erdoğan, Vladimir Putin, Donald Trump, Angela Merkel, Hillary Clinton ("Hitlery") and Barack Obama have all seamlessly been compared to Hitler. That's just a few of the more recent examples, but they clearly show just how little value such glib analogies have.

The Trump presidency has made use of the Hitler card even more 8 pronounced. Such comparisons have not just increased in frequency and intensity, however. Serious ones are now even being made by leading experts on Nazi Germany.

The British historian Jane Caplan, for example, wrote an analysis 9 in November 2016 directly addressing the question of whether or not Trump was a fascist.

Caplan didn't reach any definite conclusions, but she did point out 10 quite a few striking similarities between the rise of fascism in Germany then and the current political climate in the United States now. In short, she feels that America is in a vulnerable position right now — one that radical forces can use to their advantage.

A few months later, Yale historian Timothy Snyder published *On Tyranny*. His book similarly concludes that America under Trump bears striking similarities to Germany in the interwar period and reads like something of a how-to manual for resisting the rise of authoritarianism in today's America. 11

Respectable warning voices like these, engaging in historical analysis grounded in empirical scholarship, give the lie to any fears that Hitler is somehow being trivialized. 12

In fact, such experts are well equipped to communicate to a broader public the potential value of historical analogies. When paying close attention to historical context, analogies can become useful tools — ones that help us understand our present, and perhaps even shape it for the better. 13

Unfortunately, considered analysis on par with that of Caplan or Snyder is the exception, not the rule. That's no surprise given the frenzied, often nasty character of current political discourse. 14

FALSE EQUIVALENCY RISKS TRIVIALIZING EVIL

The Hitler comparison has, for many, become nothing more than a cudgel for branding someone or something as morally wrong or evil, for making what the Germans call a *Totschlagargument*: a "knock-out" or "killer" argument intended to end all discussion. 15

I believe there are several reasons why conversations tend to end at this point.

I believe there are several reasons why conversations tend to end at this point. For one, few people wish to trivialize Hitler. Just as important: When such accusations are made, those on the receiving end are understandably upset about the comparison. 16

While it seems that many people in the U.S. no longer feel that they're able to agree on anything — including sometimes even facts — they still seem able to agree on one point: Hitler epitomizes evil. 17

Take, for example, a recent ad campaign by the NRA featuring their spokesperson, Dana Loesch. Loesch describes the current state of American society in almost apocalyptic terms, with ominous background music and blurry pictures of street fighting helping her to make her point. 18

The United States is presented in the ad as a country coming apart at the seams because of liberal protesters. What is especially interesting here is how Loesch begins her rant: "They use their media to assassinate real news. They use schools to teach children that their president is another Hitler!" 19

Loesch clearly finds Trump comparisons to Hitler outrageous — just as Obama supporters found it outrageous when Hitler comparisons were being made about Obama. 20

Let us be clear: Hitler unleashed a war aimed at achieving global domination that resulted in the deaths of tens of millions. This included the industrialized murder of 6 million men, women and children whose only "crime" was being born Jewish. This is not to diminish the horrors wrought by tyrants like former Iraqi President Saddam Hussein or Slobodan Milošević, former president of Serbia. But the magnitude of their crimes still pales in comparison. And whatever one may think of Donald Trump, he has — although the jury is still out on this one — remained within the bounds of constitutional legality. And clearly he has not been responsible for mass death. 21

Another aspect of our shared cultural knowledge of Hitler is that negotiating with him was futile. In hindsight, historians agree that the appeasement policies of the 1930s were a failure and that forceful means were the only way to have stopped Hitler. No matter how many concessions were made to the German dictator over the course of the 1930s, he wanted more — and he wanted war. 22

This is why, as a historian of the Nazi period, I find inflated contemporary comparisons and analogies problematic. 23

False equivalencies not only risk trivializing Hitler and the horrors he unleashed. They also prevent people from engaging with the actual issues at hand — ones that urgently require our attention: immigration reform, rampant xenophobia, social and economic restructuring in a globalized world, and a loss of faith in government's ability to solve pressing problems. 24

There is an ultimate reason why the Hitler comparison should not be used as lightly as it often is nowadays. 25

Whenever we apply that political or moral comparison, we set the bar for inhumanity as high as possible. Should the abyss of World War II and the Holocaust really be the main measure for all things political? 26

The danger here is that policies only become worthy of moral outrage if they lead to genocidal violence. One would hope that in the 21st century, our society would have developed higher — or perhaps lower — standards than these. 27

VOCABULARY/USING A DICTIONARY

1. How do the definitions of *epitomize* (para. 17) and *epitome* reflect each other, and how are they different?
2. What does it mean if something is *waning* (para. 3)? What is the opposite of *waning*?
3. What is a *demagogue*? Define *demagogic* (para. 3).

RESPONDING TO WORDS IN CONTEXT

1. **Connect.** In his essay, Weingarten ("Thoughts and Prayers," p. 51) refers to the "go-to *banality*" (para. 2) of the phrase "thoughts and prayers." In her essay, Taschka describes "how little value such *glib* analogies" (para. 7) comparing modern politicians to Hitler have. Using definitions for *banal* and *glib*, can you argue that these writers are saying the same things about the language they're discussing?
2. What does Taschka mean when she says comparisons of Trump to Hitler have become almost *daily fare* (para. 3)? What is an example of a *daily fare*?
3. What do you think Taschka means when she speaks of "the *abyss* of World War II and the Holocaust" (para. 26)? What is an *abyss*?

DISCUSSING MAIN POINT AND MEANING

1. What does the author mean when she contends that such comparisons "trivialize" Hitler?
2. In Taschka's opinion, when might a comparison to Hitler hold weight?
3. What does she state is the most important reason for not using the Hitler comparison lightly?

EXAMINING SENTENCES, PARAGRAPHS, AND ORGANIZATION

1. Taschka uses a number of different adjectives to describe the Hitler comparisons being made by the public. Find two of these sentences and compare the adjectives being used. How is Taschka using adjectives to underscore her point?
2. The essay begins with words that don't belong to the essayist. Why does she start with a quotation? Why is this particular quotation important to the argument?
3. Taschka opens paragraph 21 with the phrase "Let us be clear." How does this phrase add to the paragraph she has written? Why is it at the beginning of the paragraph?

THINKING CRITICALLY

1. Consider the list of people Taschka says have been compared to Hitler in recent history. Do those comparisons illustrate how likening someone to Hitler loses effectiveness if used lightly? What do you think of the comparisons, given what you know of the people on that list?
2. Do you think the essayist is a valid authority on this subject? Why or why not?
3. Why do you think people gravitate toward Hitler when they make comparisons with politicians? Can you think of other effective comparisons to be made with officials? What might you choose?

WRITING ACTIVITIES

1. In her closing statement, Taschka insists that acts other than genocidal violence are worthy of condemnation. Write a list of acts and policies that you find objectionable in current or recent history and explain why they should be condemned, regardless of whether they recall Hitler and his Nazi regime.
2. Taschka writes, "False equivalencies not only risk trivializing Hitler and the horrors he unleashed. They also prevent people from engaging with the actual issues at hand — ones that urgently require our attention" (para. 24). Choose from one of the issues Taschka lists as pressing and write about it. Why is it an urgent topic that needs to be addressed? Did you think about this issue at all before you read about it in this article?
3. Look at the comparisons made between Hitler and Trump in paragraphs 8–11. Research the periods of German history referenced there and write a summary of that time using reputable sources, written either by the authors mentioned or by others. Following your summary, argue the validity or invalidity of the comparisons using that particular data.

AMERICA THEN . . . 1951

Langston Hughes

That Word *Black*

[*The Chicago Defender*, November 3, 1951]

Apic/Hulton Archive/Getty Images

Author Langston Hughes, photographed in 1943

When the following short essay first appeared in 1951, it was considered an insult to call an African American "black." The acceptable and respectful word at the time — the one Langston Hughes himself would have used — was Negro. *But by August 1963, when Martin Luther King Jr. delivered his famous "I Have a Dream" speech, the terms used to describe African Americans were changing. King favored the term* Negro, *but in a speech that preceded his that historic day, the twenty-three-year-old John Lewis (now a congressional leader) repeatedly used the word* black *instead of* Negro. *By the late 1960s, the word* black *had grown more popular, a result of movements like the Black Panthers and such expressions as "black is beautiful," a sentiment Hughes anticipates at the conclusion of the essay.*

One of the nation's most prolific writers, Langston Hughes (1902–1967) was born in Joplin, Missouri, but traveled east as a young man and became a leading, multitalented figure of the Harlem Renaissance. A poet, novelist, essayist, dramatist, short story writer, and journalist who also wrote many children's books, Hughes is still widely read today. In 1943, he created in his newspaper columns for the Chicago Defender *the memorable character Jesse B. Semple ("Simple"), a plain-speaking, working-class man from Harlem. The character was so engaging that Hughes went on to publish five collections of sketches:* Simple Speaks His Mind *(1950),* Simple Takes a Wife *(1953),* Simple Stakes a Claim *(1957),* The Best of Simple *(1961), and* Simple's Uncle Sam *(1965). Hughes said he based "Simple" on an actual factory worker he met in a Harlem bar in 1942.*

BEFORE YOU READ

What words or ideas do you associate with the word *black*? Would you describe the associations as positive, negative, or neutral?

WORDS TO LEARN

orators (para. 2): public speakers (noun)
blacklist (para. 4): list of people under suspicion of something (noun)
blackball (para. 4): to ostracize (verb)
blackmail (para. 4): to extort (verb)
voodoo (para 6): a religion practiced largely in the West Indies (noun)

"This evening," said Simple, "I feel like talking about the word 1
black."

"Nobody's stopping you, so go ahead. But what you really 2
ought to have is a soap-box out on the corner of 126th and Lenox where the rest of the orators hang out."

"They expresses some good ideas on that corner," said Simple, "but 3
for my ideas I do not need a crowd. Now, as I were saying, the word *black*, white folks have done used that word to mean something bad so often until now when the N.A.A.C.P. asks for civil rights for the black man, they think they must be bad. Looking back into history, I reckon it all started with a *black* cat meaning bad luck. Don't let one cross your path!

"Next, somebody got up a *black-list* on which you get if you don't 4
vote right. Then when lodges come into being, the folks they didn't want in them got *black-balled*. If you kept a skeleton in your closet, you might get *black-mailed*. And everything bad was *black*. When it came down to the unlucky ball on the pool table, the eight-rock, they made it the *black* ball. So no wonder there ain't no equal rights for the *black* man."

"All you say is true about the odium attached to the word *black*," 5
I said. "You've even forgotten a few. For example, during the war if you

bought something under the table, illegally, they said you were trading on the *black* market. In Chicago, if you're a gangster, the *Black Hand Society* may take you for a ride. And certainly if you don't behave yourself, your family will say you're a *black* sheep. Then if your mama burns a *black* candle to change the family luck, they call it *black* magic."

"My mama never did believe in voodoo so she did not burn no black candles," said Simple. 6

"If she had, that would have been a *black* mark against her." 7

"Stop talking about my mama. What I want to know is, where do white folks get off calling everything bad *black*? If it is a dark night, they say it's *black* as hell. If you are mean and evil, they say you got a *black* heart. I would like to change all that around and say that the people who Jim Crow me have got a *white* heart. People who sell dope to children have got a *white* mark against them. And all the white gamblers who were behind the basketball fix are the *white* sheep of the sports world. God knows there was few, if any, Negroes selling stuff on the black market during the war, so why didn't they call it the *white* market? No, they got to take me and my color and turn it into everything *bad*. According to white folks, black is bad. 8

"Wait till my day comes! In my language, bad will be *white*. Blackmail will be *white* mail. Black cats will be good luck, and *white* cats will be bad. If a white cat crosses your path, look out! I will take the black ball for the cue ball and let the *white* ball be the unlucky eight-rock. And on my blacklist — which will be a *white* list then — I will put everybody who ever Jim Crowed me from Rankin to Hitler, Talmadge to Malan, South Carolina to South Africa. 9

"I am black. When I look in the mirror, I see myself, daddy-o, but I am not ashamed. God made me. He did not make us no badder than the rest of the folks. The earth is black and all kinds of good things comes out of the earth. Everything that grows comes up out of the earth. Trees and flowers and fruit and sweet potatoes and corn and all that keeps mens alive comes right up out of the earth — good old black earth. Coal is black and it warms your house and cooks your food. The night is black, which has a moon, and a million stars, and is beautiful. Sleep is black which gives you rest, so you wake up feeling good. I am black. I feel very good this evening. 10

"What is wrong with black?" 11

VOCABULARY/USING A DICTIONARY

1. What is a *soap-box* (para. 2) used for?
2. What part of speech is *reckon* (para. 3) and what does it mean?
3. What does the prefix *il-* do to the word *illegally* (para. 5)? What is the opposite of *illegally*?

RESPONDING TO WORDS IN CONTEXT

1. What might *odium* (para. 5) mean, based on the words attached to *black* in paragraph 4?
2. What color do you think the *cue ball* is (para. 9)?
3. Even if you don't know what the N.A.A.C.P. is, if it asks for *civil rights* (para. 3) for the black man, what do you think it is asking for?

DISCUSSING MAIN POINT AND MEANING

1. How did negative connotations come into English expressions?
2. What expressions does Hughes include to characterize the word *black*?
3. How does Simple feel about himself? What examples does he bring in to show that black is good?

EXAMINING SENTENCES, PARAGRAPHS, AND ORGANIZATION

1. In what ways do the characters differ in speech and style of address? Why do you think this is so?
2. What advantages does Hughes gain through the use of dialogue? What would the essay be like if it took the form of an address by a single speaker?
3. What effect is created when *black* is replaced with *white* in paragraph 9? Are you surprised by the effect created?

THINKING CRITICALLY

1. What clues does Langston Hughes give to answer the question: What's wrong with *black*?
2. Why do you think Hughes names his character "Simple"? Is the character, or his argument, simple? Explain.
3. What does the essay tell you about how "black" was thought of more than sixty years ago? What is Hughes saying about the use of the word through his invented character Simple?

WRITING ACTIVITIES

1. Describe Simple's argument in a short essay. How does he arrive at his conclusion? How important are examples to his point of view? Would you argue that these are all just words and common expressions or that these words have an impact on ways we think and feel?
2. Try writing about a common word (such as *boy* or *girl*), and in a short essay examine its various connotations, looking at both negative and positive aspects of its use. You might look at the word from the perspective of different cultures and ethnic groups.

3. **Connect.** Within twenty years the word *black* became accepted usage and the word *Negro* was considered unacceptable. What do you think caused this change? How is the answer to this question reflected in Moore's "When Does Renaming a Building Make Sense?" (p. 113)? Use examples from these essays as you formulate your answer.

Discussing the Unit

SUGGESTED TOPIC FOR DISCUSSION

What's in a word? The authors in this chapter explore situations when a word is appropriate and when it is not — and all that a word comes to stand for. After reading these essays, consider the various choices we all make when we use certain words.

PREPARING FOR CLASS DISCUSSION

1. Do words matter? The authors in this chapter write about the unique power of language. As you reflect on the essays you've read, think about how words shape the thought and experience of both the individual and our society.
2. Do you habitually use words without considering their connotations? What associations do you have with the word *black*? Or with a sports team name, like the Washington Redskins? How do you react when a person compares someone to Hitler? Under what circumstances might you begin to examine words and their associations more closely?

FROM DISCUSSION TO WRITING

1. As the authors in this chapter point out, some words say too much and some say too little. Some are just right — while others create a good deal of confusion. Discuss which essays in this chapter are particularly compelling in showing when a word is illuminating and which essays are particularly convincing in pointing out when words become meaningless. Consider when words are used to create comparisons that don't hold up or are used too carelessly. Use examples from the essays to illustrate your point.
2. Gene Weingarten's "Thoughts and Prayers" (p. 51) is about using language that is reactive and inauthentic when responding to a very serious, complicated issue. Is there any connection between the thoughts and impulses behind the phrase "thoughts and prayers" and the points made in Sarah Elliott's "Women: Stop Apologizing; Be Confident" (p. 55) about women's speech ("cloaking our thoughts in superfluous disclaimers")? What point are both authors making about the way language can or should be used — and how they see it being used? Explain in a brief comparison and contrast essay.

TOPICS FOR CROSS-CULTURAL DISCUSSION

1. Does your race, gender, age, or another factor influence how you use words or what words you use? Explain your answer, citing examples from at least two of the essays in this chapter.
2. Consider what's behind the naming of a sports franchise (Washington Redskins) and the naming of the next generation (after Millennials). What happens when one particular group has control over the names of other people or things? What happens when it does not? What did "What's in a Name?" (p. 48) or "Tell Us What to Call the Generation after Millennials (Please)" (p. 61) teach you about the namer vs. the named? What is the relationship between the two?

2

Free Speech: Is It Endangered on Campus?

Free expression is such a fundamental liberty that many national charters, including the U.S. Constitution, have made it among the first rights they've expressly numbered. On college campuses, the right to hold and express dissenting views has always been considered not only an important personal freedom but also a critical component of healthy academic discourse and diversity. What happens, though, when one student's right starts to infringe on another student's well-being? Where should we draw the line?

A major battlefield in the academic free-speech wars has been what to do about content that, while it might be important to understanding a particular field or discipline, upsets students exposed to it. Some students have recently called for professors to confront this problem head-on by adopting the Internet trend of appending their courses with trigger warnings, explicit alerts that certain material on a syllabus may be upsetting, or "triggering," especially to students with past traumas.

Although it may seem from many news reports that colleges across the nation are contributing to the suppression of free speech, some schools are reacting against this perceived trend. Over the summer of 2016, the prestigious University of Chicago sent a letter to the incoming freshman class informing students in no uncertain terms that the school remains dedicated to academic freedom. "Our commitment to academic freedom," the letter said in part, "means that we do not support so-called trigger warnings, we do not cancel invited speakers because their topics might prove controversial, and we do not condone the creation of intellectual 'safe spaces' where individuals can retreat from ideas and perspectives at odds with their own."

This chapter examines the "trigger warning" and "safe-spaces" debate within the larger context of freedom of expression. A main topic in the debate — as one newspaper put it recently — is whether "a university should foster an environment where students, rather than being shielded from opposing views, are exposed to the widest variety of thought."

The James Madison Program in American Ideals and Institutions at Princeton University

Think for Yourself: Some Thoughts and Advice for Our Students and All Students

Just as the fall semester was to begin in 2017, a Princeton professor representing the university's James Madison Program in American Ideals and Institutions joined with colleagues at Yale and Harvard to offer some advice to their incoming first-year students—and, by extension, to all students. They expressed their advice in three simple words: "Think for yourself." The following brief "open letter" offered that advice and also explained why thinking for yourself can be in "today's climate" a "challenge" demanding "self discipline" and "courage." This is mainly because the "danger any student—or faculty member—faces today is falling into the vice of conformism, yielding to groupthink."

1 We are scholars and teachers at Princeton, Harvard, and Yale who have some thoughts to share and advice to offer students who are headed off to colleges around the country. Our advice can be distilled to three words:

2 **Think for yourself.**

3 Now, that might sound easy. But you will find—as you may have discovered already in high school—that thinking for yourself can be a challenge. It always demands self-discipline and these days can require courage.

4 In today's climate, it's all-too-easy to allow your views and outlook to be shaped by dominant opinion on your campus or in the broader academic culture. The danger any student—or faculty member—faces today is falling into the vice of conformism, yielding to groupthink.

5 At many colleges and universities what John Stuart Mill[1] called "the tyranny of public opinion" does more than merely discourage students from dissenting from prevailing views on moral, political, and other

[1] John Stuart Mill (para. 5): Prominent British political philosopher (1806–1873), perhaps best known today for his influential book on liberalism, *On Liberty* (1859). For more on Mill, see the Introduction, pp. 21–22.

types of questions. It leads them to suppose that dominant views are so obviously correct that only a bigot or a crank could question them.

Since no one wants to be, or be thought of as, a bigot or a crank, 6
the easy, lazy way to proceed is simply by falling into line with campus orthodoxies.

Don't do that. Think for yourself. 7

Thinking for yourself means questioning dominant ideas even 8
when others insist on their being treated as unquestionable. It means deciding what one believes not by conforming to fashionable opinions, but by taking the trouble to learn and honestly consider the strongest arguments to be advanced on both or all sides of questions — including arguments for positions that others revile and want to stigmatize and against positions others seek to immunize from critical scrutiny.

Open-mindedness, critical thinking, and debate are essential to discovering the truth.

The love of truth and the desire to 9
attain it should motivate you to think for yourself. The central point of a college education is to seek truth and to learn the skills and acquire the virtues necessary to be a lifelong truth-seeker. Open-mindedness, critical thinking, and debate are essential to discovering the truth. Moreover, they are our best antidotes to bigotry.

Merriam-Webster's first definition of the word "bigot" is a per- 10
son "who is obstinately or intolerantly devoted to his or her own opinions and prejudices." The only people who need fear open-minded inquiry and robust debate are the actual bigots, including those on campuses or in the broader society who seek to protect the hegemony of their opinions by claiming that to question those opinions is itself bigotry.

So don't be tyrannized by public opinion. Don't get trapped in an 11
echo chamber. Whether you in the end reject or embrace a view, make sure you decide where you stand by critically assessing the arguments for the competing positions.

Think for yourself. 12

Good luck to you in college! 13

POINTS TO CONSIDER

1. The letter is addressed not only to Princeton, Harvard, and Yale students — but also to you. Do you feel included by the professors? Do you agree or disagree with their educational concerns?
2. In paragraph 9, the letter defines the "central point of a college education." Do you agree or disagree with this definition? If you disagree, what definition would you offer instead?
3. Based on the letter, what do you think the authors' position would be on such campus issues as "trigger warnings" and "safe spaces"? Although they don't use these expressions, how can you infer their attitudes?

Wendy M. Williams and Stephen J. Ceci

There Are No Good Alternatives to Free Speech on Campus

[*Inside Higher Ed*, May 2, 2018]

Each year, it appears, as they prepare for graduation ceremonies, college campuses are divided by highly polarized views about commencement speakers — who is acceptable to the campus community and who isn't. And just about every year protests arise and speakers are disinvited because their presence will cause distraction and commotion at an occasion that should be celebratory. And throughout the school year invited and disinvited speakers and lecturers can provoke heated student and faculty protests. The key issues here often revolve around what can be said and who can say it.

In "There Are No Good Alternatives to Free Speech on Campus," two Cornell University psychology professors ask, "What specific topics are off-limits on college campuses today?" Reporting on their own research, they examine different surveys and look at the various "controversies surrounding recent cancellations of campus talks." Acknowledging that some speech can result in student discomfort, they nevertheless maintain that "college is an opportunity to confront divergent opinions, even if they make us uncomfortable." The selection concludes with a summary of four ways that "our colleges and universities [can] create an open atmosphere of free speech while also respecting diversity."

Wendy M. Williams is director of the Cornell University Institute for Women in Science. Stephen J. Ceci is the Helen L. Carr Professor of Developmental Psychology at Cornell. They have each authored many articles in professional journals and, in 2009, they coauthored The Mathematics of Sex: How Biology and Society Conspire to Limit Talented Women and Girls.

BEFORE YOU READ

Do you think students should debate ideas — even controversial ones — freely on a college campus? Or should college students be protected against speech that makes them feel uncomfortable?

WORDS TO LEARN

stultifying (para. 1): appearing absurd or foolish (adjective)
tangible (para. 2): substantial (adjective)
censor (para. 5): to suppress (verb)
regulate (para. 6): to fix the rate which something happens (verb)
retract (para. 8): to withdraw (verb)
inculcate (para. 10): to teach through use of repetition (verb)
arbiter (para. 10): judge (noun)
divergent (para. 11): going in different directions; diverse (adjective)
viable (para. 11): able to live (adjective)

It's difficult to determine when discussions of controversial topics became known as hate speech on college campuses across the country. But the metamorphosis has taken place all around us, and the costs are undeniable. Open debate has morphed into self-censorship and terrified silence; what used to be celebrated as an environment of fearless questioning has become a stultifying world of repression. 1

Intolerance of meaningful debate comes from both sides of the political spectrum. Talk of "black lives matter" constitutes hate speech for some, while "blue lives matter" fits the bill for others. Depending on the political leanings of their particular campus, professors, staff members and students are strongly discouraged from entertaining certain topics even privately, much less discussing them publicly on campus, because these discussions make some people uncomfortable. The risks and penalties are tangible and significant, from shaming and ostracizing, to fear of loss of tenure and jobs for professors and expulsion and dismissal for anyone else. 2

What specific topics are off-limits on college campuses today? Consider recent examples from a Cato Institute survey of over 3,000 Americans with university experience: 40 percent would ban a speaker who says men on average are better than women at math, 51 percent would ban claims that all white people are racists, 49 percent would ban statements that Christians are backward and brainwashed, 49 percent would ban speech that criticized and disrespected police, and 41 percent would ban speakers who say undocumented immigrants should be deported. 3

Our concerns over these figures is not because we agree or disagree with the statements. But shouldn't college students be exposed to arguments on both sides of these issues, as part of their journey of intellectual development? 4

The Cato survey reported a willingness to censor, regulate or punish a wide variety of expression people found offensive: 74 percent of respondents said universities should cancel speakers if students threaten violence, and 51 percent of those who self-identified as strongly liberal said it is "morally acceptable to punch Nazis in the face." 5

When older adults think about their college experience, they remember heated debates with eye-opening proclamations that deliberately challenged preconceptions and created real discomfort along the way. An essential aspect of college was broadening students' thinking in ways they could never have predicted. In the 1960s and '70s, conservative administrators were taken to task for muzzling students' free expression. Ironically, there is currently a lot of talk about free speech on college campuses, but the vast majority focuses on how to regulate it. 6

Meaningful debate on uncomfortable important topics is replaced by proclamations based on "lived experiences" and "emotional knowledge." But it is impossible to refute a person's claim of a lived experience that caused her suffering. If this rubric is how we define permissible speech, very soon nothing worthwhile qualifies. The heckler's veto reigns supreme. 7

Today's college students respond to statements that make them uncomfortable with allegations of speakers' criminal intent. Dartmouth College students railed against an op-ed published in the school's newspaper by undergraduate Ryan Spector . . . after he criticized the process that resulted in four men and 15 women being chosen as mentors. Spector argued this disparity was the result of a selection process "that sees race, gender and identity as dictating qualification." More than 30 campus organizations denounced Spector, calling his piece an "attack" on women and minorities, claiming it "endangers the lives" of students, and suggesting Spector be punished for his views. Others lamented "how violent this article is," urging the paper to retract it and require Spector to apologize and stating that allowing Spector and others like him to express their opinions endangers "the safety and well-being of marginalized students" and "only further perpetuates the culture of toxic, male, white supremacy." 8

We considered these issues in a new article in *Perspectives on Psychological Science* on the controversies surrounding recent cancellations of campus talks. We drew mainly on psychological, legal and philosophical analyses to explain the polarization of positions, focusing on phenomena known as blind-spot bias,[1] selective perception,[2] 9

---

[1] blind-spot bias (para. 9): recognizing biases in others, but not in yourself

[2] selective perception (para. 9): seeing what you want to see in media messages and events, regardless of other viewpoints

motivated skepticism,[3] my-side bias,[4] groupthink[5] and naïve realism,[6] which help explain why dueling sides overestimate support for their own position and downgrade opponents' views. In the campus disturbances, opponents did not simply interpret the same situation differently, they actually saw different things.

A number of recent campus disruptions share one or more of these biases: opponents offered different accounts about who started the violence, the role campus police played, why each side's affiliation with a cause led to the belief that it was especially enlightened whereas opponents' opposite affiliation led to their own flawed reasoning, why people on each side overestimated the strength of the evidence supporting their side, and whether protesters shouting down of speakers infringed on the audience's right to hear their views or, conversely, represented exercises in their own freedom of expression. We concluded our article with recommendations to moderate positions and inculcate a campus culture of respectful debate in which no single group appoints itself the final arbiter of what can and cannot be heard. 10

Having one's beliefs criticized — even identity-forming beliefs — is an essential aspect of a good education. College is an opportunity to confront divergent opinions, even if they make us uncomfortable; being exposed to opinions that call into question their deepest beliefs will help students develop the valuable skills needed to navigate their futures, relate to others with divergent views and contribute to society. As uncomfortable as it might be, there really is no viable alternative to allowing free speech on college campuses. 11

How can our colleges and universities create an open atmosphere of free speech while also respecting diversity? 12

First, give all sides a podium for expression. No campus group has the right to determine for the entire community what can be discussed. But protesters also have a right to be heard. Make viewpoint diversity an important component of diversity, broadly defined; ensure panels, committees and faculty and staff all contain individuals with views occupying the entire political spectrum. Psychological research shows that we all possess and must acknowledge our biases, and humility will go a long way toward accomplishing this goal. The best and most effective airing of controversy takes place within the marketplace of ideas. 13

---

[3] motivated skepticism (para. 9): being more skeptical about claims you don't like than those you do

[4] my-side bias (para. 9): evaluating evidence in a manner biased toward your own prior opinions

[5] groupthink (para. 9): a way of group decision making that discourages individual responsibility or unique opinions

[6] naïve realism (para. 9): the belief that we see the world around us objectively

Second, college experiences should involve challenges to our beliefs even when those experiences go beyond our comfort level. Colleges might begin by inculcating a culture on campus in which students are expected to become informed about controversial speakers' views, either by listening to their arguments or by reading their positions. Role-playing exercises, in which supporters of each side are asked to switch sides, can also be valuable. 14

Third, similar role-playing exercises could be woven into controversial seminars in the social sciences and humanities and even in some natural sciences (e.g., on the role of humans in climate change, safety of GMOs, theory of evolution/origin of the universe, ethics of fetal stem-cell therapies, drilling in the Arctic Refuge, and CRISPR gene editing). Researching multiple sides of a contentious argument can help prevent ideological groupthink. It can even engender empathy for others and help routinize attempts to falsify one's pet theory and supplement it with efforts to disconfirm personal bias. 15

Fourth, during freshman orientation at our university, students are informed about codes of conduct related to plagiarism, intoxication, sexual harassment and so forth. They must pass online tests based on curricula (e.g., alcohol.edu). These are important issues, and entering students must demonstrate that they have read and understood these codes. However, freshmen are not encouraged to think about issues related to free expression, hate speech, what constitutes "evidence" or what is and is not protected expression by campus speech codes — as well as by the U.S. Constitution. They should be. 16

The take-home message from college should not be that feeling uncomfortable at hearing a collection of words strung together is grounds for censoring those words. A better lesson would be to learn to endure discomfort, to listen openly to alternative sides, and to respond with reasoned and effective counterarguments (when appropriate). College students should learn that reasonable, decent people will surely disagree with them about the ideas they hold most dear. This does not mean others are correct; they may be misguided and wrong, but the answer is not censorship. 17

As the philosopher John Stuart Mill[7] noted, when we assert that a topic is too controversial to be debated, we foreclose all argument, thinking and reasoning that might ultimately derive from the unfolding debate. Considering the list of "off-limits" topics on college campuses today, we must ask if we truly want college life to deprive young minds of the opportunity to develop that would be afforded by meaningful debate on these key issues of our time. 18

[7] For more on Mill, see the Introduction, pp. 21–22.

VOCABULARY/USING A DICTIONARY

1. What part of speech is *constitutes* (para. 2)? What does it mean?
2. What does the prefix in *preconceptions* (para. 6) tell you about the word's definition?
3. Can you give a synonym for *disparity* (para. 8)? What about an antonym?

RESPONDING TO WORDS IN CONTEXT

1. What does the phrase "*black lives matter*" (para. 2) mean? What does "*blue lives matter*" (para. 2) mean?
2. What is the *rubric* referred to in paragraph 7?
3. Williams and Ceci write that "Dartmouth College students *railed against* an op-ed published in the school's newspaper" (para. 8). How would you describe the students' response based on that description?

DISCUSSING MAIN POINT AND MEANING

1. Which side do you think the authors come closest to: Do they favor unlimited free speech or speech restrictions when it is deemed offensive or violent? Explain.
2. How does the college experience of previous generations differ from the experience of the current generation?
3. Williams and Ceci offer a "take-home message" from college in paragraph 17. What is that message? (Can you rephrase it in your own words?)

EXAMINING SENTENCES, PARAGRAPHS, AND ORGANIZATION

1. Williams and Ceci incorporate a number of questions throughout their essay. Do these questions function to expand their argument, create a transition, or both? Can you identify one question in the article and explain your answer?
2. What do you think of the structure Williams and Ceci impose on their essay in paragraphs 12–16? Can you describe the difference between this section and the writing that surrounds it?
3. Why do Williams and Ceci close with a quotation by John Stuart Mill? Do you think ending this way is effective? Why or why not?

THINKING CRITICALLY

1. How can speech be described as "violent"? How do the authors interpret this violence?
2. Have you ever felt you couldn't speak out about an issue on your college campus? What issue? Why did you feel that way?
3. **Connect.** How would Wendy Kaminer ("A Civic Duty to Annoy," p. 96) respond to Williams and Ceci's argument? How do you think she'd perceive the debate over free speech on today's college campuses? Have things changed?

WRITING ACTIVITIES

1. Do you think the authors' solutions to the problem would work? Write a scenario in which you imagine offering these solutions to the opposing parties — how might they respond?
2. Williams and Ceci offer step-by-step practical advice for how to balance free speech and respect for others. Using their model as a guide, create your own outline of how such a balance might be achieved or how one side or another should be weighted (if you think one side — free speech or maintaining respectful discourse — is more important than finding a balance). What template would you offer to those in a college setting?
3. You are currently in an academic setting that either encourages free speech and debate or treads carefully around certain ideas and avoids debate. Based on your personal college experience, respond to Williams and Ceci's argument that debate and expression in college should not be censored. Do you agree with them or disagree, and how has your opinion been shaped by the atmosphere around your education?

SPOTLIGHT ON DATA AND RESEARCH

Knight Foundation

Eight Ways College Students' Views on Free Speech Are Evolving

[*Medium*, March 12, 2018]

One reason for the trend of "trigger warnings" and "safe spaces" on college campuses throughout the nation may be found in a poll conducted by the prestigious Pew Research Center in 2015. Younger people, the survey found, are more likely to favor restrictions on speech offensive to minorities than are older people. For example, 40 percent of millennials (defined as people between eighteen and thirty-four) believe that government should prevent such offensive speech, whereas only 24 percent of baby boomers (defined as those between fifty-one and sixty-nine) share that belief. More recent polls and research — such as the March 2018 Gallup/Knight Foundation survey of over three thousand U.S. college students summarized below — have confirmed the 2015 Pew report. Younger people are more troubled than older Americans when the ideal of free speech is used to protect hate speech. For example, "when asked which was more important, students chose, by narrow margin, diversity and inclusion over free speech."

The Knight Foundation describes its mission as follows: "Knight Foundation is a national foundation with strong local roots. We invest in journalism, in the arts, and in the success of cities where brothers John S. and James L. Knight once published newspapers. Our goal is to foster informed and engaged communities, which we believe are essential for a healthy democracy."

As college campuses across the United States grapple with questions surrounding the power and limits of free expression, a new Gallup-Knight Foundation survey of U.S. college students provides a view into how attitudes about the First Amendment on college campuses are evolving and what that means for our democracy. 1

The study, sponsored by Knight Foundation, the American Council on Education, the Charles Koch Foundation, and the Stanton Foundation surveyed 3,014 U.S. college students, including an oversample of 216 students at Historically Black Colleges and Universities (HBCUs). It builds on a 2016 study by Gallup, Knight Foundation and the Newseum. 2

While U.S. college students show strong support for the First Amendment, many also approve of limits on speech to foster an environment where diverse perspectives are respected. These competing views and habits can have an effect on the freedoms that the First Amendment guarantees. Understanding them will help to preserve our most fundamental rights into the future. 3

HERE ARE 8 FINDINGS THAT STOOD OUT TO US

1. Free expression is important, but so is diversity. The majority of college students say protecting free speech rights (56 percent) and promoting a diverse and inclusive society (52 percent) are both extremely important to democracy. But when asked which was more important, students chose, by narrow margin, diversity and inclusion over free speech, 53 percent to 46 percent. Women, blacks and Democrats are more likely than their counterparts to choose inclusion over free speech. 4

2. Students support free speech, but increasingly favor limits. Students (70 percent) still favor an open learning environment that allows all types of speech over one that puts limits on offensive speech, however not as widely as they did in 2016 (78 percent). Democrats, blacks and women are among the groups that are less supportive of an open environment than they were in 2016; Republicans still overwhelmingly favor an open environment (86 percent). 5

3. Confidence in the security of First Amendment rights is dropping. While the majority of college students continue to view First 6

Amendment rights as secure rather than threatened, this number has dropped since 2016. Sixty-four percent of college students say freedom of speech is secure, down from 73 percent in 2016; 60 percent, down from 81 percent, say freedom of the press is secure.

4. Political conservatives are seen as less able to express their views. 7
Students (54 percent) are more likely to think the climate on their campus prevents people from speaking their mind because others might take offense. While a majority of college students, 69 percent, believe political conservatives are able to freely express their views on campus, many more believe political liberals (92 percent) and other campus groups are able to share their opinions freely.

5. Some students say shouting down speakers and using violence 8
is sometimes acceptable. Many colleges struggle when inviting controversial figures to speak on campus. Ninety percent of college students say it is never acceptable to use violence to prevent someone from speaking, but 10 percent say is sometimes acceptable. A majority (62 percent) also say shouting down speakers is never acceptable, although 37 percent believe it is sometimes acceptable.

6. Social media can stifle free expression. Students say discussion of 9
social and political issues mostly takes place on social media (57 percent), rather than in public areas of campus (43 percent). They increasingly agree that social media can stifle free expression because people can block those whose views they disagree (60 percent) or because people are afraid of being attacked (59 percent).

7. Students believe social media companies should be responsible 10
for limiting hate speech. Eight in 10 students agree that the internet has been responsible for an increase in hate speech. Sixty-eight percent of students strongly or somewhat agree that social media platforms like Facebook and Twitter should be responsible for limiting hate speech on their platforms. While 79 percent of Democrats hold this belief, 52 percent of Republicans do. Black students are also more likely than white students to think social media companies should to limit hate speech.

8. Trust in the media varies depending on political affiliation. 11
Democratic students express significantly more trust in the news media now; 64 say they have "a great deal" or "fair amount" of trust in the media to report the news accurately and fairly versus (44 percent) in 2016. Republicans' trust remains low with 64 percent expressing "not much" or no trust in the media.

POINTS TO CONSIDER

1. Note the use of the word *evolving* in the selection's title. What does this word suggest? What if the title read "Eight Ways College Students' Views on Free Speech Are Changing"? How would that differ?
2. In several places, the Knight Foundation's summary of the poll examines political affiliation. How would you summarize the differences between Democrats and Republicans with respect to their views on speech?
3. Although the poll confirms previous surveys that show younger people "are more likely than their counterparts to choose inclusion over free speech," the Knight summary offers no explanation of why this is. What do you think the reason or reasons may be for these findings?

The American Civil Liberties Union

Speech on Campus

Since its inception in 1920, the American Civil Liberties Union (ACLU) has been a leading defender of individual freedoms and a powerful opponent of government suppression of our constitutional rights. According to its Web site, the organization, with the support of more than four million members, works tirelessly to protect the basic rights and freedoms of all Americans on a wide range of public issues: "Whether it's achieving full equality for LGBT people, establishing new privacy protections for our digital age of widespread government surveillance, ending mass incarceration, or preserving the right to vote or the right to have an abortion, the ACLU takes up the toughest civil liberties cases and issues to defend all people from government abuse and overreach."

One issue the ACLU is closely associated with is an individual's First Amendment right to free speech. Although the organization is frequently viewed as pro-liberal and antiestablishment, its uncompromising position on speech can often enrage all parties. The following statement from its Web site summarizes the organization's position on the much-debated issue of campus speech.

The American Civil Liberties Union is a nonprofit and nonpartisan organization founded in 1920 by a group of intellectuals and activists. It describes as its mission "to defend and preserve the individual rights and liberties guaranteed to every person in this country by the Constitution and laws of the United States."

BEFORE YOU READ

How do we protect our right to free speech? Should colleges be allowed to censor speech on campus?

WORDS TO LEARN

restriction (para. 1): limitation (noun)
enterprise (para. 1): a project of some importance or difficulty (noun)
scrupulous (para. 3): precise (adjective)
pervasively (para. 4): widespread (adverb)
recruit (para. 4): to enlist (verb)

The First Amendment to the Constitution protects speech no matter how offensive its content. Restrictions on speech by public colleges and universities amount to government censorship, in violation of the Constitution. Such restrictions deprive students of their right to invite speech they wish to hear, debate speech with which they disagree, and protest speech they find bigoted or offensive. An open society depends on liberal education, and the whole enterprise of liberal education is founded on the principle of free speech. 1

How much we value the right of free speech is put to its severest test when the speaker is someone we disagree with most. Speech that deeply offends our morality or is hostile to our way of life warrants the same constitutional protection as other speech because the right of free speech is indivisible: When we grant the government the power to suppress controversial ideas, we are all subject to censorship by the state. Since its founding in 1920, the ACLU has fought for the free expression of all ideas, popular or unpopular. Where racist, misogynist, homophobic, and transphobic speech is concerned, the ACLU believes that more speech — not less — is the answer most consistent with our constitutional values. 2

But the right to free speech is not just about the law; it's also a vital part of our civic education. As Supreme Court Justice Robert Jackson wrote in 1943 about the role of schools in our society: "That they are educating the young for citizenship is reason for scrupulous protection of Constitutional freedoms of the individual, if we are not to strangle the free mind at its source and teach youth to discount important principles of our government as mere platitudes." Remarkably, Justice Jackson was referring to grade school students. Inculcating constitutional values — in particular, the value of free expression — should be nothing less than a core mission of any college or university. 3

To be clear, the First Amendment does not protect behavior on campus that crosses the line into targeted harassment or threats, or that creates a pervasively hostile environment for vulnerable students. But merely offensive or bigoted speech does not rise to that level, and determining when conduct crosses that line is a legal question that requires examination on a case-by-case basis. Restricting such speech may be attractive to college administrators as a quick fix to address campus tensions. But real social change comes from hard work to address the underlying causes of 4 inequality and bigotry, not from purified discourse. The ACLU believes that instead of symbolic gestures to silence ugly viewpoints, colleges and universities have to step up their efforts to recruit diverse faculty, students, and administrators; increase resources for student counseling; and raise awareness about bigotry and its history.

VOCABULARY/USING A DICTIONARY

1. What does *violation* (para. 1) mean? In what other circumstance have you heard that word that might help you define it?
2. Can you describe the difference between someone who is *vulnerable* (para. 4) and someone who is *invulnerable*?
3. What is another word for *discourse* (para. 4)?

RESPONDING TO WORDS IN CONTEXT

1. What part of speech is *warrant* as it's used in paragraph 2? How would you define it?
2. Paragraph 2 refers to *racist, misogynist, homophobic,* and *transphobic* speech. What groups are targeted by the hate speech of each of those words?
3. If our government is allowed to *suppress* an idea (para. 2), what is the government doing to it?

DISCUSSING MAIN POINT AND MEANING

1. What part of the Constitution protects the right to free speech in this country? How does the ACLU help uphold that right?
2. What potential problem exists if our right to free speech is hindered?
3. What, noted by the ACLU, are actions *not* protected by the First Amendment?

EXAMINING SENTENCES, PARAGRAPHS, AND ORGANIZATION

1. In the discussion of free speech, what transition or change takes place between the ideas in paragraph 2 and the ideas in paragraph 3?
2. In paragraph 2, we find the following sentence: "Speech that deeply offends our morality or is hostile to our way of life warrants the same constitutional protection as other speech because the right of free speech is indivisible: When we grant the government the power to suppress controversial ideas, we are all subject to censorship by the state." Why is this sentence structured this way? What is the benefit of the colon? What would be the difference if the two halves were inverted?

3. This is a short article. Does the final paragraph feel conclusive? Explain your answer.

THINKING CRITICALLY

1. Are you surprised by Supreme Court Justice Robert Jackson's statement about the role of free speech in education? Why or why not? What has your experience been, in primary and secondary schools as well as college- or university-level learning?
2. How do you feel about censorship? Are there times or situations in which the government should be allowed to step in and censor someone's words or actions? Explain your answer.
3. What does the ACLU state is a productive way to combat bigotry on campus? Do you agree? Why or why not?

WRITING ACTIVITIES

1. **Connect.** This article states: "How much we value the right of free speech is put to its severest test when the speaker is someone we disagree with most" (para. 2). With this in mind, write about the struggle taking place on college campuses over freedom of expression. What are the arguments against free speech, and why must the right to free speech be upheld? Compare the position presented here with the one in Williams and Ceci's "There Are No Good Alternatives to Free Speech on Campus" (p. 79).
2. In writing, respond to the following questions: Do you believe in the ACLU's ability to protect your right to free speech on campus? Have you experienced any situations in which the ACLU's help would have been beneficial or was enlisted? Even if you haven't, describe a situation that might cause a problem on campus in terms of free speech and consider who the ACLU would represent and what its arguments would be. Draw from the article here to support your position.
3. Research the history of the ACLU. In writing, state its original mission and whether that mission has changed over the years. What cases has the ACLU been involved in? Paragraph 2 mentions the founding of the ACLU in 1920. Why was 1920 a year that lent itself to the founding of such an organization? What have been the organization's greatest successes and failures?

Danny Bugingo (student essay)

A Need for Safe Spaces

[*The University of Idaho Argonaut*, December 4, 2017]

Along with such topics as "trigger warnings" and "microaggressions," "safe spaces" has become one of the contentious issues in campus battles over "free speech." What exactly are "safe spaces" and do they help protect marginalized students or do they further insulate them? In "A Need for Safe Spaces," University of Idaho student Danny Bugingo examines both the merits and disadvantages of protective campus spaces, which he defines as "anywhere people who share an identity, or are sympathetic to it, can meet without needing to justify, explain, or defend themselves." As you read his argument, ask yourself: Do I agree with his definition or do I see any flaws in it?

Danny Bugingo is studying mathematics and French at the University of Idaho.

BEFORE YOU READ

Is it possible or even desirable for different people to have a safe space to go to at all times? Are safe spaces antithetical to learning or to keeping an open mind?

WORDS TO LEARN

insularity (para. 4): isolation (noun)
sympathetic (para. 5): compassionate (adjective)
cower (para. 8): to crouch fearfully (verb)
revolve (para. 12): to circle around (verb)
incompatible (para. 13): contradictory (adjective)

I've never been to a Students for Life meeting, but their Facebook page indicates they plan tabling events and building a pro-life community on a campus that can often seem hostile to their views. 1

If I were to walk into one of their meetings and begin lecturing them about bodily autonomy and reproductive rights, they would probably ask me to leave and rightly so. Our free speech rights are in no way diminished by the fact that there are spaces where debate is unproductive and unwanted. 2

Conservatives are happy to construct these spaces, for example, at church or while the national anthem plays at a football game. They recognize that certain contexts should preclude protest and debate, and is consistent with our free speech ideals. 3

When conservatives grumble about campus snowflakes insulating themselves in safe spaces, they are reacting to a real, problematic insularity on the left, but they also misunderstand safe spaces. 4

A safe space is anywhere people who share an identity, or are sympathetic to it, can meet without needing to justify, explain, or defend themselves. 5

A church retreat site where Christians can explore their faith 6
without arguing with atheists is a safe space. The African Students' Association, where students can share ideas and experiences without constantly needing to explain their culture, is a safe space. An apartment where Kardashian fans can keep up with their favorite celebrity family, free from judgement, is a safe space.

Those who most forcefully object to safe spaces are often those 7
deepest inside one, surrounded by people who look like them and think like them. When someone's identity is never called into question, they can lose sight of the way it drapes their reality, and criticize others for engaging their own identities.

The idea of safe spaces arose in the 8
LGBTQA community, among people who knew speaking freely could invite violence. They were protecting themselves — not cowering from dissenting opinions.

> **They were protecting themselves — not cowering from dissenting opinions.**

While a Kardashian fan most likely 9
doesn't need a safe space in the same way, we all need safe spaces to live normal, healthy social lives.

Some progressives, however, take this idea too far. While every- 10
where should be safe from violence and harassment, not everywhere can be a safe space.

Classrooms, in particular, cannot be safe spaces. Learning often 11
requires that identities be justified, explained, and defended. There is no shared identity among the assorted students in a given classroom that would lend itself to a corresponding safe space. In general, the larger and more diverse a space and the people inside it are, the more difficult it is to make it a safe space because of this lack of shared identity.

However, some progressives fight to build expansive safe spaces 12
surrounding their entire lives. Their friends, habits, interests and crucially, social media, begin to revolve around their politics. While there's nothing wrong with being around like-minded people, wrapping oneself in an ideological cocoon avoids the difficult, important work of dealing with people who disagree.

In a country as diverse as ours, working with people who see things 13
differently is unavoidable. But listening and talking to a wide variety of people with kindness and an open mind is by no means incompatible with making use of safe spaces.

VOCABULARY/USING A DICTIONARY

1. Do you know what it means when something is said or done within the *context* (para. 3) of something else?

2. What part of speech is *preclude* (para. 3)? What is its relationship to *include*?
3. What is the opposite of a *dissenting* opinion (para. 8)?

RESPONDING TO WORDS IN CONTEXT

1. Why would someone approach a pro-life group to discuss *reproductive rights* (para. 2)? What would those rights be?
2. What contributing factors might lead to a situation in which debate is *unproductive* and *unwanted* (para. 2)?
3. Moving from any of the ideas Bugingo presents in this essay, can you give an example of an *ideological cocoon* (para. 12) or explain what he means by this term?

DISCUSSING MAIN POINT AND MEANING

1. How does Bugingo's final paragraph summarize his main point? How would you express his point?
2. Why can classrooms not be safe spaces?
3. What is the difference between a member of the LGBTQA community and a Kardashian fan in terms of the need for a safe space?

EXAMINING SENTENCES, PARAGRAPHS, AND ORGANIZATION

1. The essay opens with a hypothetical situation. What is it? Why do you think Bugingo starts this way? Of what relevance is it to his argument?
2. Are there places where you hoped for more from Bugingo's essay (in terms of specific examples or more explanation)? If so, where? If you were confused at any point, what was your confusion about?
3. In paragraph 6, Bugingo brings in three specific examples of people who might be looking for a safe space. He explains why. How did this paragraph influence your understanding of the argument that follows? Where else do you notice specific examples like these in the essay?

THINKING CRITICALLY

1. Consider paragraph 5. How does Bugingo define a safe space? Do you agree with his definition? Is this the way you think a safe space should be defined? Is this the way it is usually defined?
2. Who are the people Bugingo refers to in paragraph 7? Why is their identity "never called into question"?
3. **Connect.** Where do Bugingo and Williams and Ceci ("There Are No Good Alternatives to Free Speech on Campus," p. 79) agree on the purpose and value of "unsafe" classrooms? Do you think Williams and Ceci share Bugingo's ideas about safe spaces outside the classroom? Explain.

WRITING ACTIVITIES

1. Bugingo criticizes both the left and the right, both progressives and conservatives. What do conservatives get wrong about "safe spaces"? What does Bugingo claim that progressives get wrong? In a brief writing assignment, compare the ways in which each side misunderstands the intention of a safe space. Try to incorporate real-world examples (be specific when illustrating a scenario with progressives or conservatives) as you write.
2. Do you agree with Bugingo's argument in paragraph 11? In your opinion, can a classroom be a safe space? Write a short persuasive essay on this topic.
3. Try to come up with a group that Bugingo hasn't mentioned in his essay that might need a safe space. Write a short piece that explains why a safe space is needed and how that need connects to the points Bugingo makes.

LOOKING CLOSELY

Moving from Specific to General

A common and effective way to develop an essay is to move from a specific instance to a general point. A writer may open an essay by looking at a former professional football player now seriously disabled as a result of multiple concussions. From this particular instance, she could go on to establish a larger point about the severe dangers athletes face in today's competitive world of sports.

Notice how University of Idaho student Danny Bugingo, who makes a case for the value of safe spaces on college campuses, begins with a particular (though hypothetical) instance of interrupting a Students for Life meeting and, after producing further examples of other groups, moves to a general conclusion about our entire country. He not only supports his argument with concrete examples along the way but also, by his clear focus on particulars, fully earns his concluding generalization. His final paragraph is not merely tacked on.

1
Opens with a strong specific instance

2
Concludes with a general observation

(1) If I were to walk into one of their meetings and begin lecturing to them about bodily autonomy and reproductive rights, they would probably ask me to leave and rightly so.

(2) In a country as diverse as ours, working with people who see things differently is unavoidable. . . .

Wendy Kaminer

A Civic Duty to Annoy

[*Atlantic*, September 1997]

Although many Americans say they applaud diversity, they also often prefer to be among people who think and feel the same way they do. Given the choice, most people would rather be around those who agree with them politically, culturally, and socially. Yet, in the following short essay that appeared in the Atlantic *in September 1997, the best-selling social critic Wendy Kaminer argues that a healthy civic life demands a great deal of disagreement and that people should be much less sensitive about expressions that may offend them. Resisting the complaints of her privileged students about being "marginalized" or "oppressed," she maintains that "sometimes nurturing students means challenging their complaints instead of satisfying their demands for sympathy." She also reminds us that "everyone is bound to feel silenced, invisible, or unappreciated at least once in a while." But is Kaminer's outlook fading as the university becomes ever more diverse? Can we, and should we, sacrifice a bit of our ability to say whatever we want for the sake of others' well-being?*

An attorney, an author, and a social critic, Wendy Kaminer has won many awards and has served as president of the National Coalition against Censorship. Her numerous articles and reviews have appeared in such publications as the New York Times, *the* New Republic, *and the* Nation. *She is the author most recently of* Worst Instincts: Cowardice, Conformity, and the ACLU *(2009).*

BEFORE YOU READ

Do you feel you have a duty to annoy others? Why might one feel such a thing is important — for everyone's well-being?

WORDS TO LEARN

provoke (para. 2): to vex (verb)
scoff (para. 2): to mock (verb)
irreverence (para. 3): lack of respect (noun)
privileged (para. 3): entitled (adjective)
systematically (para. 4): in a planned manner (adverb)
promiscuously (para. 5): indiscriminately (adverb)
melodramatic (para. 5): overdramatic (adjective)
derogatory (para. 6): disparaging (adjective)
puerile (para. 6): childish (adjective)
apt (para. 8): fitting (adjective)
solicitude (para. 8): state of being caring or protective (noun)
rectitude (para. 11): integrity or uprightness (noun)

What is there about being in a room filled with people who agree with me that makes me want to change my mind? Maybe it's the self-congratulatory air of consensus among people who consider themselves and one another right-thinking. Maybe it's the consistency of belief that devolves into mere conformity. Maybe it's just that I can no longer bear to hear the word "empower." 1

At self-consciously feminist gatherings I feel at home in the worst way. I feel the way I do at family dinners, when I want to put my feet up on the table and say something to provoke old Uncle George. To get George going, I defend affirmative action or the capital-gains tax. To irritate my more orthodox feminist colleagues, I disavow any personal guilt about being born white and middle-class. I scoff every time I hear a Harvard student complain that she's oppressed. 2

I'm not alone in my irreverence, but feminist pieties combined with feminine courtesy keep most of us in line. Radcliffe College,[1] where I am based, is devoted to nurturing female undergraduates. We're supposed to nod sympathetically, in solidarity, when a student speaks of feeling silenced or invisible because she is female, of color, or both. We're not supposed to point out that Harvard students are among the most privileged people in the universe, regardless of race or sex. 3

I don't mean to scoff at the discrimination that a young woman of any color may have experienced or is likely to experience someday. I do want to remind her that as a student at Harvard/Radcliffe or any other elite university she enjoys many more advantages than a working-class white male attending a community college. And the kind of discrimination that students are apt to encounter at Harvard — relatively subtle and occasional — is not "oppression." It does not systematically deprive people of basic civil rights and liberties and is not generally sanctioned by the administration. 4

Besides, everyone is bound to feel silenced, invisible, or unappreciated at least once in a while. Imagine how a white male middle manager feels when he's about to be downsized. Like laments about dysfunctional families, complaints about oppression lose their power when proffered so promiscuously. Melodramatic complaints about oppression at Harvard are in part developmental: students in their late teens and early twenties are apt to place themselves at the center of the universe. But their extreme sensitivity reflects frequently criticized cultural trends as 5

[1] Founded in 1879 in Cambridge, Massachusetts, Radcliffe served as the women's college of the then all-male Harvard University. It didn't fully merge with Harvard until 1999, two years after Kaminer's essay was published.

well. An obsession with identity and self-esteem has encouraged students to assume that every insult or slight is motivated by racist, sexist, or heterosexist bias and gravely threatens their well-being. What's lost is a sense of perspective. If attending Harvard is oppression, what was slavery?

Sometimes nurturing students means challenging their complaints instead of satisfying their demands for sympathy. I've heard female students declare that any male classmate who makes derogatory remarks about women online or over the telephone is guilty of sexual harassment and should be punished. What are we teaching them if we agree? That they aren't strong enough to withstand a few puerile sexist jokes that may not even be directed at them? That their male classmates don't have the right to make statements that some women deem offensive? There would be no feminist movement if women never dared to give offense. 6

When nurturing devolves into pandering, feminism gives way to femininity. Recently a small group of female students called for disciplinary proceedings against males wearing "pornographic" T-shirts in a dining hall. They found it difficult to eat lunch in the presence of such unwholesome, sexist images. Should we encourage these young women to believe that they're fragile creatures, with particularly delicate digestive systems? Should we offer them official protection from T-shirts? Or should we point out that a group of pro-choice students might someday wear shirts emblazoned with words or images that pro-life students find deeply disturbing? Should we teach them that the art of giving and taking offense is an art of citizenship in a free society? 7

That is not a feminine art. Radcliffe, for example, is an unfailingly polite institution. Criticism and dissatisfaction are apt to be expressed in a feminine mode, covertly or indirectly. It's particularly hard for many of us not to react with great solicitude to a student who declares herself marginalized, demeaned, or oppressed, even if we harbor doubts about her claim. If she seeks virtue in oppression, as so many do, we seek it in maternalism. 8

We tend to forget that criticism sometimes expresses greater respect than praise. It is surely more of an honor than flattery. You challenge a student because you consider her capable of learning. You question her premises because you think she's game enough to re-examine them. You do need to take the measure of her self-confidence, and your own. Teaching — or nurturing — requires that you gain students' trust and then risk having them not like you. 9

Sometimes withholding sympathy feels mean, insensitive, and uncaring; you acquire all the adjectives that aren't supposed to 10 attach to women. You take on the stereotypically masculine vices at a time when the feminine virtue of niceness is being revived: Rosie O'Donnell[2] is the model talk-show host, civility the reigning civic virtue, and communitarianism the paradigmatic political theory. Communities are exalted, as if the typical community were composed solely of people who shared and cared about one another and never engaged in conflict.

In fact communities are built on compromise, and compromise 11 presupposes disagreement. Tolerance presupposes the existence of people and ideas you don't like. It prevails upon you to forswear censoring others but not yourself. One test of tolerance is provocation. When you sit down to dinner with your disagreeable relations, or comrades who bask in their rectitude and compassion, you have a civic duty to annoy them.

VOCABULARY/USING A DICTIONARY

1. What is *consensus* (para. 1)? What about *solidarity* (para. 3)?
2. What part of speech is the word *devolves* (para. 1)?
3. What does the prefix of the word *disavow* (para. 2) tell you about its definition?

RESPONDING TO WORDS IN CONTEXT

1. Why do you think Kaminer can "no longer bear to hear the word 'empower'" (para. 1)?
2. What do you think Kaminer means in paragraph 3 when she refers to *feminist pieties* (a clue might be in what follows—*feminine courtesy*)?
3. What do you think Kaminer means by *maternalism* in paragraph 8, and why do you think that word was chosen?

DISCUSSING MAIN POINT AND MEANING

1. According to Kaminer's title, it is our "civic duty to annoy." What does she mean by that? Point to specific sentences or paragraphs that support your thinking.
2. What example does Kaminer bring in to make the distinction between oppression and a lesser degree of discrimination?
3. What are the necessary aspects of teaching, according to Kaminer?

---

[2] Comedian and LGBTQ+ activist Rosie O'Donnell (b. 1962) hosted a popular television show from 1996 to 2002.

EXAMINING SENTENCES, PARAGRAPHS, AND ORGANIZATION

1. What do you notice about Kaminer's opening sentence? How does it help characterize her as an author?
2. In paragraph 11, she writes, "In fact communities are built on compromise, and compromise presupposes disagreement." Where else in the essay has Kaminer presented those ideas — that communities are built on compromise or that compromise presupposes disagreement? Identify particular passages.
3. Kaminer introduces a number of questions throughout her essay. Choose one (or a few) and explain why she is using a question instead of a statement. What effect is she trying to achieve?

THINKING CRITICALLY

1. **Connect.** Kaminer seems to believe that our society has gone too far to protect people from criticism and disappointment in college and social life. Consider how her essay from 1997 overlaps with the more recent ideas presented about college life in Williams and Ceci's "There Are No Good Alternatives to Free Speech on Campus" (p. 79). Identify a message or messages that you find shared between them.
2. What, for Kaminer, is a test of tolerance? What is achieved by such a test?
3. Do you agree that "criticism sometimes expresses greater respect than praise" (para. 9)? If yes, how so? If no, why not?

WRITING ACTIVITIES

1. Have you ever exercised your "civic duty to annoy" as Kaminer did when "to irritate [her] more orthodox feminist colleagues," she would "disavow any personal guilt about being born white and middle-class" and "to provoke old Uncle George," she would "defend affirmative action or the capital-gains tax" (para. 2)? If so, write a short essay describing a time you've exercised this duty. Or if not, explain what held you back.
2. Write a direct response to Kaminer. Do you agree or disagree with her perspective? Do you think things have changed since 1997 when this was written, for better or for worse? Incorporate your thinking about historical changes into the response. While you can respond to her specifically (using "I" and "you"), this is not a letter but a reasoned response that should refer to her points and include your own supporting evidence.
3. Consider Kaminer's essay in the light of political correctness, trigger warnings, microaggression awareness, and the #MeToo movement. Using some sort of visual mapping or outline, identify Kaminer's main points and hold these newer ideas or protections against them. What happens to Kaminer's points when these are introduced? What does the argument look like when extended through time and how might she circle back to these ideas if she were to rewrite the essay today?

Discussing the Unit

SUGGESTED TOPIC FOR DISCUSSION

While it is constitutionally protected, our right to free speech does not mean we can say anything we want whenever or wherever we want. Should speech be entirely free on a college campus? Why is encouraging free speech important, particularly for university-level learning? Are students today encouraged to speak freely or do we need to protect the student body from certain ideas?

PREPARING FOR CLASS DISCUSSION

1. Today's campuses are divided over whether having one's beliefs challenged is a productive part of the college experience. How is the challenging of beliefs and introduction of many perspectives a valuable part of one's educational experience? What about Bugingo's argument about the importance of safe spaces?
2. Does your campus tolerate free speech and a free exchange of ideas regardless of whether those ideas are popular or potentially harmful? Have there been times when free speech has been limited or when students have been shielded from certain ideas or messages on your campus? How are these questions raised and these moments discussed in the essays in this chapter?

FROM DISCUSSION TO WRITING

1. Does this chapter provide clues about how past generations of students might have responded to words and situations that would cause discomfort when free speech is practiced? Do you think we are less interested today in protecting free speech on campus?
2. Are the writers who favor protecting students from certain ideas or language hindering anyone's education? Is there anything that any writer or writers say on the topic of circumscribing free speech or creating safe spaces that strikes you as particularly persuasive?

TOPICS FOR CROSS-CULTURAL DISCUSSION

1. Some articles in this chapter state that shielding students from certain ideas does them a disservice. Can you make a case against that idea by comparing it with an argument from another essay in this chapter? Do gender and race play a part in that argument? Are gender and race important considerations? Why or why not?
2. Today's professors must navigate the increasingly murky waters of when to shield students from particular materials—and what materials those would be. Look closely at articles discussing free speech on college campuses and

the free exchange of ideas. Where do the debating authors show sensitivity or insensitivity to students suffering from psychological difficulties? Using readings in this chapter, make a case that colleges should or should not make accommodations for students suffering from conditions including post-traumatic stress disorder by using trigger warnings, or should or should not protect students from microaggressions. Should there be safe spaces on campus for students or are those spaces likely to be used as a way to avoid engaging with the ideas of others?

3

U.S. History: How Do We Remember Our Past?

Chapter 2 looked at the state of free speech on America's campuses. And just as students and instructors grapple with the ways they communicate in an ever more diverse setting, another problem hovers over the conversation — the campuses themselves. Many of America's universities were built at a time when racism, sexism, and other forms of discrimination were the default in American life. The names enshrined on college walls and the people celebrated with statues on college greens sometimes carry a dark legacy from a less inclusive past. Universities, like all institutions, want to pay homage to the men and women who built and nurtured them, but this puts students, especially minority students, in a difficult position: Should they blithely accept in their midst monuments and dedications to people who might have denied them their education? Or should they object to things that are largely symbolic, an effort other students sometimes see as petulant and pointless?

Recent years have seen several high-profile flare-ups at American schools over their physical and historical legacies. Many schools, under pressure from students and faculty, renamed buildings and institutions originally named after people who had supported slavery and white supremacy in the past. Amherst College officially shelved its mascot, Lord Jeffery Amherst, an eighteenth-century governor who promoted genocide of Native Americans. Harvard stopped calling faculty leaders of its residential houses "masters." Although it insisted the word had nothing to do with slavery in its context, the university acknowledged it was troubling to many students. Other efforts have failed to bring about change. Students and faculty at the University of Virginia, founded in 1819 by Thomas Jefferson, America's third president, have called for images of and references to the founder, who owned slaves, to be scrubbed. Members of the communities of the University of Missouri and the College of William and Mary, which also have Jefferson statues, joined the call. So far, those efforts have foundered; Jefferson's image as an intellectual leader seems, for the moment, to trump the more troubling elements of his legacy on campus. In 2019, the University of Notre Dame decided to cover a large mural of Christopher Columbus in one of its main halls because of its "demeaning" portrayal of Native Americans.

In this chapter, we will examine how the call for a reevaluation of our public history has played out in the country as a whole.

Bill Bramhall

Mt. Rushmore: Student Activists Demanded Their Removal

[*New York Daily News*, November 23, 2015]

Mount Rushmore, a massive statue in the Black Hills of South Dakota where the faces of four American presidents seem to spring out of the natural world, is one of the country's most famous and enduring national monuments. In this cartoon, Bill Bramhall imagines its somewhat grotesque removal as a reflection on the "cleansing" of history by taking down statues and names some people find offensive. A park ranger tells some clearly disappointed tourists that the four faces — all of older white men who have been in charge of the country — have been toppled, because "student activists demanded their removal."

POINTS TO CONSIDER

1. Why does the park ranger refer to "student activists"? Mount Rushmore is not on a college campus, and university movements to remove markers of the past considered offensive include both students and faculty. How

does limiting the complainants to students subtly discredit the movement Bramhall is imagining? How does the word *demanded* further argue against the students' point of view?

2. The means of dismantling Mount Rushmore that the cartoon imagines—blowing up the presidents' heads—is especially violent. What does this achieve for the cartoonist and his point of view?
3. Why does Bramhall use Mount Rushmore as his extreme example? Why does removing the massive granite memorial seem so obviously unreasonable? Do you agree with Bramhall that removing the heads would be unreasonable? What arguments might there be for "their removal"?

Ernest B. Furgurson

The End of History?

[*The American Scholar*, Autumn 2015]

In the "real," off-campus world, perhaps nothing has provoked more debate than symbols of the Confederacy. After a white supremacist who flew the Confederate flag on his social media pages killed nine people in a historically black Charleston church, South Carolina finally took the controversial flag down from its statehouse grounds. But the flag represents only one symbol; scattered all over the nation are monuments and memorials honoring those (such as Generals Robert E. Lee or Stonewall Jackson) who fought for or defended the Confederacy during the Civil War. And many buildings carry the names of Southern statesmen who supported slavery.

Historian and journalist Ernest B. Furgurson may disagree with much of the protest against the display of Confederate history, but he urges us to seek balance and caution in our consideration of historical symbols. "Before we send out the wrecking ball," he says in "The End of History?," "let's do nuance: Where do we start, and where do we stop?" Furgurson urges liberals to apply their very own principles—inclusivity, thoughtfulness, and understanding—to the symbols they would tear down.

Ernest B. Furgurson is a former correspondent and columnist for the Baltimore Sun. *A historian and biographer, Furgurson has written a number of books, including* Chancellorsville 1863 *(1993),* Ashes of Glory *(1997),* Not War but Murder *(2001), and* Freedom Rising *(2005).*

BEFORE YOU READ

Where do you stand in the debate over war memorials, particularly Civil War memorials? How do you think history should be honored?

WORDS TO LEARN

nuance (para. 2): a subtle difference (noun)

obelisk (para. 3): a tall, four-sided stone column that tapers at the top (noun)

rearguard (para. 8): describing an action that protects the back of the troops (often during retreat) (adjective)

vigorous (para. 8): strong or active (adjective)

eloquently (para. 11): fluently or expressively (adverb)

egregious (para. 12): glaring or flagrant (adjective)

conspicuously (para. 12): noticeably (adverb)

With the lowering of the Confederate battle flag in South Carolina and elsewhere, some diehards still insist that the banner had nothing to do with race, that it was just a symbol of their Southern heritage. Other Americans long offended by the Confederate monuments that stand all across Dixie are urging that those memorials come down along with the flag. Still others clarify the matter in three words: black lives matter, spray-painted on monuments north and south. Somewhere amid all this, I am trying to place myself. 1

So far, the debate lacks nuance. It seems simple: The Confederate States of America existed to preserve slavery, so anything honoring its memory should be erased from modern America. But before we send out the wrecking ball, let's do nuance: Where do we start, and where do we stop? 2

What about statues that were cast to mourn for the dead, erected not by the Ku Klux Klan or its descendants, but by grieving widows? Should those in graveyards be allowed to stand? What about the memorial in Green Hill Cemetery in my hometown, Danville, Virginia? It's a tall obelisk erected in 1878 by the Ladies Memorial Association, standing in what is today a mostly black neighborhood. It's a monument to the dead, but it's by no means neutral. It features bas-reliefs of Robert E. Lee and Stonewall Jackson, and says, 3

> Patriots! Know that these fell in the effort to establish just government and perpetuate Constitutional Liberty. Who thus die, will live in lofty example.

If it should go, what about the simple government-issued headstone nearby, which identifies my Civil War great-grandfather as "1st Sgt Co I 53rd Va Infantry," and thousands of others like it? 4

5 What about Monument Avenue in Richmond, with its grand likenesses of Lee, Jackson, Jefferson Davis, J. E. B. Stuart, Matthew Fontaine Maury? Might we differentiate between fiery politicians such as Davis, who wasn't even a Virginian, and the generals they dragged into war? If the generals should go, then what about the privates who marched because their neighbors did, defending slavery even though they never owned a slave? What about the statues of Confederate soldiers standing before hundreds of county courthouses? Most face north defiantly, muskets at the ready. But others, like the one facing south in the center of Alexandria, Virginia, are unarmed, hats off, heads bowed, clearly mourning fallen comrades. Shall we appoint committees to decide what each sculptor was thinking? You're right: this could get silly.

6 But suppose we did decide to tear those down — what about all the other reminders of our shameful past? Mount Vernon, Monticello, Montpelier, and the other homes of our slave-owning presidents? What about the statues of Confederate soldiers on every Civil War battlefield site?

7 To take down every offensive monument in the South willy-nilly reminds me of the wholesale de-Stalinization campaign that I witnessed in the old Soviet Union, and the destruction of ancient monuments by ISIS and Taliban fanatics today. Totalitarian states may decree that the painful past never happened, but any such official effort in our country, even one executed selectively, would be tragic.

> **So far, the debate lacks nuance.**

8 Saying all this, and considering my ancestors, I might be shrugged off as just another rearguard Rebel. I qualify four times over for membership in the Sons of Confederate Veterans, vigorous defenders of their heritage and its symbols. Because I'd written Civil War history, I was invited about 20 years ago to speak to the SCV camp in Alexandria. In my talk, I recalled my great-grandfather who died of smallpox in the Yankee prison at Fort Delaware, and the three others who were wounded later in the war. The Sons were impressed. And then I told them that the Confederate battle flag was a provocation that should be retired to the museum. I haven't been invited back.

9 The punch line of that talk was a pale version of everything I've said and written about race and racism since I did my first column for the late, lamented *Danville Commercial Appeal* at the age of 18. Yet, because I remain concerned that I might be misunderstood when I suggest going slow in the current debate, I've let others say what I've been thinking.

10 Mayor Stephanie Rawlings-Blake of Baltimore, with hard-earned experience trying to cool public anger, has wisely punted these matters by naming a committee to dig into the issue and stir public dialogue. Roger

Davidson Jr., a professor at Baltimore's Coppin State University — who, like the mayor, is African American — thinks that demolishing the monuments would be "horrible" because they can be teaching tools about a chapter still misunderstood by too many people.

New York Times editorialist Brent Staples [see p. 229], who has written eloquently about growing up black, strongly supports removing statues of villains like Confederate general Nathan Bedford Forrest, who was a postwar organizer of the Klan. Such efforts are not "bad-faith attempts to rewrite history," he says, but reflections on "how to honor history . . . and rightly deciding that some figures who were enshrined as heroes in the past do not deserve to be valorized in public places." 11

Interesting that Staples says "some figures," which may suggest just the most egregious offenders, or just Confederates. But neither he nor the mayor nor the professor nor I want to start bulldozing without serious "reflections on how to honor history." For me, that should mean enshrining other heroes at least as conspicuously as the ones who now stir such passions. 12

Imagine Martin Luther King Jr. standing tall in the capital of every state in the old Confederacy, indeed the whole Union . . . Move Arthur Ashe's token memorial off Monument Avenue and put a grander one on the broad Boulevard nearby, renaming it Ashe Boulevard. Along it, raise Powhatan Beaty, Decatur Dorsey, and Edward Ratcliff, who fled slavery in Virginia to join the U.S. Colored Troops and won the Medal of Honor fighting for freedom . . . Erect Thurgood Marshall, Sojourner Truth, Frederick Douglass, Medgar Evers, Crispus Attucks, A. Philip Randolph, Dred Scott, Rosa Parks, Harriet Tubman . . . The list stretches from 1619 into tomorrow. 13

If we're going to honor our history, let us honor all of it. 14

VOCABULARY/USING A DICTIONARY

1. What is a *widow* (para. 3)?
2. How would you describe something that happens *willy-nilly* (para. 7)?
3. What is the definition of *totalitarian* (para. 7)? What part of speech is it?

RESPONDING TO WORDS IN CONTEXT

1. If the soldiers depicted are mourning their *comrades* (para. 5), whom are they mourning?
2. If a matter is *punted* (para. 10), what does that mean? When is the word *punted* likely to be used?
3. What is the meaning of *provocation* (para. 8)? From what language does it derive?

DISCUSSING MAIN POINT AND MEANING

1. What two main questions does Furgurson believe are important to ask before we decide how to rethink our memorials?
2. Does Furgurson suggest we should remove all offensive memorials? Why or why not?
3. How does Furgurson think history should be honored?

EXAMINING SENTENCES, PARAGRAPHS, AND ORGANIZATION

1. What do you notice about Furgurson's conclusion? Why do you think he ends his essay the way he does?
2. In his opening paragraph, Furgurson outlines different positions taken on war memorials and the idea of reconsidering their place in our public spaces. He states, "Somewhere amid all this, I am trying to place myself" (para. 1). Does he explore these positions thoroughly in his body paragraphs?
3. It is fine for a writer to take different positions into account in an essay — often it makes an essay stronger — but many essays present one particular position, known as the thesis. In Furgurson's essay, which sentence do you think is closest to his thesis?

THINKING CRITICALLY

1. Why does Furgurson hesitate to get rid of Confederate memorials?
2. Is it surprising that Furgurson moves from a discussion of removing Confederate monuments to a discussion of getting rid of Mount Vernon, Monticello, and Montpelier? Why or why not?
3. Based on the arguments Furgurson presents, do you think Mayor Rawlings-Blake will find any consensus by forming "a committee to dig into the issue and stir public dialogue" (para. 10)? Explain.

WRITING ACTIVITIES

1. Copy the names of the other heroes Furgurson suggests. If you don't recognize a name, do a quick online search to familiarize yourself. Choose one name and make a case in writing for why that person's contributions were valuable to society and why a statue or memorial should be erected in his or her honor. Describe the sort of memorial you envision and where it would be placed.
2. Looking at the names you copied for question 1, think about another person *not already on the list* whom the public might want to see honored with a memorial. Would that person's name fit in this particular list? Why or why

not? Regardless of whether the name belongs in this list, write a portrait of the individual you have chosen and explain why that person's contributions were valuable to society. In small groups, discuss the reasons for a memorial, as if you and your classmates were members of a committee choosing to honor one individual. In discussion, determine if any of your reasons for wanting to memorialize someone are the same as those of the other group members.

3. Create an outline of the main points Furgurson uses in his essay. What is this essay about? What conclusion does Furgurson reach at the end? Furgurson states in the beginning: "Somewhere amid all this, I am trying to place myself" (para. 1). Construct an *if... then* statement that reflects Furgurson's position at the end of the essay.

SPOTLIGHT ON DATA AND RESEARCH

Rosalind Bentley

Are Southerners Losing Support for the Confederate Flag?

[*The Atlanta Journal-Constitution*, December 18, 2018]

For decades, the Confederate flag has been a hotly contested social, political, and cultural issue, with those who support it believing it displays southern pride and those who oppose it arguing that it endorses an ugly history of slavery, racism, and white supremacism. It was not until July 5, 2015, that South Carolina removed the controversial flag from its statehouse after nine African American churchgoers were gunned down in Charleston by a young white supremacist who flaunted the flag. But the nationally covered statehouse removal was not without protests by those who lamented the loss of what they regard as a cherished symbol.

Although not entirely, the issue was and still remains largely confined to the southern states. The following news item from the Atlanta Journal-Constitution *reports on the results of a poll that surveyed approximately one thousand Southerners to see how they felt about the flag and several other issues (omitted here). The poll showed that 46 percent of all southerners hold a "somewhat or very unfavorable" view of the Confederate flag. But the poll also demonstrated that the flag remains divisive along racial lines.*

A little more than half of the people living in 11 Southern states 1
want to address the issue of Confederate statues and monuments in public spaces, but they disagree over how that should be done, according to a new Winthrop University Southern Focus poll.

The results of the Winthrop Southern Focus Survey, released 2
Tuesday, also show that 46 percent of all Southerners now hold a "somewhat or very unfavorable" view toward the Confederate battle flag. But the degree to which a Southerner has unfavorable feelings about Confederate iconography has much to do with the individual's race. . . .

The survey comes at a time when 3
Southern states and cities, including Atlanta, are deciding what to do with Confederate monuments, statues and street names. In Atlanta, the city changed the name of Confederate Avenue to United Avenue this fall. And the debate has sometimes taken a deadly turn, as with the killing of a counterprotester at a white supremacists rally in Charlottesville, Va., in August 2017. The rally was over the city's plan to remove a statue of Confederate Gen. Robert E. Lee from a public park near downtown.

The survey comes at a time when Southern states and cities, including Atlanta, are deciding what to do with Confederate monuments, statues and street names.

With the battle flag question, 58 percent of African-Americans 4
said they view the flag unfavorably, while only 44 percent of the white respondents felt that way. Similarly, a majority of African-Americans saw the battle flag as a divisive image, while a majority of whites saw it as a representation of "Southern pride."

While some cities such as Richmond, Va., and Atlanta have explored 5
adding contextual markers to Confederate monuments as opposed to removing the monuments altogether, poll respondents had strong opinions about the marker strategy. In most cases, the proposed markers would address slavery and the legacy of legal segregation.

When it comes to monuments and statues that honor the 6
Confederate war dead, 42 percent of all respondents, black and white, said they should be left as they are without markers. Thirty-one percent of white respondents, however, said they should be left alone but markers added. Only 16 percent of African-Americans agreed with that approach. African-Americans, however, did support removing monuments and statues to the Confederate war dead, with 55 percent of black respondents saying the statuary should be placed in museums or removed altogether. Only 20 percent of whites agreed with that approach.

When it came to statues that honored segregationists, 63 percent of African-Americans said they should be placed in museums or removed completely from public view. Only 33 percent of whites supported those two approaches. 7

As for the cause of the Civil War, a debate that is still ongoing in the South, the results were by some measures surprising. When asked whether the war was caused by slavery, concerns over states' rights or both equally, just under half of all Southerners polled, 49 percent, said it was "both equally." Thirty percent of African-Americans said slavery was the main reason, and 26 percent of whites said it was solely a question of states' rights. 8

POINTS TO CONSIDER

1. Do you think the Winthrop Southern Focus Survey clearly demonstrates that the Confederate flag is losing appeal among Southerners? Why or why not? How do you interpret the numbers?
2. What do the numbers reported here tell you about how the races differ in their reaction to the flag? In your opinion, how significant are the differences?
3. The poll also asked about responses of both races to Confederate monuments and statues. How do those numbers compare to the numbers regarding the flag alone? What differences can you see between how African Americans and whites approach the question of what to do about the statues and monuments?

Dasia Moore (student essay)

When Does Renaming a Building Make Sense?

[*The Nation*, February 17, 2017]

As a first-year student at Yale, Dasia Moore was dismayed to see herself surrounded by stereotypical images of African Americans in a college building named to honor one of its graduates, John C. Calhoun. One of the South's leading defenders of slavery, Calhoun (1782–1850) was also one of the most influential politicians behind the concept of secession. His political theories would justify the dissolution of southern states from the Union and ultimately result in the Civil War.

In "When Does Renaming a Building Make Sense?," Moore reports on her role as a part of a university committee to "create standards for renaming buildings." Her essay covers the struggles with coming to a decision and, at the same time, makes her readers aware that "what and whom we choose to memorialize from the past also serve as powerful symbols of the present."

Dasia Moore graduated from Yale in 2018 with a degree in Ethics, Politics, and Economics. She currently works as a news associate for Katie Couric Media.

BEFORE YOU READ

Have you ever seen something memorialized from the United States' past that made you angry or ashamed? What tipping point must be reached in such a case before changing the name of a place — whether it's a college or other building or memorial?

WORDS TO LEARN

intact (para. 1): whole (adjective)
chastise (para. 3): to criticize harshly (verb)
convene (para. 3): to come together (verb)
marginalized (para. 8): sidelined; made unimportant (adjective)
demarcate (para. 8): to set the boundaries of (verb)
iconography (para. 8): symbolic representation (noun)
fundamentally (para. 10): in a basic way (adverb)
tumult (para. 10): uproar (noun)
exclusion (para. 11): the state of being kept apart (verb)

The image that greets me is one that will go on to make headlines nearly two years later when a black dining-hall employee named Corey Menafee takes a broom to the window and shatters it into 27 pieces. When asked why he did it, Menafee will say to the *New Haven Independent,* "It's 2016. I shouldn't have to come to work and see things like that." But it is 2014, during my second week at Yale, and the window is still intact. I am transfixed by what I see: two black figures, an enslaved man and woman — the only black woman I have seen depicted in art at Yale so far — with baskets on their heads, picking cotton. Other details of the room start to come into focus: the portrait of John C. Calhoun hanging over one mantel, the minstrel show–like image of a man in blackface eating a watermelon, the panels dedicated to South Carolina plantation scenery. I feel like crying or running away — doing anything besides eating lunch and chatting with my new roommate. I struggle through the meal and quietly promise myself to avoid Calhoun College as best I can for the next four years. 1

I did not end up keeping my promise. My sophomore year, Calhoun wove in and out of conversations with friends, in class, and even with people back home following the announcement by Yale's president that the university would consider renaming Calhoun, in the aftermath of the massacre at Emanuel A.M.E. Church. I grew up in Charleston and attended elementary school directly across the street from Mother Emanuel, on Calhoun Street. It was coming of age in a historic city that taught me the importance of remembering the past. It was standing on Calhoun's namesake street after the shooting, crying with family and strangers, that convinced me that what and whom we choose to memorialize from the past also serve as powerful symbols of the present. 2

After a year of community conversations and demonstrations, in May of 2016 Yale decided not to change the name of Calhoun. In the spring and summer after that announcement, columns chastised, letters pleaded, and the window in the dining hall depicting the two slaves was shattered. The decision turned out not to be final: In August, the Yale community received an e-mail from President Salovey saying that a committee would be convened to create standards for renaming buildings, standards that would be applied to a revisited case for renaming Calhoun College. There was one spot on the committee for an undergraduate. I applied, and just before my junior year began, my non-engagement pact with Calhoun definitively ended. 3

Over the course of four months, I spoke in person with 188 undergraduates about Calhoun and the question of renaming more generally. These conversations were supplemented by reports, articles, personal writings, e-mails, and meeting transcripts that drew from hundreds more student voices that had spoken out about Calhoun the previous year. Beyond community engagement, the committee read through thousands of pages on the history and theory of public memory and renaming. 4

Why do all of this? Why not just scrap Calhoun or preserve Calhoun and then move on? While there were days I asked myself these questions, I was reminded time and time again throughout the committee's process that the situation Yale had found itself in was about more than Calhoun, more than even the scores of namesakes honored around campus. Our community was engaged in an important struggle over how symbolism and history assert themselves in our lives, and how they impact diverse communities differently. On these issues, my peers spoke with incredible passion, insight, and a profound love for the Yale community that turned even the sharpest criticisms of the university into salves for its deepest wounds. 5

Many undergraduates appealed to what they saw as Yale's highest values — community, learning, and diversity of experience and thought among them — just as they expressed a pervasive sentiment that Yale as an institution did not always live up to those values. One student, a black student, said that racist and otherwise hurtful symbols he confronted on campus did not surprise him at an old university so entwined with our nation's murky history: "I expected things like this," he told me with a shrug. At one listening session, a student offered a different perspective. She cited Yale's "obsession with its own history" as a crucial impediment to the school's progression into the future. Her comment resonated with others in the room who took a moment to look around the imitation-Gothic stonework, the leaded windows, the dark fireplaces that had spent most of their lives sealed in — all built in the 1930s. 6

Students were invested in history, of course, and felt strongly that Yale was obligated to teach and preserve the past in all its glory and shame, but most believed that Yale could carry out its responsibility to history without compromising its commitment to its present-day student body. Every single listening session, meeting, and individual conversation about renaming and symbolism eventually circled around to the importance of community. Yale students love the residential colleges, the places where we study, live, eat, make friends, play Frisbee, meet our professors, and feel at home. Many students stressed the importance, or even sacredness, of the colleges in particular as spaces where they and all their peers should feel welcomed. Your home is not the place to engage in a battle with history, many argued, it is the place to rest after fighting that battle in the classroom and the rest of the world. 7

In particular, students of color and those with other marginalized identities spoke to the power symbols and memorials have to announce priorities and demarcate the boundaries of inclusive and exclusive spaces. Many shared stories that mirrored my experience freshman year — loss of appetite or loss of a sense of belonging at Yale after seeing the windows in Calhoun or similar iconography, learning that the namesake of a building or room would not have wanted them in it, or else confronting the serious lack of representation of their identity on campus. Many emphasized that symbolism has as much to do with absences as it does presence. People described the struggle to exist in a space that had historically excluded us, as well as the desire to see evidence of our existence — in the names etched on buildings, in the portraits hanging proudly on walls. 8

> **People described the struggle to exist in a space that had historically excluded us, as well as the desire to see evidence of our existence. . . .**

For decades now, students of color, women, low-income students, those with disabilities, and so many others have fought to make a home at Yale, and many felt it was time to feel the fruits of that labor, both through the recognition and reconsideration of the painful symbols that picked at the scabs of painful histories and through increased diversity in symbols that could mirror the community's range of members.

Had it been possible, I might have spent an eternity talking with my peers about building names, just to take in the passion and thoughtfulness that make up the spirit of Yale. The committee had to start making decisions, however, and by late November, we had a draft of principles. The final report was over 20 pages — the most condensed a fair account of the complexity and range of considerations surrounding renaming could be. In the report, we played a balancing game that involved assuaging fears of both the most conservative and liberal, young and old members of the community, while offering principles that were fair to both the historic legacy of Yale and the Yale of today and the future. We began with an assumption against renaming, one that honored the university's commitment to history and continuity, and transitioned into the special circumstances that would warrant removing a name. 9

Like the undergraduates who had called for change at Yale, the committee report appealed to the institution's values: "Is a principal legacy of the namesake fundamentally at odds with the mission of the University?" If the answer was yes, three further principles offered circumstances under which a name change on the basis of values would be especially appropriate: if the namesake's actions and ideas were a subject of debate even in their own lifetime, if the university knowingly acted against its own mission in choosing a certain namesake, and if the building was central to community life and unity. It was not the committee's job to decide whether to rename Calhoun, and the principles themselves avoided specific reference to him. Still, in the days following the report's release, there seemed to be no doubt in anyone's mind that under those principles, John C. Calhoun was unfit to be the namesake of a residential college at Yale. Our community had already undergone a year of highly publicized tumult. After the report release, the campus settled into relative peace and quiet while we all awaited the final word on Calhoun. Just last week, the news came, and the college on the corner of Elm and College Streets will now be called Grace Murray Hopper. The decision on campus was met with a full day of celebration and relief. 10

Universities everywhere, cities, states, and the country as a whole continue to struggle to preserve history without perpetuating inequality and prejudice. Though none of these challenges will be met easily, I believe firmly that possibilities exist, and we must pursue them with the confidence that we can build communities that welcome all people of all 11 backgrounds home. To find these solutions, we must engage in thoughtful dialogue and compromise, but we cannot settle for others' exclusion, or our own. I, for one, will no longer be promising myself to avoid eating in the college formerly known as Calhoun.

VOCABULARY/USING A DICTIONARY

1. How might you be able to define the word *transfix* (para. 1) based on the parts of the word?
2. Define the word *salve* (para. 5). From what language does it derive?
3. What is an *impediment* (para. 6)?

RESPONDING TO WORDS IN CONTEXT

1. What does Moore mean when she refers to Calhoun's *namesake* street (para. 2)?
2. If something is *residential* (para. 7), like the colleges Moore speaks of, what does it feel like to be there?
3. What is implied when Moore says she wishes she could have spent an *eternity* (para. 9) talking to the Yale community about building names?

DISCUSSING MAIN POINT AND MEANING

1. What moment reveals the value to Moore of careful thought and discretion to whom we memorialize in order to empower ourselves in the present?
2. Though the writer is focused on one particular building on one college campus, how does she expand this specific case into a larger issue?
3. What is the central conflict Moore faces in the debate over Calhoun College?

EXAMINING SENTENCES, PARAGRAPHS, AND ORGANIZATION

1. Note the many times the writer refers to "community." Why is that concept important to our understanding of her argument?
2. What is the link between Yale and Charleston, South Carolina, in paragraph 2?
3. What does Moore's final sentence mean? Can you paraphrase it?

THINKING CRITICALLY

1. How do you understand Moore's first experience of Calhoun College? What would your reaction be?
2. **Connect.** Do you think Niman ("As Confederate Flags Fall, Columbus Statues Stand Tall," p. 121) would be sympathetic to Moore and her experience? Explain why you think so or why you do not.
3. Do you think Yale should reconsider names of other buildings? Why or why not? What might be grounds for the possibility of renaming?

WRITING ACTIVITIES

1. When does renaming a building make sense? Create your own argument in answer to this question. Feel free to include personal anecdotes as Moore does, if helpful.
2. Do some research on John C. Calhoun. In writing, explain why he might be memorialized. Then explain why such memorializing could be considered objectionable.
3. Who is Grace Murray Hopper? Write a brief biographical sketch of Hopper and explain whether you think she's a fitting replacement for John C. Calhoun at Yale University.

LOOKING CLOSELY

Effective Argument: Organizing Points Systematically

When writing an argument essay, especially a longer one, it is always a good idea to set down key points in a systematic fashion. This not only helps you organize your thoughts but also helps your reader follow your argument more easily. Your argumentative points can serve as an outline for the entire essay or, as in Moore's essay, can be used to unify a paragraph. The points need not be explicitly numbered, but they should all be in a logical order and they should all be related to a central claim or position.

In "When Does Renaming a Building Make Sense?" Yale student Dasia Moore sets down the four guidelines her committee used to determine whether the naming of a campus building was inappropriate. She lists the four criteria clearly and concisely in a way that enforces her conclusion: "There seemed to be no doubt in anyone's mind that under those principles, John C. Calhoun was unfit to be the namesake of a residential college at Yale."

1
Primary guideline clearly stated

(1) Is a principal legacy of the namesake fundamentally at odds with the mission of the University?

2
Three other criteria that would be applied

(2) If the namesake's actions and ideas were a subject of debate even in their own lifetime; if the university knowingly acted against its own mission in choosing a certain namesake; and if the building was central to community life and unity.

STUDENT WRITER AT WORK

Dasia Moore

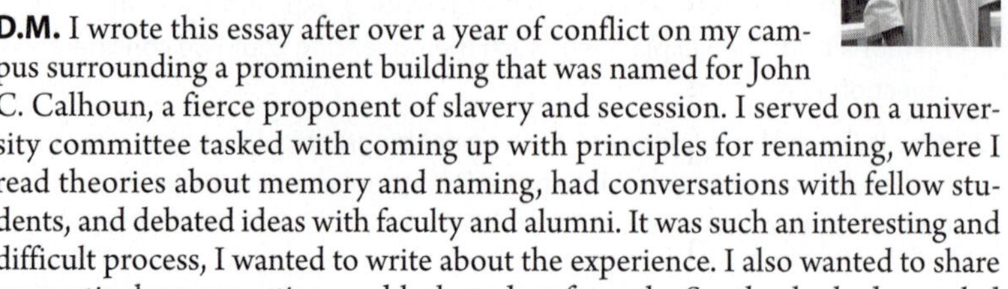

Courtesy of Dasia Moore

R.A. What inspired you to write your essay? And publish it?

D.M. I wrote this essay after over a year of conflict on my campus surrounding a prominent building that was named for John C. Calhoun, a fierce proponent of slavery and secession. I served on a university committee tasked with coming up with principles for renaming, where I read theories about memory and naming, had conversations with fellow students, and debated ideas with faculty and alumni. It was such an interesting and difficult process, I wanted to write about the experience. I also wanted to share my particular perspective as a black student from the South who had grappled with the legacy of Calhoun long before attending college.

R.A. What response have you received to this piece? Has the feedback you have received affected your views on the topic you wrote about?

D.M. I received mostly positive feedback! One personal writing mentor sensed that I had been cautious about being argumentative in this piece and encouraged me to have the confidence to take more of a stand in the future; I've tried to take those words to heart.

R.A. How long did it take for you to write this piece? Did you revise your work? What were your goals as you revised?

D.M. It took a few days to write the piece, followed by a process of revising alongside an editor for *The Nation*. As I revised, clarifying my ideas was the primary goal. I also had to cut words, because I tend to write too much at first.

R.A. Do you generally show your writing to friends before submitting it? Do you collaborate or bounce your ideas off others? To what extent did discussion with others help you develop your point of view on the topic you wrote about?

D.M. In general, I share my writing with one or two people before pitching or submitting a piece. Usually I choose to write about things that I have already discussed extensively with my friends because those are the topics at the forefront of my mind. This piece is a great example: I had discussed with dozens of classmates and other community members for over a year!

R.A. What topics most interest you as a writer?

D.M. For journalistic writing and essays, I am interested in writing about policy — especially surrounding poverty and inequality — and history. Much of my writing is creative and dwells on concepts of home and memory from a perspective rooted in black womanhood.

R.A. What advice do you have for other student writers?

D.M. My advice is to let what you love guide you! As a low-income student in college, I worried a lot about whether writing was a viable career path for me. I also struggled with the very real challenge that many campus publications require a great deal of free time, which might not be compatible with working during school. You can practice writing in unconventional ways that fit with your schedule — through your club's newsletter, policy briefs for your job, a poetry class, editing translated essays. Any writing and editing you can get your hands on, do it! You'll stretch your skill set and build your experience.

Michael I. Niman

As Confederate Flags Fall, Columbus Statues Stand Tall

[*The Public*, October 12, 2015]

Although, as Yale student Dasia Moore reminds us, Confederate memorials can be found anywhere in the U.S. — even on a northern Ivy League campus — such memorials and symbols appear largely in one region of the country. Yet what about our shared national legacy? In "As Confederate Flags Fall, Columbus Statues Stand Tall," Michael I. Niman takes on one of our most visible national heroes, Christopher Columbus. Niman rebukes the argument of Furgurson (see above) and others that we should keep statues up so that we can consider the figures they represent, warts and all. He maintains that our continued celebration of Columbus Day is inextricably linked to racism, genocide, and other forms of oppression. To insist on the idea of Columbus as a great explorer distracts us from the fact that his "most significant contribution to history was as father of the transatlantic slave trade, who presided over a brutal reign of murder and rape shortly after arriving in the new world."

Michael I. Niman is a professor of journalism and critical media studies at Buffalo State College whose work has appeared in Truthout, The Humanist, Artvoice, AlterNet, *and* ColdType, *among many other publications. He is the author of* People of the Rainbow: A Nomadic Utopia *(2nd ed., 2011).*

BEFORE YOU READ

Many people in the United States identify the Confederate flag as a racist symbol and question its presence in public places. Do you believe statues of Christopher Columbus should be subject to the same deliberation? What do you know about Columbus? How has he been presented to you as a historical figure?

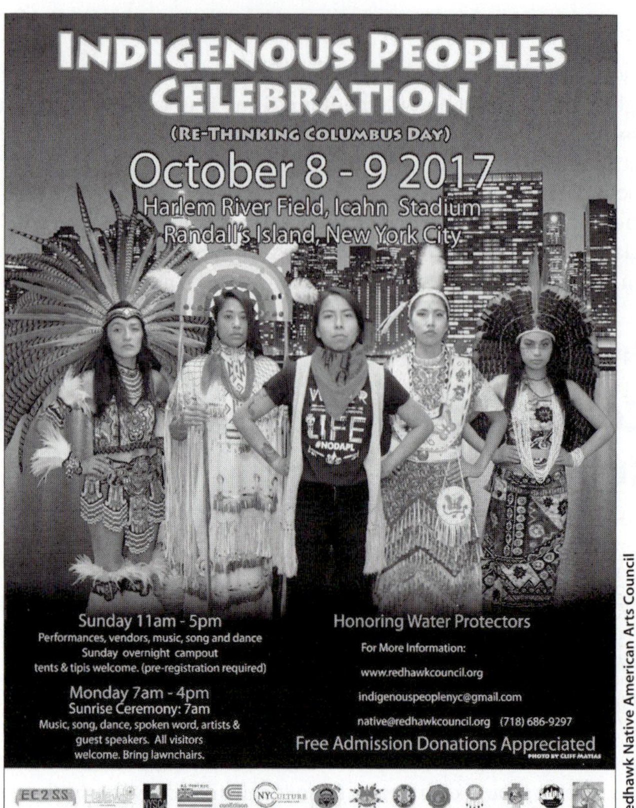

Redhawk Native American Arts Council

This poster advertises a celebration, sponsored by the Redhawk Native American Arts Council, of "Native American culture through song, dance, works of art, food and more."

WORDS TO LEARN

treasonous (para. 1): traitorous (adjective)
resurgence (para. 1): growth or increase (noun)
desegregation (para. 1): the process of ending a law or practice that kept people separate (noun)
subjugation (para. 1): enslavement (noun)
genocidal (para. 2): having to do with the extermination of a group that shares a common identity (adjective)
moniker (para. 2): name (noun)
boycott (para. 2): protest (by refusing to buy or participate in something) (noun)
vandalism (para. 4): the act of deliberately destroying property (noun)
snitch (para. 4): to inform on someone (verb)

recap (para. 6): to give a concise summary (verb)
meticulous (para. 6): careful and exact (adjective)
commodity (para. 7): something bought and sold (noun)
subsequent (para. 7): happening after something else (adjective)
graphically (para. 8): clearly (adverb)
forte (para. 9): one's strong point (noun)
persistence (para. 10): perseverance (adjective)
infrastructure (para. 15): underlying framework (noun)
municipal (para. 16): relating to local government (adjective)
contentious (para. 16): quarrelsome (adjective)

South Carolina removed the Confederate battle flag from its state- 1
house grounds this summer. Walmart removed it from its stores. Virginia is removing it from vanity license plates. Ridding popular culture of this racist symbol is long overdue, considering the stars and bars first rose to support a treasonous rebellion in support of state-supported white supremacy, manifested in the most grotesque fashion as legally sanctioned enslavement, wanton murder, and rape of black Americans. The flag later had a resurgence beginning in the 1940s, with white supremacists raising it in opposition to civil rights and desegregation. It's not the Southern heritage of lemonade and hospitality that Confederate symbol represents, but this darker heritage of white privilege and the horrific subjugation of blacks — and no number of *Dukes of Hazzard*[1] reruns can erase that.

Also this year, the Lancaster, New York, school board voted unani- 2
mously to change the racist name of their high school sports teams. The original name began its life in the 19th century, referring to the dried scalp-skins of Native Americans which could be exchanged for cash by bounty hunters during a genocidal period of American history. Supporters of the racist name protested and, in a last-ditch effort to keep their town in the middle 1800s, imported a rather random Native American from South Dakota and a Cuban Indian impersonator from Connecticut to testify that they were okay with the racist moniker. The school board, however, feeling the tidal pull of the 21st century — and, probably more importantly, confronting a growing boycott of their teams by other schools — ditched the name.

It seemed like we were finally confronting the enduring symbols of 3
our racist past, albeit with tiny baby steps.

[1] *The Dukes of Hazzard* (para. 1): A long-running TV show that aired in 1979 about two country boys who were outlaws. Their getaway car, known as the General Lee, had a large Confederate flag on its hood.

PECCA VESTRA EXPONUNTUR

Sometime over the Labor Day weekend, someone, or some group of 4
people, painted a rather accurate history lesson on the City of Buffalo's Christopher Columbus statue, located in Columbus Park on the city's Lower West Side, adjacent to a neighborhood that hosts one of New York State's largest urban Native American communities. Three local TV news crews covered the story on September 7 (Time Warner Cable News) and 8 (WIVB and WGRZ), all contextualizing the incident as vandalism and asking viewers to snitch out the writers to police, with two reports broadcasting a tip line number.

The writers painted the word "rape" across the front of the statue's 5
base, "slaver" on one side, "genocide" on another. Most interestingly, they wrote the Latin phrase "*pecca vestra exponuntur*," which translates to "your sins are exposed," across the back of the base. All three television crews chose to ignore this last message; one (WIVB) also ignored "slaver," while another (TWC) misstated it as "slave," which would reverse the meaning. None of the reporters expressed any understanding of the context of the story — why, in the run-up to Columbus Day, these messages appeared, or why other writers have been painting similar messages on this statue for decades.

To quickly recap the history behind the Columbus myth: The char- 6
acter of Christopher Columbus, "the great discoverer," was created in 1828 by the American writer, Washington Irving, as a piece of historical fiction based on the life of Cristóbal Colón. Colón, along with other members of the "voyages of discovery," kept logs and took meticulous notes in journals, leaving a strong record of evidence describing events from multiple perspectives. These logs and journals exist to this day in the Spanish archives and paint a pretty damning picture of Colón. Far from being the fabled explorer who argued to an unbelieving world that the earth was round, Colón actually lived out his life arguing that it was pear-shaped even though the concept of a round earth was well accepted by 1492. His most significant contribution to history was as the father of the transatlantic slave trade, who presided over a brutal reign of murder and rape shortly after arriving in the new world.

When he did not find gold in the Caribbean, Colón looked for an 7
alternative commodity to satisfy his investors and win funding for subsequent voyages. That commodity turned out to be his hosts, the Taino people. Colón, impressed by their friendliness, generosity, and peaceful nature, wrote in his journal that "They are the best people in the world and above all the gentlest." What this meant, he wrote, was that "with 50 men they could all be subjected and made to do all that one might wish." The Taino, he explained, were "fit to be ordered about, to sow, and do everything else that may be needed."

Colón captured up what he described as "seven head of women, young ones and adults, and three small children" to bring back to Spain as cargo, along with exotic birds and fruits. This act by Colón, who claimed previous experience as a slave trader in Africa, laid the precedent and foundation for one of the darkest chapters in world history — the transatlantic slave trade, which, after most of the indigenous population in the Caribbean was worked to death or killed by genocide and disease, thrived bringing captured Africans to the Americas. The journals from Colón's voyages graphically document acts of rape and depraved brutality, beyond the pale even for 15th-century Europe. There is no place in any American city for a statue of this man, much less a holiday in his honor. 8

The TWC reporter sought his explanation for the Columbus statue "vandalism" from a confused passerby, who explained to viewers that the writers must be "ignorant people with small minds" who "do stupid things," which, he added, "doesn't make any sense." Seeking out folks for comment based solely on the fact that they are clueless on the subject matter seems to be a forte of Buffalo television news reporters. 9

The fact that news producers chose to broadcast this embarrassing idiocy speaks volumes not only about the crisis of journalism but about the epidemic of ignorance regarding issues of racism. One of the most noticeable aspects of white privilege is the privilege to remain ignorant of, or just not give a damn about, the persistence of racism. TWC's interview subject concluded that "The statue isn't bothering anybody and has been there for years." The ignorance exemplified by this reporting clues us in to why it's still there. . . . 10

There are Columbus statues and place names around the United States; only George Washington has more cities, roads, parks, etc. named after him. As more people continue to become historically literate about the Colón legacy, the continued existence of these tributes has become more controversial and offensive to larger segments of the population. 11

In Buffalo, TWC interviewed Niagara District Councilman David Rivera on camera about the writing on the Columbus statue. Rivera promised, "We're going to be looking at what we can do to find the folks" who did the writing. The TWC reporter also claimed in their report that "with Columbus Day approaching next month, Rivera says the statue's historical value should still be respected." In an interview for this column, Rivera denies this interpretation of what he said, which doesn't appear on-camera on TWC's televised report. Instead he explained that he is fully aware of the history surrounding Colón and is sympathetic to complaints about the statue and the name of the park. 12

BRING IT ON

Rivera went on to explain how the Buffalo City Council voted unanimously in June of this year to change the name of an island in the Niagara River from Squaw Island to Unity Island after Seneca Nation leaders complained about the racist and misogynist name — a name that dates back more than three centuries. Rivera's complaint about the painting of the Columbus statue, he reiterated, is against the method of protest, which he considers damaging public property, rather than the sentiment of the protest or the accuracy of the message. Yes, "Columbus" was a rapist and slaver, but the statue honoring his legacy is protected public property. Rivera suggests that activists protest legally and petition the city government with any demands or complaints regarding the statue. 13

Buffalo's Columbus statue, like others around the country, is literally anchored by a deep foundation. Once erected, it's hard to muster the funding and political capital to tear such things down, no matter what they represent and whom they offend. Rivera uses the Unity Island case, however, to argue that city government is open to responding to protests and petitions. What they would be willing to do, however, would likely depend on the strength of the protests and political threats generated by such protests. Anything is possible. The Unity Island name change came after more than three centuries. In historical terms, the Columbus statue, despite being anchored in stone, is just an adolescent, dating back only 63 years. 14

Given our nation's history, many cities are saddled with such racist infrastructure. As the political class in the country becomes more diverse, there increase the demands to end the whitewashing of American history and challenge the mythology that distorts the teaching of history. How municipalities deal with this infrastructure is revealing. Government officials in Alabama still refuse to change the name of the Edmund Pettus Bridge, for example, despite the fact that the high-visibility bridge, scene to historic 1965 police attacks on civil rights protesters, is named after a grand dragon of the Ku Klux Klan. 15

Given our nation's history, many cities are saddled with such racist infrastructure.

PLYMOUTH ROCKS

By contrast, the town of Plymouth, Massachusetts, erected a monument near their historic rock, honoring the National Day of Mourning, which is a Native American alternative to Thanksgiving. Cast in bronze, the monument explains why many Native Americans don't celebrate the 16 arrival of the Pilgrims, referencing how, to Native Americans, Thanksgiving "is a reminder of the genocide of millions of their people, the theft of their lands, and the relentless assault on their culture." The Plymouth monument goes on to explain that the National Day of Mourning honors "Native ancestors and the struggles of Native peoples to survive today . . . as well as a protest of the racism and oppression which Native Americans continue to experience." In a similar vein, Neto Hatinakwe Onkwehonwe, a Native American arts and cultural organization, erected a monument in Buffalo at a public park at the mouth of Lake Erie. The Neto monument offers an alternative to an older municipal monument emblazoned with a historically contentious narrative about warlike Indians. Five years ago, however, the City of Buffalo hired a Missouri restoration firm to renew its Columbus statue.

In an era when Confederate flags and racist team names are regularly being challenged around the country; when the narratives on other historical monuments meet empirical challenges cast in bronze and stone; and decades after Eastern Europeans demonstrated how statues, in their case hundreds of statues of Lenin, can be torn down, our Columbus statues continue to stand tall as enduring symbols of racism beyond the reach of change. 17

VOCABULARY/USING A DICTIONARY

1. What does it mean to be in *opposition* (para. 1) to something or someone?
2. What does an *impersonator* (para. 2) do?
3. What sort of word is *albeit* (para. 3)?

RESPONDING TO WORDS IN CONTEXT

1. If a school board voted *unanimously* (para. 2) to change the name of its high school team, what percentage of members voted in favor of changing the name?
2. What is a *last-ditch* (para. 2) effort?
3. What is a *fabled* (para. 6) explorer?

DISCUSSING MAIN POINT AND MEANING

1. What two events give Niman hope that we are confronting our past and dealing with symbols of past racism?
2. Does Niman understand and accept the journalists' confusion about and reaction to what happened to the Columbus statue? How do you know?
3. Does this essay "challenge the mythology" (para. 15) of what we're taught about our history? Where does it do that?

EXAMINING SENTENCES, PARAGRAPHS, AND ORGANIZATION

1. The essay's subjects are grouped in several distinct parts. What are they?
2. The title is "As Confederate Flags Fall, Columbus Statues Stand Tall." Is this title misleading? Why or why not?
3. What is the effect of including Christopher Columbus's own words in the essay?

THINKING CRITICALLY

1. The Buffalo news channels seem conflicted about what to make of it, but why do you think the messages "*pecca vestra exponuntur,*" "rape," "slaver," and "genocide" were painted on a Christopher Columbus statue?
2. What is the biggest revelation about Christopher Columbus, "fabled explorer" (para. 6), in this essay?
3. What is the National Day of Mourning? Why was a monument erected near Plymouth Rock to honor the National Day of Mourning?

WRITING ACTIVITIES

1. Write an outline for an essay describing the vandalism of the Christopher Columbus statue. Given the information that you know, what do you want to be sure to include in your essay? What questions do you want to try to answer in your essay? Take some notes on what you know about Columbus, as well as notes that attempt to place the vandalism story in historical context.
2. Niman refers to the "whitewashing of American history" in paragraph 15. What does this mean? Think of the history you know. Is it "whitewashed"? Write down a few examples of history that you learned about from a common source like schools, books, or television. Discuss the examples you've chosen. Explain why you think the history you learned is, or is not, whitewashed.
3. In a freewriting exercise, consider the phrase *pecca vestra exponuntur*. Write down some questions as prompts before you begin. For instance, why would someone choose to write a message in Latin? What is the weight of each word ("your sins are exposed")? What does this phrase have to do with Columbus? Why would someone write on his statue?

Michele de Cuneo

Violence in the Virgin Islands

Less than a year after Christopher Columbus made his famed discovery of the New World on October 12, 1492, he set out on a second voyage that he hoped would prove more commercially successful for Spain than the first. Columbus, of course, did not "discover" new lands; the native peoples he found on his voyages already had. But Columbus was the first European to discover that the world was larger than geographers imagined and that it contained lands that no one previously knew existed. The Vikings had landed at Newfoundland in the year 1000, but that expedition had no impact on future exploration, and it is very possible that mariners and fishermen had frequently made unrecorded landings in North America for quite some time before Columbus. Although he never knew exactly what he had found, it was Columbus's voyages that led to the exploration and eventual colonization of North and South America.

On the second voyage, Columbus encountered Puerto Rico, parts of Cuba, Jamaica, the Virgin Islands, and the Lesser Antilles. To his great disappointment, once again he found no gold or silver and no wealthy cities with which to establish a lucrative trade. No official log or journal of that voyage remains, but we have a vivid and at times lurid account of that second expedition. Though he sailed for Spain, Columbus was an Italian and on his second trip he brought with him a friend from the Genoa region, Michele de Cuneo. A few years after he returned to Italy, de Cuneo wrote a long report to another friend describing the details of the second voyage. Written in Italian in 1495, the original report has disappeared, but a copy made in 1511 was made public in 1885. The translation of the portion below is provided by Elissa Weaver of the University of Chicago.

Note: In de Cuneo's original report, he refers to the indigenous people as Camballi, *which can be translated as "Caribs" or "Cannibals." It is generally believed that the word* cannibal *came about as a linguistic corruption of* Carib.

BEFORE YOU READ

What do you know of Columbus and his contemporaries' trips to the New World? Are you surprised or not surprised by first-person accounts of the voyage?

WORDS TO LEARN

plains (para. 1): land areas distinguished by their flatness (noun)

deserted (para. 1): abandoned (adjective)

gestures (para. 1): expressive movements of the body used to communicate something (noun)

exhibit (para. 2): a display (noun)

fertile (para. 3): able to produce something (adjective)

On the island of Santa Maria la Gallante we got water and wood. The island is uninhabited even though it's full of trees and plains. We set sail from there that day and arrived at a large island inhabited by Caribs, who fled immediately to the mountains when they saw us. We landed on this island and stayed about six days since eleven of our men, who had banded together in order to steal, went five or six miles into the deserted area by such a route that when they wanted to return, they were unable to find their way, even though they were all sailors and could follow the sun, which they couldn't see well for the thick and full woods. When the admiral[1] saw that these men had not returned and were nowhere to be found, he sent two hundred men divided into four squadrons with trumpets, horns, and lanterns but even they were unable to find the lost men, and there was a time when we were more worried about the two hundred men than the others before them. But, as it pleased God, the two hundred returned with great difficulty and greater hunger; we judged that the eleven had been eaten by the Caribs as they are wont to do. However, after five or six days, the eleven men, as it pleased God, when there remained little hope of ever finding them, built a fire on a cape; seeing the fire, we judged it to be them and we sent a boat and in that way recovered them. Had it not been that an old woman showed them the way back with gestures, they'd have been done for since we had planned to set sail on the following day. 1

On that island we took twelve very beautiful and fat females about fifteen or sixteen years old and two boys of the same age whose genital member had been cut off down to their belly; and we judged that this had been done to keep them from mixing with their women or at least to fatten them and then eat them. These boys and girls had been picked by the Caribs for us to send to Spain to the king as an exhibit. The admiral named this island Santa Maria di Guadalupe. 2

[1] Admiral (para. 1): Columbus

We set sail from this island of Santa Maria di Guadalupe, the Island of Caribs, on November tenth and on the fourteenth we reached another beautiful and fertile island of Caribs and came to a very beautiful port. When the Caribs caught sight of us they fled, as the others had, to the mountains and abandoned their houses where we went and took what we liked. In these few days we found many islands where we didn't disembark, but others where we did — for the night. When we didn't leave the ship we kept it tied, and this we did so we wouldn't travel on and out of fear of running aground. Because these islands were closely adjoining, the admiral called them the Eleven Thousand Virgins, and the previous one, Santa Croce.[2] 3

We had anchored and gone ashore one day when we saw, coming from a cape, a canoe — that is, a boat, for so it is called in their speech — and it was beating oars, as though it were a well-armed brigantine.[3] On it there were three or four male Caribs with two female Caribs and two captured Indian slaves — so the Caribs call their other neighbors from those other islands; they had also just cut off their genital member down to their belly and so they were still sick. Since we had the captain's boat ashore with us, when we saw this canoe we quickly jumped into the boat and gave chase to the canoe. As we approached it, the Caribs shot hard at us with their bows, and if we had not had our Pavian shields[4] we would have been half destroyed. I must also tell you that a companion who had a shield in his hand got hit by an arrow, which went through the shield and into his chest three inches, causing him to die within a few days. We captured this canoe with all the men. One Carib was wounded by a lance-blow and thinking him dead we left him in the sea. Suddenly we saw him begin to swim away; therefore we caught him and with a long hook we pulled him aboard where we cut off his head with an axe. We sent the other Caribs together with the two slaves to Spain. 4

VOCABULARY/USING A DICTIONARY

1. What is a *squadron* (para. 1)?
2. What is the opposite of *disembark* (para. 3)? What does the prefix tell you about the word?
3. How is *adjoining* (para. 3) defined?

---

[2] Santa Croce (para. 3): Now St. Croix

[3] This incident took place at the current site of Salt River, St. Croix.

[4] Pavian shields (para. 4): Large shields made in Pavia, Italy

RESPONDING TO WORDS IN CONTEXT

1. What is the difference between the islands de Cuneo visits that are *uninhabited* or *inhabited* (para. 1)?
2. Describe the shape of a *cape* (para. 4) as a land mass. What are its distinguishing features?
3. De Cuneo is unfamiliar with the term *canoe* for boat (para. 4). What is the difference between the boat he is on and a canoe, given what you know and the context?

DISCUSSING MAIN POINT AND MEANING

1. What does de Cuneo think has happened to the eleven men sent to pillage the island?
2. How do the Caribs seem to react to de Cuneo and his men?
3. Are de Cuneo and his men attacked, or are they the attackers? How do they treat the Caribs?

EXAMINING SENTENCES, PARAGRAPHS, AND ORGANIZATION

1. **Connect.** How is de Cuneo's account like a story? How is it different from other essays in this book? As you answer, compare with another reading.
2. How does de Cuneo talk about the people? When he talks about the Caribs, what is his tone? Is it different from when he speaks about his own men?
3. De Cuneo's report was composed not as an "official" account of the expedition but as a letter to a friend. What elements of his account strike you as "unofficial"? That is, what details do you think might not have found their way into an official report to the authorities who sponsored the trip?

THINKING CRITICALLY

1. What do you think of Columbus as a leader based on how he appears within the context of de Cuneo's report?
2. At the time de Cuneo was writing, democratic governments did not exist and slavery was not universally condemned. Do you believe this justifies or mitigates the conduct of de Cuneo and Columbus's crew? Why or why not?
3. **Connect.** Think about the topic of neocolonialism from the perspective of Michael I. Niman's "As Confederate Flags Fall, Columbus Statues Stand Tall" (p. 121). How does that idea link to what's described in de Cuneo's writing? How has the historical context around the colonialism of de Cuneo's time and the neocolonialism of the present day changed (or not)? Do you think the sort of behavior and thinking described by de Cuneo is still present and/or allowed today?

WRITING ACTIVITIES

1. Try writing a narrative. Choose a trip you have taken recently or just write about daily activities (as if you are keeping a journal). Stick to the details and facts of your day — try to avoid reflecting on what's happening. When you've written one to two full pages, read them and notice both the tone and the meaning of what's there. How is it different from writing in which you analyze or consider the meaning of what's there?
2. Did de Cuneo's account make you think or feel differently about the holiday named after Columbus? What has changed after reading an account of the time in which he lived and explored? Write a short piece about the reasons for or against honoring Columbus on a federal holiday and refer to de Cuneo's narrative as you write.
3. Imagine the Caribs' experience that de Cuneo captures in his report. In a short writing assignment, try to give words to their narrative. What would they report on? How would they describe what's happening and how would they view these men arriving on their shores?

Discussing the Unit

SUGGESTED TOPIC FOR DISCUSSION

There is an old saying that history is written by the victors. However, the authors in this chapter suggest new approaches that provide new windows of perspective on historical events and how we respond to them. Is history fixed and one-sided? How can we promote a broader, more inclusive understanding of our past?

PREPARING FOR CLASS DISCUSSION

1. When you enjoy a national holiday (Presidents Day, Columbus Day, Thanksgiving), how do you identify with who or what is being celebrated? Do you ever feel that your history is not represented or that something, or someone, is missing?
2. Who are your historical heroes? Where do you find them represented or memorialized? Do you think more should be done to promote their presence in our national consciousness, whether they are currently established or emerging historical figures?

FROM DISCUSSION TO WRITING

1. What associations do you have of Christopher Columbus and the "discovery" of America? Do your associations match or conflict with what is presented in Niman's essay, and how do you respond to the de Cuneo piece from

1493? Write a reflective essay that explores your personal associations with Columbus and their intersection with or divergence from what you read in these essays.

2. Keeping in mind the perspectives of Michael Niman, Rosalind Bentley, Dasia Moore, Ernest B. Furgurson, as well as the cartoon by Bill Bramhall, ask yourself whether more changes should be made to whom we honor in history. Explain your answer in a brief essay that responds directly to the ideas in at least two of the essays mentioned.

TOPICS FOR CROSS-CULTURAL DISCUSSION

1. Many of the essays in this chapter clearly pinpoint both regional and racial differences in how history is remembered. Using examples from an essay concerned with a moment in American history, discuss the role of gender and/or race in the argument to preserve or dismantle certain ideas about the historical experience.

2. What is the effect when one particular group has control over how history is perceived? What changes when it does not? Discuss these questions, using any two essays from this chapter to support your answers.

4

Immigration: Is It Our Most Serious Issue?

For centuries, Americans have referred to their country as a "melting pot," a place where people of all backgrounds, colors, and creeds come to live and work together freely and harmoniously. Today, there is often heated debate about the concept of citizenship in general, the extent to which immigrant groups should assimilate or retain their distinctive ethnic or racial differences, and the legitimacy of borders. Each political party expresses different views on the topic of immigration. Is diversity still a relevant category of discourse? Or should Americans be focusing on what brings us together more than on what separates us?

Current debates over immigration have focused on a number of issues, among them whether the United States needs better security over the length of the Mexican border, whether people in the country without proper documentation (some estimates run to twelve million) should be subject to mass deportation, how to treat asylum seekers, and whether amnesty should be granted to many undocumented workers and their families. The range of topics under discussion and dispute would require an entire book to cover fairly, but this chapter touches on some of the major issues: citizenship, assimilation, the value of diversity, and borders.

Francie Diep

Why Did We Ever Call Undocumented Immigrants "Aliens"?

[*Pacific Standard*, August 12, 2015]

In 2015, California removed the term "alien" from the state's labor code. "How did 'alien' come to be a term for immigrants in the first place?" asks Francie Diep in "Why Did We Ever Call Undocumented Immigrants 'Aliens'?" Her short essay explains the origins of the term in U.S. history and goes on to note its eventual "science-fiction definition" along with the word's dehumanizing connotations.

Francie Diep is a science journalist who has contributed to many publications, including Scientific American, Popular Science, *and* Smithsonian.

Yesterday [April 11, 2015], California Governor Jerry Brown signed a law that removes the word "alien" from the state's labor code. It's a change that's largely symbolic — Brown signed other laws yesterday that make a more concrete difference — but the vocabulary shift is still important to many. "Alien is now commonly considered a derogatory term for a foreign-born person and has very negative connotations," as California Senator Tony Mendoza, who introduced the bill, told the *Los Angeles Times*. How did "alien" come to be a term for immigrants in the first place? American politicians have actually used the word to denote foreign nationals for more than 200 years. Legally speaking, it doesn't have anything to do with an immigrant's documentation status. You can be an alien whether you entered the United States with or without papers. 1

Between the 1950s and the 1990s, however, newspapers began using the phrase "illegal alien" more frequently, as sociology student Edwin Ackerman documents in a paper published in the journal *Ethnic and Racial Studies* in 2012. The rise in the phrase's popularity paralleled the emergence in the American political consciousness that how an immigrant entered the U.S. mattered, Ackerman argues. In other words, before the 1970s or so, most Americans didn't much care whether people entered the country legally or illegally. They found other reasons to worry about, and discriminate against, immigrants. But in the 1970s, federal agencies in charge of immigration played up illegality in hopes 2 of increasing their budgets, Ackerman argues. He cites an analysis of *Los Angeles Times* articles from that period, which found that more than one in five border officials quoted in news stories talked about how agencies needed more money, and how a greater number of undocumented immigrants were entering the U.S. than ever. Meanwhile, official estimates of the number of undocumented immigrants varied wildly, Ackerman writes, suggesting the numbers were unreliable.

At the same time, labor-union leaders saw undocumented workers 3
as strike-breakers, and ethnicity-based organizations sought to reduce discrimination against their members by separating themselves from undocumented immigrants, Ackerman writes. The combination of all of these forces — which weren't trying to work together — made the idea of undocumented immigrants being a problem a particularly powerful cultural force. By 1994, 90 percent of newspaper articles addressed undocumented immigrants as "illegal aliens." Coincidentally, "alien" gained its science-fiction definition with the Space Age in the 1950s. So now we have a word that once meant foreign national, but has taken on implications of being criminal, potentially even less than human.

By 1994, 90 percent of newspaper articles addressed undocumented immigrants as "illegal aliens."

Does it matter what we call immigrants? One recent study found 4
that what terms news media use to refer to immigrants doesn't affect what immigration policies readers support. Maybe banning words doesn't cause changes in policy, but it is a reflection of shifting public perception. After all, California laws are among the most inclusionary of immigrants, as *Pacific Standard* recently reported. The "California Package" of laws offers immigrants of all stripes unique freedom of movement and opportunity. It's no wonder the Golden State should pioneer symbolic, cultural changes as well as legal, material ones.

POINTS TO CONSIDER

1. What comes first to mind when you hear the word *alien*? Do you form a picture? In your opinion, did California make the right decision to remove the word from the state's labor code?
2. Diep says that the removal of the word is "largely symbolic" (para. 1). What does that mean to you? Does that make the change less significant? Why might it still be important?
3. Do you agree that "what terms news media use to refer to immigrants doesn't affect what immigration policies readers support" (para. 4)? Why or why not?

Laila Lalami

Blending In

[*The New York Times Magazine*, August 6, 2017]

Aside from the economic and legal issues it so often raises, immigration is often promoted culturally and intellectually because it helps increase diversity, a contemporary public value that—according to some critics—often goes unquestioned in our quest to achieve multiculturalist ideals. Yet, at the same time that "diversity" is applauded as a national goal, many Americans still seem to support another goal: assimilation. But are "assimilation" and "diversity" opposing goals? In "Blending In," the renowned author Laila Lalami takes a very close look at assimilation: What does the word mean exactly? What do Americans want it to mean? "One reason immigration is continuously debated in America," she says, "is that there is no consensus on whether assimilation should be about national principles or national identity." Her essay demonstrates the critical importance of this distinction.

A native of Morocco, Laila Lalami moved to the United States in 1992 and received her PhD in linguistics at the University of Southern California. Her novel The Moor's Account *was an American Book Award winner and a finalist for the Pulitzer Prize in 2015.*

BEFORE YOU READ

What are your feelings about when and how immigrants should assimilate into American society? Do you think they should leave their national characteristics and norms behind when they come to the United States, or does carrying these traits into their new country benefit the United States and its citizens?

WORDS TO LEARN

undefined (para. 2): indefinite; unspecific (adjective)
pragmatic (para. 2): practical (adjective)
dynamic (para. 2): energetic (adjective)
connotation (para. 2): additional meaning of a word beyond the primary meaning (noun)
pretext (para. 4): excuse; ruse (noun)
deter (para. 7): to prevent (verb)
aggrieved (para. 9): offended (adjective)
lament (para. 10): to express sorrow (verb)
unprecedented (para. 11): never before experienced (adjective)
objective (para. 11): unbiased (adjective)

The problem is," my seatmate said, "they don't assimilate." We were about 30,000 feet in the air, nearly an hour from our destination, and I was beginning to regret the turn our conversation had taken. It started out as small talk. He told me he owned a butcher shop in Gardena, about 15 miles south of Los Angeles, but was contemplating retirement. I knew the area well, having lived nearby when I was in graduate school, though I hadn't been there in years. "Oh, it's changed a lot," he told me. "We have all those Koreans now." Ordinarily, my instinct would have been to return to the novel I was reading, but this was just two months after the election, and I was still trying to parse for myself what was happening in the country. "They have their own schools," he said. "They send their kids there on Sundays so they can learn Korean." 1

What does assimilation mean these days? The word has its roots in the Latin "simulare," meaning to make similar. Immigrants are expected, over an undefined period, to become like other Americans, a process metaphorically described as a melting pot. But what this means, in practice, remains unsettled. After all, Americans have always been a heterogeneous population — racially, religiously, regionally. By what criteria is an outsider judged to fit into such a diverse nation? For some, assimilation is based on pragmatic considerations, like achieving some fluency in the dominant language, some educational or economic success, some familiarity with the country's history and culture. For others, it runs deeper and involves relinquishing all ties, even linguistic ones, to the old country. For yet others, the whole idea of assimilation is wrongheaded, and integration — a dynamic process that retains the connotation of individuality — is seen as the better model. Think salad bowl, rather than melting pot: Each ingredient keeps its flavor, even as it mixes with others. 2

Whichever model they prefer, Americans pride themselves on being a nation of immigrants. Starting in 1903, people arriving at Ellis Island were greeted by a copper statue whose pedestal bore the words, "Give me your tired, your poor, your huddled masses yearning to breathe free." One of this country's most cherished myths is the idea that, no matter where you come from, if you work hard, you can be successful. But these ideals have always been combined with a deep suspicion of newcomers. 3

In 1890, this newspaper ran an article explaining that while "the red and black assimilate" in New York, "not so the Chinaman." Cartoons of the era depicted Irish refugees as drunken apes and Chinese immigrants as cannibals swallowing Uncle Sam. At different times, the United States barred or curtailed the arrival of Chinese, Italian, Irish, Jewish and, most recently, Muslim immigrants. During the Great Depression, as many as 4 one million Mexicans and Mexican-Americans were deported under the pretext that they were to blame for the economic downturn.

The pendulum between hope and fear continues to swing today. "We are a country where people of all backgrounds, all nations of origin, all languages, all religions, all races, can make a home," Hillary Clinton told an immigrant-advocacy conference in New York in 2015. By contrast, Donald Trump warned on the campaign trail that "not everyone who seeks to join our country will be able to successfully assimilate." Last November, one of these visions of assimilation won out. 5

The pendulum between hope and fear continues to swing today.

Immigrants contribute to America in a million different ways, from growing the food on our tables to creating the technologies we use every day. They commit far fewer crimes than native-born citizens. But hardly a week goes by when poor assimilation isn't blamed for offenses involving immigrants — and the entire project of immigration called into question. In Michigan, an Indian-American emergency-room doctor who belongs to the Dawoodi Bohra community, a Shiite Muslim sect, was charged with performing female genital mutilation on several young girls. In Minnesota, a black police officer, the first Somali-American cop in his precinct, shot an unarmed Australian woman. Both incidents were immediately seized upon by the far right as examples of the inability — or refusal — of Muslims to assimilate. So far this year, American police officers have killed more than 500 people, but for the commentator Ann Coulter, the shooting in Minnesota would never have happened in Australia because "they have fewer than 10k Somalis. We have >100k." Earlier this month, the *Fox News* personality Tucker Carlson ran a segment in which he said citizens of a small town in Pennsylvania claimed that several dozen Roma who had been resettled there "defecate in public, chop the heads off chickens, leave trash everywhere." (The police said they issued citations where relevant.) "The group doesn't seem at all interested in integrating," Carlson complained. "You have to assume it's a statement." 6

One reason immigration is continuously debated in America is that there is no consensus on whether assimilation should be about national principles or national identity. Those who believe that assimilation is a matter of principle emphasize a belief in the Constitution and the rule of law; in life, liberty and the pursuit of happiness; and in a strong work ethic and equality. Where necessary, they support policy changes to further deter any cultural customs that defy those values. For example, 7

Rick Snyder, the governor of Michigan, signed a new law that increases existing penalties for anyone who performs female genital mutilation on a minor.

But for those who believe that assimilation is a matter of identity — as many on the far right do — nothing short of the abandonment of all traces of your heritage will do. The alt-right pundit Milo Yiannopoulos, an immigrant himself, told a campus group in January that "the hijab is not something that should ever be seen on American women." The perception that visible signs of religious identity are indicators of deep and sinister splits in society can lead to rabid fears of wholly imaginary threats. Several states have passed anti-Shariah measures, in fear that Muslims will seek to impose their own religious laws on unsuspecting Americans. The fact that Muslims make up 1 percent of the U.S. population and that such an agenda is both a statistical and a Constitutional impossibility has done nothing to temper this fear. It is no longer a fringe belief: The white nationalist Richard Spencer told a reporter that he once bonded with Stephen Miller, now a senior White House adviser, over concerns that immigrants from non-European countries were not assimilating. 8

Debates about assimilation are different from debates about undocumented immigration, even though they are often mixed together. Concerns about undocumented immigration typically center on competition for jobs or the use of public resources, but complaints about assimilation are mostly about identity — a nebulous mix of race, religion and language. In May, a survey by the Public Religion Research Institute and *The Atlantic* found that white working-class voters were 3–5 times more likely to support Donald Trump if they reported feeling "like a stranger in their own land." My seatmate on that airplane was a small-business owner, yet he did not seem worried about Korean-Americans taking business away from him; he seemed more aggrieved that their children studied two languages, or that his community featured store signs and church marquees in an alphabet he could not read. Others might object to their neighbors' wearing skullcaps, or eating fermented duck eggs, or listening to Tejano music — and call these concerns about assimilation, too. 9

It should be clear by now that assimilation is primarily about power. In Morocco, where I was born, I never heard members of Parliament express outrage that French immigrants — or "expats," as they might call themselves — eat pork, drink wine or have extramarital sex, in plain contradiction of local norms. If they do adopt the country's customs or speak its language, they aren't said to have "assimilated" but to have "gone native." In France, by contrast, politicians regularly lament that 10 people descended from North African immigrants choose halal food options for school lunches or want to attend classes in head scarves. One result is a daily experience of rejection, which only makes assimilation more difficult.

America is different from Europe in one significant way: It has a long and successful history of integrating its immigrants, even if each new generation thinks that the challenges it faces are unique and unprecedented. It is a nation in which people will wear green on St. Patrick's Day without thinking much about the periods during which the Irish were accused of contaminating the nation with their foreign habits. Because there is no objective measure of assimilation, many people end up throwing up their hands and saying, "I know it when I see it." The question is: Who is doing the judging here? 11

VOCABULARY/USING A DICTIONARY

1. How do you define *assimilate* (para. 1)?
2. What is the opposite of *heterogeneous* (para. 2)?
3. Do you know what a *nebula* is? Can you use your knowledge of that word to help you define *nebulous* (para. 9)?

RESPONDING TO WORDS IN CONTEXT

1. What part of speech is *minor* (para. 7)? What is the definition of *minor* within the context of Lalami's sentence?
2. What part of speech is *rabid* (para. 8)? What does it mean? In what other context might you have heard something referred to as *rabid*?
3. When Lalami writes in paragraph 4 that immigration was "barred or curtailed" at different times, what is she saying happened to the immigrants trying to enter the country? What is the difference between *barring* and *curtailing* something?

DISCUSSING MAIN POINT AND MEANING

1. Why is the topic of assimilation in the United States particularly pressing and controversial (as opposed to considering assimilation in another country, like Morocco or France)?
2. What does Lalami's seatmate think the kids in the neighborhood should do differently? Where should they go to school? What should they not do?
3. What similarities does Lalami note between attitudes in the 1890s and the current climate in the United States?

EXAMINING SENTENCES, PARAGRAPHS, AND ORGANIZATION

1. Why do you think the author starts with a conversation on a plane? How does this help her introduce her topic? What about the seatmate's conversation makes her uncomfortable?
2. Lalami interjects a rhetorical question and then a dictionary definition in paragraph 2. What is the effect of this? Consider the paragraph if those two things were deleted. How would the experience of her paragraph, and her introduction, be different?
3. In paragraph 3, Lalami writes, "Starting in 1903, people arriving at Ellis Island were greeted by a copper statue whose pedestal bore the words, 'Give me your tired, your poor, your huddled masses yearning to breathe free.'" What effect is she creating and why does she word the sentence in this way?

THINKING CRITICALLY

1. Central to Lalami's argument about assimilation is the distinction between "national principles" and "national identity" (paras. 7–8). Which side of these opposing views does Lalami appear to take? How can you tell?
2. Consider Lalami's use of specific examples and data in paragraph 6. Do you find her use of this material convincing? Why or why not?
3. What do you think Lalami means when she says in paragraph 10 that "assimilation is primarily about power"? Using examples from Lalami's text, argue how it is about power, and also argue how it is about sameness. In what way do these two ideas overlap?

WRITING ACTIVITIES

1. In a short writing exercise, explain where Lalami stands on assimilation. Using examples from the text, discuss how measured her argument is. Explain how, in paragraph 5, she is endorsing Clinton's view of immigration over Trump's. Discuss the contrast and her image of the "pendulum."
2. Write an essay on a topic of national significance or a current event that begins with a personal anecdote (using Lalami's introduction as an example). In class, read the personal introductions out loud and discuss their effectiveness. Can classmates guess the issue under discussion?
3. **Connect.** In a succinct written response, explain how "The Muslims Are Coming!" (p. 180) is used to promote the identity of a group (Muslim immigrants). Discuss the poster as an argument against assimilation. Where you can, draw from Lalami's essay to support your position.

Sravya Tadepalli (student essay)

Say It Right: When People Mispronounce Your Name

[*Oregon Humanities*, November 29, 2018]

Assimilation — as discussed in the previous selection — can perhaps be made easier if one's name looks and sounds "American." But what if it doesn't? In the following selection, a University of Oregon student reports on her constant struggle with hearing her name spoken incorrectly. Yet, why not just simply accept the fact and explain how it should be pronounced? In "Say It Right: When People Mispronounce Your Name," Sravya Tadepalli offers a bit of linguistic advice, explores her heritage, and tries to understand why the mispronunciation makes her angry.

Sravya Tadepalli is a student at the University of Oregon. Her work has appeared in Teaching Tolerance, Skipping Stones Magazine, *and* Brown Girl Magazine, *where she enjoys writing primarily about the two taboo subjects: politics and religion. A 2018 Truman Scholar, she hopes to pursue a career working in foreign policy and national security.*

BEFORE YOU READ

Have you ever met someone with a name you found difficult to pronounce? Were they of a different ethnicity or from a different country? What made it hard to pronounce?

WORDS TO LEARN

infallible (para. 8): incapable of error (adjective)

nuisance (para. 10): an annoyance (noun)

persistent (para. 11): tenacious (adjective)

anglicize (para. 12): to make English (verb)

colonizer (para. 12): someone who establishes or takes part in a colony (noun)

"Come on, how do you say it? Teach me how to say it?" My high school principal pestered me after five minutes of trying to pronounce my last name. "Ta-day-PA-lee? That's right, right?" 1

"No." 2

"I want to learn how to say it — I'm going to have to say it at senior awards," he continued. 3

"You can say it however you want to say it. But I'm not going to tell you that you're saying it right when you're not." 4

"Well, how would a person like me say it?" 5

A person like you? 6

When non-Indian people pronounce my name wrong, I tell them that 7
they're pronouncing it wrong.

I don't believe in lying to people to make them feel comfortable. It 8
won't kill anyone to feel uncomfortable once in a while — uncomfortable with the fact that they are not as infallible as they think they are, and uncomfortable that I deny them the privilege of comfort.

Most people simply can't pronounce my last name. Tadepalli — 9
pronounced "THA-day-pa-lee," with an emphasis on the "THA," schwa on the "pa," and a hooked connection between "pa" and "lee" that lasts for an extra moment in time, the "l" resting on the top teeth for just an extra millisecond before letting go. This isn't an accent thing. My name, written in Telugu, is pronounced exactly how it is spelled in Telugu, the emphases, the schwas, and the hooked connections all factored in. The name translates to "village of the palm trees," a combination of *palli* (village) and *tade* (palm trees).

Sometimes people can say it — after I repeat it sound by sound, 10
fifteen times, grimacing the whole way. Then they can say it, abruptly pausing between each syllable. That's much more of a nuisance than simply mispronouncing it, because teaching others to say my last name wastes my time. I have better things to do than to deal with the poor maneuverability of English-speaking tongues — especially when they may forget how to say it moments after they get it right once.

My high school principal was particularly persistent. 11

I knew what he meant by a person like him — he meant, how 12
would an English-speaking person say it. How do you anglicize the pronunciation? Can you just rip the *tade* from the soil, burn the *palli* to the ground, toss out all the *gunintalu* and *vattulu,* the little ornaments added to the main letters that describe the sound, and give whatever remains back to the colonizers who already stole the wealth the *tade* and *palli* had created? There was nothing I could teach him with regard to that.

"You're saying it like a person like you 13
would say it."

We went in a circle as everyone in the class tried to say my last name and I tried to contain my anger.

In my university, I had a professor who 14
insisted on calling everyone "Mr." or "Ms." and their last name.

"Is this how you say it? Ta-DAY-PA-lee." 15

"No." 16

"THA-day-PAA-lee." 17

"No." 18

"Can anyone in the class try to say this individual's last name?" 19

We went in a circle as everyone in the class tried to say my last name and I tried to contain my anger. 20

I didn't know where that anger came from. It seemed objectively silly to be upset about the attention given to my last name when there were a million other larger problems in the world. I tried to figure out why this bothered me. Was it because I constantly had to hear my name mispronounced? Or was it because the professor refused to call me by my first name, always choosing to point at me and stare as a means of acknowledgment, choosing to blindly obey a code of formality instead of one of respect? Or was it because I was so tired of white people acting out their discomfort: so tired of hearing my name being treated like a game, so tired of having to explain to people how to pronounce it, so tired of it that I sometimes thought about— 21

"You should really change your name," the professor chortled one day. 22

Out of the obstacles that I will face in my life, I know that one of the toughest will be my Telugu last name that forever brands me as being from somewhere else. I don't want to anglicize it, but I think about changing it to Kodali, my great-grandfather's last name, and a much easier name for an English speaker to say. My great-grandfather was a freedom fighter—I'd be honoring someone who brought freedom to the country my parents came from. Kodali would be a good name to settle for. 23

But he fought imperialism so Indian culture and language could be honored—wouldn't it counter his efforts if I changed my name to better fit into a white society? To be better accepted by the colonizers? To make white people feel more comfortable? To protect myself from their discomfort? 24

VOCABULARY/USING A DICTIONARY

1. How long is a *millisecond* (para. 9)?
2. What is a *schwa* (para. 9)?
3. What is the root of the word *maneuverability* (para. 10)? What part of speech is it?

RESPONDING TO WORDS IN CONTEXT

1. What's the difference between *principal* (para. 1) and *principle*? What definition is Tadepalli using?

2. What do you think she means by "the *privilege* of comfort" (para. 8)?
3. What *imperialism* (para. 24) was Tadepalli's grandfather fighting?

DISCUSSING MAIN POINT AND MEANING

1. In what ways does Tadepalli's essay introduce issues that go beyond pronunciation? How is the mispronunciation of her name linked to broader issues? What are those issues?
2. What happens to Tadepalli's name if she anglicizes it?
3. Whose name does Tadepalli consider taking? Why does she ultimately reject this idea?

EXAMINING SENTENCES, PARAGRAPHS, AND ORGANIZATION

1. In paragraphs 21–23, Tadepalli considers changing her name. In her account, what would be the advantages in doing so? Yet, in the next, and final, paragraph she raises an objection to doing that. Why do you think she raises those objections in the form of questions? How do you interpret those questions?
2. Two characters are introduced in this essay: Tadepalli's high school principal and a university professor. How would you characterize these two? What adjectives come to mind?
3. Do paragraphs 9 and 12 help the readers who have no connection to Tadepalli's Indian background? What does it teach them about the language? Explain.

THINKING CRITICALLY

1. Tadepalli writes that some people ask her how her name is pronounced. Why doesn't she view that as a polite gesture instead of a hostile one?
2. Tadepalli writes that she doesn't know where the anger comes from. What do you think causes the anger, based on the information available in the essay?
3. She says, at the end of the essay, that she doesn't want to fit herself into "white society" or "make white people more comfortable." How is her argument about racial discord and inequality? How does she show the problem as based in race, not just language?

WRITING ACTIVITIES

1. Many people from different language backgrounds have serious difficulty correctly pronouncing names and words from languages they are unfamiliar with. How annoyed would you be if a non-native speaker pronounced your name incorrectly? Would you be annoyed at all? Does Tadepalli acknowledge this common phonetic difficulty? Write briefly about the problems one might have based on differences in language and various reactions.

2. **Connect.** In the text following paragraph 6, Tadepalli's notions of discomfort can be linked to the discussions of safe spaces and speech in Chapter 2. What do you think of Tadepalli's comments about not caring how people feel if she corrects them? Can you relate? What are the positives and negatives of such a scenario? Write a short response to these questions, drawing from essays in both chapters.
3. Why does it bother Tadepalli that people pronounce her name incorrectly? Can you think of reasons why they don't or can't? List all you can think of.

LOOKING CLOSELY

Posing a Question

Effective essays often pose a question and then attempt to answer it. An essayist might ask what can be done about a certain problem: How can we make police forces more responsible to a community? What can human populations do to improve their environment? But such questions need not only be about public affairs; they can also be personal, as Sravya Tadepalli aptly demonstrates in "Say It Right: When People Mispronounce Your Name."

She begins paragraph 18 wondering why the mispronunciations make her angry and acknowledges that, with "a million other larger problems in the world," being upset about her name seems "objectively silly." But as she tries to figure out her anger, she introduces a number of questions that may help explain her emotions. As she seeks an answer, these questions also add to her essay the process of discovery. Essays often reflect the process of thinking something through and this paragraph provides a solid example of how a writer can express that mental and emotional activity.

1
States she doesn't understand her anger.

2
Poses several questions that might help explain it.

(1) I didn't know where that anger came from. It seemed objectively silly to be upset about the attention given to my last name when there were a million other larger problems in the world. I tried to figure out why this bothered me. (2) Was it because I constantly had to hear my name mispronounced? Or was it because the professor refused to call me by my first name, always choosing to point at me and stare as a means of acknowledgment, choosing to blindly obey a code of formality instead of one of respect? Or was it because I was so tired of white people acting out their discomfort: so tired of hearing my name being treated like a game, so tired of having to explain to people how to pronounce it. . . .

STUDENT WRITER AT WORK

Sravya Tadepalli

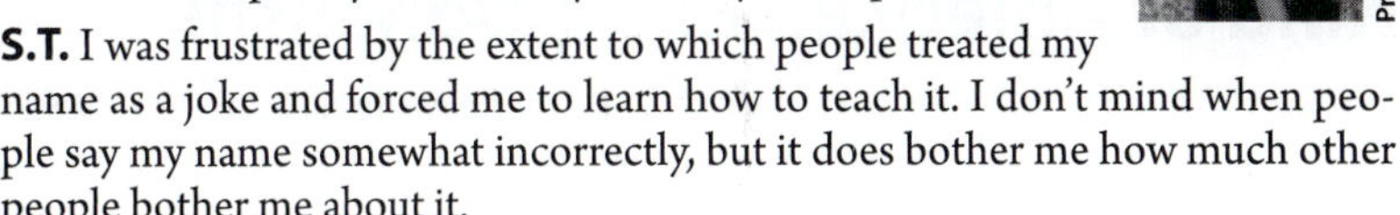

Prasad Tadepalli

R.A. What inspired you to write your essay? And publish it?

S.T. I was frustrated by the extent to which people treated my name as a joke and forced me to learn how to teach it. I don't mind when people say my name somewhat incorrectly, but it does bother me how much other people bother me about it.

R.A. What was your main purpose in writing this piece?

S.T. I wanted to just get my feelings on paper. I was so frustrated by people treating my name like it was exotic or a game. I was tired of white people insisting on learning how to say my name "authentically." I felt that they were just trying to feel better about themselves. I was tired of people treating me like an "other" and felt the need to just get it all out.

R.A. Who was your prime audience?

S.T. My prime audience was really myself. I was writing for myself in order to process my own thinking.

R.A. What response have you received to this piece? Has the feedback you have received affected your views on the topic you wrote about?

S.T. I read some of the comments and I was surprised that people were saying things like "Don't get offended when people say your name wrong." I think some people misinterpreted the piece, thinking that I get offended when people say my name wrong. You'll notice throughout the piece, I never actually tell anyone to "say it right." If I were to rewrite the piece, I'd probably try to make the point of my piece clearer. I'd try to make my "why I'm writing this" more clear.

R.A. Did you revise your work? What were your goals as you revised?

S.T. The first time I revised it was to proofread and improve the flow. The second time was more of a check on the content and tone; I made the tone a bit less confrontational and removed certain identifying details.

R.A. What topics most interest you as a writer?

S.T. I am most interested in topics related to social and political issues, particularly race relations.

R.A. What advice do you have for other student writers?

S.T. The less afraid you are to dig deep into your own sentiments, ask the questions of others you really want to ask, and put everything you feel and learn onto paper, the better your writing will be and the bigger impact it can have. Question everything: what others say, as well as your own feelings, thoughts, and beliefs. Have a clear sense of why you are writing and what impact you are trying to create and try to write so that the audience gets it.

Eric Foner

Birthright Citizenship Is the Good Kind of American Exceptionalism

[*The Nation*, August 27, 2015]

In the following selection, we look at one key issue that for centuries has been taken for granted but was recently raised amid much controversy during the presidential debates in 2015–2016 and has been recently reintroduced as an option to control immigration. Should the Fourteenth Amendment to the Constitution, which grants automatic citizenship to any person born in the United States, regardless of the legal status of the parents, be repealed or revised? In "Birthright Citizenship Is the Good Kind of American Exceptionalism," historian Eric Foner discusses the origins of the "birthright" principle (unique in much of the world) and explains why it "remains an eloquent statement of what our country is or would like to be."

Eric Foner is a Pulitzer Prize–winning historian who has been on the faculty of Columbia University's history department since 1982. His specialties include American political history and the post–Civil War Reconstruction Era.

BEFORE YOU READ

Why is birthright citizenship part of our Constitution? Do you think anyone born here should be considered an American citizen?

WORDS TO LEARN

principle (para. 1): a basic truth or rule (noun)
ratification (para. 1): confirmation (noun)
exceptionalism (para. 2): uniqueness (noun)
delineate (para. 3): to indicate or portray (verb)
naturalization (para. 4): the act of becoming a citizen (noun)
associate (para. 5): to be connected with others (verb)
repudiation (para. 6): rejection (noun)
undifferentiated (para. 6): not showing difference (adjective)
jurisdiction (para. 7): area where particular laws are used (noun)
minuscule (para. 7): very small (adjective)
invalidate (para. 8): to discredit (verb)
specter (para. 8): apparition (noun)
polygamists (para. 9): people who have more than one wife at a time (noun)
subsequent (para. 9): happening later (adjective)
titanic (para. 10): having great power (adjective)

Birthright citizenship — the principle that any person born in the United States is automatically a citizen — has been embedded in the Constitution since the ratification of the 14th Amendment[1] in 1868. This summer, it has suddenly emerged as a major issue in the Republican presidential campaign. Following the lead of Donald Trump, candidates like Rick Santorum, Bobby Jindal, Ted Cruz, and Rand Paul have called for the repeal or reinterpretation of the amendment, to prevent children born to undocumented immigrants from being recognized as American citizens. 1

The situation abounds in ironies. Now a Republican target, the 14th Amendment was for many decades considered a crowning achievement of what once called itself the party of Lincoln. Today, moreover, birthright citizenship stands as an example of the much-abused idea of American exceptionalism, which Republicans have berated President Obama for supposedly not embracing. Many things claimed as uniquely American — a devotion to individual freedom, for example, or social opportunity — exist in other countries. But birthright citizenship does make the United States (along with Canada) unique in the developed world. No European nation recognizes the principle. Yet, oddly, those most insistent on proclaiming their belief in American exceptionalism seem keenest on abolishing it. 2

Why is birthright citizenship part of our Constitution? Until after the Civil War, there existed no commonly agreed-upon definition of American citizenship or the rights that it entailed. The original Constitution mentioned citizens but did not delineate who they were. The individual states determined the boundaries and rights of citizenship. 3

The Constitution does, however, empower Congress to create a system of naturalization, and a law of 1790 offered the first legislative definition of American nationality. Although the new nation proclaimed itself, in the words of Thomas Paine, an "asylum for mankind," that law restricted the process of becoming a citizen from abroad to any "free white person." Thus, at the outset, ideas of American citizenship were closely linked to race. 4

Slaves, of course, were not part of the body politic. But in 1860, there were half a million free blacks in the United States, nearly all of them born in this country. For decades, their citizenship had 5

---

[1] 14th Amendment (para. 1): Amendment to the Constitution that grants birthright citizenship. The amendment was passed as part of Reconstruction after the Civil War and granted citizenship to former slaves.

been hotly contested. Finally, in the Dred Scott[2] decision of 1857, the Supreme Court declared that no black person could be a citizen. The framers of the Constitution, Chief Justice Roger Taney insisted, regarded blacks, free and slave, as "beings of an inferior order, and altogether unfit to associate with the white race . . . and so far inferior, that they had no rights which the white man was bound to respect." (This statement, the Radical Republican leader Thaddeus Stevens later remarked, "damned [Taney] to everlasting fame; and, I fear, to everlasting fire.")

The destruction of slavery in the Civil War, coupled with the service 6 of 200,000 black men in the Union Army and Navy, put the question of black citizenship on the national agenda. The era of Reconstruction produced the first formal delineation of American citizenship, a vast expansion of citizens' rights, and a repudiation of the idea that these rights attached to persons in their capacity as members of certain ethnic or racial groups, rather than as part of an undifferentiated American people. Birthright citizenship is one expression of the commitment to equality and the expansion of national consciousness that marked Reconstruction.

In June 1866, Congress approved and sent to the states the 14th 7 Amendment, whose opening section declares that "all persons born or naturalized in the United States, and subject to the jurisdiction thereof, are citizens of the United States and of the state wherein they reside." What persons are not subject to national jurisdiction? The debates in Congress in 1866 make clear that the language was meant to exclude Native Americans, still considered members of their tribal sovereignties. Two minuscule other groups were mentioned: children born in the United States to the wives of foreign diplomats, and those fathered by members of occupying armies (fortunately, the latter case hasn't arisen since the amendment's ratification).

While the immediate purpose of this part of the 14th Amendment 8 was to invalidate the Dred Scott decision, the language says nothing about race — it was meant to establish a principle applicable to all. Opponents raised the specter of Chinese citizenship, or citizenship for "gypsies"; one senator said that he'd heard more about gypsies during the debate than in his entire previous life. Lyman Trumbull, chairman of the Senate Judiciary Committee, made it crystal clear that "all persons"

[2] Dred Scott (para. 5): The Dred Scott decision refers to a Supreme Court case that resulted in the decision that African Americans, slave or free, were not citizens. Dred Scott was a slave taken by his masters to free states, where he tried to sue for his freedom.

meant what it said: Children born to Chinese, gypsies, or anybody else one could think of would be citizens.

What about the children of "illegal aliens" today? No such group existed in 1866; at the time, just about anyone who wished to enter the United States was free to do so. Only later did the law single out certain groups for exclusion: prostitutes, polygamists, lunatics, anarchists, and, starting in 1882, the entire population of China. In fact, the closest analogy to today's debate concerns children born to the 50,000 or so Chinese in the United States in 1866, all of whose parents were ineligible for citizenship. The authors of the amendment, and subsequent decisions by the Supreme Court, made it clear that these children must be considered American citizens. The legal status of the parents does not determine the rights of the child; anyone born here can be a good American. These are the principles the Republicans now seek to overturn. 9

The authors of the amendment, and subsequent decisions by the Supreme Court, made it clear that these children must be considered American citizens.

The 14th Amendment, as Republican editor George Curtis wrote, was part of a process that changed the U.S. government from one "for white men" to one "for mankind." Birthright citizenship is one legacy of the titanic struggle of the Reconstruction era to create a genuine democracy grounded in the principle of equality. It remains an eloquent statement of what our country is or would like to be. We should think long and hard before abandoning it. 10

VOCABULARY/USING A DICTIONARY

1. What does it mean to *berate* (para. 2) someone?
2. If a person is *keenest* (para. 2) to do something, how eager is that person?
3. What part of speech is *empower* (para. 4)? What does it mean?

RESPONDING TO WORDS IN CONTEXT

1. What is a *body politic* (para. 5)?
2. If Americans have a *devotion* (para. 2) to individual freedom, how do they feel about it?
3. If there is a "*legislative* definition of American nationality" (para. 4), who provided it?

DISCUSSING MAIN POINT AND MEANING

1. Is Foner trying to persuade us of anything? If so, what does he want to persuade us of?
2. What does Foner find ironic about the position of many of the most recent Republican candidates?
3. Does legal status of the parents matter in deciding the baby's nationality when the baby is born in the United States?

EXAMINING SENTENCES, PARAGRAPHS, AND ORGANIZATION

1. Describe the construction of Foner's first sentence. Why do you think he begins with this sentence?
2. Explain how Foner transitions between the ideas in paragraphs 2, 3, and 4. Are his transitions effective?
3. Which particular paragraph does the conclusion reflect back upon with the statement "Birthright citizenship is one legacy of the titanic struggle of the Reconstruction era to create a genuine democracy grounded in the principle of equality" (para. 10)?

THINKING CRITICALLY

1. Why would birthright citizenship have been of particular importance to slaves?
2. Why do some recent Republican presidential candidates want to repeal or reinterpret the Fourteenth Amendment? To whom don't they want to provide the benefit of birthright citizenship?
3. What is meant by "American exceptionalism"? Why does Foner say it is a "much-abused idea" (para. 2)?

WRITING ACTIVITIES

1. Do you think birthright citizenship is a good or bad policy for the United States to have in place? Using Foner's argument as a starting point, explain your own view on birthright citizenship. You can explore both sides of the story (explaining why it is both good and bad) if you wish, but you need to bring in solid examples and evidence to support what you say.
2. What do you think about the desire to overturn or rewrite an amendment to the Constitution? Some people feel that amendments are inviolable (consider how staunchly some people defend the Second Amendment). But there is at least one amendment that was passed and then repealed—the Eighteenth Amendment. Discuss your feelings about amendments to the Constitution: what they represent, when they should be questioned, how

important they are to the country. Include in your response a consideration of what it might mean to repeal the Fourteenth Amendment.

3. In two or three paragraphs, summarize Eric Foner's essay. Remember that a summary does not need to include all points made in an essay — only the main points.

SPOTLIGHT ON DATA AND RESEARCH

Scott Rasmussen

The Immigration Mess

[*Townhall*, June 28, 2018]

In "The Immigration Mess," the pollster and columnist Scott Rasmussen summarizes and interprets the results of recent polls about America's immigration problems. As his summary shows, Rasmussen does not believe our public dialogue on immigration is "serious" and he attempts to redirect the avenues of the debate. Immigration is not just a current problem but, as he argues, will continue to be a problem "in election after election until significant changes are made." He is optimistic that we can find a solution. "While difficult, it is quite possible to build a consensus around policies that respect America's great tradition as both a nation of immigrants and a nation of laws."

Scott Rasmussen is the founder and publisher of the public-opinion site ScottRasmussen.com, which tracks public mood by offering daily reports and analyses. He is the author, most recently, of The Sun Is Still Rising: Politics Has Failed But America Will Not.

Problems with U.S. immigration policy played a big role in the 2016 presidential election and are likely to do so in election after election until significant changes are made. It's a serious issue worthy of substantial public debate. However, what passes for a public dialogue on the issue is anything but serious. 1

It is, for example, heartbreaking to hear about and see pictures of young children separated from their parents at the U.S. border. According to a CBS poll, only 4 percent of Americans support that approach for dealing with families who enter the country illegally. But beyond that, there's not a clear consensus on what should be done. 2

Under the Obama Administration, families who entered the coun- 3
try illegally were released into the United States and required to report back for a hearing on their status at a later date. Not surprisingly, many failed to report as promised. Also not surprising is the fact that only 21 percent of Americans support that policy.

Roughly half of all Americans believe that families who enter the 4
U.S. illegally should simply be returned to their home country. While understandable, that approach raises the question of how we will ensure that those sent home won't try again to illegally enter the United States. Since coming to the United States could offer a better future for their children, it's reasonable to assume that caring parents won't give up after just one try.

Clearly, a debate focused around the narrow question of how to deal 5
with families entering the U.S. illegally will not lead to a lasting solution for the current immigration mess.

Instead, the starting point for a serious debate would focus on 6
what sort of legal immigration the nation is willing to encourage or accept. Most Americans support a generally welcoming immigration policy so long as those who come here can support themselves and do not pose a national security or criminal threat. Such concerns cannot be lightly dismissed. Sixty-one percent believe that some of those seeking to enter the country illegally are criminals and gang members. Sixty-seven percent believe that some are seeking handouts and welfare payments.

> **[T]he starting point for a serious debate would focus on what sort of legal immigration the nation is willing to encourage or accept.**

Coming up with a policy to address those concerns raises an import- 7
ant subset of questions. Do we prioritize those who have valuable skills or relatives of U.S. citizens? How much legal immigration should we allow? What exceptions should be allowed for humanitarian purposes? How do we classify seasonal workers who want to legally enter the country and then return home? Should the states or federal government determine how many such workers are allowed? How long should new immigrants be required to live in the United States before being eligible for citizenship? The list could go on and on.

While difficult, it is quite possible to build a consensus around 8
policies that respect America's great tradition as both a nation of immigrants and a nation of laws. As on most issues, there is far more common ground among the American people on immigration than the elites would like to admit.

A key part of that common ground is a belief that a functioning system of legal immigration must be supported by a rational program for preventing illegal immigration. 9

POINTS TO CONSIDER

1. Some commentators on today's immigration issues are reluctant to use the word *illegal*. Some avoid it altogether, while others use "unauthorized" or "undocumented." What does Rasmussen's consistent use of "legal" and "illegal" suggest about his overall policy?
2. Why does Rasmussen think that a "debate focused around the narrow question of how to deal with families entering the U.S. illegally will not lead to a lasting solution for the current immigration mess" (para. 5)? What does he see wrongheaded about that focus?
3. In his conclusion, Rasmussen clearly believes a "common ground" can be found to solve the immigration problem. Do you think his final paragraph accurately describes that "common ground"? Why or why not?

William C. Anderson

Solidarity Abolishes Borders

[*Truthout*, November 17, 2018]

When Scott Rasmussen in the selection above suggests that Americans can find "common ground" to solve the issues of legal and illegal immigration, he doesn't take into account that some people believe there is no such thing as illegal immigration because they do not believe in national borders in the first place. This is the opinion expressed in the following essay by the political writer William C. Anderson. In "Solidarity Abolishes Borders," he uses the recent caravans from Honduras to paint a larger picture of an unstable global situation. To do so, he relies on the philosophy of community solidarity proposed by one of the founders of the Black Panther Party, Huey P. Newton. As Williams argues: "If we don't believe in borders and hope to abolish them, we can challenge their existence by viewing struggle through an intercommunal lens that brings together communities worldwide, and doesn't affirm states or their boundaries."

William C. Anderson writes on politics, race, class, and immigration for a wide variety of publications. He is coauthor of As Black as Resistance *(2018).*

BEFORE YOU READ

Do you think borders create problems or solutions? What would happen if borders disappeared?

WORDS TO LEARN

terrain (para. 3): land (noun)
caravan (para. 4): group of travelers moving together for safety (noun)
repression (para. 5): the act of checking or suppressing something (noun)
coup (para. 5): a sudden action in government that changes things (by force) (noun)
migrate (para. 6): to shift location (verb)
denounce (para. 12): to criticize or disapprove of something openly (verb)

Borders are imaginary lines that have very real, violent implications. These dividers of nations block movement in the name of security and sovereignty, but they're often a threat to the very things they're theoretically supposed to protect, including people. Rejecting borders, instead of people, should be a top priority. 1

Many of us who reject borders seek out real ways to abolish them in our daily lives, as we work toward a broader movement for border abolition. One way we can reject the violence of borders is by being fully aware of what's happening outside of the ones that have been drawn around us. In addition to this, it's important to know what's happening at them and because of them. This awareness can provide us with the necessary tools to develop a worldview that challenges state violence at its core. 2

Many members of the public sincerely do not understand what would drive people to risk their own lives or those of their family to trek across harsh terrain toward uncertainty. If anything is guaranteed along the way, it's danger and suffering. That tells us a lot about what sorts of situations people are leaving if they're willing to take such a risk. 3

Caravans and large groups of people making their way to Western nations have recently drawn publicity. In Europe, the so-called "migrant crisis" has driven a variety of reactions ranging from state violence to "reception centers" (places where migrants, immigrants and refugees are detained) to right-wing vigilante efforts. The violence and destruction that the Global North has inflicted on the home countries of those fleeing is hardly an afterthought in the mainstream narrative. What we know to be true about how European military aggression, economic exploitation, and climate change are pushing people from their homes regularly gets left out of the conversation. The same can be said regarding the U.S. 4

Thousands of people heading toward the U.S. in a caravan from 5
Honduras were described by the Associated Press as "a ragtag army of the poor." However, there was no mention of, for example, the army-backed, U.S.-supported coup that ousted democratically elected Honduran president Manuel Zelaya in 2009. After this regime change, the murder rate dramatically worsened in Honduras from 60.8 per 100,000 in 2008 to 90.4 in 2012. Death squads and political repression, including assassinations, have taken place since the now legitimized post-coup government has gotten comfortable. The most vulnerable people in Honduras have been under great duress because of the growing violence. This was highlighted by the tragic murder of environmentalist and human rights activist Berta Cáceres in 2016. The situation at hand is no accident, and it was made worse by the forces of an empire that now attacks the victims who are approaching its gates.

The problem is similar for the people leaving their homes through- 6
out the Middle East, Asia, the African continent, South and Central America, and more. One of the products of empire is displacement. Another, it seems, is the shameless violence that empires deploy against the people whose lives have been turned upside down by the imperial powers' accumulation of capital and resources. People who are forced to migrate are portrayed as "freeloaders" by states that freeload off the rest of the world.

For those of us who live inside of the confines of empire, our sol- 7
idarity with communities on the outside is of the utmost importance. Solidarity can delegitimize borders. By taking up an informed perspective and decentering empire, we can shift public consciousness. Simply knowing what's happening — in terms of both the actions of empire and the resistance to it — beyond the neighborhoods, cities, states, and nations, where we reside, is important. Solidarity-based organizing grows from this kind of knowledge. We can learn from other struggles and respond to global repression against oppressed people all over the globe.

The premise of invalidating borders through solidarity is a view 8
that's consistent with Huey P. Newton's intercommunalism. Newton, the cofounder of the Black Panther Party, once stated:

> We say that the world today is a dispersed collection of communities. A community is different from a nation. A community is a small unit with a comprehensive collection of institutions that exist to serve a small group of people. And we say further that the struggle in the world today is between the small circle that administers and profits from the empire of the United States, and the peoples of the world who want to determine their own destinies.

If we don't believe in borders and hope to abolish them, we can 9
challenge their existence by viewing struggle through an intercommunal lens that brings together communities worldwide, and doesn't affirm states or their boundaries. States don't deserve our affirmation, loyalty, or love; people that states oppress do. Solidarity and awareness transcend borders and bring us closer to what we need, which is the end of racial capitalism.

States rely on our ignorance of the struggles of those around us, 10
inside and outside the nations we inhabit. They want us to be ignorant of what's happening because ignorance disadvantages our organizing and weakens our movements. Believing in borders looks like us not knowing what's happening outside of them, not because we're not allowed or prevented from knowing, but because we're not well informed. Campaigns for the sake of a global collective of oppressed people should disseminate the needed information to everyone they can reach. The more that we know about each other, the stronger we can become.

The more that we know about each other, the stronger we can become.

We might also unintentionally affirm borders by romanticizing 11
other places outside them as well. Other countries like Canada, New Zealand, and Scandinavian nations in Europe have become increasingly tempting to people in the U.S. considering flight. Rather than fighting to eliminate the global system of inequality and exploitation and its dependence on national borders, some consider merely relocating inside of new nation-states that are more fitting before conditions worsen where they live. People living inside of empire, particularly those who are empowered or privileged by class and race, must acknowledge that the world is not their playground or a giant tourist destination for achieving comfort.

Of course, we should not ignore our immediate needs to an 12
extent that's damaging. This wouldn't be beneficial to us at all. But we can denounce capitalism as a practice that prioritizes some communities over others based on borders, walls, and other dividers. We can and we do build movements that work with, not against other people fighting the same or similar problems. Cutting capitalism out of relationships includes transforming the relationships that we have in the name of solidarity.

There's no purpose in seeking a perfect movement free from conflict 13
and internal problems. There is purpose in seeking to form informational networks that strengthen our organizing. It's time for us to abolish borders and focus on communities — and people.

VOCABULARY/USING A DICTIONARY

1. What part of speech is *theoretically* (para. 1)? What does it mean?
2. How do you define the word *abolish* (para. 2)? In what other contexts have you heard this word or variants of it used?
3. What is the word *vigilante* (para. 4)? From what language is it taken?

RESPONDING TO WORDS IN CONTEXT

1. Anderson says "rejecting borders, instead of people, should be a *top priority* (para. 1). What does this mean?
2. What's another way to phrase Anderson's idea about "imperial powers' *accumulation* of capital and resources" (para. 6)? How else might that be put?
3. "Solidarity can *delegitimize* borders" (para. 7). Can you explain what this means, focusing on the difference between *legitimizing* or *delegitimizing* something?

DISCUSSING MAIN POINT AND MEANING

1. What association does Anderson see between borders and violence?
2. In the quotation by Huey P. Newton, what distinction does Newton make between nations and communities? In what ways is this distinction key to Anderson's argument?
3. In Anderson's opinion, what must happen before we can abolish borders? What role does being informed play? What has "solidarity" to do with it, and how does he see solidarity as being achieved?

EXAMINING SENTENCES, PARAGRAPHS, AND ORGANIZATION

1. Why do you think Anderson cites Huey P. Newton in paragraph 8? What does that citation add to Anderson's essay?
2. Anderson writes, "It's time for us to abolish borders and focus on communities — and people" (para. 13). What effect does the em-dash have on the reader of this sentence? Why do you think Anderson chose to end on this note?
3. What words would you use to describe Anderson's paragraphs? Once you have a list of descriptive words, find their opposites — what would happen to Anderson's paragraphs if they were changed in this way?

THINKING CRITICALLY

1. What is the relationship between borders and capitalism?
2. What does Anderson think of U.S citizens relocating to other countries? What is your reaction to the idea that people who are in places of more

privilege "must acknowledge that the world is not their playground or a giant tourist destination for achieving comfort" (para. 11)?

3. **Connect.** How do you think Anderson would respond to Lalami's article ("Blending In," p. 138) about assimilation? How does the idea of "dispersed . . . communities" (para. 8) connect to her idea of retaining identity? Do states and borders encourage ignorance? How do you understand Anderson's argument in paragraph 10 (considered also in the light of Lalami's discussion of America as a melting pot)?

WRITING ACTIVITIES

1. Why does Anderson regard borders as "imaginary"? Of what importance is it to his argument that they be considered imaginary? In a short written statement, explain what arguments might be made that far-from-imaginary borders are geographically real.
2. Consider the sentence: "The more that we know about each other, the stronger we can become" (para. 10). Brainstorm a moment when you've believed this to be true, either in your personal life or the world at large. In small groups, discuss the evidence you've compiled to support Anderson's statement.
3. Gather research on two countries that border each other. Write an article that examines the relationship between those countries and if or how the border affects their relationship (think in terms of language, commerce, tension/conflict, travel, etc.).

AMERICA THEN . . . 1883

Emma Lazarus

The New Colossus

The New York City–born Emma Lazarus wrote "The New Colossus" in 1883 to help raise funds for the construction of a pedestal for the Statue of Liberty. Twenty years later, the sonnet would be engraved on a bronze plaque at that pedestal. The poem once reflected what many Americans felt was their nation's welcoming attitude toward all immigrants, especially with the following lines that became well-known throughout the world: "Give me your tired, your poor, / Your huddled masses yearning to breathe free." Today, with all the bitter controversy over immigration, the famous lines may seem quaint or ironic.

Lazarus was also an activist who promoted social, economic, and immigrant causes. Unfortunately, she is so well known for this one poem that all her other work has largely been obscured by it. "The New Colossus" is a reference to the statue of a god constructed on the ancient Greek island of Rhodes in the third century BC. As the tallest statue of its time, it became known as one of the Seven Wonders of the Ancient World, though it was destroyed by an earthquake just some fifty years after its construction. As you read the poem, consider why Lazarus compares the new Statue of Liberty to the ancient colossus. What qualities does the new colossus embody?

BEFORE YOU READ

Do you associate the words of Lazarus's poem with the Statue of Liberty? Is the United States still the "mother of exiles"?

WORDS TO LEARN

astride (line 2): on either side of (preposition)
mighty (line 4): huge or exceptional (adjective)
exile (line 6): someone forced to leave his or her homeland (noun)
huddled (line 11): gathered close together (adjective)

Not like the brazen giant of Greek fame,
With conquering limbs astride from land to land;
Here at our sea-washed, sunset gates shall stand

A mighty woman with a torch, whose flame
Is the imprisoned lightning, and her name
Mother of Exiles. From her beacon-hand

Glows world-wide welcome; her mild eyes command
The air-bridged harbor that twin cities frame.
"Keep, ancient lands, your storied pomp!" cries she

With silent lips. "Give me your tired, your poor,
Your huddled masses yearning to breathe free,
The wretched refuse of your teeming shore.

Send these, the homeless, tempest-tost to me,
I lift my lamp beside the golden door!"

VOCABULARY/USING A DICTIONARY

1. How does someone who is *brazen* (line 1) act?
2. What is a *beacon* (line 6)?
3. If something is *teeming* (line 12), is it full or empty?

RESPONDING TO WORDS IN CONTEXT

1. What is meant by *storied pomp* (line 9)?
2. In line 12, what is *refuse* (noun)? How is it different from *refuse* (verb)?
3. Even if you can't find *tempest-tost* (line 13) in a dictionary, what do you think it means, based on context?

DISCUSSING MAIN POINT AND MEANING

1. What is the name of the "woman with a torch" (line 4)? (What is she called by the world, and what is she called in Lazarus's poem?)
2. Is Lazarus's new Colossus threatening or welcoming? Explain.
3. How are immigrants arriving at their destination in this poem? (Try to identify, line by line, all the images that give this away.)

EXAMINING SENTENCES, PARAGRAPHS, AND ORGANIZATION

1. Lazarus's poem is a sonnet. Why is the form important? How is the sonnet form working to convey Lazarus's message?
2. Why does Lazarus refer to immigrants as "wretched refuse" in line 12? How is that characterization different from "huddled masses" in the line above?
3. Arguably, Lazarus's most famous line from this poem is "Your huddled masses yearning to breathe free" (line 11). What might explain why it is so memorable and famous?

THINKING CRITICALLY

1. This poem is about the "new Colossus." Who or what was the "old Colossus"? How is the Statue of Liberty like Colossus?
2. What is meant by the "golden door" (line 14)? Is it always golden, or even a door? Explain Lazarus's interpretation of U.S. immigration based on this image.
3. **Connect.** How do you think Lazarus viewed immigration? Was her view accurate? What in the poem leads you to your conclusion? Is immigration still viewed in the same way in the United States today? Is this idealism at odds with the stories Lalami ("Blending In," p. 138) tells of backlash against immigrants in her essay? Explain.

WRITING ACTIVITIES

1. In a freewriting, begin with Lazarus's line: "Your huddled masses yearning to breathe free" and explore all the words and images that come to mind when you think about immigrants to the United States, past and present.

2. Research the building of the Statue of Liberty. Who built it? Why did it end up in New York harbor? What does it have to do with immigration or the immigrant experience? Write a brief history of the statue and end with a consideration of how this statue has come to represent the ideas in Lazarus's poem.

3. There are many descriptive adjectives in Lazarus's poem. Try crossing out the adjectives and rewrite the poem without them. Read the poem out loud, both as it is and without the adjectives. In small groups, discuss what changes when the adjectives are removed. How is it a different poem? What do the adjectives add?

Discussing the Unit

SUGGESTED TOPIC FOR DISCUSSION

America is supposedly the land of the immigrant, but there are wide differences in perceptions across the country about immigrants. Immigrants do not always feel immediately welcome in American society. There are so many types of immigrants (legal, illegal, the refugee) and they come from countries all over the globe. While reading these essays, try to identify reasons people might come to America to make a new life, and decide whether Americans and American culture respond to them appropriately.

PREPARING FOR CLASS DISCUSSION

1. If you are an American who isn't strictly Native American, at some point there is immigration in your family history. Which members of your family were immigrants? How long ago did they emigrate from their home country? Why did they immigrate? Do you think your immigrant relatives or ancestors had regrets?

2. Who do you think of when you think of American immigrants? What do they look like? What language do they speak? How does this compare to your concept of yourself as an American? Should immigrants strive to be a certain way that's deemed "American"?

FROM DISCUSSION TO WRITING

1. How do authors in this chapter approach the question of assimilation? What are their opinions on whether immigrant identity should match the lifelong citizen's identity? Do you think of America as the great melting pot, or are there divisions between groups of people (immigrant versus citizen, for example) that are too great to mend? Explain, using examples from the text.

2. How well is American immigration working? What does this question mean to you? Write your response to this question, citing at least three essays (including Lazarus's poem) from the chapter that support your position.

TOPICS FOR CROSS-CULTURAL DISCUSSION

1. How many of our reactions to immigrants and immigration are based on race? Why do you think so? Write a brief essay that explores this question and, as you write, bring in at least two essays from this chapter that support your argument.
2. What, in your opinion, makes us American? Pay special attention to the conflicting answers these authors give in this chapter. Which authors do you side with? Whose opinion is most similar to yours? Why do you think this is so?

5

Identity: How Does It Shape Our Sense of Self?

Jean de Crèvecoeur, a Frenchman who moved to America in the eighteenth century (see p. 193), wrote that an immigrant to the United States "becomes an American by being received in the broad lap of our great alma mater. Here individuals of all nations are melted into a new race of men." As we saw in Chapter 4, the metaphor of a melting pot, in which people of various origins are blended together to become one unified compound, has remained a popular image of our society. Attempts to forge a truly homogeneous American society, however, have met with limited success — and consistent opposition.

One challenge is that racial and ethnic identity are deeply felt and persistent, not only for recent immigrants but also for their children and grandchildren. In a society in which defining oneself is increasingly important, our cultural and geographic roots, even when they are generations old (note the continued success of ancestry.com), are becoming a significant source of self-understanding as well as personal pride. But they can also be a source of confusion and displacement and, especially in recent years, have led to a constant racial and ethnic tension. In this chapter, we will examine both the personal and the public sides of racial and ethnic identity, how identity shapes an individual's sense of self as well as how it leads to the larger social and cultural issues that today commonly go by the term "identity politics."

Gish Jen

A New High School Course: Identity 101

[*The Washington Post Magazine*, October 29, 2017]

The concept of identity brings many people together: If they can "identify" with one another, they will see themselves in many ways as the same. But when a society is composed of many different identities, then it's very likely that identity will result in an emphasis on differences — people will start seeing a world divided by "them" and "us." In "A New High School Course: Identity 101," the prominent Chinese American author Gish Jen proposes that "in the interest of a more functional nation," it would be a good idea for students to learn about "culture" in general. In this very brief essay, she poses a number of questions that she believes we need to ask ourselves in order to overcome our cultural differences and divides.

A graduate of Harvard University and the University of Iowa Writers' Workshop, Gish Jen is an award-winning novelist and short story writer. Her most recent nonfiction book is The Girl at the Baggage Claim: Explaining the East-West Culture Gap *(2017).*

Race, class, gender. These lenses on society have proved revelatory, and no one would ever deny their importance. And yet to this holy trinity, I would like to add a fourth lens: culture. 1

Cultural difference has riven our culture. We are aware that there are cultural divides. We are aware that we have trouble talking across these divides. We are aware that there seems to be no convincing some people of their essential wrongness and our essential rightness. We are aware that some part of the problem is unrelated to our objective interests — that some part of the problem is a matter of how we just think things should be. We are aware that some of us do not see the same things at all. We are aware that we can bug others as much as they bug us. And yet the nature of culture itself — of what drives these differences, of what drives our ideals and focus and irritation — is poorly understood. 2

In the interest of a more functional nation, then, I propose a new high school requirement. Every student should be required to take, not a course in foreign culture — not a course in Italian food, or Japanese gardens, or Central American weaving — but a course on the nature of culture: on meta-culture. We could call it Identity 101. What part of identity 3 is culture? Where does our culture come from? How has it helped us? Do we have selves independent of culture? Does anyone? How can we know what our culture is? Is that culture immutable? And if it changes, how does it change? It goes without saying that an understanding of what exactly culture is will help us deal with the rest of the globe, but its value begins at home. To understand the nature of culture will not solve our problems. But understanding that we all have scripts — to which we may or may not adhere but which are ours nonetheless — might at least help us begin to see ourselves as the actors that we are, and to speak to other actors in a new way.

Do we have selves independent of culture?

POINTS TO CONSIDER

1. Why do you think Gish Jen proposes a "new high school requirement" (para. 3)? What motivates her to think one is needed?
2. Note that her third paragraph is composed largely of unanswered questions. Why do you think she raises these questions? What do the questions suggest about what we need to learn?
3. How do you interpret her conclusion? In what way do we all follow a script? How does thinking of ourselves as "actors" help us understand the "nature of culture"?

Susan Power

Native in the Twenty-First Century

[*World Literature Today,* May–August 2017]

Identity isn't, as the following essay shows, an issue confronting only immigrants and their descendants. It also affects the lives of those who were the first Americans. In "Native in the Twenty-First Century," Susan Power, a member of the Standing Rock Sioux, reflects on the ways her ancestry has affected her life and the nation's. "I've always been Native first and American second," she writes, as she resists the "tired, inadequate labels that obliterate the rich histories of America's other-class citizens."

Susan Power won the PEN/Hemingway Award for The Grass Dancer *(1994). A graduate of both Harvard University and Harvard Law School, she is the author of two other works of fiction,* Roofwalker *(2002) and* The Sacred Wilderness *(2014).*

BEFORE YOU READ

Can you see the value of a varied perspective from mixed ancestry that Power is describing here? Have you ever found yourself traveling in the "circles beyond circles" (para. 2) that she recounts, or known someone who has?

WORDS TO LEARN

inadequate (para. 2): insufficient (adjective)
caricatures (para. 2): exaggerated portraits that accentuate defects or differences (noun)
ancestor (para. 3): a person one is distantly descended from (noun)
mysticism (para. 4): beliefs and ideas based on spiritual intuition (noun)
turf (para. 4): a layer of earth (noun)
wasting (para. 5): devastating or ravaging (adjective)
generation (para. 5): group of people born and living around the same time period (noun)
exploit (para. 5): to use unfairly to one's own advantage (verb)

I'm mixed but that doesn't mean I'm mixed up — it just means my parents fell in love across a racial and cultural divide that split my blood. When I was young I looked like my dad, my brown hair tipped red in summer — anyone could think I was white, only white, and never Yanktonai Dakota and a little Hunkpapa. But as I get older I look more like Mom, which means I'm mistaken for a variety of ethnicities (people placed bets on their guesses in front of me and never guessed right), which means in small towns or small-minded neighborhoods I experience a taste of Ye Old-School Racism — the kind that shadowed my mother from her first steps, the kind my father couldn't believe until he saw it in action when they traveled to Rapid City after my aunt's murder. 1

I've always been Native first and American second, but in youth people forgot that when they looked at me, so I traveled in circles beyond circles — felt like a Dakota spy perched at my listening post to gather information on what the dominant society *really* felt about us, whatever term it is we're using now, "minorities," "people of color," the tired, inadequate labels that obliterate the rich histories of America's other-class citizens. I heard what the good people were saying, and the angry ones, the fearful ones, the lazy-minded who think it's fine to yuck it up at stereotypes and caricatures ("lighten up, already, my God, can't you take a joke, what's the harm in a few laughs at some outsider's expense?"). I would speak up then, I would speak down, around, 2 and sideways, near stand on my head to show there was another way of seeing the world, but damn, it made me tired and dizzy. At least I could shift perspective in a world that said, "Look through the viewfinder and see the Truth," though that 3D ViewMaster was made of plastic, told sugar-coated stories I knew were myths laid across truth like a carpet to hide all the bones and blood, and the prophets who died in the making of that particular film.

3 We're often told, "You've come a long way, baby," and we have, a hundred years followed a hundred years and extermination failed. I'm a citizen of the country my ancestors inhabited before the so-called Founding Fathers moved here and learned from the Six Nations Confederacy the intricate political system that governs us now. If I'd been born a hundred years ago I wouldn't be a citizen yet because, well, you know, that's the way it is when you play Manifest Destiny with loaded dice. So why are we grumbling? is the new refrain. Why are we angry after all these years and acres and deaths? And I slap my head with my hand because sometimes I'd like to be lazy, too, look ahead toward the vanishing point and never behind; pretend my feet on this ground are my feet on this ground rather than my ancestor's brave work. It's not "magical realism" to see how time resists those easy straight lines. Can't you see how the past shapes the present and future? How we live what our grandfathers said and our grandmothers sang?

4 It's summer again in the twenty-first century as Hollywood gears up for its Blockbuster vision, all Action to keep us distracted with noise. It's Tonto time and we're supposed to be grateful because a good-looking actor who may be part Cherokee was inspired by a flying crow in a painting; decided to plunk it on his head, wear the face paint of a Crow man, though his character is Comanche — heck, they're all "C" tribes, what's the difference? An Indian is an Indian is an Indian, and we belong to the collective unconscious, we belong to the masses, we belong to everyone but our own selves. Oh, Tonto, I know you had fun imagining what Indian "mysticism" meant to you for a shoot 'em up show, but you'd better take care, our spiritual turf isn't a playground and sometimes the spirits fight back.

5 The good news is that Natives are on the move, Idle No More, in a country that's dying from a wasting disease. We're standing up for Turtle Island and the waters, we're standing up for the future we refuse to gamble away as if it doesn't matter, as if it should be someone else's story, someone else's problem. We may not be Skins in Space but we invented Science Fiction — the awareness that almighty science divorced from wisdom is a reckless beast. The dominant society made a fiction of our science though their breakthroughs are leading them back to what we knew all along, what

we tried to tell them in the very beginning. They've been educating us for years, for several lost generations, but we're up-ending that one-sided desk, that one-sided conversation that can only tell stories in a single direction. Don't tell us we're finding our voices in some new academic-artistic renaissance you can study at conferences or exploit in pages on Amazon.com — we've been speaking all along as poets and rappers, counselors and prophets, healers and politicians. The problem was, no one was listening to our parents and grandparents, and for certain not our great-grandparents who were too busy facing down guns to hand over their dissertation. You may not want to listen now, but that's okay, we've learned your language and can ride our ponies through communication highways that cross reservation lines. Our ancestors never gave up and they're singing us awake. We're inside and outside, listening and speaking, standing up and dancing, connecting and reaching — we've got a world to save, yours as well as ours.

> **[W]e've been speaking all along as poets and rappers, counselors and prophets, healers and politicians.**

VOCABULARY/USING A DICTIONARY

1. What is the opposite of *dominant* (para. 2)?
2. What is a *dissertation* (para. 5)?
3. What part of speech is *obliterate* (para. 2)?

RESPONDING TO WORDS IN CONTEXT

1. How would you characterize the tone of the phrase *yuck it up* (para. 2)? What does it mean?
2. What is Power referring to in paragraph 3 when she says *extermination* failed?
3. What does Power mean when she says "[we] can ride our ponies through *communication highways* that cross *reservation lines*" (para. 5)?

DISCUSSING MAIN POINT AND MEANING

1. How does Power see the world and understand "truth"? How is her experience different from the way she thinks most people see the world and understand "truth"?

2. Power asks in paragraph 3: "Why are we angry after all these years and acres and deaths?" Does her essay provide an answer to the question? Why do you think she is angry? What is she angry about?
3. **Connect.** Power says, "I've always been Native first and American second, but in youth people forgot that when they looked at me, so I traveled in circles beyond circles" (para. 2). What does Power have in common with Faruqi's daughter ("Cut from the Same Cloth," p. 174)? What do you think she might say to Faruqi's daughter about their particular experience of their identities and their heritage?

EXAMINING SENTENCES, PARAGRAPHS, AND ORGANIZATION

1. Power uses *allusion* in her essay to strengthen the ideas she's conveying. Can you identify any allusions and explain what she's referring to?
2. A parenthetical is incorporated in paragraph 2. Why do you think Power includes it? What effect does it have within the paragraph?
3. Overall, this is a short (five-paragraph) essay. What are the major issues Power covers? Does her first line connect to her last line? Explain.

THINKING CRITICALLY

1. In the final paragraph, Power writes, "You may not want to listen now." Who does Power mean by "you"?
2. Power says at times she looked more like her father, and sometimes more like her mother. What advantage does Power's appearance give her in discussions with people she encounters?
3. Who is Power's intended audience? How do you know?

WRITING ACTIVITIES

1. In a writing exercise, discuss the role of the "past" in Power's argument. What particular meaning or import does the past have for her?
2. On her mother's side, Power is part of the Standing Rock Sioux tribe of North Dakota. Write a short research paper on this particular tribe as well as any information you find on Susan Power's ancestry. Does your research shed any light on why Power is writing about this subject, or her argument?
3. Power says, "I've always been Native first and American second." Write a brief response to this statement. What is your own experience of identity? Do you relate to how Power sees herself? Include your answers in your response.

Saadia Faruqi

Cut from the Same Cloth

[*The Texas Observer*, June 2017]

"Why do you wear that thing on your head?" That question asked by a cashier at a Subway sandwich shop in Northwest Houston inspired the following reflections by a Muslim woman who chooses to wear a hijab, or head scarf. In "Cut from the Same Cloth," Saadia Faruqi, realizes it's a question on the minds of many Americans who see the hijab as something foreign or confrontational, even frightening. Yet, to her, "It is an expression of faith, a profession of modesty and decorum, and increasingly, a political statement." Her answer to the cashier's question is directed, surprisingly, not only to all those who may wonder about the head scarf but to her own daughter as well.

An interfaith activist, Saadia Faruqi is the author of the short story collection, Brick Walls: Tales of Hope & Courage from Pakistan.

BEFORE YOU READ

Which of your habits or choices (about clothing, pastimes, food, and so on) contribute to your identity? Do you make identifications or judgments about others based on their appearance and demeanor?

WORDS TO LEARN

theological (para. 2): having to do with religion, religious study (adjective)
observance (para. 4): a practice or ritual (noun)
oppression (para 4): persecution or abuse (noun)
diverse (para. 5): showing variety (adjective)
controversy (para. 8): dispute or quarrel (noun)
context (para. 10): circumstances or conditions around an event or idea (noun)
oath (para. 11): a solemn promise or pledge (noun)
trepidation (para. 11): feeling of fear or dread (noun)
aspire (para. 11): to desire or aim toward a goal (verb)

Sometimes a piece of fabric is just a piece of fabric. Not so the hijab, the head cover worn by many Muslim women like myself. The hijab is a conversation starter and a conversation killer. It is a way to make friends, but also to make enemies who glare at you from the other side of the bus or yell "Aren't you hot in there?" at the beach. And sometimes it stands between a woman and her sandwich. 1

Not long ago, a trip to a Subway sandwich shop in northwest Houston almost turned into a theological debate. As I stood in line with my children, hungry and running late, the cashier held my receipt and asked, "Why do you wear that thing on your head?" For a moment I debated what to do, though he wasn't the first stranger to ask me that question, nor will he be the last. I couldn't shake my head and pretend not to speak English, because he'd already heard me order. I didn't want to joke, "What, my sunglasses?" 2

I looked at him again, and saw something in his eyes. Sincerity. Curiosity. I turned and looked at my 8-year-old daughter standing next to me, waiting for my response. It's a question she's asked many times, perhaps in a more sensitive way. But it's a question on the minds of many, and sometimes I'm the only person within a 10-mile radius with any sort of answer. 3

The hijab — head scarf, veil, burqa — is one of the most visible forms of faith one could possibly have. Muslim women who choose to cover themselves are set apart by this simple act of religious observance, and for us, a piece of fabric is never just a piece of fabric. It is an expression of faith, a profession of modesty and decorum, and increasingly, a political statement. Since 9/11, the hijab has become an easy target for oppression. The news is full of legislation against it, such as the head scarf ban in Germany and the burkini ban in France. Each terrorist attack in America results in hate crimes against Muslim women wearing the hijab, leading to a rise in self-defense classes for women in mosques and civic groups. 4

Houston is the most diverse metro area in the nation. There are more than 157,000 Muslims here, more than anywhere else in Texas. Still, worries about how people will perceive me are always at the back of my mind, and these fears have become only more pronounced after the election of President Trump. I feel more self-conscious in public because the dislike and suspicion toward me is more obvious. I feel more stares at my back, more grumblings around me when I stand in line at the grocery store. Thankfully, I haven't been targeted by an attack, verbal or physical, but my life seems to be suspended in some sort of terrible anticipation. When will it happen? How? Will I be calm or scared? Will my children be with me, and how will I defend them? 5

All this seems too much to explain at Subway. There are other people waiting in line behind us, and the cashier is getting dirty looks. I smile graciously — or so I hope — and reply, "It's for modesty" and hurry away. In the parking lot, my daughter looks at me disapprovingly. "I don't think you did a good job back there, Amma," she told me. "What does modesty even mean?" 6

It's a valid question. I'm sure the Subway cashier didn't understand me either. Frustrated, I sigh. An opportunity lost. I am a writer with a host of bylines on this very subject. I am a public speaker routinely invited to teach churches, synagogues, civic organizations and law enforcement about Islam. I should have done a better job. But to be honest, I am so tired of being the representative of more than a billion people. I just want to eat a sandwich in peace, go to the mall without being harassed, write about a completely unrelated topic without feeling guilty that I wasn't using my time and skills to help people understand the hijab a little better. 7

I am so tired of being the representative of more than a billion people.

I wonder how the controversy around the hijab will affect my daughter when she is older. Will she decide to wear the hijab, or will she reject it as so many other women in my family have done? Will she be able to ignore the naysayers and angry looks on the street? She watches me wind the hijab around my head when we leave the house, shops with me for new colors and designs at Old Navy and Stein Mart. She asks questions similar to the ones my training audiences ask: Why do girls wear it, what's the point of it, what does it say in the Quran? Anyone with an internet connection can answer those questions, but what she's really asking for is my personal story. 8

My story is simple. I worked at a nonprofit about 13 years ago, and one day my supervisor stopped me in the middle of a conversation to ask, abruptly, "Why don't you wear that thing I've seen other Muslim women wear?" I felt startled and unsure, just as I would at Subway a decade later. Why didn't I wear that thing? What was holding me back; why couldn't I commit to it when I had committed to the praying and fasting and everything else that makes me Muslim? I don't remember what I replied to my supervisor, but on the way home that evening I stopped to buy a few headscarves to try on. It took a few more years until I wore it regularly, but that's where it all began. 9

Not long ago, after I'd spent an hour volunteering at my daughter's school, I waited in the pickup lane as usual. She sat down in a huff in the backseat and announced, "Can you please not volunteer at my school anymore? Everyone asks me questions about your clothes." Ah, the worry apparent in her little voice. I could have been hurt or upset, but I understood her so completely. I took that opportunity to talk to her about the hijab in the larger context of being confident, as a woman and as an American, that we are free to wear what we want, even if it doesn't make sense to her classmates. "The hijab trains us to forget about 10 appearances, sweetheart," I told her. "To stop looking at the outside and see into people's hearts." The radio was on, and she pretended to sing along, but I knew she was listening. Her eyes were fixed on mine in the rearview mirror.

Since then, I've thought about it more. I finally have an answer for that Subway cashier, my former boss and even my daughter. I wear the hijab not because it is easy but because it is difficult. I wear it with perseverance in 100-degree Houston weather, while hiking at Sam Houston National Forest with my family, and at a business dinner with my husband's coworkers. I wore it with pride at my citizenship oath ceremony and with only slight trepidation when I trained thousands of Houston police officers. The hijab is a part of me, an expression of who I am and who I aspire to be, and hopefully my daughter will see that as she makes her own decision one day. 11

VOCABULARY/USING A DICTIONARY

1. How would you define the word *sincere*? What part of speech is *sincerity* (para. 3)?
2. Look up definitions or descriptions of *hijab* and *burqa* (para. 4). Are they the same thing? How are they similar and how are they different?
3. Pull apart the compound word *naysayer* (para. 8). Looking at its parts, how would you define it?

RESPONDING TO WORDS IN CONTEXT

1. Faruqi writes that wearing the hijab is "a profession of *modesty* and *decorum*" (para 4). What do words like those indicate about the wearer? Is there a difference between *modesty* and *decorum*?
2. The head scarf ban in Germany and the burkini ban in France are examples of "legislation against" (para. 4) the hijab. With those example in mind, give your definition of legislation.
3. Faruqi wears the hijab with "perseverance in 100-degree Houston weather" (para. 11). What part of speech is *perseverance*, and what does it mean for one to *persevere*?

DISCUSSING MAIN POINT AND MEANING

1. How do you interpret the essay's title? How does it relate to the essay's opening sentences? Aside from the literal meaning of a fabric, what larger issue does the title suggest?
2. Faruqi says, "I just want to eat a sandwich in peace, go to the mall without being harassed, write about a completely unrelated topic without feeling

guilty that I wasn't using my time and skills to help people understand the hijab a little better" (para. 7). Why does she discuss the reason she wears her hijab, both in conversation and in writing, if it is a bother to do so?

3. How is wearing the hijab different from "praying and fasting and everything else that makes [Faruqi] Muslim" (para. 9)? Where in her essay does Faruqi elaborate on how wearing the hijab is different from these things?

EXAMINING SENTENCES, PARAGRAPHS, AND ORGANIZATION

1. Faruqi begins her essay with the ways in which the hijab isn't "just a piece of fabric." She immediately goes on to describe the unique force of this article of clothing. In what ways do the descriptions that follow illustrate the hijab and its power?
2. The daughter is introduced in various spots in the narrative. Identify where in the essay she's mentioned. What would be lost if Faruqi's daughter wasn't part of the narrative?
3. Look at the words the author uses to describe her experience of life as a Muslim in Houston in paragraph 5. Write down words that create or indicate a specific tone. How do Muslims like Faruqi sometimes feel? How does the introduction of questions at the end also influence the tone she is creating about her feelings in that paragraph?

THINKING CRITICALLY

1. How does Faruqi use the exchange in the car with her daughter as a way to teach her daughter how wearing the hijab is important to Faruqi as a Muslim *and* as an American?
2. What significance does the question asked by the cashier at a Houston Subway shop (para. 2) have to the essay as a whole? What is your reaction to the way Faruqi responds to the question? Does it anger her? Why or why not?
3. Were you surprised to learn why Faruqi started wearing the hijab? What aspects, if any, of that story surprised you?

WRITING ACTIVITIES

1. Faruqi is asked by her supervisor why she *doesn't* wear the hijab. She's asked in Subway why she *does* wear the hijab. Do you think in either situation the asker should feel free to ask Faruqi questions about why she chooses to dress the way she does? Do you find their questions helpful? Valuable? Rude? An invasion of privacy? In a brief essay, please make a case for why

you feel the way you do. Use examples from Faruqi's story to make your argument, but also feel free to pull in examples from your own life to support your writing.

2. Consider a time the dress, speech, or behavior of a grown-up embarrassed you as a child in front of your peers. What was it about that dress, speech, or behavior that stood out, and what made you self-conscious or ashamed? What were you afraid would be noticed by others? Write a short narrative about an incident you remember from childhood and include as many details as you can remember — both about the adult in question and about your relationship with your peers or the others involved in the incident.

3. **Connect.** In her article, Fields ("Submerged in a Din of Identity Politics," p. 187) quotes Barack Obama who said, "Democracy demands that we're able also to get inside the reality of people who are different from us . . . so we can understand their point of view. Maybe we can change their minds, but maybe they'll change ours." How do you see Obama's statement reflected in the situation Faruqi finds herself in with the Subway employee? In a brief essay, explain whether you think this transaction of changing minds took place — if you think Faruqi and the Subway employee understand anything more about the other's point of view. In what way, with time, might their minds eventually be changed by what took place?

Negin Farsad and Dean Obeidallah

The Muslims Are Coming!

[Vaguely Qualified Productions, April 28, 2015]

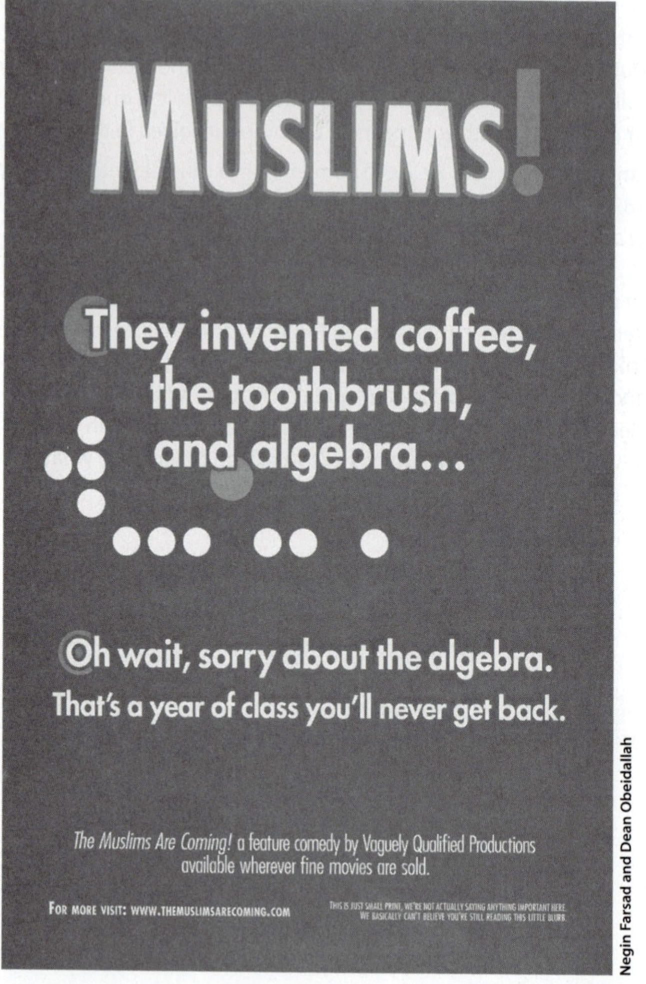

Negin Farsad and Dean Obeidallah

This poster is one of a series of ads that appeared in numerous New York City subway stations in the spring of 2016. The posters were designed to promote *The Muslims Are Coming!*, an award-winning documentary covering a national tour of Muslim American comedians. At first, New York City refused to allow the ads to be posted, but eventually the comedians won their case. Do you think the strategy behind the posters is correct — that we can fight negative stereotypes with humor?

Tadeu Velloso (student essay)

Brown

[*Portland Magazine*, University of Portland, Summer 2014]

A U.S. citizen born to Brazilians in California, Tadeu Velloso lived an immigrant life that even included learning English as a second language. In his essay "Brown," written while he was a student at the University of Portland, we see how difficult it can be, even for those born here, to form a stable American identity. As he writes, "There are weird transition phases that the children of immigrants go through, most notably the declaration of our United States American identity over our other identities. We become cultural straddlers."

Tadeu Velloso is a 2014 graduate of the University of Portland and is now an attorney in Washington State.

BEFORE YOU READ

Are race relations in America particularly problematic for the children of immigrants? What challenges do they face in terms of determining their own identities or understanding the perceptions of others?

WORDS TO LEARN

avid (para. 1): ardent; enthusiastic (adjective)

declaration (para. 6): announcement; formal statement (noun)

implications (para. 7): suggestions; associations (noun)

advocacy (para. 9): active pleading for something (noun)

predominantly (para. 10): preeminently (adverb)

rehabilitation (para. 11): restoration (noun)

incarcerated (para. 11): imprisoned (adjective)

collaboratively (para. 12): cooperatively (adverb)

extant (para. 12): in existence (adjective)

Growing up I always dealt with the question What are you? From my earliest years I knew this was a loaded question — people weren't asking if I was an avid reader, an adventurer, a jokester; they wanted to know who I was racially, so that they could classify me and figure out how to interact with me. 1

I am American, the son of Brazilian immigrants. I grew up first in California, where I was constantly mixing with immigrants from 2

El Salvador, Mexico, and Guatemala. When I was four, we moved to Brazil. I returned to the States at age seven. By the time I returned to the States I didn't speak any English, so from second grade I was foreign and international and an English as a second language student, even though I was, as I tried to say, a United States American, when people asked me What are you?

But my answer wasn't good enough. No one believed it. My skin 3
color and my accent didn't add up to United States American in their minds.

"I'm Brazilian," I'd try. But that didn't work either — I had adopted 4
too many attributes of the "white" culture, whatever that is, to claim Latino identity.

I began to notice how differently people looked at me if I was with 5
my Latino friends' families or black families as opposed to with a white family. Curious eyes were trying to figure out what the relation was between white family and brown boy.

There are weird transition phases that the children of immigrants 6
go through, most notably the declaration of our United States American identity over our other identities. We become cultural straddlers. I felt that I had to choose one. In a culture that shames immigrants on a daily basis, I tried my hardest to claim my United States American identity, and rid myself of my Latino identity.

This grew complicated once I began to learn about the civil rights 7
movement. Seeing the images of segregated places made me think, if I was alive during this time would I have been considered black or white? I began to realize the implications that claiming blackness or brownness historically had on people in the United States; at the same time I grew increasingly fascinated by the possibilities of a world where race could be embraced positively.

In California, however, where I spent the next ten years of my child- 8
hood, there are clear and definite divisions among whites and people of color. In my schools, immigrants and the children of immigrants were often assumed to be gangbangers and troublemakers. Though I was neither, I was aware from an early age that people I was growing up with were seen as threats and probable criminals simply because of their color or ancestry. At age 14, I took part in my first public protest against those divisions — an immigrant rights march. A group of us kids left school and marched around our town. This was a monumental moment for me. It was the first time

A group of us kids left school and marched around our town. This was a monumental moment for me.

that I embraced the fact that my mom was an immigrant, that my mom had an accent, that my mom was a part of a rich culture, and that all those things were a part of me as well. For the first time in my life, I was proud of being Latino; I was proud of being brown.

That realization has shaped my life since then. I have been dedicated to advocacy and social justice awareness since that moment. I worked with migrant workers, people experiencing homelessness, low-income families. I always approached it from the perspective that I was engaging with a community, and separated myself from any ideology that I was somehow capable of saving anyone. 9

When I came to the university, a traditionally white space, in Portland, a predominantly white space, I began to engage with social justice in an academic way also, particularly modern race relations and the reflections of modern race relations through music like hip-hop. But after going on the Moreau Center's[1] civil rights immersion through the South, I really struggled with everything I had witnessed, and felt that I needed to find something to do to make a change. 10

For me it became criminal justice reform, the rehabilitation of formerly incarcerated people, and the push for systemic racial equity. One of the most obvious and ignored forms of institutional racism is the criminal justice system. Low-income communities and communities of color are disproportionately affected by incarceration and its consequences — which include, if prisoners are even freed, inability to find employment, inability to qualify for assistance with housing and food and student loans, and inability to vote. 11

I have tried to figure out tangible ways to get people talking about these issues, while also directly helping people affected by incarceration; and so came the idea of a "transparent" clothing company — one that told the stories and struggles of people in prison making the clothes, while also helping those same incarcerated people learn job skills, work collaboratively and productively, and get a rare chance to be proud of their work. After a while I discovered an extant company called Stripes. I connected with them about my vision for a brand of clothing that would empower incarcerated people while also telling their story to the wider world, and we went into business together. I'll be working with Stripes after I graduate, working to introduce this new business model to the market, and looking for more ways to help create a world where race isn't ignored but celebrated in honest and productive ways. It's been a racially brutal world for a long time; it doesn't have to stay that way. 12

---

[1] Moreau Center (para. 10): A division of the University of Portland that offers service opportunities to students as well as justice and leadership learning.

VOCABULARY/USING A DICTIONARY

1. What part of speech is *formerly* (para. 11)? What does it mean?
2. What is a synonym for *transparent* (para. 12)?
3. What does *systemic* (para. 11) mean?

RESPONDING TO WORDS IN CONTEXT

1. What is meant by *Latino* (para. 5)?
2. How would you define *cultural straddlers* (para. 6)?
3. What do *migrant workers* (para. 9) do?

DISCUSSING MAIN POINT AND MEANING

1. Why is Velloso asked "What are you?"
2. What sort of assumptions are made about the essayist because he is part of a community of immigrants and children of immigrants?
3. What activity does Velloso engage in that he describes as monumental in changing how he views himself?

EXAMINING SENTENCES, PARAGRAPHS, AND ORGANIZATION

1. Why is the first paragraph important to the essay?
2. Why is the essay called "Brown"?
3. Why does Velloso repeat "What are you?" in paragraphs 1 and 2?

THINKING CRITICALLY

1. Why do you think Velloso took an interest in social justice in college?
2. What attributes mark the essayist as an immigrant? What attributes mark the essayist as an American?
3. What is eye-opening about the "immigrant rights march" (para. 8)? What does it teach Velloso about himself?

WRITING ACTIVITIES

1. Consider the question "What are you?" How would you answer this question? What aspects of yourself do you highlight when answering this question? Try answering it in a freewriting exercise in which you write for ten to fifteen minutes without stopping. When you've finished, try to craft a personal narrative about what (not who) you are that mines your freewriting for material.
2. What assumptions do we make about what it means to be an American? Using Velloso's narrative as research, write a brief essay about who Americans are and how presuppositions can be misleading.

3. In small groups, discuss the ending of Velloso's essay. In a collaborative effort, write an essay that considers Velloso's interest in incarceration as a form of institutional racism and how he chooses to combat that form by creating a "'transparent' clothing company" (para. 12). Do you and other members of the group think this is an effective way to bring attention to incarceration and racism? How does this bring the issue to light? Does it help those institutionalized? Does it help the rest of the world think about prisoners differently?

LOOKING CLOSELY

Describing a Defining Moment

In personal essays, writers often turn to moments in their lives that had a major impact on their perspectives, choices, and careers. Years ago, students were often given writing assignments that asked them to describe a "turning point" in their lives. Sometimes, especially in literature, such moments are called "epiphanies," referring to a life-altering "sudden realization."

In his personal essay, "Brown," University of Portland student Tadeu Velloso memorably describes such "a monumental moment." Note that he first establishes a context by observing that the children of immigrants, like him, are often stereotyped as "probable criminals." Then he introduces a specific moment that altered his life — an immigrant rights march that he joined as a means to protest against the "divisions" he had become conscious of. At fourteen, he realized that he was proud of both his origins and the color of his skin. His essay then goes on to show how this sudden realization has ultimately "shaped" his life since then.

1
Sets the context for his defining moment

2
Introduces the specific event that led to it

3
Clearly describes the defining moment

(1) In my schools, immigrants and the children of immigrants were often assumed to be gangbangers and troublemakers. Though I was neither, I was aware from an early age that people I was growing up with were seen as threats and probable criminals simply because of their color or ancestry. (2) At age 14, I took part in my first public protest against those divisions — an immigrant rights march. A group of us kids left school and marched around our town. (3) This was a monumental moment for me. It was the first time that I embraced the fact that my mom was an immigrant, that my mom had an accent, that my mom was a part of a rich culture, and that all those things were a part of me as well. For the first time in my life, I was proud of being Latino; I was proud of being brown.

STUDENT WRITER AT WORK

Tadeu Velloso

R.A. What inspired you to write this essay? And publish it?

T.V. I wrote the essay before graduating from the University of Portland. During my time as a student, there were several incidents of explicit and implicit racism. However, the institution wasn't doing anything to address or teach its students about racism. I was approached to write this piece about my work with a company (with which I am no longer affiliated). I believe that incarcerated people deserve a second chance, and I believe that my conviction about this second chance stems from my experience as a person of color. As a student of color, I felt as if I wasn't often afforded the benefit of the doubt; that I had to go above and beyond to prove my credibility. Given that people of color are disproportionately represented in the criminal justice system and face serious collateral consequences upon their release, it is important for me to be an advocate to ensure that everyone, regardless of their mistakes, can live a meaningful life.

At the University of Portland, people weren't talking about race. But by ignoring race, I (as a student of color) felt like the institution was ignoring me. Our identities shape who we are and how we see the world, so dismissing those experiences is a complete disservice to your students.

R.A. Do you generally show your writing to friends before submitting it? Do you collaborate with others or bounce your ideas off them? To what extent did discussion with others help you develop your point of view on the topic you wrote about?

T.V. When it's something so personal, I usually won't show it to friends. When writing about my own experience, I make sure to reflect on the message. What point am I trying to make? What stories will illustrate my point? I want my work to be fueled by passion, but I also understand that I need to lead the reader throughout the piece.

R.A. What advice do you have for other student writers?

T.V. Don't be scared. Sometimes you need to write about things that are unpopular, but your writing often needs to exist in the world. I had a lot of great supporters and mentors at the University of Portland, but I wanted them to know that I am proud of being a person of color.

Suzanne Fields

Submerged in a Din of Identity Politics

[*Townhall*, July 27, 2018 (*The News & Advance*, August 1, 2018)]

In a speech honoring the one hundredth anniversary of the birth of South African leader Nelson Mandela, former president Barack Obama maintained that, among other things, "democracy demands that we're also able to get inside the reality of people who are different than us so we can understand their point of view. Maybe we can change their minds, but maybe they'll change ours." In her essay "Submerged in a Din of Identity Politics," the syndicated columnist Suzanne Fields cites Obama's comment as a way to resist what she sees as a swerve toward a fractious polarization of Americans based on various identity groups. "It's us against them," she argues, "and a mean spirit becomes a contagion, splintering us into subgroups of animosity left and right, culturally and politically."

Suzanne Fields is an author and a widely syndicated columnist for the Washington Times. *In addition to writing, she has appeared on CNN and on* Nightline, Larry King Live, The Oprah Winfrey Show, The Today Show, *and* Good Morning America, *among other programs.*

BEFORE YOU READ

What words or ideas come to mind when you hear the phrase "political identity"? How does identity used in the political arena divide and alienate instead of bringing individuals closer together?

WORDS TO LEARN

gratifications (para. 1): satisfactions (noun)
dilute (para. 2): to water down (verb)
animosity (para. 5): hostility (noun)
polarization (para. 7): division into two opposing beliefs (noun)
animate (para. 8): to bring to life (verb)
multicultural (para. 8): made up of several cultural or ethnic groups (adjective)
congenial (para. 9): agreeable (adjective)
revival (para. 10): a resurgence (noun)
deleterious (para. 10): harmful (adjective)
reconciliation (para. 11): restoration of friendship or goodwill (noun)
redeem (para. 11): to save or to regain (verb)

The human animal seems hard-wired for tribalism, and the ties that bind are shaped by our compelling need to group together, obeying calls for loyalties and exclusions. Some groupings not only contribute to the gratifications of bonding, whether in family, clubs, choirs or loyalty to sports teams, but also provide the glue that holds a community together. 1

But tribes become the "factions" that former President George Washington warned against in his Farewell Address, heightening differences and rivalries that the Founding Fathers hoped to dilute through checks and balances in the three branches of government. In the age of the internet, tribalism asserts itself in the flood of outrage stories that bombard us hourly, and make us angry and hostile toward those with whom we disagree. 2

Former President Barack Obama, who had all but vanished from public life, opened a conversation about identity politics in a speech in South Africa the other day during the 100th anniversary of the birth of Nelson Mandela, warning that democracy is served poorly when identity is the organizing principle. 3

"But democracy demands that we're able also to get inside the reality of people who are different than us," he said, "so we can understand their point of view. Maybe we can change their minds, but maybe they'll change ours." 4

It's tempting to dismiss an argument offered by a former president and the current one if we don't like things that are said, even when it's reasonable. There's no room for debate, and everyone is quickly labeled as either hateful or stupid for expressing a different point of view. It's us against them, and a mean spirit becomes a contagion, splintering us into subgroups of animosity left and right, culturally and politically. 5

"A shift in tone, rhetoric, and logic has moved identity politics away from inclusion — which had always been the left's watchword — toward exclusion and division," writes Yale Law professor Amy Chua in *Political Tribes: Group Instinct and the Face of Nations*. Facebook now lists over 50 genders ("sexes," they used to be called) for argument, "from genderqueer to intersex to pangender," as it competes to take equal opportunity offense. The competition for victimization has become a crowded field. 6

Jonathan Haidt, author of *The Righteous Mind*, who has studied political polarization since 2007, observes that both sides of the political spectrum show increasing dislike for the other and think the other a threat to the country. The parties, which once included an uneven mix of conservatives and liberals, contrive now to be so ideologically "pure" that opposing voices within are quickly silenced. 7

8 The term “identity politics” is heard often in the news and on social media to animate our own ideas and prejudices, some good, some not so good, in our multicultural country. But what does “identity politics” actually refer to? Whose identity? Whose politics? The questions run through conversations on the beach, at a bar and around the barbecue grill, overheard in the swimming pool or on a picnic blanket, addressed casually between men and women of different ages, and in different locations where people congregate.

> **But what does “identity politics” actually refer to? Whose identity? Whose politics?**

9 Summer brings people together from many walks and places of life, backgrounds and traditions. They once could meet during the happy and laid-back season without the baggage that disrupts and angers debate on politics and current events. But now, not so much. Politics seems to be permanently polarized. After old friends and summer acquaintances move through congenial conversations about family, relationships, work, play, baseball, sometimes soccer, the scorching heat or the dreary rainy day, identity politics emerges as a common theme. It asserts itself like a snake coiling around the base of a tree and becomes a dangerous disruption of neighborly cohesion. Whether black, white, Hispanic, Asian, male, female, gay, straight, Jewish, Christian or Muslim, identity politics forces us to think in terms of differences and not the many good things we cherish and hold in common.

10 The imperfect melting pot that once united us as unhyphenated Americans has boiled over into an indigestible stew, giving people heartburn and indigestion and no longer providing a way for smoothing over differences. The temperature of social discourse inevitably rises. Identity politics and the revival of a tribal mentality may be the most deleterious affliction with which we as individuals and as a nation must contend.

11 When Martin Luther King Jr. led the civil rights struggle, he aimed for a national reconciliation to redeem an inclusive American dream. Former President Abraham Lincoln, who sought healing in the few days he had left after the Civil War, urged us to listen to “the better angels of our nature.” But those angels, as he knew, are fragile and easily destroyed in the din of identity.

VOCABULARY/USING A DICTIONARY

1. What is the root of the word *tribalism* (para 1)? What does that root indicate about the idea being presented?

2. What does the word *contagion* (para. 5) mean? In what context is that word usually used?
3. What is a *din* (para. 11)? Is it unusual that Fields ascribes it to identity? Why?

RESPONDING TO WORDS IN CONTEXT

1. Fields says, "Tribalism asserts itself in the flood of outrage stories that bombard us hourly" (para. 2). What do you think that means? Can you give an example of asserting yourself in a situation?
2. What part of speech is *congregate* (para. 8)? Can you think of a noun that shares the root of the word *congregate* that might help you come up with its definition in this context?
3. When Fields refers to the soup in America's "imperfect melting pot" as an "indigestible stew" (para. 10), what do you think she's saying about how people get along with each other? What is your definition of *indigestible*?

DISCUSSING MAIN POINT AND MEANING

1. What appears to be Fields's main reason to be opposed to "identity politics"? How does she express that opinion in paragraph 9? What does "summer" have to do with her argument?
2. If we are "hard-wired for tribalism" (para. 1), is there anything we can do to fight against the divisions of identity politics? What possible alternatives to that tribalism does Fields introduce, if any?
3. What is Fields's point in bringing up the multiplicity of genders in paragraph 6?

EXAMINING SENTENCES, PARAGRAPHS, AND ORGANIZATION

1. Explain whether material from Amy Chua (para. 6) and Jonathan Haidt (para. 7) contributes to the argument. Why would Fields add them to her conversation about identity politics?
2. What is Fields's strategy of introducing Martin Luther King Jr. and Abraham Lincoln in her conclusion? What do these two individuals represent?
3. Fields introduces questions in paragraph 8. What effect do those questions have, placed where they are?

THINKING CRITICALLY

1. Why is identity politics becoming so pronounced at this moment in our history? Does Fields give any hints at why it is resurfacing now and becoming such a problem? Can you think of other reasons why identity politics might be an issue at this time?

2. **Connect.** Do you think that in identity politics, divisions are as clear cut as Fields suggests? Do you think that's the case for Susan Power ("Native in the Twenty-First Century" p. 169)? Name all the ways Power might identify, and explain your thinking, looking to both Fields's and Power's articles for guidance.
3. Do you think that the United States is particularly susceptible to the dangers of identity politics? More so than other countries? Why or why not?

WRITING ACTIVITIES

1. Write a response to this article, explaining how persuasive you find Fields's argument. Do you think those who endorse identity politics would be convinced by her plea to set aside our differences?
2. Choose either Martin Luther King Jr. or Abraham Lincoln, and write a brief essay that examines his work and his attempts to avoid identity politics. Discuss how his attempts were successful as well as how they were unsuccessful.
3. Look at the life and times of Martin Luther King Jr. and Abraham Lincoln that Fields invokes in her article. How did their political moment shape the work they were trying to do? In a comparison and contrast essay, show how each faced his challenges with identity politics and how successful each was in surmounting them, within the context of the time in which each lived.

SPOTLIGHT ON DATA AND RESEARCH

Matthew Bulger

What Makes an American?

[*The Humanist*, July 2, 2015]

One of the common functions of journalism is to describe and interpret the results of scientific polls and research reports. In "What Makes an American?," a columnist for the Humanist *magazine, Matthew Bulger, interprets a recent survey taken by the Public Religion Research Institute. Founded in 2009, this organization describes itself as "a nonprofit, nonpartisan organization dedicated to research at the intersection of religion, values, and public life." Its "mission is to help journalists, opinion leaders, scholars, clergy, and the general public better understand debates on public policy issues and the role of religion and values in American public life by conducting high quality public opinion surveys and qualitative research." The* Humanist *magazine is a publication of the American Humanist Association, which was founded in 1941 and is located in Washington, D.C. According to its Web site, "The American Humanist Association advocates progressive values and equality for humanists, atheists, freethinkers, and the non-religious." The association's motto is "Good without a God."*

As the Fourth of July rapidly approaches, red, white, and blue banners (as well as hundreds of tacky Independence Day–themed advertisements for bars and nightclubs) seem to be everywhere in our nation's capital. While patriotic fireworks and large quantities of alcohol tend to mark the way we celebrate our country's independence on this special day, discussions regarding patriotism and the American identity reveal disagreement on just what and who we're celebrating. 1

Coming from conservative Texas, I've heard more than my fair share of xenophobic remarks regarding immigrants and other communities that weren't seen as authentically "American." But what exactly do Americans think constitutes being American? 2

According to a recent Public Religion Research Institute survey, several factors contribute to making a person seem distinctly American. By far the most important factor according to the study is the ability to speak English, with 89 percent of participants saying this was necessary for a person to be considered truly American. This is a bit strange, considering that our country does not maintain English as our official language and because we have more Spanish speakers than any country in the world excluding Mexico (but including Spain). 3

Another strange finding was that 58 percent of respondents said being born in the United States is a requirement to be considered a real American. Sadly, this means that only 42 percent of people recognize and respect our country's proud history as a nation of immigrants. 4

But strangest of all was the survey's finding on the relationship between religious belief and American identity. Sixty-nine percent of those surveyed said that a belief in God is required to be a true American, while 53 percent believe only Christians can be true Americans. 5

There are a few ways to look at these numbers. On a positive note, 31 percent of Americans don't make a connection between religious beliefs and American identity, which is a higher number than the roughly 23 percent of Americans who are religiously unaffiliated. That means there are a significant number of Americans who maintain a belief in a god or gods, but who don't see their religion, or any religion for that matter, as a prerequisite for being considered an American. And while nearly 71 percent of Americans identify as Christian, only half of those surveyed think that being specifically Christian is a fundamental part of being an American. 6

Still, these numbers do seem to show that for a significant amount of Americans, religious beliefs, and a specific type of religious belief at that, are required for an individual to be considered an American. By doing so, many of those surveyed alienated Jews, Muslims, Hindus, and Buddhists, as well as humanists and atheists, from a community that is ostensibly open to all regardless of religious beliefs. 7

Our nation has a proud history of religious diversity, but this survey shows that many Americans are either unaware of that history or are opposed to the values that made this country what it is today. As the growth of the nonreligious continues, it's unlikely that religion will continue to remain so intertwined with American identity. But until that day arrives, it's crucially important that attempts to wed patriotism with religious belief and with perceptions of national identity be exposed both as theocratically intolerant and historically inaccurate. 8

POINTS TO CONSIDER

1. Given the goal of the *Humanist* magazine, as described in the lead-in to the selection, why do you think it took an interest in this particular survey?
2. Why do you think Bulger links his report to the Fourth of July holiday? From the tone of the opening paragraph, what attitude do you detect on the part of the author?
3. What does the author find most distressing about the result of the survey? Do you agree with him? Do you think the poll numbers that show a link between "religious belief and American identity" (para. 5) are a cause for concern? Why or why not?

AMERICA THEN . . . 1782

J. Hector St. Jean de Crèvecoeur

The Melting Pot

[*Letters from an American Farmer*, 1782]

Is there really such a thing as an "American"? In the previous selection, we saw a 2015 survey that surprisingly found that many Americans considered a belief in God, along with speaking English and native birth, to be essential components of an American identity. The question, however, goes back a long way, to before there was a United States of America.

"What then is the American, this new man?" With that question, a French-born aristocrat who had made New York State his home launched one of the first inquiries into the puzzling nature of the American identity. In 1782, J. Hector St. Jean de Crèvecoeur (1735–1813) published a book of a dozen epistolary essays called Letters from an American Farmer *that made him an instant literary success. The most important of the letters is the third, "What Is an American?" The short excerpt below (the original essay is quite long) is often reprinted and remains one of the most famous passages of early*

American literature. In this passage, he also formulates the famous concept of the "melting pot." "Here," Crèvecoeur forecasted, "individuals of all nations are melted into a new race of men."

BEFORE YOU READ

How did early American immigrants experience their change of life from the Old World to the New World? Do you think Crèvecoeur's experience is how most immigrants would describe their emigration?

WORDS TO LEARN

emigrant (para. 1): person who leaves one country to live permanently in another (noun)
motto (para. 1): an aphorism (noun)
posterity (para. 1): future generations (noun)
exuberance (para. 1): quality of cheerfulness, energy, and excitement (adjective)
ample (para. 1): more than enough (adjective)

What attachment can a poor European emigrant have for a country where he had nothing? The knowledge of the language, the love of a few kindred as poor as himself, were the only cords that tied him; his country is now that which gives him land, bread, protection, and consequence: *Ubi panis ibi patria* [Where there is bread, there is my country], is the motto of all emigrants. What then is the American, this new man? He is either a European, or the descendant of a European, hence that strange mixture of blood, which you will find in no other country. I could point out to you a family whose grandfather was an Englishman, whose wife was Dutch, whose son married a Frenchwoman, and whose present four sons have now four wives of different nations. He is an American, who leaving behind him all his ancient prejudices and manners, receives new ones from the new mode of life he has embraced, the new government he obeys, and the new rank he holds. He becomes an American by being received in the broad lap of our great alma mater. Here individuals of all nations are melted into a new race of men, whose labors and posterity will one day cause great changes in the world. Americans are the Western pilgrims, who are carrying along with them that great mass of arts, sciences, vigor, and industry which began long since in the East; they will finish the great circle. The Americans were once scattered all over Europe; here they are incorporated into one of the finest systems of population which has ever appeared, and which will hereafter become distinct by the power of the different climates they inhabit. The American ought therefore 1 to love this country much better than that wherein either he or his forefathers were born. Here the rewards of his industry follow with equal steps the progress of his labor; his labor is founded on the basis of nature, self-interest; can it want a stronger allurement? Wives and children, who before in vain demanded of him a morsel of bread, now, fat and frolicsome, gladly help their father to clear those fields whence exuberant crops are to arise to feed and to clothe them all; without any part being claimed, either by a despotic prince, a rich abbot, or a mighty lord. Here religion demands but little of him; a small voluntary salary to the minister, and gratitude to God; can he refuse these? The American is a new man, who acts upon new principles; he must therefore entertain new ideas and form new opinions. From involuntary idleness, servile dependence, penury, and useless labor he has passed to toils of a very different nature, rewarded by ample subsistence — this is an American.

VOCABULARY/USING A DICTIONARY

1. What is a *descendant* (para. 1)? What clue lies within the root of the word?
2. The words *alma mater* (para. 1) are in what language? What does it mean?
3. If someone lives in *penury* (para.1), how is that person living?

RESPONDING TO WORDS IN CONTEXT

1. What part of speech is *kindred* (para. 1) in this context?
2. What do you think Crèvecoeur means when he refers to the land that gives him *consequence* (para. 1)?
3. What's another way of saying *mode of life* (para. 1)?

DISCUSSING MAIN POINT AND MEANING

1. Why is "*Ubi panis ibi patria*" described as the motto of all emigrants?
2. Crèvecoeur describes Americans as a "new race of men" (para. 1). What do they leave behind? How are they made new?
3. Who is the boss of the new American? Who is not?

EXAMINING SENTENCES, PARAGRAPHS, AND ORGANIZATION

1. Look at the writing in Crèvecoeur's essay. How would you describe it? Consider the use of pronouns, the density of the paragraph, and the use of punctuation as you formulate your answer.
2. Crèvecoeur begins the passage with a question. Does he answer it? What is the effect of the many questions scattered throughout this passage?

3. "Wives and children, who before in vain demanded of him a morsel of bread, now, fat and frolicsome, gladly help their father to clear those fields whence exuberant crops are to arise to feed and to clothe them all; without any part being claimed, either by a despotic prince, a rich abbot, or a mighty lord," writes Crèvecoeur. What is the tone of this passage? Is it reflective of Crèvecoeur's tone throughout?

THINKING CRITICALLY

1. **Connect.** Look at Crèvecoeur's statements about how he feels as a man living in a new world. What do you notice about the way old and new, immigrant and citizen, interact in his America? Look at the writing of Emma Lazarus's poem "The New Colossus" (p. 162), written about 100 years later. How do the two view the immigrants who come to America and the New World they've come to? What are the similarities and differences in their perspectives on America and the immigrants who come here? Explain how you think their perspectives converge and diverge and why this might be so.
2. Do you think Crèvecoeur's description of the immigrant experience and mood reflects the truth of the situation or does he paint a picture of emigration that can never live up to reality for many? Why might Crèvecoeur choose to describe life in America this way?
3. Why will the new American love his new country more than his old one? Do you think the reason Crèvecoeur gives is sufficient? Why or why not?

WRITING ACTIVITIES

1. Was Crèvecoeur right in 1782, when he wrote: "Here individuals of all nations are melted into a new race of men, whose labors and posterity will one day cause great changes in the world"? In a brief essay, describe the ways in which Crèvecoeur was correct in his description of the immigrant experience and contribution to America.
2. **Connect.** Look at the differences between Crèvecoeur's description of being an immigrant and Faruqi's description in "Cut from a Different Cloth" (p. 174). In a short comparison essay, consider how Faruqi might respond to Crèvecoeur's idea of the melting pot. Do they view immigration to America the same way? How would Faruqi feel about the new mode of life that Crèvecoeur holds up for the new American?
3. What is your ancestry? Is it similar to what Crèvecoeur describes for Americans or is it different? Write about the people you come from and think about what your forebears gave up or held onto if they immigrated here. If you are Native American, describe that heritage, and if you are a citizen of another country, think about what, if anything, of Crèvecoeur's description applies to you.

Discussing the Unit

SUGGESTED TOPIC FOR DISCUSSION

How do we forge our identity? From race? Nationality? Gender? Sexual orientation? Political leanings? We are a nation made up of many immigrants and cultures; national identity is often complicated or in flux. Individual Americans have always had, and are becoming more entrenched in, an "us" against "them" attitude — polarized by politics and the very diversity that defines us as a nation.

PREPARING FOR CLASS DISCUSSION

1. Who decides what it means to be an American? Is there a standard or set of traits to which we aspire? Can the word contain different meanings and values?
2. How do you identify yourself? What makes up your identity? Is it something handed down to you from your parents? Does your identity hinge on how you are different from others? "Identify" implies similarity with another, but consider the ways in which it implies difference.

FROM DISCUSSION TO WRITING

1. Discuss how Power and Faruqi have a strong sense of identity even though they must often hold contradictory parts of themselves as part of that identity. How would you describe them in terms of who they are — who they are at their core? Are Power and Faruqi's identities alike in any way? Explain.
2. Identity is a way to understand who you are in relation to the world. Find two essays that show the authors knowing themselves well, and that knowledge being an advantage, a powerful tool in the world. Discuss how these essays speak to you and your own sense of yourself. Use specific examples from the text when talking about your own identity.

TOPICS FOR CROSS-CULTURAL DISCUSSION

1. Think about Suzanne Fields's very contemporary argument about identity politics in America. Do you think identity politics is particular to America? Do any readings in this chapter support your position?
2. Fields's conclusion suggests that we'd be better off without the fragmentation of identity politics. Do you agree or disagree? How does identity politics add to, or support, your sense of who you are and your voice as a citizen of this country? How does identity politics hinder you?

6

Race: Why Does It Still Matter?

For as long as America has existed, race has been one of its most challenging issues. After the election of Barack Obama in 2008, some observers felt the nation's racial tensions were coming to an end, claiming that we now live in a "post-racial" America. In this new America, the systematic oppression of certain ethnic groups by others would no longer continue as a serious problem. It seemed as though Martin Luther King Jr.'s dream of a society that judges its individuals "not by the color of their skin but by the content of their character" had come true.

But that vision of progress was short-lived. Many critical observers argue that racial injustice still plagues American society and, in particular, that African Americans and other minorities are the persistent victims — sometimes unknowingly — of "institutional racism," persecution that's not direct (as was legal segregation) but systemic. Such systemic racism can be seen throughout society in both large and small ways, from the murder of unarmed African American citizens by white police officers (incidents that gave birth to the Black Lives Matter movement) to the "microaggressive" behavior of white people who may be unaware of the racist attitudes they bring to their everyday encounters with persons of color.

This chapter will explore a few of the many ways that obvious and subtle, visible and invisible racism infects our entire society.

Claudia Rankine

You and Your Partner . . .

In the following prose poem, the prominent poet Claudia Rankine uses a single compressed incident to show how racial prejudice can insinuate itself into the ordinary moments of everyday life. With a keen eye and ear, along with a remarkable sensitivity to nuance, Rankine dramatizes the unsettling and often hidden ways that racism emerges in everyday life even among people who abhor racism.

A New York Times *best seller and the winner of numerous poetry awards, Claudia Rankine's 2014 book* Citizen: An American Lyric *is a meticulous exploration in poetry and prose of what it means to be black in a supposedly post-racial society.*

You and your partner go to see the film *The House We Live In.* You ask a friend to pick up your child from school. On your way home your phone rings. Your neighbor tells you he is standing at his window watching a menacing black guy casing both your homes. The guy is walking back and forth talking to himself and seems disturbed. 1

You tell your neighbor that your friend, whom he has met, is babysitting. He says, no, it's not him. He's met your friend and this isn't that nice young man. Anyway, he wants you to know, he's called the police. 2

Your partner calls your friend and asks him if there's a guy walking back and forth in front of your home. Your friend says that if anyone were outside he would see him because he is standing outside. You hear the sirens through the speakerphone. 3

Your friend is speaking to your neighbor when you arrive home. The four police cars are gone. Your neighbor has apologized to your friend and is now apologizing to you. Feeling somewhat responsible for the actions of your neighbor, you clumsily tell your friend that the next time he wants to talk on the phone he should just go in the backyard. He looks at you a long minute before saying he can speak on the phone wherever he wants. Yes, of course, you say. Yes, of course. 4

POINTS TO CONSIDER

1. In your own words, describe exactly what has happened in Rankine's account. What mistake was made? How do you interpret the mistake?
2. How does Rankine herself compound the mistake? Why do you think she uses the word *clumsily* to describe what she tells her friend in the last paragraph?
3. What is the effect of Rankine's final words? Why does she repeat them? What does the repetition suggest about the entire incident?

Robin DiAngelo

White America's Racial Illiteracy: Why Our National Conversation Is Poisoned from the Start

[*The Good Men Project*, April 9, 2015]

In a much less compressed form than the previous selection, the well-known author and lecturer Robin DiAngelo offers a systematic account of how and why even well-intentioned white people — those who do not believe they hold racist views — are clueless when it comes to detecting their own privileges and entitlements, which they too often take for granted. In "White America's Racial Illiteracy: Why Our National Conversation Is Poisoned from the Start," she argues that "white people have extremely low thresholds for enduring any discomfort associated with challenges to our racial worldviews." She then clearly enumerates all the challenges to a dominant white perspective.

Robin DiAngelo was a professor of multicultural education at Westfield State University and now serves as a lecturer at the University of Washington. For more than two decades, she has been a trainer and consultant on racial and social justice issues. She is the author of What Does It Mean to Be White? *(2012) and* White Fragility: Why It's So Hard for White People to Talk about Racism *(2018).*

BEFORE YOU READ

Do you think of yourself as living in an inherently racist society? What aspects of daily life might we take into consideration when we define the word *racist*?

WORDS TO LEARN

mainstream (para. 1): belonging to the prevailing or dominant culture or group (adjective)
hierarchies (para. 3): ranking systems (noun)
adaptive (para. 4): having capacity to change (adjective)
insulate (para. 6): to keep separate (verb)
benign (para. 6): not harmful (adjective)
solidarity (para. 7): unity (noun)
centrality (para. 7): the state of being in the center (noun)
equilibrium (para. 8): balance (noun)
platitudes (para. 10): statements expressing ideas that are not new (noun)
binary (para. 14): based on two things (noun)
penalization (para. 16): punishment (noun)
antidote (para. 21): something that corrects or fixes a problem (noun)
certitude (para. 24): freedom from doubt (noun)

I am white. I have spent years studying what it means to be white in a society that proclaims race meaningless, yet is deeply divided by race. This is what I have learned: Any white person living in the United States will develop opinions about race simply by swimming in the water of our culture. But mainstream sources — schools, textbooks, media — don't provide us with the multiple perspectives we need. 1

Yes, we will develop strong emotionally laden opinions, but they will not be informed opinions. Our socialization renders us racially illiterate. When you add a lack of humility to that illiteracy (because we don't know what we don't know), you get the breakdown we so often see when trying to engage white people in meaningful conversations about race. 2

Mainstream dictionary definitions reduce racism to individual racial prejudice and the intentional actions that result. The people that commit these intentional acts are deemed bad, and those that don't are good. If we are against racism and unaware of committing racist acts, we can't be racist; racism and being a good person have become mutually exclusive. But this definition does little to explain how racial hierarchies are consistently reproduced. 3

Social scientists understand racism as a multidimensional and highly adaptive *system* — a system that ensures an unequal distribution of resources between racial groups. Because whites built and dominate all significant institutions (often at the expense of and on the uncompensated labor of other groups), their interests are embedded in the foundation of U.S. society. 4

While individual whites may be against racism, they still benefit from the distribution of resources controlled by their group. Yes, an individual person of color can sit at the tables of power, but the overwhelming majority of decision-makers will be white. Yes, white people can have problems and face barriers, but systematic racism won't be one of them. This distinction — between individual prejudice and a system of unequal institutionalized racial power — is fundamental. One cannot understand how racism functions in the U.S. today if one ignores group power relations. 5

This systemic and institutional control allows those of us who are white in North America to live in a social environment that protects and insulates us from race-based stress. We have organized society to reproduce and reinforce our racial interests and perspectives. Further, we are centered in all matters deemed normal, universal, benign, neutral, and good. Thus, we move through a wholly racialized world with an unracialized identity (e.g., white people can represent all of humanity, people of color can only represent their racial selves). 6

Challenges to this identity become highly stressful and even intolerable. The following are examples of the kinds of challenges that trigger racial stress for white people: 7

- Suggesting that a white person's viewpoint comes from a racialized frame of reference (challenge to objectivity);
- People of color talking directly about their own racial perspectives (challenge to white taboos on talking openly about race);
- People of color choosing not to protect the racial feelings of white people in regards to race (challenge to white racial expectations and need/entitlement to racial comfort);
- People of color not being willing to tell their stories or answer questions about their racial experiences (challenge to the expectation that people of color will serve us);
- A fellow white not providing agreement with one's racial perspective (challenge to white solidarity);
- Receiving feedback that one's behavior had a racist impact (challenge to white racial innocence);
- Suggesting that group membership is significant (challenge to individualism);
- An acknowledgment that access is unequal between racial groups (challenge to meritocracy);
- Being presented with a person of color in a position of leadership (challenge to white authority);

- Being presented with information about other racial groups through, for example, movies in which people of color drive the action but are not in stereotypical roles, or multicultural education (challenge to white centrality).

Not often encountering these challenges, we withdraw, defend, cry, argue, minimize, ignore, and in other ways push back to regain our racial position and equilibrium. I term that push back *white fragility.* 8

This concept came out of my ongoing experience leading discussions on race, racism, white privilege, and white supremacy with primarily white audiences. It became clear over time that white people have extremely low thresholds for enduring any discomfort associated with challenges to our racial worldviews. 9

We can manage the first round of challenge by ending the discussion through platitudes — usually something that starts with "People just need to," or "Race doesn't really have any meaning to me," or "Everybody's racist." Scratch any further on that surface, however, and we fall apart. 10

Socialized into a deeply internalized sense of superiority and entitlement that we are either not consciously aware of or can never admit to ourselves, we become highly fragile in conversations about race. We experience a challenge to our racial worldview as a challenge to our very identities as good, moral people. It also challenges our sense of rightful place in the hierarchy. Thus, we perceive any attempt to connect us to the system of racism as a very unsettling and unfair moral offense. 11

The following patterns make it difficult for white people to understand racism as a *system* and lead to the dynamics of white fragility. While they do not apply to every white person, they are well-documented overall: 12

Segregation. Most whites live, grow, play, learn, love, work, and die primarily in social and geographic racial segregation. Yet, our society does not teach us to see this as a loss. Pause for a moment and consider the magnitude of this message: We lose nothing of value by having no cross-racial relationships. In fact, the whiter our schools and neighborhoods are, the more likely they are to be seen as "good." The implicit message is that there is no inherent value in the presence or perspectives of people of color. This is an example of the relentless messages of white superiority that circulate all around us, shaping our identities and worldviews. 13

The good/bad binary. The most effective adaptation of racism over time is the idea that racism is conscious bias held by mean people. If we are not aware of having negative thoughts about people of color, don't tell racist jokes, are nice people, and even have friends of color, then we 14 cannot be racist. Thus, a person is either racist or not racist; if a person is racist, that person is bad; if a person is not racist, that person is good. Although racism does of course occur in individual acts, these acts are part of a larger system that we all participate in. The focus on individual incidences prevents the analysis that is necessary in order to challenge this larger system. The good/bad binary is the fundamental misunderstanding driving white defensiveness about being connected to racism. We simply do not understand how socialization and implicit bias work.

Individualism. Whites are taught to see themselves as individuals, 15
rather than as part of a racial group. Individualism enables us to deny that racism is structured into the fabric of society. This erases our history and hides the way in which wealth has accumulated over generations and benefits us, *as a group*, today. It also allows us to distance ourselves from the history and actions of our group. Thus, we get very irate when we are "accused" of racism, because as individuals, we are "different" from other white people and expect to be seen as such; we find intolerable any suggestion that our behavior or perspectives are typical of our group as a whole.

We find intolerable any suggestion that our behavior or perspectives are typical of our group as a whole.

Entitlement to racial comfort. In the dominant position, whites 16
are almost always racially comfortable and thus have developed unchallenged expectations to remain so. We have not had to build tolerance for racial discomfort and thus when racial discomfort arises, whites typically respond as if something is "wrong," and blame the person or event that triggered the discomfort (usually a person of color). This blame results in a socially sanctioned array of responses toward the perceived source of the discomfort, including: penalization; retaliation; isolation; and refusal to continue engagement. Since racism is necessarily uncomfortable in that it is oppressive, white insistence on racial comfort guarantees racism will not be faced except in the most superficial of ways.

Racial arrogance. Most whites have a very limited understanding 17
of racism because we have not been trained to think in complex ways about it and because it benefits white dominance not to do so. Yet, we have no compunction about debating the knowledge of people who have thought complexly about race. Whites generally feel free to dismiss these informed perspectives rather than have the humility to acknowledge that they are unfamiliar, reflect on them further, or seek more information.

Racial belonging. White people enjoy a deeply internalized, largely 18
unconscious sense of racial belonging in U.S. society. In virtually any

situation or image deemed valuable in dominant society, whites belong. The interruption of racial belonging is rare and thus destabilizing and frightening to whites and usually avoided.

Psychic freedom. Because race is constructed as residing in people of color, whites don't bear the social burden of race. We move easily through our society without a sense of ourselves as racialized. Race is for people of color to think about — it is what happens to "them" — they can bring it up if it is an issue for them (although if they do, we can dismiss it as a personal problem, the race card, or the reason for their problems). This allows whites much more psychological energy to devote to other issues and prevents us from developing the stamina to sustain attention on an issue as charged and uncomfortable as race. 19

Constant messages that we are more valuable. Living in a white dominant context, we receive constant messages that we are better and more important than people of color. For example: our centrality in history textbooks, historical representations, and perspectives; our centrality in media and advertising; our teachers, role models, heroes, and heroines; everyday discourse on "good" neighborhoods and schools and who is in them; popular TV shows centered around friendship circles that are all white; religious iconography that depicts God, Adam and Eve, and other key figures as white. While one may explicitly reject the notion that one is inherently better than another, one cannot avoid internalizing the message of white superiority, as it is ubiquitous in mainstream culture. 20

These privileges and the white fragility that results prevent us from listening to or comprehending the perspectives of people of color and bridging cross-racial divides. The antidote to white fragility is ongoing and lifelong, and includes sustained engagement, humility, and education. We can begin by: 21

- Being willing to tolerate the discomfort associated with an honest appraisal and discussion of our internalized superiority and racial privilege.
- Challenging our own racial reality by acknowledging ourselves as racial beings with a particular and limited perspective on race.
- Attempting to understand the racial realities of people of color through authentic interaction rather than through the media or unequal relationships.
- Taking action to address our own racism, the racism of other whites, and the racism embedded in our institutions — e.g., get educated and act.

"Getting it" when it comes to race and racism challenges our very identities as good white people. It's an ongoing and often painful process 22 of seeking to uncover our socialization at its very roots. It asks us to rebuild this identity in new and often uncomfortable ways. But I can testify that it is also the most exciting, powerful, intellectually stimulating, and emotionally fulfilling journey I have ever undertaken. It has impacted every aspect of my life — personal and professional.

I have a much deeper and more complex understanding of how society works. I can challenge much more racism in my daily life, and I have developed cherished and fulfilling cross-racial friendships I did not have before. 23

I do not expect racism to end in my lifetime, and I know that I continue to have problematic racist patterns and perspectives. Yet, I am also confident that I do less harm to people of color than I used to. This is not a minor point of growth, for it impacts my lived experience and that of the people of color who interact with me. If you are white I urge you to take the first step — let go of your racial certitude and reach for humility. 24

VOCABULARY/USING A DICTIONARY

1. What do you think *socialization* (para. 2) means?
2. What is an *uncompensated* (para. 4) worker paid?
3. What is a *meritocracy* (para. 7)?

RESPONDING TO WORDS IN CONTEXT

1. What is the difference between *everyday* (para. 20) and *every day*?
2. What does DiAngelo mean when she says that "racism and being a good person have become mutually exclusive" (para. 3)?
3. DiAngelo talks about "religious iconography that depicts God, Adam and Eve, and other key figures as white" (para. 20). What do you think *iconography* means?

DISCUSSING MAIN POINT AND MEANING

1. When the word *racism* is used, what does it usually mean? How are we beginning to rethink what it means to be a racist person?
2. What are some of the factors that lead to what DiAngelo terms "white fragility" (para. 8)?
3. What are some of the dynamics of white fragility, as outlined by DiAngelo?

EXAMINING SENTENCES, PARAGRAPHS, AND ORGANIZATION

1. What information does DiAngelo establish in her introductory paragraph? Why do you think she starts with this information?
2. DiAngelo uses bullet points and subheadings at different points in her essay. Why does she do this? Are they effective?

3. You may have heard that it is effective to start an essay with a definition. DiAngelo's essay tries to redefine *racism*, and she includes a dictionary definition in paragraph 3. What would be the effect of starting her essay with that paragraph? Why do you think she chose to begin the essay as she did?

THINKING CRITICALLY

1. Do you understand DiAngelo's reaction against the mainstream definition and mainstream understanding of racism and what it means to be racist? Does her definition place more emphasis on the individual or on society—or on both?
2. If you are white, do you think it is important to understand what DiAngelo calls "a deeply internalized sense of superiority and entitlement" (para. 11)? If you do not identify as white, do you perceive this sense in whites as "white fragility" (para. 8)? Why or why not?
3. Not everyone thinks of Americans as living in a segregated society (segregation was abolished in the United States in 1964). However, DiAngelo includes segregation as one of the things whites do when they feel unsettled by the challenges of confronting a racialized world. Do you see segregation in your world? Does it match what DiAngelo identifies as segregation (para. 13)?

WRITING ACTIVITIES

1. Choose one of the "dynamics of white fragility" (para. 12) that DiAngelo identifies in her essay. Write an analysis of how you see this dynamic working on your own college campus or in your community. You can write about it generally or you can provide very specific examples and/or narrative.
2. DiAngelo says she doesn't expect racism to end in her lifetime, and she suggests that combating white fragility is "ongoing and lifelong, and includes sustained engagement, humility, and education" (para. 21). Do you agree that racism is unlikely to end in the near future (or hasn't ended yet)? Do you think her solution to racism is the right one? Take some notes about what you think on these matters and write some responses to DiAngelo's points; then argue your position in a short essay.
3. Create a list of acts of racism, both those perpetrated by an individual and those perpetrated by a society. After you have generated a list of possible acts (these can be acts you've read about in the news, acts you've heard about anecdotally, things you've perceived to be racist in daily interactions, or events that you've studied in school), label them as either "individual" or "society." Decide, after considering how you've labeled them, whether most racist acts occur on an individual level or are part of a greater system of societal racism, as DiAngelo suggests.

Dawn Lundy Martin

Weary Oracle

[*Harper's Magazine*, March 2016]

Looking at college campuses across the country, Dawn Lundy Martin, a poet and professor, sees an apparently serene "ivy-encrusted" world in which African American students confront enormous pressures that transform leisure into labor. In "Weary Oracle," she explains the "labor of having to name racism when it is already nakedly visible; the labor of being perpetually suspect, never afforded the possibility of neutral innocence; . . . the very special labor of pretending (because you are tired) that everything is fine."

Poet and activist Dawn Lundy Martin is currently an associate professor in the University of Pittsburgh's English department. Her most recent collection of poetry, Good Stock, *was published in 2016.*

BEFORE YOU READ

Why do you think people process race trauma so differently? Do you understand why race is an important (or hot-button) topic on campuses today?

WORDS TO LEARN

derogatory (para. 1): disparaging (adjective)
disparage (para. 1): to belittle (verb)
reducible (para. 2): able to be reduced (adjective)
redress (para. 3): compensation (noun)
stoicism (para. 3): conduct that represses emotion and shows little concern for pleasure or pain (noun)
incorporate (para. 4): to introduce or include (verb)
serenity (para. 5): sereneness (noun)
manicured (para. 5): well trimmed and cared for (adjective)
intimately (para. 5): personally (adverb)
perpetually (para. 5): continuously (adverb)

My mother, who was born more than eighty years ago, deep in the Jim Crow[1] South, insists that she has never experienced a single moment of racism. I have never heard her say a derogatory word about white people as a race or use the word "white" as an insult. When she calls people "black," she does not do so affectionately, 1

[1] Jim Crow (para. 1): Jim Crow laws enforced racial segregation from Reconstruction until 1965.

to suggest kinship, community, or belonging. And she gets visibly annoyed when black people organize around black*ness*, as though claiming the category that is also used to disparage them were a criminal act. Why excite the ghost? Why call its hideous name? Yet when I ask her whether she remembers black people getting lynched, she says, "Yeah, they did sometimes."

That is what race trauma looks like — although it is not reducible 2
to that.

At Claremont McKenna College, a young woman's voice cracks 3
as she speaks into a megaphone handed to her by protesters who seek redress for the racial slights that they believe have been encouraged by the culture of the campus. Instead of talking about her own experiences of racism, the woman testifies to the more generalized experiences of others. She weeps; her whole body vibrates. Against my mother's stoicism, the weeping almost reads as performance. It has the texture of a sleeve pulled up to reveal a sore and disgust the viewer. *Put it away.*

But the pitch of the reactions on cam- 4
puses is not a display of "excessive vulnerability" resulting in "self-diminishment," as some critics of student tactics claim. Something is pressing on these students, making them burst at the seams, and it's not imaginary. They are like oracles whose bodies bear the collective weight of what others do not — or will not — see: the lynchings my mother cannot incorporate into her worldview, the black boy the police shot down in the street just yesterday. They feel all of it when, for example, a white person mistakes them for another brown person who looks nothing like them.

Something is pressing on these students, making them burst at the seams, and it's not imaginary.

It is not unreasonable for college students to desire to be care- 5
fully held by the universities that courted them. In fact, universities and colleges imply a promise, in their mottoes of "Light and Truth," in their ivy-encrusted buildings, in the serenity around their lakes and on their manicured greens, and especially in their invitations for students to engage in the leisure of intellectual work. That's one place where I think students of color hurt: right where leisurely study becomes labor. As a professor who has spent more than half my life on college campuses, I know this labor intimately — the labor of having to name racism when it is already nakedly visible; the labor of being perpetually suspect, never afforded the possibility of neutral innocence; the labor of negotiating others' racially offensive speech; or the very special labor of pretending (because you are tired) that everything is fine. Instead of

being protected by the institution that you see your white counterparts inhabiting so casually, you find the institution protected from you. That it is guarded by historical figures such as Woodrow Wilson, a KKK sympathizer whose name is emblazoned on a campus building, is not lost on you. Still, folks want to know, why are you so enraged, what is causing your pain, why do you act so insane?

VOCABULARY/USING A DICTIONARY

1. What is another word for *lynch* (para. 1)?
2. When might you have heard the word *oracle* (para. 4) before? In what context?
3. What word embedded in the word *collective* (para. 4) gives you a clue to its meaning?

RESPONDING TO WORDS IN CONTEXT

1. What does Martin mean by the phrase *race trauma* (para. 2)?
2. What is the opposite of a *generalized* experience (para. 3)?
3. When Martin writes that Woodrow Wilson's name is *emblazoned* (para. 5) on a school building, what is she suggesting about its presence?

DISCUSSING MAIN POINT AND MEANING

1. Has Martin's mother ever experienced racism? How do you know?
2. What is Martin referring to when she writes about a sore revealed to "disgust the viewer" (para. 3)? What is the sore?
3. At college, what work are students of color engaged in that white students don't have to do?

EXAMINING SENTENCES, PARAGRAPHS, AND ORGANIZATION

1. Martin brings the example of her mother into the first paragraph. How does her example connect to what the essay is about? Do you think the essay is more or less effective with that example in the introduction?
2. Look at Martin's use of the words *labor* and *leisure* in paragraph 5. How does she create the contrast between them? What activities does she connect with those two words? Does she see college as a place of "labor" or "leisure"?
3. Does the essay feel finished? Why or why not?

THINKING CRITICALLY

1. Why do you think Martin's mother denies experiences of racism? Why might her responses be considered an expression of race trauma?

2. Is campus the place for expressing one's feelings about race trauma? Why or why not?
3. Do you think people experience and express experiences of racism differently? Do you think the differences between Martin's experiences and responses and those of her mother are due to a generational difference or something else? What else might cause these kinds of differences?

WRITING ACTIVITIES

1. Martin ends her essay with a question. Imagine if Martin had more to say in this fairly short essay. Outline where the essay might go from here.
2. In writing, respond to Martin's statement, "It is not unreasonable for college students to desire to be carefully held by the universities that courted them" (para. 5). Do you think this statement is true? In what ways, or under what circumstances, should students be "carefully held"?
3. Martin gives examples of "race trauma" that college students are responding to, acting as "oracles" for others. Write down some of the examples she offers in this essay and then try to come up with some others, based on personal experience or generalized experience. Look around your campus and ask yourself if there is anything else that might be added to Martin's essay. Consider current events as you write.

Destry Adams (student essay)

Why Students Should Care about Affirmative Action

[*Technician* (North Carolina State University), January 21, 2019]

One of the longest-lasting campus controversies over race has been the issue of affirmative action, the policy that allows educational institutions the right to take race, ethnicity, class, and other pertinent factors into account when making admission decisions. The idea is to provide equal opportunities for all applicants while acknowledging that many minority applicants may be disadvantaged by past discrimination. In the following column, North Carolina State University student Destry Adams reports on one of the nation's recent challenges to affirmative action policies: a lawsuit advanced against Harvard University by the activist group Students for Fair Admissions (SFFA). The lawsuit claims that Harvard discriminates against Asian American students. According to Adams, Harvard discriminates against this group "by holding them to an unfair standard compared to other applicants." Adams, like many other commentators on this case, believes that it will eventually wind up in the Supreme Court and could jeopardize the ideals of diversity and equality of opportunity that affirmative action policies were designed to protect.

Destry Adams is a staff columnist for the Technician, *the student newspaper of North Carolina State University.*

BEFORE YOU READ

What role, if any, should affirmative action play in college admissions? Do you know why it is part of the process for many schools?

WORDS TO LEARN

conservative (para. 1): (politically) tending toward traditional values and resistant to change; cautious or staying within reasonable limits (adjective)

rely (para. 3): to depend upon (verb)

factor (para. 5): to work into result (verb)

undermine (para. 6): to attack or weaken (verb)

As many students have heard, Harvard is currently facing a lawsuit over potential discrimination against Asian Americans. The group Students for Fair Admissions (S.F.F.A.) claims that Harvard is discriminating against Asian Americans by holding them to an unfair standard compared to other applicants and wants the university to adopt a race-neutral admissions process. The lawsuit could go on to decide the future of affirmative action. It seems plausible that this case will eventually go to the Supreme Court. Since there are five conservative judges on the bench, they are likely to rule against Harvard, which could mean the end of affirmative action, particularly in college admissions. 1

Many are afraid if affirmative action ends it will be difficult for disenfranchised groups of people to be admitted into college. Although affirmative action isn't perfect, students need to care about its future. Students should be concerned about the future of affirmative action to ensure that everyone has an equal chance to be admitted into college and be successful in the workforce. 2

In its current state, affirmative action is a process in which colleges or jobs can factor race, sex or other socio-economic factors when admitting students or hiring potential employees. Part of the reason affirmative action exists is to atone for various racist and discriminatory practices whose effects are still prevalent today. However, because colleges can't establish racial quotas, they rely on affirmative action to diversify the student population. 3

The problem with this argument is that it assumes everybody had equal education opportunities.

Race-blind admission is touted by 4
those against affirmative action to give everyone a fair and equal chance during the process. The problem with this argument is that it assumes everybody had equal education opportunities. To this day, unequal education is still a problem that persists in America, and it primarily affects disenfranchised minority groups. By not factoring race in the admissions process, it would be difficult for people from a poor socio-economic background to be admitted into college.

The University of California at Berkeley doesn't factor race when 5
admitting students. As a result, the university has seen a decline in African American and Latino students. With race-blind strategies, it will be very difficult for students who come from poor backgrounds to be admitted into college, inhibiting them from receiving a job in today's economy.

The same situation could happen to colleges across North Carolina. 6
NC State uses affirmative action in their admissions process. Out of the student population, 74% of students are Caucasian. If affirmative action was to be removed from the admissions process, then there could be practically no diversity at NC State in a couple of generations. A big part of college is to be exposed to new ideas from people who come from different backgrounds, and removing affirmative action from the admissions process undermines this completely.

Clearly, affirmative action isn't perfect. It has the potential to uninten- 7
tionally discriminate against certain groups of people, as seen with Asian Americans. However, adopting race-blind strategies have been proven to decrease diversity in colleges, which would be an even worse effect. If the case goes to the Supreme Court it could have huge consequences. Students absolutely have to be aware of the risk to diversity present at NC State and other universities as a result of this court case and its impact.

VOCABULARY/USING A DICTIONARY

1. If something is *plausible* (para. 1), is it believable?
2. What does the word *affirmative* (para. 1) have at its root? What does that suggest about the meaning of the word?
3. What is the opposite of *exposed* (para. 6)?

RESPONDING TO WORDS IN CONTEXT

1. If affirmative action affects *disenfranchised* (para. 2) groups, who do you think makes up those groups?

2. What do you think Adams means by *diversity* in paragraph 6? Why do you think so?
3. If affirmative action has the potential to *unintentionally* (para. 7) discriminate against certain people, what does that mean?

DISCUSSING MAIN POINT AND MEANING

1. Why is Harvard facing a lawsuit?
2. How will the Harvard case affect affirmative action? Why?
3. What will happen to affirmative action if the Supreme Court rules against Harvard?

EXAMINING SENTENCES, PARAGRAPHS, AND ORGANIZATION

1. This essay is short and easy to outline. What is the basic argument, if you outline the essay?
2. Do you think the writing is balanced, even though this article is considered an opinion piece? Why or why not? How would the article be different if written by the students bringing the lawsuit against Harvard or by Harvard administrators defending their admissions policies?
3. Consider the words Adams chooses: "many are *afraid*" and "students should be *concerned*" (para. 2). How does that influence the tone of the article? Are there other passages that sway the tone? What are they?

THINKING CRITICALLY

1. Do you agree that limiting or removing affirmative action will affect students adversely by limiting diversity on campus? Explain your thinking.
2. **Connect.** Adams writes, "Many are afraid if affirmative action ends it will be difficult for disenfranchised groups of people to be admitted into college" (para. 2). Based on what you read in Gordon-Reed's article, "America's Original Sin" (p. 217), explain why this fear is valid. Consider affirmative action in terms of the legacy of slavery that Gordon-Reed writes about.
3. Do you think race should play a role in college admissions? Are there other factors that affirmative action puts forward to play a role in admissions (besides race)? Others that you can think of that aren't under the umbrella of affirmative action? What are they?

WRITING ACTIVITIES

1. Do you think Adams adequately explains why students should care about affirmative action? In a short writing assignment, outline the argument that's here and add other reasons or add to points already made. Discuss the

other reasons in a paragraph or two, and/or elaborate in your own words on the ones already here.

2. Adams acknowledges, "Clearly, affirmative action isn't perfect" (para. 7). Do you think Adams has indicated the ways in which affirmative action is problematic? Write down how it is flawed or can pose problems.
3. Research the Supreme Court and affirmative action. Can you find a case that discusses the benefits and problems of affirmative action in a way that you understand? Write a paper on one of the cases that you find and discuss what it tells you about affirmative action and the reasons why others are for or against it.

LOOKING CLOSELY

Conceding the Merits of an Opposing Viewpoint

In any argument or debate, it is rare that one side is 100 percent right and other side 100 percent wrong. Therefore, when writing opinion essays, it is often a good idea to notice and acknowledge that the position you disagree with possesses some merits or to concede that the opposing position has some justification. Making concessions shows that a writer is being reasonable and is not simply intent on demonizing the opposition as being entirely in the wrong.

Note how North Carolina State University columnist Destry Adams acknowledges that the organization he opposes, the Students for Fair Admissions, has some merits to its argument. He does this by emphasizing through repetition that affirmative action policies are not "perfect" and by conceding that Asian Americans in this instance are in fact being discriminated against. He does this while at the same time he hopes to persuade his readers that affirmative action is still a necessary educational policy.

1
Concedes that affirmative action isn't perfect

(1) Although affirmative action isn't perfect, students need to care about its future. (para. 2)

2
Admits that alleged discrimination does exist

(2) Clearly, affirmative action isn't perfect. It has the potential to unintentionally discriminate against certain groups of people, as seen with Asian Americans. (para. 7)

Annette Gordon-Reed

America's Original Sin: Slavery and the Legacy of White Supremacy

[*Foreign Affairs*, January–February 2018]

It is an often-forgotten fact that our nation's much-revered Constitution — so often regarded as a "sacred" document by all political parties — exists mainly because it accepted the institution of slavery. In "America's Original Sin: Slavery and the Legacy of White Supremacy," the Harvard historian Annette Gordon-Reed reminds us of the "fateful compromise" that established the United States of America and at the same time "protected slavery." Her essay takes us on a guided tour of how "American slavery was tied inexorably to white dominance" and explains how slavery's legacy has endured throughout U.S. history. To understand America's past and its future, we must understand the linkage between slavery and white supremacy. "Americans must come to grips with both," Gordon-Reed concludes, "if they are to make their country live up to its founding creed."

A professor of history at Harvard University, Annette Gordon-Reed is also the Charles Warren Professor of American Legal History at Harvard Law School. Her book Thomas Jefferson and Sally Hemings: An American Controversy *(1997) won numerous awards.*

BEFORE YOU READ

What is the legacy of slavery in the United States? How has the racial hierarchy established by slavery been perpetuated through the country's history?

WORDS TO LEARN

espoused (para. 1): taken up as a cause (verb)
preamble (para. 1): introductory statement (noun)
abolition (para. 2): the act of doing away with something (noun)
inexorably (para. 6): unalterably (adverb)
pivotal (para. 10): crucial (adjective)
purported (para. 10): alleged (adjective)
explicitly (para. 12): clearly; unreservedly (adverb)
prominent (para. 13): standing out (adjective)
doctrine (para. 14): government policy or principle (noun)
carnage (para. 16): slaughter of a large number of people (noun)
emancipation (para. 16): the act of freeing someone or the state of being freed (noun)
monopoly (para. 17): exclusive control (noun)
adherents (para. 17): supporters (noun)
creed (para. 19): system or doctrine of belief (noun)

The documents most closely associated with the creation of the United States — the Declaration of Independence and the Constitution — present a problem with which Americans have been contending from the country's beginning: how to reconcile the values espoused in those texts with the United States' original sin of slavery, the flaw that marred the country's creation, warped its prospects, and eventually plunged it into civil war. The Declaration of Independence had a specific purpose: to cut the ties between the American colonies and Great Britain and establish a new country that would take its place among the nations of the world. But thanks to the vaulting language of its famous preamble, the document instantly came to mean more than that. Its confident statement that "all men are created equal," with "unalienable Rights" to "Life, Liberty, and the pursuit of Happiness," put notions of freedom and equality at the heart of the American experiment. Yet it was written by a slave owner, Thomas Jefferson, and released into 13 colonies that all, to one degree or another, allowed slavery. 1

The Constitution, which united the colonies turned states, was no less tainted. It came into existence only after a heated argument over — and fateful compromise on — the institution of slavery. Members of the revolutionary generation often cast that institution as a necessary evil that would eventually die of its own accord, and they made their peace with it to hold together the new nation. The document they fought over and signed in 1787, revered almost as a sacred text by many Americans, directly protected slavery. It gave slave owners the right to capture fugitive slaves who crossed state lines, counted each enslaved person as three-fifths of a free person for the purpose of apportioning members of the House of Representatives, and prohibited the abolition of the slave trade before 1808. 2

As citizens of a young country, Americans have a close enough connection to the founding generation that they look to the founders as objects of praise. There might well have been no United States without George Washington, behind whom 13 fractious colonies united. Jefferson's language in the Declaration of Independence has been taken up by every marginalized group seeking an equal place in American society. It has influenced people searching for freedom in other parts of the world, as well. 3

Yet the founders are increasingly objects of condemnation, too. Both Washington and Jefferson owned slaves. They, along with James Madison, James Monroe, and Andrew Jackson, the other three slave-owning presidents of the early republic, shaped the first decades of the United States. Any desire to celebrate the country's beginning quickly runs into the tragic aspects of that moment. Those who wish 4 to revel without reservation in good feelings about their country feel threatened by those who note the tragedies and oppression that lay at the heart of this period. Those descended from people who were cast as inferior beings, whose labor and lives were taken for the enrichment of others, and those with empathy for the enslaved feel insulted by unreflective celebration. Learning how to strike the right balance has proved one of the most difficult problems for American society.

WHY SLAVERY'S LEGACY ENDURES

The issue, however, goes far beyond the ways Americans think and talk 5
about their history. The most significant fact about American slavery, one it did not share with other prominent ancient slave systems, was its basis in race. Slavery in the United States created a defined, recognizable group of people and placed them outside society. And unlike the indentured servitude of European immigrants to North America, slavery was an inherited condition.

As a result, American slavery was tied inexorably to white domi- 6
nance. Even people of African descent who were freed for one reason or another suffered under the weight of the white supremacy that racially based slavery entrenched in American society. In the few places where free blacks had some form of state citizenship, their rights were circumscribed in ways that emphasized their inferior status — to them and to all observers. State laws in both the so-called Free States and the slave states served as blueprints for a system of white supremacy. Just as blackness was associated with inferiority and a lack of freedom — in some jurisdictions, black skin created the legal presumption of an enslaved status — whiteness was associated with superiority and freedom.

The historian Edmund Morgan explained what this meant for 7
the development of American attitudes about slavery, freedom, and race — indeed, for American culture overall. Morgan argued that racially based slavery, rather than being a contradiction in a country that prided itself on freedom, made the freedom of white people possible. The system that put black people at the bottom of the social heap tamped down class divisions among whites. Without a large group of people who would always rank below the level of even the poorest, most disaffected white person, white unity could not have persisted. Grappling with the legacy of slavery, therefore, requires grappling with the white supremacy that preceded the founding of the United States and persisted after the end of legalized slavery.

Consider, by contrast, what might have happened had there been 8
Irish chattel slavery in North America. The Irish suffered pervasive discrimination and were subjected to crude and cruel stereotypes about

their alleged inferiority, but they were never kept as slaves. Had they been enslaved and then freed, there is every reason to believe that they would have had an easier time assimilating into American culture than have African Americans. Their enslavement would be a major historical fact, but it would likely not have created a legacy so firmly tying the past to the present as did African chattel slavery. Indeed, the descendants of white indentured servants blended into society and today suffer no stigma because of their ancestors' social condition.

9 That is because the ability to append enslaved status to a set of generally identifiable physical characteristics — skin color, hair, facial features — made it easy to tell who was eligible for slavery and to maintain a system of social control over the enslaved. It also made it easy to continue organized oppression after the 13th Amendment ended legal slavery in 1865. There was no incentive for whites to change their attitudes about race even when slavery no longer existed. Whiteness still amounted to a value, unmoored from economic or social status. Blackness still had to be devalued to ensure white superiority. This calculus operated in Northern states as well as Southern ones.

CONFEDERATE IDEOLOGY

10 The framers of the Confederate States of America understood this well. Race played a specific and pivotal role in their conception of the society they wished to create. If members of the revolutionary generation presented themselves as opponents of a doomed system and, in Jefferson's case, cast baleful views of race as mere "suspicions," their Confederate grandchildren voiced their full-throated support for slavery as a perpetual institution, based on their openly expressed belief in black inferiority. The founding documents of the Confederacy, under which the purported citizens of that entity lived, just as Americans live under the Declaration of Independence and the Constitution, announced that African slavery would form the "cornerstone" of the country they would create after winning the Civil War. In 1861, a few weeks before the war began, Alexander Stephens, the vice president of the Confederacy, put things plainly:

> The new constitution has put at rest, forever, all the agitating questions relating to our peculiar institution — African slavery as it exists amongst us — the proper status of the negro in our form of civilization. This was the immediate cause of the late rupture and present revolution. Jefferson in his forecast had anticipated this as the "rock upon which the old Union would split." He was right. . . . The prevailing ideas entertained by him and most of the leading statesmen at the

> time of the formation of the old constitution, were that the enslavement of the African was in violation of the laws of nature; that it was wrong in principle, socially, morally, and politically. . . . Those ideas, however, were fundamentally wrong. They rested upon the assumption of the equality of races. This was an error.
>
> Our new government is founded upon exactly the opposite idea; its foundations are laid, its cornerstone rests, upon the great truth that the negro is not equal to the white man; that slavery — subordination to the superior race — is his natural and normal condition.

Despite the clarity of Stephens' words, millions of Americans today are unaware of — or perhaps unwilling to learn about — the aims of those who rallied to the Confederate cause. That ignorance has led many to fall prey to the romantic notion of "the rebels," ignoring that these rebels had a cause. Modern Americans may fret about the hypocrisy and weakness of the founding generation, but there was no such hesitancy among the leading Confederates on matters of slavery and race. That they were not successful on the battlefield does not mean that their philosophy should be ignored in favor of abstract notions of "duty," "honor," and "nobility"; Americans should not engage in the debate that the former Confederates chose after the war ended and slavery, finally, acquired a bad name. 11

To confront the legacy of slavery without openly challenging the racial attitudes that created and shaped the institution is to leave the most important variable out of the equation.

It has taken until well into the twenty-first century for many Americans to begin to reject the idea of erecting statues of men who fought to construct an explicitly white supremacist society. For too long, the United States has postponed a reckoning with the corrosive ideas about race that have destroyed the lives and wasted the talents of millions of people who could have contributed to their country. To confront the legacy of slavery without openly challenging the racial attitudes that created and shaped the institution is to leave the most important variable out of the equation. And yet discussions of race, particularly of one's own racial attitudes, are among the hardest conversations Americans are called on to have. 12

This issue of the Confederacy's legacy was made tragically prominent in 2015, when the white supremacist Dylann Roof shot 12 black parishioners in a church in Charleston, South Carolina, killing nine of them. History had given the worshipers in Emanuel African Methodist Episcopal Church every reason to be suspicious of the young man 13 who appeared at their doorstep that day, yet they invited him in to their prayer meeting. Although they had, Roof said, been "nice" to him, they had to die because they (as representatives of the black race) were, in his words, raping "our women" and "taking over our country." Their openness and faith were set against the images, later revealed, of Roof posing with what has come to be known as the Confederate flag and other white supremacist iconography. The core meaning of the Confederacy was made heartbreakingly vivid. From that moment on, inaction on the question of the display of the Confederate flag was, for many, no longer an option. Bree Newsome, the activist who, ten days after the shooting, scaled the flagpole in front of the South Carolina State House and removed the Confederate flag that flew there, represented the new spirit: displaying symbols of white supremacy in public spaces was no longer tolerable.

And those symbols went far beyond flags. Monuments to people 14
who, in one way or another, promoted the idea of white supremacy are scattered across the country. Statues of Confederate officials and generals dot parks and public buildings. Yet proposals to take them down have drawn sharp opposition. Few who resist the removal of the statues openly praise the aims of the Confederacy, whatever their private thoughts on the matter. Instead, they raise the specter of a slippery slope: today, Jefferson Davis and Robert E. Lee; tomorrow, George Washington and Thomas Jefferson. Yet dealing with such slopes is part of everyday life. The problem with the Confederacy is not just that its leaders owned slaves. The problem is that they tried to destroy the Union and did so in adherence to an explicit doctrine of slavery and white supremacy. By contrast, the founding generation, for all its faults, left behind them principles and documents that have allowed American society to expand in directions opposite to the values of the South's slave society and the Confederacy.

It is not surprising that colleges and universities, ideally the site of 15
inquiry and intellectual contest, have grappled most prominently with this new national discussion. Many of the most prestigious American universities have benefited from the institution of slavery or have buildings named after people who promoted white supremacy. Brown, Georgetown, Harvard, Princeton, and Yale have, by starting conversations on campus, carrying out programs of historical self-study, and setting up commissions, contributed to greater public understanding of the past and of how the country might move ahead. Their work serves as a template for the ways in which other institutions should engage with these issues in a serious fashion.

RECONSTRUCTION DELAYED

For all the criticism that has been leveled at him for the insufficient radicalism of his racial politics, Abraham Lincoln understood that the central question for the United States after the Civil War was whether blacks could be fully incorporated into American society. Attempting to go forward after the carnage, he returned to first principles. In the Gettysburg Address, he used the words of the Declaration of Independence as an argument for the emancipation of blacks and their inclusion in the country's "new birth of freedom." What Lincoln meant by this, how far he was prepared to take matters, will remain unknown. What is clear is that Reconstruction, the brief period of hope among four million emancipated African Americans, when black men were given the right to vote, when the freedmen married, sought education, and became elected officials in the South, was seen as a nightmare by many white Southerners. Most of them had not owned slaves. But slavery was only part of the wider picture. They continued to rely on the racial hierarchy that had obtained since the early 1600s, when the first Africans arrived in North America's British colonies. Rather than bring free blacks into society, with the hope of moving the entire region forward, they chose to move backward, to a situation as close to slavery as legally possible. Northern whites, tired of "the Negro problem," abandoned Reconstruction and left black people to the mercy of those who had before the war seen them as property and after it as lost possessions.

The historian David Blight has described how the post–Civil 17
War desire for reconciliation between white Northerners and white Southerners left African Americans behind, in ways that continue to shape American society. The South had no monopoly on adherents to the doctrine of white supremacy. Despite all that had happened, the racial hierarchy took precedence over the ambitious plan to bring black Americans into full citizenship expressed in the 13th, 14th, and 15th Amendments to the Constitution. In a reversal of the maxim that history is written by the victors, the losing side in the Civil War got to tell the story of their slave society in ways favorable to them, through books, movies, and other popular entertainment. American culture accepted the story that apologists for the Confederacy told about Southern whites and Southern blacks.

That did not begin to change until the second half of the twenti- 18
eth century. It took the development of modern scholarship on slavery and Reconstruction and a civil rights movement composed of blacks, whites, and other groups from across the country to begin moving the needle on the question of white supremacy's role in American society.

Since then, black Americans have made many social and economic gains, but there is still far to go. De jure segregation is dead, but de facto segregation is firmly in place in much of the country. The United States twice elected a black president and had a black first family, but the next presidential election expressed, in part, a backlash. African Americans are present in all walks of life, up and down the economic scale. But overall, black wealth is a mere fraction of white wealth. Police brutality and racialized law enforcement tactics have shown that the Fourth Amendment does not apply with equal force to black Americans. And the killing of armed black men in open-carry states by police has called into question black rights under the Second Amendment. To understand these problems, look not only to slavery itself but also to its most lasting legacy: the maintenance of white supremacy. Americans must come to grips with both if they are to make their country live up to its founding creed. 19

VOCABULARY/USING A DICTIONARY

1. What is the difference between *reflective* and *unreflective* (para. 4)?
2. Can you give a synonym for *fractious* (para. 3)? What part of speech is it?
3. What is another word for *chattel* (para. 8)?

RESPONDING TO WORDS IN CONTEXT

1. How is *indentured servitude* (para. 5) different from slavery?
2. Gordon-Reed refers to "corrosive" (para. 12) ideas about race that perpetuated slavery. What else might be described as *corrosive*, or where might you have heard that word before? What do you think it means?
3. Gordon-Reed says Dylann Roof was pictured with "white supremacist iconography" (para. 13). What do you think *iconography* refers to?

DISCUSSING MAIN POINT AND MEANING

1. What contradiction does Gordon-Reed note between the words of the Declaration of Independence and the world it was released into?
2. How was slavery in the United States different from other slave systems?
3. How were Confederate ideas reflected in the thinking of Dylann Roof in 2015?

EXAMINING SENTENCES, PARAGRAPHS, AND ORGANIZATION

1. In what ways do section titles scattered through the article help organize Gordon-Reed's material?

2. Gordon-Reed begins her article with a very thorough thesis statement. Why does her thesis start the article and why does Gordon-Reed extend it the way she does?
3. There are many sentences that condemn the early leaders of the country, but there are moments when Gordon-Reed acknowledges that even the flawed leaders of the United States are able to leave room for the country to grow and grapple with its history of slavery. Can you identify one of these sentences?

THINKING CRITICALLY

1. What do you make of Gordon-Reed's inclusion of Edmund Morgan's argument (that racially based slavery in the United States "made the freedom of white people possible" para. 7)? What difficulties does a country with this type of slavery in its history face in trying to achieve racial equality?
2. How do you understand the term "white supremacy"? Does Gordon-Reed's discussion of white supremacy match your understanding or change it in any way?
3. When you think about Confederate history, what do you think about? Do you agree that its cause and experience has been romanticized and has ignored its roots in white supremacy?

WRITING ACTIVITIES

1. Read Jefferson's "Declaration of Independence." Write a short analysis of how it can be read as a document that supports the rights of all. Then write an analysis of how it can be read as a document that supports only the rights of certain people. Examine the language closely. How is it possible that it can be read in different ways?
2. **Connect.** Consider how Americans must struggle with their history of slavery as presented by Gordon-Reed. Consider also Moore's experience of Calhoun College at Yale, and the struggle both Moore and that university faced ("When Does Renaming a Building Make Sense?" p. 113). In a short essay, discuss how Moore's experience reflects ideas presented by Gordon-Reed. Where do you see the two writers discussing the same issues?
3. Why is it so hard for Americans to have conversations about race or to discuss their own racial attitudes? Write on this question in an essay that examines your personal experiences in terms of race and what has shaped your attitudes on race.

Chandra D. L. Waring

Black and Biracial Americans Wouldn't Need to Code-Switch If We Lived in a Post-Racial Society

[*The Conversation*, August 17, 2018]

Everybody "code-switches," that is, interacts (mostly verbally) with different groups in different ways. Most teens, for example, talk to parents and teachers differently than they talk to each other. Sports figures talk to the media differently than they talk to fellow teammates. So why is code-switching considered an issue when it's performed by African Americans? In "Black and Biracial Americans Wouldn't Need to Code-Switch If We Lived in a Post-Racial Society," sociology professor Chandra D. L. Waring uses the example of a popular film to explain why "code-switching" reveals "the magnitude of racial and class oppression." According to Waring, "there's much more incentive for people of color to code-switch — to adapt to the dominant culture to improve their prospects."

Chandra D. L. Waring is assistant professor of sociology and race and ethnic studies at the University of Wisconsin–Whitewater.

Boots Riley's new film *Sorry to Bother You* does anything but apologize. In telling the story of Cassius, a young black man who becomes an extraordinarily successful telemarketer after he starts using his "white voice," it showcases the magnitude of racial and class oppression. Colloquially, Cassius' use of a "white voice" is known as code-switching, and the film highlights something that most African-Americans could probably tell you: The ability to code-switch is often a prerequisite to becoming a successful black person in America. 1

As a race scholar and sociologist, I've studied biracial Americans who engage in code-switching. I found that the ability to deftly code-switch has some real advantages. But it also has its fair share of pitfalls. More broadly, it has led me to wonder what the persistence of code-switching tells us about race, opportunities and making connections in America today. 2

ADAPTING TO THE DOMINANT CULTURE

Code-switching is the practice of interacting in different ways depending on the social context, and it isn't limited to race. Most of us interact differently when hanging out with friends than we would during a job interview. However, due in large measure to structural inequality and centuries of segregation, different cultural norms and ways of speaking have emerged among white and black Americans. 3

But because dominant culture is white, whiteness has been baked into institutions as natural, normal and legitimate. So there's much more incentive for people of color to code-switch — to adapt to the dominant culture to improve their prospects. White people rarely, if ever, feel this same pressure in their daily lives. 4

For this reason, the notion of a person of color deploying a "white voice" in the workplace (or anywhere in American society) isn't a new phenomenon. 5

Biracial people create somewhat of a different dynamic due to their backgrounds. Often they have to navigate groups that are either all white or all black. In each instance, they're outsiders who need to send certain signals — or avoid certain landmines — to fit in. 6

In my research, I explain how black and white biracial Americans deploy what I call "racial capital." 7

I interviewed 60 black-white biracial Americans and asked them how their lives were shaped by race. I soon realized that they seemed to be pulling from a repertoire of resources in order to break down racial barriers and establish in-group membership among whites and blacks. 8

I categorized this repertoire into four areas: knowledge, experiences, meanings and language. 9

The language category involves code-switching. For example, one of my interviewees bragged about her ability to code-switch: "To some people, I'll say 'He was handsome!' versus 'He fine as hell, girl!' And I think I'm the baddest because I can talk to this group and that group in the same way that they talk." 10

But this doesn't always work. One person I interviewed explained that when he didn't dap properly at his predominately black barbershop, the other patrons laughed at him and treated him like an outsider. Other times, people are "caught in the act," meaning people witness them interacting differently in ways that are shaped by race. This makes others question their authenticity, which ultimately jeopardizes any connection. 11

One participant in my study told me that he is perpetually self-conscious about code-switching out of fear that someone would witness 12 his behavior and question his authenticity. Another participant echoed his concern: "I feel almost bad sometimes when someone sees [me code-switch]," she said, "because they are like 'What's going on?' Especially my boyfriend — he'll be like 'Who are you?'" And one person I spoke with said that it was "humiliating" when others saw him code-switch because people "just don't understand."

These are the costs of code-switching, and my participants continually risked being misunderstood and treated as outsiders. Because of societal pressures, it's a risk black and biracial people are clearly willing to keep taking. 13

AN OPPRESSIVE SCRIPT

Code-switching would not be necessary if white privilege hadn't been embedded in every social institution in American society for centuries. More and more, researchers have been able to show how racism has been rooted in how American society is organized. 14

In the workplace, black people face more obstacles to career advancement and a growing racial wage gap. In education, schools in poor black neighborhoods receive less resources, while teachers mete out disproportionately harsh disciplinary treatment for students of color. In politics, we see a lack of proportional representation among elected officials and recently witnessed the election of a president who routinely disparages people of color. In entertainment, there is a lack of diverse, nuanced, fully human characters of color. Even in religion, deities have been whitewashed. 15

Despite this documented reality, there are those who think that racism in America is a myth, that reverse racism is a threat or that our society is largely colorblind — a convenient way to avoid grappling with the severe discrepancy between societal values like equality and the reality of structural, intergenerational inequality. 16

I argue that there would be no need for racial capital if we were truly in a "post-racial" society — that is, a society where race carried no meaning. Why would black and biracial Americans feel compelled to change the way they interact — the words they use — if race no longer mattered? 17

Although my study is about biracial Americans engaging in code-switching to bond with whites and blacks — and *Sorry to Bother You* is about a monoracial black man engaging in code-switching to perform well in his job — for everyone involved, code-switching serves the same purpose: to create a connection that will generate opportunities. 18

Yet the fact that code-switching is blatantly referred to as the "white voice" in the film underscores the power of whiteness — and the persistence of white privilege. Even though we are becoming more racially 19 and ethnically diverse, we are seeing racial tensions rise. Rampant racial inequality is evidence that white privilege continues to prevail.

In the film, Cassius' manager fervently urges him to "stick to the script." There is no room for individuality, nuance or variation, which precisely captures the oppression of being compelled to code-switch. Whiteness is the script, and code-switching is merely a strategy to adapt. Race relations will continue to deteriorate unless our society's script undergoes some serious revisions. 20

POINTS TO CONSIDER

1. Waring could have made her point about code-switching without reference to the film *Sorry to Bother You*. Why do you think she refers to the movie? How effective do you think it is for her argument?
2. Why does Waring's study focus only on "black-white biracial Americans" (para. 8)? What reasons does she give for concentrating on the experiences of only this single group?
3. After reading Waring's report of her research, what do you think of code-switching? Do its advantages outweigh the disadvantages? Or do you see more benefits than costs from such shifting of identities? For example, most people would consider it an advantage to be fluent in two languages, so why doesn't that apply to code-switching? What is Waring's central point?

AMERICA THEN . . . 1986

Brent Staples

Just Walk On By: A Black Man Ponders His Power to Alter Public Space

[*Ms. Magazine*, 1986]

This modern classic essay begins: "My first victim was a woman — white, well dressed, probably in her early twenties." But it's not what you may think. In "Just Walk On By: A Black Man Ponders His Power to Alter Public Space," essayist Brent Staples plays with our conventional ideas of victim and victimizer as well as with our notions of the threatening and the threatened. As a young graduate student at the University of Chicago, Staples discovered during his habitual nightly walks that he possessed an uncanny power. Years later, as he reflected on that power, he composed one of the great American essays on the connection between race and fear.

A member of the New York Times *editorial board since 1990, Brent Staples has contributed essays to many American magazines. He incorporated "Just Walk On By" into his 1994 memoir,* Parallel Time.

BEFORE YOU READ

Do you think someone should alter his or her appearance or behavior in a public setting in order to make another person feel more comfortable? By doing so, does the person make him- or herself feel more comfortable as well? What if the person makes those changes because of his or her race?

WORDS TO LEARN

menacingly (para. 1): threateningly (adverb)
taut (para. 4): tight (adjective)
duplicate (para. 8): to copy (verb)
labyrinthine (para. 10): like a labyrinth or maze (adjective)
paranoid (para. 12): as if suffering from the mental disorder paranoia (adjective)
skittish (para. 13): tending to startle (adjective)
congenial (para. 13): agreeable (adjective)
constitutional (para. 14): a walk (noun)

My first victim was a woman — white, well dressed, probably in her early twenties. I came upon her late one evening on a deserted street in Hyde Park, a relatively affluent neighborhood in an otherwise mean, impoverished section of Chicago. As I swung onto the avenue behind her, there seemed to be a discreet, uninflammatory distance between us. Not so. She cast back a worried glance. To her, the youngish black man — a broad six feet two inches with a beard and billowing hair, both hands shoved into the pockets of a bulky military jacket — seemed menacingly close. After a few more quick glimpses, she picked up her pace and was soon running in earnest. Within seconds she disappeared into a cross street. 1

That was more than a decade ago. I was twenty-two years old, a graduate student newly arrived at the University of Chicago. It was in the echo of that terrified woman's footfalls that I first began to know the unwieldy inheritance I'd come into — the ability to alter public space in ugly ways. It was clear that she thought herself the quarry of a mugger, a rapist, or worse. Suffering a bout of insomnia, however, I was stalking sleep, not defenseless wayfarers. As a softy who is scarcely able to take a knife to a raw chicken — let alone hold it to a person's throat — I was surprised, embarrassed, and dismayed all at once. Her flight made me feel like an accomplice in tyranny. It also made it 2 clear that I was indistinguishable from the muggers who occasionally seeped into the area from the surrounding ghetto. That first encounter, and those that followed, signified that a vast, unnerving gulf lay between nighttime pedestrians — particularly women — and me. And I soon gathered that being perceived as dangerous is a hazard in itself. I only needed to turn a corner into a dicey situation, or crowd some frightened, armed person in a foyer somewhere, or make an errant move after being pulled over by a policeman. Where fear and weapons meet — and they often do in urban America — there is always the possibility of death.

In that first year, my first away from my hometown, I was to become thoroughly familiar with the language of fear. At dark, shadowy intersections in Chicago, I could cross in front of a car stopped at a traffic light and elicit the *thunk, thunk, thunk, thunk* of the driver — black, white, male, or female — hammering down the door locks. On less traveled streets after dark, I grew accustomed to but never comfortable with people who crossed to the other side of the street rather than pass me. Then there were the standard unpleasantries with police, doormen, bouncers, cabdrivers, and others whose business is to screen out troublesome individuals *before* there is any nastiness. 3

I moved to New York nearly two years ago and I have remained an avid night walker. In central Manhattan, the near-constant crowd cover minimizes tense one-on-one street encounters. Elsewhere — visiting friends in Soho,[1] where sidewalks are narrow and tightly spaced buildings shut out the sky — things can get very taut indeed. 4

Black men have a firm place in New York mugging literature. Norman Podhoretz[2] in his famed (or infamous) 1963 essay, "My Negro Problem — And Ours," recalls growing up in terror of black males; they "were tougher than we were, more ruthless," he writes — and as an adult on the Upper West Side of Manhattan, he continues, he cannot constrain his nervousness when he meets black men on certain streets. Similarly, a decade later, the essayist and novelist Edward Hoagland extols a New York where once "Negro bitterness bore down mainly on other Negroes." Where some see mere panhandlers, Hoagland sees "a mugger who is clearly screwing up his nerve to do more than just *ask* for money." But Hoagland has "the New Yorker's quick-hunch posture for broken-field maneuvering," and the bad guy swerves away. 5

---

[1] Soho (para. 4): A district of lower Manhattan known for its art galleries.

[2] Norman Podhoretz (para. 5): A well-known literary critic and editor of *Commentary* magazine.

I often witness that "hunch posture," from women after dark on the warrenlike streets of Brooklyn where I live. They seem to set their faces on neutral and, with their purse straps strung across their chests bandolier style, they forge ahead as though bracing themselves against being tackled. I understand, of course, that the danger they perceive is not a hallucination. Women are particularly vulnerable to street violence, and young black males are drastically overrepresented among the perpetrators of that violence. Yet these truths are no solace against the kind of alienation that comes of being ever the suspect, against being set apart, a fearsome entity with whom pedestrians avoid making eye contact. 6

It is not altogether clear to me how I reached the ripe old age of twenty-two without being conscious of the lethality nighttime pedestrians attributed to me. Perhaps it was because in Chester, Pennsylvania, the small, angry industrial town where I came of age in the 1960s, I was scarcely noticeable against a backdrop of gang warfare, street knifings, and murders. I grew up one of the good boys, had perhaps a half-dozen fistfights. In retrospect, my shyness of combat has clear sources. 7

Many things go into the making of a young thug. One of those things is the consummation of the male romance with the power to intimidate. An infant discovers that random flailings send the baby bottle flying out of the crib and crashing to the floor. Delighted, the joyful babe repeats those motions again and again, seeking to duplicate the feat. Just so, I recall the points at which some of my boyhood friends were finally seduced by the perception of themselves as tough guys. When a mark cowered and surrendered his money without resistance, myth and reality merged — and paid off. It is, after all, only manly to embrace the power to frighten and intimidate. We, as men, are not supposed to give an inch of our lane on the highway; we are to seize the fighter's edge in work and in play and even in love; we are to be valiant in the face of hostile forces. 8

Unfortunately, poor and powerless young men seem to take all this nonsense literally. As a boy, I saw countless tough guys locked away; I have since buried several, too. They were babies, really — a teenage cousin, a brother of twenty-two, a childhood friend in his midtwenties — all gone down in episodes of bravado played out in the streets. I came to doubt the virtues of intimidation early on. I chose, perhaps even unconsciously, to remain a shadow — timid, but a survivor. 9

The fearsomeness mistakenly attributed to me in public places often has a perilous flavor. The most frightening of these confusions occurred in the late 1970s and early 1980s when I worked as a journalist in Chicago. One day, rushing into the office of a magazine I was writing for with a deadline story in hand, I was mistaken for a burglar. The office manager called security and, with an ad hoc posse, pursued me through 10 the labyrinthine halls, nearly to my editor's door. I had no way of proving who I was. I could only move briskly toward the company of someone who knew me.

> **I had no way of proving who I was. I could only move briskly toward the company of someone who knew me.**

Another time I was on assignment for a local paper and killing time before an interview. I entered a jewelry store on the city's affluent Near North Side. The proprietor excused herself and returned with an enormous red Doberman pinscher straining at the end of a leash. She stood, the dog extended toward me, silent to my questions, her eyes bulging nearly out of her head. I took a cursory look around, nodded, and bade her good night. Relatively speaking, however, I never fared as badly as another black male journalist. He went to nearby Waukegan, Illinois, a couple of summers ago to work on a story about a murderer who was born there. Mistaking the reporter for the killer, police hauled him from his car at gunpoint and but for his press credentials would probably have tried to book him. Such episodes are not uncommon. Black men trade tales like this all the time. 11

In "My Negro Problem — And Ours," Podhoretz writes that the hatred he feels for blacks makes itself known to him through a variety of avenues — one being his discomfort with that "special brand of paranoid touchiness" to which he says blacks are prone. No doubt he is speaking here of black men. In time, I learned to smother the rage I felt at so often being taken for a criminal. Not to do so would surely have led to madness — via that special "paranoid touchiness" that so annoyed Podhoretz at the time he wrote the essay. 12

I began to take precautions to make myself less threatening. I move about with care, particularly late in the evening. I give a wide berth to nervous people on subway platforms during the wee hours, particularly when I have exchanged business clothes for jeans. If I happen to be entering a building behind some people who appear skittish, I may walk by, letting them clear the lobby before I return, so as not to seem to be following them. I have been calm and extremely congenial on those rare occasions when I've been pulled over by the police. 13

And on late-evening constitutionals along streets less traveled by, I employ what has proved to be an excellent tension-reducing measure: I whistle melodies from Beethoven and Vivaldi and the more popular classical composers. Even steely New Yorkers hunching toward nighttime destinations seem to relax, and occasionally they even join in the tune. Virtually everybody seems to sense that a mugger wouldn't be warbling bright, sunny selections from Vivaldi's *Four Seasons*. It is my 14 equivalent of the cowbell that hikers wear when they know they are in bear country.

VOCABULARY/USING A DICTIONARY

1. What is the opposite of *affluent* (para. 1)?
2. What is a *bandolier* (para. 6)?
3. If something feels *perilous* (para. 10), is that an enjoyable feeling?

RESPONDING TO WORDS IN CONTEXT

1. If Staples's effect on people is called an *unwieldy* (para.2) inheritance, what does that suggest about what he's inherited?
2. What do you think Staples means by the "language of fear" (para. 3)?
3. What distinction is made when Staples refers to Podhoretz's "famed (or infamous)" (para. 5) essay, "My Negro Problem — and Ours"?

DISCUSSING MAIN POINT AND MEANING

1. What does the woman in the introductory paragraph assume about Staples? What do we know about him? Is there any intersection between what she assumes and what we know? What is it?
2. Why does Staples consciously change his behavior when walking at night?
3. What is the effect of Staples's whistling classical tunes?

EXAMINING SENTENCES, PARAGRAPHS, AND ORGANIZATION

1. What is your reaction to Staples's first sentence: "My first victim was a woman — white, well-dressed, probably in her early twenties" (para. 1)? What does that sentence conjure up in your imagination?
2. What clues does Staples offer in his writing (not just his actions) to indicate that he is well-educated, cultured, and able to blend in with his audience if they are white? Do you think that is important? Why or why not?
3. Identify the paragraphs in which Staples discusses fear. Whose fear is it? How does he organize these paragraphs in the essay as a whole?

THINKING CRITICALLY

1. **Connect.** Think about how we view people as "other" or "not-other" ("same") in social situations. How is Brent Staples's behavior here, his attempts to blend in or become "not-other," a contrast to Power's experience of blending in until she is able to speak up for the "other" in "Native in the Twenty-First Century" (p. 169)? How is Power able to travel in "circles beyond circles" in ways that Staples cannot?

2. Staples is once suspected of being a burglar. What situations, either from personal experience or from the news, does this suspicion remind you of? What are the connections, in your opinion?
3. Staples talks about the "precautions" he takes in certain situations or at certain times of day. Do you think these "precautions" are for himself, or for the people around him? Explain.

WRITING ACTIVITIES

1. Write a paper in which you describe a time you changed something about yourself to make someone else respond to you differently. Do you think the changes you made were more about you and your comfort, or about the other person? Explain your answer.
2. Do you think the situations Staples describes about himself are the ones young black men today continue to find themselves in? Write down ways in which times have changed and ways in which they have not. Based on your writing, would Staples continue to behave in public spaces the way he did then? Would he have to do more or less for the same result?
3. Take a few minutes to write your responses to the following questions: What other techniques, similar to Staples's, do people use to make others feel more comfortable in public situations that might seem threatening? Or if you have ever been perceived as a threat, what do you do to make people feel more comfortable? Are there things you find threatening about others? What are they, and why do you think you feel the way you do? Are there things people have felt are threatening about you that you can't fathom? What are they, and why do you not understand their perception?

Discussing the Unit

SUGGESTED TOPIC FOR DISCUSSION

Americans would like to think that the United States is no longer a racist society, all these years after the end of slavery and the introduction of the civil rights movement. However, racism lingers in the nation's historical consciousness. How do the writers in this chapter approach the subject of race in America? What do they tell us about the history of blacks and whites, our perception of race, and the continued experience of racism in this country?

PREPARING FOR CLASS DISCUSSION

1. Do you think of yourself as prejudiced? Do you identify as a particular race? How does your experience of race influence your thinking about yourself and others? Have you witnessed racially motivated actions or speech that

made you pause and think more deeply about the racism that continues to exist in this country?

2. When you consider race or learn more about the experience of race and racism in this country, do you respond more to poetry, narrative, argument, or straight data? All these forms are offered in this chapter. Why do you think you respond more to one form of writing over another? What do you find particularly persuasive about one form or other?

FROM DISCUSSION TO WRITING

1. Does our racial identity affect how we understand and relate to our fellow human beings? Is our reaction specific to the race with which we identify? Using three essays — Robin DiAngelo's "White America's Racial Illiteracy" (p. 201), Annette Gordon-Reed's "America's Original Sin: Slavery and the Legacy of White Supremacy" (p. 217), and Dawn Lundy Martin's "Weary Oracle" (p. 209) — write about how different races respond to each other. Where do those responses come from? How might they be explained?
2. What do you know about the Black Lives Matter movement? Do you think it is a positive or negative movement? Write an essay about your response to the Black Lives Matter movement, but add to your own understanding by drawing material from at least three essays from this chapter.

TOPICS FOR CROSS-CULTURAL DISCUSSION

1. What is America like in the time Claudia Rankine ("You and Your Partner . . .") is writing? What is America like in Gordon-Reed's description in "America's Original Sin: Slavery and the Legacy of White Supremacy"? Explain what these writings tell us about racial bias, then and now, and about the racial divide in America.
2. Claudia Rankine and Dawn Lundy Martin are African American women, African American poets. Does their writing reflect their experience or does it transcend it? Do you react to their writing from your own gender or race, and do you feel welcomed in or held at a distance? Consider and explain your response.

7

Guns: Can the Second Amendment Survive?

To the perpetual confusion of this country, its founders wrote in the Second Amendment to the Constitution that "a well regulated Militia, being necessary to the security of a free State, the right of the people to keep and bear Arms, shall not be infringed." The precise meaning of this right, and whether it still applies to modern society, has been for decades the subject of heated debate. In particular, tragic public events like the 2015 shootings in San Bernardino, California (sixteen dead), the 2016 nightclub massacre in Orlando, Florida (forty-nine dead), along with the 2017 Las Vegas music festival shootings (fifty-nine dead) and the 2018 attack on a high school in Parkland, Florida (seventeen dead), have raised the question of whether the nation's public safety outweighs our liberty to own powerful weapons.

This chapter examines a persistent problem that never seems to get resolved and that grows more contentious after every violent incident. For example, according to Gallup polls (see the "Spotlight" feature, p. 261), 13 percent of Americans considered guns "the country's most pressing problem" shortly after the Parkland, Florida, school attack in February 2018, but a month later only 6 percent thought so.

As you read through this chapter, keep in mind the attention to issues of individual freedom and public safety, a common and persistent conflict in American public affairs.

Jane Vincent Taylor

New Law Makes Local Poet Nervous

[*This Land*, February 1, 2013]

On November 1, 2012, Oklahoma passed an "open carry" law, allowing people to carry guns in public. According to the online journal ThinkProgress, *"Oklahoma's new 'open carry' law allows individuals with permits to openly carry guns in public and into many types of businesses including restaurants, grocery stores and banks, unless they post a sign prohibiting guns." Writing in the Oklahoma literary journal* This Land, *poet Jane Vincent Taylor summarizes the conflict between public safety and the "open carry" laws a number of states are putting into place. "New Law Makes Local Poet Nervous" tells a subtle story of fear and surprise in consequence of the law allowing private citizens to carry unconcealed weapons.*

Jane Vincent Taylor's work has appeared in This Land, Nimrod, *and* Still Point Quarterly, *among other periodicals. Her most recent book of poetry is* Pencil Light *(2015). She teaches creative writing at Ghost Ranch, a retreat and education center in New Mexico.*

Others have book fests, opera
and garden expos.
We have gun shows. Ammo.
Freedom
and now more freedom: open carry.

Like an old decoy I sit in my local coffee shop.
Post-holiday parents, toddlers in tow, order the special—
peppermint pancakes, dollar-size.
Megan fills the ketchup bottles.
Poinsettias wrinkle and curl. The radio plays Reba.

In walks a vested cowboy sporting a leather holster.
I react the way a gun insists: with fear. But nearer now,
I see his fancy shoulder bag
holds only oxygen,
precious sips of life—protection,

safety—openly carried, so we can all
breathe a little easier.

POINTS TO CONSIDER

1. Whom do you think Taylor refers to in the first word — who are the "Others"? And whom would "We" refer to in the third line?
2. How does the common expression "breathe a little easier" take on additional significance within the context of the poem?
3. Consider the words *protection* and *safety*. What sense do they have here? How do they refer to a larger argument about guns? How would you explain the poet's position on the topic?

The New York Times Editorial Board

End the Gun Epidemic in America

[*The New York Times*, December 5, 2015]

Advocates of gun control — government efforts to ban or restrict private ownership of guns — often respond to terrible mass shootings by declaring that tighter control of firearms might have averted the many tragedies. Supporters of tighter regulations would specifically restrict the purchase of certain types of weapons they deem more suitable for combat than for hunting or private safety. Immediately after the slaughter in San Bernardino, the New York Times *ran an editorial saying, "It is a moral outrage and a national disgrace that civilians can legally purchase weapons designed specifically to kill people with brutal speed and efficiency." To underscore the urgency of this issue, the paper ran the editorial on the front page; it was the first time an editorial appeared on page one since 1920.*

The New York Times *is a daily newspaper, founded and published in New York City since 1851. It has won 127 Pulitzer Prizes.*

BEFORE YOU READ

Are we encouraging an epidemic of gun violence in this country by not working harder to control gun ownership and use? Have recent events shown that the Second Amendment must be reconsidered?

WORDS TO LEARN

premium (para. 2): value (noun)
unfettered (para. 2): freed from restraints (adjective)
disgrace (para. 3): shame (noun)
abet (para. 5): to encourage or support (verb)
drastically (para. 5): extremely; extensively (adverb)

All decent people feel sorrow and righteous fury about the latest slaughter of innocents, in California. Law enforcement and intelligence agencies are searching for motivations, including the vital question of how the murderers might have been connected to international terrorism. That is right and proper. 1

But motives do not matter to the dead in California, nor did they in Colorado, Oregon, South Carolina, Virginia, Connecticut and far 2 too many other places. The attention and anger of Americans should also be directed at the elected leaders whose job is to keep us safe but who place a higher premium on the money and political power of an industry dedicated to profiting from the unfettered spread of ever more powerful firearms.

It is a moral outrage and a national disgrace that civilians can legally 3
purchase weapons designed specifically to kill people with brutal speed and efficiency. These are weapons of war, barely modified and deliberately marketed as tools of macho vigilantism and even insurrection. America's elected leaders offer prayers for gun victims and then, callously and without fear of consequence, reject the most basic restrictions on weapons of mass killing, as they did on Thursday. They distract us with arguments about the word *terrorism*. Let's be clear: These spree killings are all, in their own ways, acts of terrorism.

These spree killings are all, in their own ways, acts of terrorism.

Opponents of gun control are saying, as they do after every killing, 4
that no law can unfailingly forestall a specific criminal. That is true. They are talking, many with sincerity, about the constitutional challenges to effective gun regulation. Those challenges exist. They point out that determined killers obtained weapons illegally in places like France, England and Norway that have strict gun laws. Yes, they did.

But at least those countries are trying. The United States is not. 5
Worse, politicians abet would-be killers by creating gun markets for them, and voters allow those politicians to keep their jobs. It is past time to stop talking about halting the spread of firearms, and instead to reduce their number drastically — eliminating some large categories of weapons and ammunition.

It is not necessary to debate the peculiar wording of the Sec- 6
ond Amendment. No right is unlimited and immune from reasonable regulation.

Certain kinds of weapons, like the slightly modified combat rifles 7
used in California, and certain kinds of ammunition, must be outlawed for civilian ownership. It is possible to define those guns in a clear and effective way and, yes, it would require Americans who own those kinds of weapons to give them up for the good of their fellow citizens.

What better time than during a presidential election to show, at long 8
last, that our nation has retained its sense of decency?

VOCABULARY/USING A DICTIONARY

1. If something has been *modified* (para. 3), what has happened to it?
2. Where does the word *macho* (para. 3) come from?
3. What part of speech is *callously* (para. 3)?

RESPONDING TO WORDS IN CONTEXT

1. What is a *vigilante*? If you can define *vigilante*, can you guess the meaning of *vigilantism* (para. 3)?
2. Have you ever heard of a shopping spree? What is it? If you can define *shopping spree*, what might a *spree killing* (para. 3) be?
3. What does *immunity* mean? In what context is the term usually used? What do the writers mean when they say, "No right is unlimited and *immune* from reasonable regulation" (para. 6)?

DISCUSSING MAIN POINT AND MEANING

1. What has spurred the *New York Times* staff to write this editorial?
2. What argument do opponents of gun control make against changing the current laws about guns?
3. What change does the editorial board of the *New York Times* hope to see happen?

EXAMINING SENTENCES, PARAGRAPHS, AND ORGANIZATION

1. The editorial begins, "All decent people feel sorrow and righteous fury about the latest slaughter of innocents, in California" (para. 1). What do you notice about the diction in the first sentence? How is the reader being influenced by the language used here?
2. What do you notice about sentence structures and the organization of the argument in paragraph 4?
3. How would you describe the organization of this essay? If you put it in outline form, how might it look?

THINKING CRITICALLY

1. Why did the editorial board decide to write this editorial in December 2015? Why was it important to voice these concerns before a presidential election?
2. Do opponents of gun control have valid points in their argument? Where does the editorial board differ from its opponents?
3. Do you agree that slightly modified combat rifles are not necessary for civilians to own? Why or why not?

WRITING ACTIVITIES

1. The editorial "End the Gun Epidemic in America" was the first front-page editorial published in the *New York Times* since 1920. In your own words, write about the arguments over gun control in this country, explain why it has become such an important issue, and explain how and why the issue is getting significant media attention. Is there a gun epidemic? If so, what does that mean to you?
2. Write a paragraph in which you make an argument on a subject of your choice. Then, in another paragraph, offer a clear counterargument (one that you can articulate in writing). Once you have written both of these, structure a paragraph that imitates paragraph 4 in this editorial. Then use your counterargument and give credit where credit is due: What points does your opponent make that are valid?
3. Choose one sentence that you agree or disagree with in this editorial and offer a brief written response. As you write, bring in your own examples to support your position.

John A. Fry

Allowing Guns Won't Make Campuses Safer

[*The Philadelphia Inquirer*, October 19, 2015]

Responding to the numerous campus shootings in recent years and various calls to allow students and faculty to carry weapons for self-protection, John A. Fry, the president of Philadelphia's Drexel University, stressed the dangers of such a policy. In "Allowing Guns Won't Make Campuses Safer," Fry wonders if "someone with a gun" at the Oregon community college where nine students were killed and nine wounded in October 2015 "could have intervened in the recent massacre." He concludes that "the odds are very small that another person with a gun would have been in a position to stop it." "The best answer to the shootings," he believes, "is fewer guns, not more."

BEFORE YOU READ

What can we do to make campuses safer from the gun violence we see happening across the country? What are some of the suggestions raised in this essay and elsewhere on how to make colleges safer?

WORDS TO LEARN

volatile (para. 4): explosive (adjective)
exacerbate (para. 4): to aggravate (verb)
preposterous (para. 7): absurd (adjective)
mayhem (para. 8): random violence; disorder (noun)
prominent (para. 10): standing out (adjective)

Just eight days after a gunman massacred nine people at a community college in Oregon, two more students were killed in separate shootings on college campuses in Texas and Florida. In many parts of the country, the shootings prompted a call to arm students and faculty. Only in America do we respond to shootings with the need for more guns. Arming college campuses will do little to reduce mass attacks, and will likely lead to more shooting deaths. There are already 300 million civilian firearms in the United States. That's more than one for every adult. At what point do Americans say enough is enough? 1

It didn't happen last year after a student killed six and injured 13 near the University of California, Santa Barbara. It didn't happen in 2013 after a 23-year-old shot his father and brother before killing three others at Santa Monica College. It didn't happen in 2012 when a 43-year-old former student shot and killed seven people and injured three others at Oikos University in Oakland, Calif. And it obviously didn't happen after a senior killed 32 people at Virginia Tech University in 2007 — the largest campus massacre ever. 2

It defies logic to think that allowing students, faculty, and administrators to carry guns will somehow make college campuses safer. Indeed, experts from the Harvard School of Public Health found that wherever there are more guns, there are more murders. 3

> **It defies logic to think that allowing students, faculty, and administrators to carry guns will somehow make college campuses safer.**

Many college campuses are already confronting thorny issues of how best to combat suicide, sexual assault, and binge drinking. Introducing more guns into that volatile mix will only exacerbate the problems. 4

Yet, in the past few years, campus-carry bills have been introduced in almost half the states. Thankfully, most of the measures have failed. 5

But starting in August, students and faculty members at universities in Texas will be allowed to carry handguns into classrooms, dormitories, and other campus buildings. 6

Supporters claim the so-called concealed-carry law will make cam- 7
puses safer by allowing gun owners to defend themselves, and possibly save lives, should a mass shooting occur. Some have even made the preposterous claim that legalizing guns on college campuses will help women defend themselves from sexual assault.

The reality is that allowing more guns will lead to more fear and 8
mayhem, while having a chilling effect on campus life. Will students be willing to engage in thoughtful debate if they know a fellow classmate has a gun in his backpack? Will professors meet with struggling students to discuss their grades if the person is armed?

If anything, allowing guns on college campuses will likely lead to 9
more accidental shootings and suicides. Just imagine all the things that could go wrong with gun-carrying students at a fraternity party or concert.

There's a reason why the U.S. military bars most troops from carry- 10
ing weapons on their bases outside of combat zones. In fact, one of the most prominent opponents of the campus-carry bill is a former commander of the U.S. Special Operations forces who directed the raid that killed Osama bin Laden.

Adm. William McRaven is now the chancellor at the University of 11
Texas and a gun owner. Yet, he opposed allowing guns on college campuses in Texas.

"I feel the presence of concealed weapons will make a campus less 12
safe," McRaven wrote in a letter to the Texas legislature.

In all, eight states allow the carrying of concealed weapons on pub- 13
lic college campuses. Nineteen states ban concealed weapons on campus, and 23 others leave the decision to the individual colleges or state board of regents.

Oregon is one of the states that allows guns on college campuses, 14
though not in classrooms. Perhaps someone with a gun could have intervened in the recent massacre. But the odds are very small that another person with a gun would have been in a position to stop it. The best answer to the shootings is fewer guns, not more. Witness how strict gun laws in other developed countries have resulted in fewer deaths by firearms.

Short of that, the best way to reduce campus shootings is to increase 15
efforts to identify and treat disturbed students, while preventing them from buying guns. A well-trained, well-equipped campus police force is also critical to campus safety.

Other sensible steps include universal background checks, tighter 16
regulation of gun dealers, safe storage requirements, and prohibiting gun ownership for anyone convicted of domestic violence or assault.

There are many steps that can be taken to make college campuses safe. But allowing more guns on campus is not one of them. 17

VOCABULARY/USING A DICTIONARY

1. What is a *thorn*? What is a *thorny* (para. 4) situation or problem?
2. Who might a state board of *regents* (para. 13) be?
3. What is the opposite of *reduce* (para. 15)?

RESPONDING TO WORDS IN CONTEXT

1. What part of speech is *massacred* (para. 1)?
2. How is the word *bars* (para. 10) used in this essay?
3. When Fry speaks of *disturbed students* (para. 15), what kind of students do you think he means?

DISCUSSING MAIN POINT AND MEANING

1. What is the usual response in the United States to shootings around the country, according to Fry?
2. What is Fry's response to the impulse to arm people on college campuses?
3. Does the military encourage carrying weapons outside of combat zones? Why or why not?

EXAMINING SENTENCES, PARAGRAPHS, AND ORGANIZATION

1. How does Fry begin his essay? Is his introduction effective? What would you think if he started instead with paragraph 4?
2. Do you think Fry spends enough time suggesting the alternative to guns on campus? Why or why not?
3. Fry includes the sentence "Thankfully, most of the measures have failed" in paragraph 5. He is commenting on the introduction of campus-carry bills in various states. Can you tell Fry's position on campus carry based on the wording of his sentence?

THINKING CRITICALLY

1. Does it surprise you that campus-carry bills are being introduced? What, if anything, surprises you? If you aren't surprised by this, explain why not.
2. What will be the effect of arming students and faculty on college campuses? Why do you think this is so?

3. What are some of the ways Fry suggests helping students (besides giving them guns)? What do you think of Fry's call to help students? Would it reduce gun violence on campuses?

WRITING ACTIVITIES

1. Write a short piece that expresses your feelings and beliefs about guns on campus. Once you have written it, try to rewrite it imitating Fry's style — short paragraphs, one or two sentences long (you may need to cut and/or rearrange your draft to do this effectively). Then write it again with longer, denser paragraphs (again, you may need to write more or cut portions that don't carry as much weight). In small groups, discuss which version you prefer and why.
2. Outline Fry's essay. Your outline should have anywhere from five to twenty points that cover the ideas in Fry's paragraphs, and you should use only words and phrases (rather than complete sentences) to indicate what each part is about.
3. Analyze Fry's concerns about what carrying guns on campus will do. Do you think his concerns are valid? Which of his concerns are convincing, and which are not convincing? Why?

Brittney Christ (student essay)

We Should Be Allowed to Protect Ourselves

[*The State Hornet*, California State University, Sacramento, June 25, 2015]

California State University, Sacramento, student Brittney Christ expressed her opinions on the subject just months before the Oregon school shootings that Fry refers to in the preceding selection, but in "We Should Be Allowed to Protect Ourselves," she offers an opposing view. She argues that "allowing guns on campuses will not only make students feel more secure, but hopefully eliminate a potential school shooting that ends up in the death of innocent people."

Brittney Christ served as the State Hornet's *opinion editor and graduated from California State University, Sacramento, in 2015 with a degree in English.*

BEFORE YOU READ

What do you know about campus-carry bills that have been passed in states like Texas? Would allowing people on campus to carry guns make you feel more or less secure when you are there?

WORDS TO LEARN

infamous (para. 1): known for evil deeds (adjective)
hype (para. 5): publicity used to promote something (noun)
potential (para. 6): possible (adjective)

Guns on college campuses in particular have become a hot topic in the last few years because of infamous shootings such as Columbine High School in '99 and Virginia Tech in '07. These massacres have sparked debate over gun control laws as well as gun violence involving youth. 1

Texas lawmakers have passed a campus-carry bill that could come into action in August 2016 for universities and August 2017 for community colleges. Those in support of this bill, such as women who have been assaulted on campus or students who just feel unsafe and want the right to protect themselves against another Virginia Tech incident, claim this new law will give gun owners the security to know that they have the right to defend themselves in overtly dangerous situations. 2

According to the University of Iowa, 53 percent of students think guns should not be allowed, and would be upset if they were legal to have on campus. In addition, many professors are worried about frenzied students coming into their offices and threatening the professors over bad grades. However, surely there will be rules to allow these guns to be carried onto campus. The popular phrase that comes to mind is, "Guns don't kill people, people kill people." There have been many hilarious memes about gun control. One in particular that has gotten people talking is the picture of the newspaper clipping of the man who says that he left his gun on the porch all day and it never shot anyone. 3

> **The popular phrase that comes to mind is, "Guns don't kill people, people kill people."**

The man behind the photo, Donald Martin, said, "Can you imagine 4 how surprised I was, with all of the hype about how dangerous guns are and how they kill people? . . . Either the killing is by people misusing guns or I'm in the possession of the laziest gun in the world. So now I'm off to check my spoons, because I heard they make people fat."

Allowing guns on campuses will not only make students feel more 5 secure, but hopefully eliminate a potential school shooting that ends up in the death of innocent people. Of course, every school within the eight states (Texas, Colorado, Idaho, Kansas, Mississippi, Oregon, Utah, and Wisconsin) allowing this bill will have strict rules about gun usage and will have training courses in addition to those required to own a gun in the first place. Furthermore, gun registration will probably be required as well. So why is everyone worrying so much?

Let's promote self-defense and stop shaming those who want to 6 exercise their Second Amendment rights.

VOCABULARY/USING A DICTIONARY

1. What is an example of an *overtly* (para. 2) dangerous situation? What is the opposite of *overt* or *overtly*?
2. What is a *meme* (para. 3)?
3. What part of speech is *eliminate* (para. 5)? What does it mean?

RESPONDING TO WORDS IN CONTEXT

1. What is Christ describing when she speaks of *frenzied* (para. 3) students?
2. Donald Martin says that maybe he's "*in the possession of* the laziest gun in the world" (para. 4). What does the phrase *in the possession of* mean?
3. In her last sentence, Christ says, "Let's . . . stop *shaming* those who want to exercise their Second Amendment rights" (para. 6). What does she mean? How might people who want to exercise their Second Amendment rights be *shamed* in the conversation about gun control?

DISCUSSING MAIN POINT AND MEANING

1. Why does Christ think it is okay for guns to be carried on campus, despite various objections to that possibility?
2. What do the statistics Christ cites suggest about how many people view campus carry?
3. How will guns keep schools safer, according to Christ?

EXAMINING SENTENCES, PARAGRAPHS, AND ORGANIZATION

1. In paragraph 3, Christ looks at some data from the University of Iowa. She ends the paragraph with her response to this data. How does she indicate the introduction of a different point of view?
2. Does the mid-essay anecdote about the meme (para. 3) support Christ's position or further her argument about campus carry? Explain your answer.
3. Do you think Christ's one-sentence conclusion is sufficient as an ending to the essay? Why or why not?

THINKING CRITICALLY

1. How have incidents like Columbine and Virginia Tech influenced ideas about gun control laws and violence?
2. Does the meme Christ includes work in favor of campus carry? Why or why not?
3. Does Christ explain how allowing guns on campus will make students feel more secure? What about the claim that it will "hopefully eliminate a potential school shooting that ends up in the death of innocent people" (para. 5)? Are you convinced by Christ's essay?

WRITING ACTIVITIES

1. How do you feel about campus-carry bills that allow students, faculty, and staff to have guns on campus? What potential drawbacks to allowing campus carry can you think of? What sort of rules would you put in place to make you feel safer (whether you are for or against campus carry)?
2. Come up with your own gun control meme. What would it look like? What would the text be? What is the message you are trying to convey?
3. How do you understand the wording of the Second Amendment? Is it literal and inviolable? How do you interpret what it says? Answer these questions in one to three short paragraphs.

LOOKING CLOSELY

Effective Openings: Establishing a Clear Context for an Argument

When writing an essay that advances an opinion about a current issue, one of the best approaches a writer can take is to summarize the general context or situation that gave rise to the issue. This approach is effectively demonstrated in Brittney Christ's "We Should Be Allowed to Protect Ourselves." Note how her opening paragraph sets out in a clear and direct fashion the situation that has prompted her essay — the debate about whether students should be permitted to carry guns on campus for self-protection. She not only establishes her main topic in her first sentence but also efficiently provides a reason for why it is a "hot topic." Her opening paragraph takes us directly into the debate, and she will express her opinions on the issue in the body of her paper.

1
Establishes her topic

2
Shows specific examples that fueled the debate

(1) Guns on college campuses in particular have become a hot topic in the last few years (2) because of infamous shootings such as Columbine High School in '99 and Virginia Tech in '07. These massacres have sparked debate over gun control laws as well as gun violence involving youth.

STUDENT WRITER AT WORK

Brittney Christ

Courtesy of Brittney Christ

R.A. What inspired you to write this essay? And publish it?

B.C. Campus shootings were the hot topic to talk about and I wanted to share my take on it, especially since it is not a common opinion to have. It was also one of my first pieces as an editor on the paper, so I got to really express my thoughts without too much censoring.

R.A. What was your main purpose in writing this piece?

B.C. Campus shootings were extremely prevalent during this time, and a campus-carry law was passed by Texas lawmakers, which in turn sparked a debate in many classrooms.

R.A. Are your opinions unusual or fairly mainstream, given the general climate of discourse on campus?

B.C. My views were widely out of place for the environment. Most people I came into contact with wanted more gun control and fewer guns in America in general.

R.A. What topics most interest you as a writer?

B.C. I am very passionate about social issues such as feminism, gay pride, and the environment. Issues such as fracking, abortion, and equal rights are the types of topics I love to dig into.

R.A. Are you pursuing a career in which writing will be a component?

B.C. Yes, in every job I take I make sure that writing is a component. I plan to one day become a best-selling fiction author!

R.A. What advice do you have for other student writers?

B.C. You need to write from the heart and make it authentic. You should pick something you are passionate about. You need to find your niche and stick with it. Trust me, someone out there in the world is writing about whatever it is that you have set your heart on.

Dahleen Glanton

Stop Saying We Can't Do Anything to Stop Mass Shootings. We Can.

[*Chicago Tribune*, February 19, 2018]

Why does nothing ever seem to be done to reduce the number of mass shootings that have taken so many innocent American lives? That is the central question asked by a Chicago columnist shortly after the Parkland, Florida, attack on February 14, 2018. In "Stop Saying We Can't Do Anything to Stop Mass Shootings. We Can," Dahleen Glanton praises the young survivors of the shootings and their mission to demand more effective gun control. "Why are we so quick," she wonders, "to let lawmakers off the hook for shirking their duty to pass responsible gun laws?"

Dahleen Glanton has served as a news columnist for the Chicago Tribune *since 1989. Her special interests involve civil rights, race, and violence.*

BEFORE YOU READ

How does politics get in the way of passing sensible gun control legislation? Is there anything we, the American people, can do to prevent more school shootings?

WORDS TO LEARN

deranged (para. 1): insane (adjective)
depiction (para. 7): picture (noun)
potential (para. 7): having the capacity to become something (adjective)
lackadaisical (para. 12): passionless; without spirit (adjective)
zeal (para. 12): fervor (noun)
complacent (para. 16): self-satisfied (adjective)
partisan (para. 16): supporting only a particular party (adjective)
unprecedented (para. 17): new

Seventeen more people died last week at the hands of a deranged shooter wielding a semiautomatic rifle. Don't tell me there is nothing we could have done to stop it. 1

Don't tell me that this is simply what our country has become. That is a lie. 2

We are a nation of compassionate and dutiful people, of citizens who more often than not choose to protect rather than harm. We have seen Americans come to each other's aid time and time again in the aftermath of hurricanes, tornadoes and floods. 3

What makes mass shootings so different? Why do so many of us 4
dig our heels in the sand and choose our guns over the safety of our children? Why are we so quick to let lawmakers off the hook for shirking their duty to pass responsible gun laws?

We owe it to our children to be better than that. 5

After a 19-year-old gunman used an AR-15 in a massacre at a Park- 6
land, Fla., high school last week, I decided to have a conversation with a man who owns an AR-15. He is a good and caring person, a retired educator with school-age grandchildren whom he adores.

He purchased his high-powered rifle a few days after the mass shoot- 7
ing at the Pulse nightclub in Orlando, Fla., in 2016, where 49 people were killed. He bought it, he says, in protest of the media's depiction of all gun owners as potential deranged shooters who are likely to flip out and go on a killing rampage.

He is a responsible, law-abiding citizen, he told me, who believes 8
that the U.S. Constitution gives him the right to own any kind of gun he wants. He feels no kinship to anyone who misuses that freedom and shoots up a school.

And, he said, he enjoys shooting it. "I love going to the gun range," 9
he told me.

He admits, however, that he only visited the gun range once last 10
year. The rest of the time, the $600 rifle sits on a shelf in his closet unloaded and collecting dust alongside his six handguns.

"As long as AR-15s are legal, no one can tell me that I can't own one," 11
he said. "But if they were illegal, I would be the first to give mine up."

It would not be surprising to find many other law-abiding gun own- 12
ers who have a similar lackadaisical attitude about assault weapons. Many of them likely don't share the National Rifle Association's zeal for turning America into a free-for-all gun society.

According to a Gallup Poll in late 2017, 13
a growing majority of Americans support passing new gun control legislation. The poll, taken after the October massacre in Las Vegas that killed 58, found that 51 percent of Americans favored increasing legislation.

How to go about it, though, was split 14
along party lines. About 81 percent of Democrats favored calls for new legislation, while 73 percent of Republicans preferred to impose existing laws more strictly.

So why not stand together and force lawmakers in Congress and every local statehouse to do the right thing?

So why not stand together and force lawmakers in Congress and 15
every local statehouse to do the right thing?

On March 24, young people plan to march in cities across the country, doing what most adults have been too complacent to do. They will demand that Americans put aside their partisan loyalties and compromise for the good of the nation. 16

In an unprecedented call for action, the teenagers will push the backs of adults against the wall and force them to choose sides. 17

Adults will have to look young people in the eye and admit that firing a high-powered weapon at the gun range is just too much fun to give up, even if it means their children and grandchildren might never feel safe at school. 18

Adults will have to decide if it's more important to use an assault rifle to hunt for deer or to stop a teenager from going classroom to classroom with an AR-15 hunting for children. 19

And adults will have to finally acknowledge that their Second Amendment right to own any kind of firearm they choose is more important than a child's right to know that a crazed maniac would no longer be able to legally obtain any kind of gun he wants and use it on them. 20

Cameron Kasky, a 17-year-old junior at Marjory Stoneman Douglas High School where last week's massacre occurred, summed it up perfectly on the Sunday morning news shows. 21

"You're either with us or against us," he said. 22

VOCABULARY/USING A DICTIONARY

1. The word *compassionate* (para. 3) comes from *compassion*. From what language does that word derive?
2. If someone is *shirking* his or her duty (para. 4), what is that person doing?
3. What type of language is *flip out* (para. 7)? What does it mean, and is it a good way to describe what it means? Explain your answer.

RESPONDING TO WORDS IN CONTEXT

1. Glanton calls us a *compassionate* and *dutiful* people (para. 3). How do those words indicate that there is something about us that wants to protect and help? How do you define those words?
2. A *deranged* shooter might go on a killing *rampage* (para. 7). What type of person might be characterized as *deranged*? Who or what else might be said go on a *rampage*?
3. What is the definition of *kinship* (para. 8)? What does the AR-15 owner mean when he says he feels no *kinship* to anyone who misuses a gun?

DISCUSSING MAIN POINT AND MEANING

1. A man who owns an AR-15 spoke to Glanton. Why did he buy his weapon?
2. What does the data about the Democratic and Republican voters tell you about the positions of those two parties on the gun control debate? Be specific in your answer.
3. The action we can take to stop shootings becomes the focus of the last half of the essay. What action does Glanton describe?

EXAMINING SENTENCES, PARAGRAPHS, AND ORGANIZATION

1. Glanton writes very short paragraphs. What is the effect of these short paragraphs on the reader? Is it appropriate for her subject and audience?
2. What is different about paragraph 4? Why do you think Glanton constructs it that way?
3. The man who owns a high-powered rifle (para. 6) is described as "a retired educator with school-age grandchildren whom he adores." Why does Glanton include these details in this sentence?

THINKING CRITICALLY

1. Why do you think Glanton includes her conversation with an anonymous AK-15 owner? What purpose does it serve?
2. **Connect:** Glanton calls the Parkland shooter "a 19-year-old gunman" (para. 6). She doesn't mention his name. Do you think she agrees with Mona Charen's argument in "No Names" (p. 257)?
3. Do you believe Glanton's suggestion that "it would not be surprising to find many other law-abiding gun owners who have a similar lackadaisical attitude about assault weapons" (para. 12)? Why do you believe or disbelieve it?

WRITING ACTIVITIES

1. Note that Glanton turns her argument at the end not to gun advocates versus gun opponents but to adults versus children. In a short writing assignment, explain whether you think this is an effective way to endorse gun control.
2. Consider the Parkland shooting survivor Kasky's statement that concludes the essay: "You're either with us or against us." Write an essay that defends that sort of position on the gun control debate or argues that it won't work. Bring in facts about the history of gun control (about either tightening or loosening gun control laws) or the history of public/mass shootings to make your point.
3. Collect one to three pages of data on gun owners and the ease with which a gun can be purchased in your state. Do you feel safer or less safe once you review this information? Write a personal response to the data you've collected, and feel free to imitate the structure of Glanton's article as you write.

Mona Charen

No Names

[*Townhall*, February 15, 2018 (*The New Hampshire Union Leader*, February 16, 2018)]

Gun violence in America is often referred to as an "epidemic" (see the New York Times *editorial, "End the Gun Epidemic," on p. 240). In "No Names," columnist Mona Charen takes the term literally: "Mass killings," she writes, "like viruses, seem to be contagious." Hesitant to think that legislation would help and reluctant to compromise anyone's Second Amendment rights, she proposes a solution — based on her "contagion" theory — that she believes is worth trying.*

Let news organizations limit the publicity she believes many mass killers seek. In her opinion, the news media should refrain from coverage that turns the killer into a celebrity: "There is no need, for example, for cable news to feature images of the accused, nor to repeat his name dozens of times within 24 hours."

Mona Charen is a widely syndicated conservative columnist and a political analyst. She is the author of three books: Useful Idiots *(2003),* Do-Gooders *(2005), and* Sex Matters *(2018).*

BEFORE YOU READ

Can we take steps to avoid mass shootings that go beyond stricter gun control or more security measures? What role does a media spotlight play in encouraging such shootings?

WORDS TO LEARN

epidemic (para. 4): rapidly spread; widespread (adjective)
cinematic (para. 4): suggestive of the flourish of motion pictures (adjective)
contagious (para. 5): easily transmitted by contact (adjective)
copycat (para. 5): an imitator (noun)
predecessor (para. 6): one who precedes another (noun)
decry (para. 7): to express disapproval (verb)
atrocity (para. 8): something that is shockingly bad or atrocious (noun)

An orgy of mutual disgust now greets every mass shooting in America. Liberals despise conservatives who, they predict, will offer only insipid "thoughts and prayers" in the face of what they conceive to be preventable massacres. Conservatives scorn liberals who, they believe, will propose "feel-good" gun measures that would have no effect on any mass shooting. 1

But there is something that we can try to prevent these horrific killings. It doesn't require legislation. It won't cost a penny. It doesn't require compromising anyone's gun rights, and it's more concrete than "see something, say something." 2

First, the scale of the problem. While overall gun deaths have been declining in recent years, mass shootings have been increasing. According to the Harvard Injury Control Research Center, the number of days separating mass shootings declined from an average of 200 between 1983 and 2011 to 64 between 2011 and 2014. The five deadliest mass shootings in U.S. history have occurred in the past 11 years. These shocking attacks have become so common that their locations and dates blur — Sutherland Springs, Blacksburg, Sandy Hook, Las Vegas, Orlando, Binghamton, Aurora, Dallas, Washington Navy Yard. The randomness of these massacres, and their quotidian locations — schools, movie theaters, concerts — amplify the horror. 3

Every possible cause is considered to explain the epidemic of cinematic violence: the overabundance of guns, violent video games and films, family decline, the waning influence of churches, inadequate mental health policies. Perhaps all of these contribute, and all require long-term social reforms. 4

But then there is this insight: Mass killings, like viruses, seem to be contagious. It isn't news that behaviors are catching. Sociologists have long known that suicide, for example, prompts imitators, especially among the young. Researchers at Arizona State University have studied mass murders (particularly school shootings) and found that each new episode does inspire copycats. 5

We also know that some of the mass shooters have expressed fascination with their predecessors. The Oregon shooter, for example, had written of another: "A man who was known by no one, is now known by everyone. . . . Seems the more people you kill, the more you're in the limelight." 6

The second Fort Hood shooter, weirdly enough, seemed to decry the attention paid to killers. He posted on Facebook: "These bastards have perfected their way of attacking by studying previous massacres to gain publicity and their minute of fame as a villain." He then went on to commit a mass shooting himself. An Everett, Washington, man was arrested on Wednesday after his grandparents reported to police that he was "learning from past shooters." 7

The sick desire for fame — even when purchased through atrocity — seems to be at work in many of these cases. Would denying them the attention they seek diminish the attraction? 8

The proposal is straightforward. It's outlined at www.nonotoriety.com. News organizations and law enforcement officers should voluntarily limit the use of the names of mass killers. It's not possible in the internet era to keep the names secret, but news organizations can dramatically reduce the attention a killer receives. There is no need, for example, for cable news to feature images of the accused, nor to repeat his name dozens of times within 24 hours. Newspapers should not publish the manifestos of diseased minds. Investigators can comb through his social media rants, but the media should shun them. TV channels may get ratings by repeating the grievances of killers, but they are also providing a platform that other borderline personalities may find irresistible. 9

Investigators can comb through his social media rants, but the media should shun them.

We expect our presidents to serve as national grief counselors in these moments. But it's just possible that this attention is also putting too much power into the hands of mass killers. While a presidential visit may comfort the grieving, is it worth it if it also gratifies the murderer's rage for attention — and spurs some future attention-seeking monster? 10

Some homicidal types are motivated by political objectives. Of the 69 mass shootings since Columbine High School, four were committed by Islamic extremists, and others (the Sikh temple, Charleston) by racists. But the overwhelming majority were the work of men whose motivations probably include a lust for fame. 11

Perhaps this is wrong. Perhaps denying mass killers the attention they seek won't have any effect on this epidemic of violence. But what would be lost by trying? 12

VOCABULARY/USING A DICTIONARY

1. What part of speech is *insipid* (para. 1)? What does it mean?
2. How do you define the word *amplify* (para. 3)?
3. How would you describe the action of *waning* (para. 4)?

RESPONDING TO WORDS IN CONTEXT

1. What do you think Charen means by an "*orgy* of mutual disgust" (paragraph 1)?
2. How are schools, movie theaters, and concerts *quotidian* locations (para. 3)?
3. Charen says, "Newspapers should not publish the *manifestos* of diseased minds" (para. 9). How might you rephrase that sentence?

DISCUSSING MAIN POINT AND MEANING

1. What precisely is Charen suggesting might be a chief cause of mass shootings in the United States?
2. What does Charen suggest we should do to prevent further shootings?
3. Specifically, what would change after a shooting if we were to follow Charen's suggestions?

EXAMINING SENTENCES, PARAGRAPHS, AND ORGANIZATION

1. How does Charen characterize different political parties in paragraph 1? Is this characterization important?
2. Isolate one of Charen's paragraphs. In it, take out any descriptive adjectives she uses. Read the paragraph without it/them. What effect is created by adding or removing these adjectives?
3. In her next to last paragraph, Charen mentions that some shootings are motivated by "political objectives" or are "racist." Why does she introduce these factors, and what is the effect of ending with them? How do they affect her argument?

THINKING CRITICALLY

1. What does "contagion" have to do with the cause of mass shootings in the United States? Do you think Charen offers sufficient evidence to establish this cause?
2. **Connect:** How far do you think Charen would go in asking the media to scale back attention from mass shootings? How do you think she would feel about Glanton's essay ("Stop Saying We Can't Do Anything to Stop Mass Shootings. We Can," p. 253)? Do you think she'd object to giving greater media attention to Cameron Kasky (para. 21, Glanton) or other Parkland shooting survivors? Why or why not?
3. Do you agree that many mass shootings are driven by the murderer's "lust for fame" (para. 11)? Do you think Charen backs up this assertion in her essay?

WRITING ACTIVITIES

1. In what way is Charen's explanation of mass shootings a criticism of the media? How does she think the media should react to the shootings? In a brief essay, compare the role the media plays in mass shootings with the role she thinks the media could play. Feel free to insert your own opinions (as long as you distinguish them from Charen's).
2. After you finish the essay addressing the first question, note that Charen concludes she could be wrong and her explanation could have no effect

on the shootings. But she ends by asking, "What would be lost by trying?" Do you think this conclusion effectively clinches her case about naming the shooters? Can you think of anything that might be lost by denying the murderers media attention? Formulate written answers to these questions.

3. Write an argument that insists we should give a little or a lot of media attention to mass shootings. Then write one that insists the opposite. Write one final paragraph in rebuttal, and consider whether the idea you believe is strengthened or weakened by including an opposing argument.

SPOTLIGHT ON DATA AND RESEARCH

Megan Brenan

Ten Takeaways about Americans' View of Guns

[*Gallup News*, May 2, 2018 (updated September 19, 2018)]

The following report summarizes the most important findings of a 2018 Gallup poll taken shortly after the February Parkland, Florida, school shooting that left seventeen dead. Although it indicates that public reaction fades over time and that an enormous divide exists between Democrats and Republicans on gun control, the report also concludes that, since the most recent attacks in Parkland and Las Vegas, "more Americans support stricter gun laws than at any point in the last 25 years."

The National Rifle Association's annual meeting in Dallas, Texas this week May 5, 2018 comes after three of the deadliest mass shootings in U.S. history, which have all occurred in the past seven months. These three massacres — at an outdoor concert in Las Vegas, Nevada, a church in Sutherland Springs, Texas and a high school in Parkland, Florida — have reignited debate across the country about gun control. President Donald Trump, who has made conflicting statements about his position on gun control in recent months, is scheduled to address NRA members for the fourth consecutive year at this week's meeting. 1

In the aftermath of the recent mass shootings, Gallup conducted several polls to gauge the public's attitudes toward guns. A poll conducted several days after the Las Vegas shooting in October found strengthened support for stricter gun laws. Yet, many Americans, particularly those 2 whose opinions align with the NRA, remain staunchly opposed to any changes to existing gun laws.

The most recent Gallup polling about guns was conducted after the 3
Florida school shooting in February. In addition to several nationwide polls gauging the public's attitudes toward guns and preventing mass shootings, a nationally-representative poll of teachers provided unique insights into their opinions.

Here are some of the key takeaways from this recent polling on guns: 4

1. Support for stricter gun laws reached 67% in March, the 5
highest percentage since 1993. This reading came several weeks after the Parkland, Florida school shooting claimed the lives of 17 people. It marked a seven-point increase from an October 2017 poll, which was also elevated following the Las Vegas mass shooting of 58 people.

2. Partisans' views of the need for stricter gun laws diverge, but 6
Republicans' and independents' support of restrictions increased after the Florida school shooting. Still, the difference is stark as **90% of Democrats but only 41% of Republicans want the laws covering the sale of firearms to be made stricter**.

3. Gun control does not typically rank high on the list of the nation's 7
most important problems, but a March Gallup poll found **a record high 13% of Americans cited guns or gun control as the country's most pressing problem**. However, by early April, guns had fallen to 6%.

4. When Gallup last asked Americans for their opinions of the 8
National Rifle Association in October 2015, 58% viewed the organization favorably and 35% unfavorably. Although Gallup has not asked the question recently, CNN did so in the week after the Florida school shooting using the same wording as Gallup. In the CNN poll, **41% viewed the NRA favorably and 49% unfavorably, indicating its image had taken a hit.**

5. In the weeks after the Florida shooting, Gallup polling addressed 9
guns and schools and found broad public support for a number of approaches to prevent mass shootings in schools. **With near unanimity, Americans favored more training for first responders to active shootings and background checks for all gun sales.** Increased security at schools and programs to manage students deemed a potential threat also received broad bipartisan support. Americans were least likely to favor arming teachers and school officials, something fewer Democrats (22%) favor than Republicans (69%).

6. In a parallel series of questions, Gallup asked the public to rate 10
the *effectiveness* of the same seven proposals. Again, more training

for first responders and background checks were viewed as the most effective measures that could be undertaken to combat future casualties in the nations' schools. **But, despite being advocated by Trump and the NRA after the Parkland shooting, only 27% of Americans said arming teachers and school officials with guns would be a very effective or somewhat effective way to limit school shootings.**

7. Several of Gallup's long-term trends about guns, though these 11
questions have not been asked since October 2017 after the Las Vegas shooting, provide some valuable insight into the direction of public opinion. Americans' support for handgun possession has been consistently in majority territory for two decades. **But support for banning assault weapons, which have been used in some of the deadliest U.S. mass shootings, including those in the past seven months, has been much less consistent.** While 61% of Americans opposed a law that would make it illegal to manufacture, sell or possess semi-automatic guns known as assault rifles in 2016, Americans were evenly divided in their support for such a ban after the Las Vegas shooting.

8. Gallup's in-depth look at the opinions of U.S. teachers in March 12
found **73% of teachers opposed the proposal to have qualified teachers and staff carry guns in school buildings**. About seven in 10 teachers also did not see this as an effective way to limit the number of casualties in the event of a shooting at school, and nearly six in 10 teachers believed arming teachers would result in less safe schools.

9. Four in 10 U.S. teachers do not think their school has ade- 13
quate security to keep potential shooters out. The same percentage think their school is not prepared to protect students and staff if an armed shooter is inside the school. Meanwhile, 36% of teachers say they are personally at least somewhat worried about the possibility of being a victim of a shooting in school, and slightly more, 45%, have the same fear for their students. High school teachers were the most likely to say their students talk about school shootings — 45% said it was discussed at least a moderate amount. The events in Parkland, Florida mobilized survivors there to start an antigun movement that sparked student-led protests all around the country.

10. There is broad agreement among teachers on the effec- 14
tiveness of several measures aimed at reducing the frequency and severity of school shootings, including background checks on all gun sales (87%), a nationwide ban on semiautomatic assault rifles (75%) and banning "bump stocks" that convert ordinary guns to fire at nearly the same rate as machine guns (74%).

BOTTOM LINE

15 The mass shootings in recent months have altered many Americans’ opinions of guns in the U.S. as more Americans support stricter gun laws than at any point in the last 25 years. Mass shootings, particularly those occurring in schools, have typically ignited national debate about guns and increased the public’s appetite for tighter gun regulations. Yet, the most recent high school shooting sparked a new phenomenon — the mobilization of student anti-gun activists across the country. If lawmakers try to pass legislation that would reduce gun violence, they will need to find common ground with gun rights’ advocates, including some of those at this week’s NRA meeting.

POINTS TO CONSIDER

1. What impact do high-profile shootings, such as those that took place in Parkland, Florida, and Las Vegas have on the public? How do they affect the poll numbers? In your opinion, if mass shootings decline significantly in the future, will there be less public interest in gun reform?
2. Takeaway #2 (para. 6) reports on the wide gap between Democrats and Republicans on the issue of gun legislation. How do you account for this difference? What does it mean for the passage of stricter legislation?
3. Five of the takeaways involve school shootings. How would you summarize the findings? Which protective measures appear to have the most support? Which the least?

AMERICA THEN . . . 1981

Paul Fussell

A Well-Regulated Militia

[*The New Republic*, June 27, 1981]

The Second Amendment to the U.S. Constitution consists of a fairly brief sentence: "A well regulated Militia, being necessary to the security of a free State, the right of the people to keep and bear Arms, shall not be infringed." For centuries, this amendment seemed straightforward and was rarely a legal issue. Yet in the politically turbulent 1960s, following the shooting deaths of President John F. Kennedy, his brother Senator Robert Kennedy, and civil rights leader Martin Luther King Jr., an anti-gun sentiment began growing. The anti-gun movement gained momentum with the attempted assassination of President Ronald Reagan in 1981, when one of the men also shot in the incident, James Brady, initiated a congressional bill that would subject gun buyers to a federal background check. Hotly contested by such pro-gun organizations as the National Rifle Association (founded in 1871 but not an influential lobbying group until 1975), the Brady Act was finally enacted in 1993. Today, with an estimated 300,000 firearm-related deaths a year—and with one highly publicized school shooting following right on the heels of another—an accurate understanding of the Second Amendment has become more important than ever: What did the framers mean by a militia and by the phrase "to keep and bear Arms," and does the Second Amendment guarantee the right of individual citizens or only those who are part of a "militia" to own weapons? Many legal scholars, historians, and journalists have covered this issue but few with the concision, wit, and irony of Paul Fussell. At a time when many believe the Second Amendment should itself be amended, given its increasingly costly consequences, Fussell argues that it should not be revised or abolished but just be taken literally and enforced.

An eighteenth-century scholar who taught for many years at Rutgers University before moving to the University of Pennsylvania, Paul Fussell (1924–2012) wrote numerous academic studies—on such topics as poetic meter, rhetoric, and eighteenth-century literature. But after winning the National Book Award in nonfiction for The Great War and Modern Memory *in 1975 (Fussell served in the infantry in World War II), he began writing essays on a variety of topics for a general public. One of those essays, "A Well-Regulated Militia," was published in the* New Republic *in 1981.*

BEFORE YOU READ

Do you know what the Second Amendment says? Do you think we miss part of what it says when we talk about our right to gun ownership?

WORDS TO LEARN

façade (para. 1): superficial appearance; front of a building (noun)
crucial (para. 2): critical (adjective)
unadvertised (para. 2): kept secret (adjective)
bivouac (para. 4): encampment (noun)
negotiation (para. 4): discussion of terms (noun)
amend (para. 5): to alter (verb)
stigmatize (para. 6): to place stigma upon (verb)
compose (para. 6): to form or create (verb)

In the spring Washington swarms with high school graduating classes. They come to the great pulsating heart of the Republic—which no one has yet told them is Wall Street—to be impressed by the White House and the Capitol and the monuments 1 and the Smithsonian and the space capsules. Given the state of public secondary education, I doubt if many of these young people are at all interested in language and rhetoric, and I imagine few are fascinated by such attendants of power and pressure as verbal misrepresentation and disingenuous quotation. But any who are can profit from a stroll past the headquarters of the National Rifle Association of America, its slick marble façade conspicuous at 1600 Rhode Island Avenue, NW.

There they would see an entrance flanked by two marble panels offering language, and language more dignified and traditional than that customarily associated with the Association's gun-freak constituency, with its T-shirts reading GUNS, GUTS, AND GLORY ARE WHAT MADE AMERICA GREAT and its belt buckles proclaiming I'LL GIVE UP MY GUN WHEN THEY PRY MY COLD DEAD FINGERS FROM AROUND IT. The marble panel on the right reads, "The right of the people to keep and bear arms shall not be infringed," which sounds familiar. So familiar that the student naturally expects the left-hand panel to honor the principle of symmetry by presenting the first half of the quotation, namely: "A well-regulated Militia, being necessary to the security of a free state, . . ." But looking to the left, the inquirer discovers not that clause at all but rather this lame list of NRA functions and specializations: "Firearms Safety Education. Marksmanship Training. Shooting for Recreation." It's as if in presenting its well-washed, shiny public face the NRA doesn't want to remind anyone of the crucial dependent clause of the Second Amendment, whose latter half alone it is so fond of invoking to urge its prerogatives. (Some legible belt buckles of members retreat further into a seductive vagueness, reading only, "Our American Heritage: the Second Amendment.") We infer that for the Association, the less emphasis on the clause about the militia, the better. Hence its pretense on the front of its premises that the quoted main clause is not crucially dependent on the now unadvertised subordinate clause — indeed, it's meaningless without it. 2

Because flying .38- and .45-caliber bullets rank close to cancer, heart disease, and AIDS as menaces to public health in this country, the firearm lobby, led by the NRA, comes under liberal attack regularly, and with special vigor immediately after an assault on some conspicuous person like Ronald Reagan or John Lennon. Thus the *New Republic*, in April 1981, deplored the state of things but offered as a solution only the suggestion that the whole Second Amendment be perceived as obsolete and amended out of the Constitution. This would leave the NRA with not a leg to stand on. 3

But here as elsewhere a better solution would be not to fiddle with the Constitution but to take it seriously, the way we've done with the First Amendment, say, or with the Thirteenth, the one forbidding open 4 and avowed slavery. And by taking the Second Amendment seriously I mean taking it literally. We should "close read" it and thus focus lots of attention on the grammatical reasoning of its two clauses. This might shame the NRA into pulling the dependent clause out of the closet, displaying it on its façade, and accepting its not entirely pleasant implications. These could be particularized in an Act of Congress providing:

1. that the Militia shall now, after these many years, be "well-regulated," as the Constitution requires.

2. that any person who has chosen to possess at home a gun of any kind, and who is not a member of the police or the military or an appropriate government agency, shall be deemed to have enrolled automatically in the Militia of the United States. Members of the Militia, who will be issued identifying badges, will be organized in units of battalion, company, or platoon size representing counties, towns, or boroughs. If they bear arms while not proceeding to or from scheduled exercises of the Militia, they will be punished "as a court martial may direct."

3. that any gun owner who declines to join the regulated Militia may opt out by selling his firearms to the federal government for $1,000 each. He will sign an undertaking that if he ever again owns firearms he will be considered to have enlisted in the Militia.

4. that because the Constitution specifically requires that the Militia shall be "well regulated," a regular training program, of the sort familiar to all who have belonged to military units charged with the orderly management of small arms, shall be instituted. This will require at least eight hours of drill each Saturday at some convenient field or park, rain or shine or snow or ice. There will be weekly supervised target practice (separation from the service, publicly announced, for those who can't hit a barn door). And there will be ample practice in digging simple defense works, like foxholes and trenches, as well as necessary sanitary installations like field latrines and straddle trenches. Each summer there will be a six-week bivouac (without spouses), and this, like all the other exercises, will be under the close supervision of long-service noncommissioned officers of the United States Army and the Marine Corps. On bivouac, liquor will be forbidden under extreme penalty, but there will be an issue every Friday night of two cans of 3.2 beer, and feeding will follow traditional military lines, the cuisine consisting largely of shit-on-a-shingle, sandwiches made of bull dick (baloney) and choke-ass (cheese), beans, and fatty pork. On Sundays and holidays, powdered eggs for breakfast. Chlorinated water will often be available, in Lister Bags. Further obligatory exercises designed to toughen up the Militia will include twenty-five-mile hikes and the negotiation of obstacle courses. In addition, there will be instruction of the sort appropriate to other lightly armed, well-regulated military units: in map-reading, the erection of double-apron barbed-wire fences, and the rudiments of military courtesy and the traditions of the Militia, beginning with the Minute Men. Per diem payments will be made to those participating in these exercises.

5. that since the purpose of the Militia is, as the Constitution says, to safeguard "the security of a free state," at times when invasion threatens (perhaps now the threat will come from Nicaragua, national security no longer being menaced by North Vietnam) all units of the Militia will be trucked to the borders for the duration of the emergency, there to remain in field conditions (here's where the practice in latrine-digging pays off) until Congress declares that the emergency has passed. Congress may also order the Militia to perform other duties consistent with its constitutional identity as a regulated volunteer force: for example, flood and emergency and disaster service (digging, sandbag filling, rescuing old people); patrolling angry or incinerated cities; or controlling crowds at large public events like patriotic parades, motor races, and professional football games.

6. that failure to appear for these scheduled drills, practices, bivouacs, and mobilizations shall result in the Militiaperson's dismissal from the service and forfeiture of badge, pay, and firearm.

Why did the Framers of the Constitution add the word *bear* to the 5
phrase "keep and bear arms"? Because they conceived that keeping arms at home implied the public obligation to bear them in a regulated way for "the security of" not a private household but "a free state." If interstate bus fares can be regulated, it is hard to see why the Militia can't be, especially since the Constitution says it must be. The *New Republic* has recognized that "the Second Amendment to the Constitution clearly connects the right to bear arms to the eighteenth-century national need to raise a militia." But it goes on: "That need is now obsolete, and so is the amendment." And it concludes: "If the only way this country can get control of firearms is to amend the Constitution, then it's time for Congress to get the process under way."

I think not. Rather, it's time not to amend Article II of the Bill of 6
Rights (and Obligations) but to read it, publicize it, embrace it, and enforce it. That the Second Amendment stems from concerns that can be stigmatized as "eighteenth-century" cuts little ice. The First Amendment stems precisely from such concerns, and no one but yahoos wants to amend it. Also "eighteenth-century" is that lovely bit in Section 9 of Article I forbidding any "Title of Nobility" to be granted by the United States. That's why we've been spared Lord Annenberg and Sir

Leonard Bernstein, Knight.[1] Thank God for the eighteenth century, I say. It understood not just what a firearm is and what a Militia is. It also understood what "well regulated" means. It knew how to compose a constitutional article and it knew how to read it. And it assumed that everyone, gun lobbyists and touring students alike, would understand and correctly quote it. Both halves of it.

VOCABULARY/USING A DICTIONARY

1. What part of speech is *customarily* (para. 2)? What does it mean?
2. What is the difference between *infer* (para. 2) and *imply* (para. 5)?
3. What does it mean if something is *obligatory* (para. 4)?

RESPONDING TO WORDS IN CONTEXT

1. What is *rhetoric* (para. 1)? Do you think it pairs well with *languages*, as Fussell pairs them?
2. What is a *dependent clause* (para. 2)? How can you tell from the example Fussell uses?
3. What might Fussell mean by *seductive vagueness* (para. 2)? How is the belt buckle he refers to an example of it?

DISCUSSING MAIN POINT AND MEANING

1. What does Fussell note about the NRA's use of the Second Amendment?
2. Does Fussell expect that the NRA will be interested in the incorporation of a Militia (the details of which he has carefully outlined)? How can you tell?
3. Why did the framers of the Constitution add the word *bear* to the phrase "keep and bear arms"?

EXAMINING SENTENCES, PARAGRAPHS, AND ORGANIZATION

1. Is it important that Fussell mentions the NRA building in the early part of his essay? Why? What would happen if he didn't mention it?
2. How does Fussell use humor in his essay? Where is he being serious?
3. Fussell sets off numbered points in the middle of his essay when describing a militia. Is this technique effective? Why or why not?

---

[1] Lord Annenberg . . . Knight (para. 6): Walter H. Annenberg (1908–2002) was a controversial billionaire publisher, known both for his philanthropy and for using his publication for direct personal or political ends; Leonard Bernstein (1918–1990) was a massively influential composer whose many works include the score for *West Side Story*.

THINKING CRITICALLY

1. Do you think the Second Amendment should be taken literally? Do you think the proposal and raising of such a militia was possible in 1981 (or that Fussell thinks it's possible)? Do you think it is possible now?
2. Do you think Fussell is for or against gun control? Explain your answer using examples from the text to support your thinking.
3. **Connect:** In Glanton's essay "Stop Saying We Can't Do Anything to Stop Mass Shootings. We Can." (p. 253), she quotes a gun owner who says, "As long as AR-15s are legal, no one can tell me that I can't own one. . . . But if they were illegal, I would be the first to give mine up." Do you think this gun owner would be willing to be part of Fussell's Militia? Why or why not? Do Fussell and Glanton share similar ideas at any point? Where?

WRITING ACTIVITIES

1. No matter where you stand on gun control, write a response to Fussell's piece. You can either take his words literally and write your response or write a similarly humorous response.
2. Do you think we've learned anything about guns and gun control legislation and about how to interpret the Second Amendment since 1981? Explain your answer in writing. You might choose to look at some of the scenarios (gun supporter t-shirts) and events Fussell mentions and bring in some that you can think of from current events.
3. Where do you stand on gun control? Try writing an introduction that leads to your thesis statement on the topic — but use an avenue similar to Fussell's. Begin with a description or narration that winds its way to your position (use Fussell's opener as a model).

Discussing the Unit

SUGGESTED TOPIC FOR DISCUSSION

Should we take the wording in the Second Amendment at face value? What would a literal interpretation look like? This chapter includes essays that present arguments made by writers both for and against gun control. Some believe that the Second Amendment provides us with the right to own — and carry — guns for our protection, at any time, in any place. Others believe that hazards are associated with citizens' owning guns and that relaxed gun laws decrease public safety. Still others question how to interpret the Second Amendment. There are also arguments about how we should respond to gun violence and mass shootings.

PREPARING FOR CLASS DISCUSSION

1. Do you believe it is inherently dangerous for a person to be able to own a gun? Why or why not? What rules, if any, do you think should be in place for purchasing, owning, and carrying a gun? Are you concerned about gun violence? Why or why not?
2. What are some of the reasons for wanting to own a gun? Does owning a gun make the owner safer or put him or her in more danger? Explain your answer.

FROM DISCUSSION TO WRITING

1. What do you think the Second Amendment means? Write a short paper in which you examine the wording of the Second Amendment and explain what right(s) you think it secures, and why. Choose two essays from this section to support your interpretation of the Second Amendment.
2. The current debate is over not only gun ownership but the right to carry a gun in public places, either as a concealed weapon or as open carry. How do the authors in this chapter debate this issue? In a comparison paper, show how two of the authors in this chapter argue for and against carrying guns in public. Which viewpoint do you agree with most, and why?

TOPICS FOR CROSS-CULTURAL DISCUSSION

1. Do any of the articles in this chapter address the question of inner-city violence in their examination of gun rights and the gun debate? What about mass shootings—school shootings in particular? Which ones look at this issue and how would you characterize their arguments? What aspect of the gun question is their focus? In a short response, address these questions using specific passages from the essays as examples.
2. Do any of these authors describe what the issues might have been when the Founding Fathers drafted the Second Amendment? How have our reasons for wanting to own or carry a gun changed? Where in these essays are examples of the change in our lives and thinking most apparent?

8

Feminism Today: What Are the Challenges?

It's hardly controversial to say that women have faced a long, difficult journey in America. From the Salem witch trials to the suffrage movement, women confronted systematic legal oppression and discrimination at just about every juncture of American history. Many people forget that it was not until 1920 that—after persistent demonstrations—women finally won the right to vote. As they strove to be treated equally in the workforce, they hurdled an enormous cultural and social obstacle as well. But have women finally arrived as equals to men in American culture, or is there still a long way to go?

Many contemporary supporters of the rights of women have taken to Twitter and tumblr with the phrase "I need feminism because . . ." to remind us that oppression still exists within what they call the "patriarchy," or the male-dominated traditional hierarchy of American power. Like the advocacy for minorities we observed in Chapter 6, today's feminist movement often seeks to point out hidden, systemic forms of oppression although obvious ones still exist. For example, after the 2018 midterms, newly elected women to the Massachusetts legislature were often publicly mistaken for aides. Feminists often point out that, though major legal battles like suffrage may be over, forms of gender inequality persist in daily life. Most recently, the highly publicized #MeToo movement has reawakened feminism and alerted the nation to these many inequalities, especially in the workplace.

This chapter will examine some of the leading issues associated with feminism and the feminist movement today.

We Should All Be Feminists

[*Harper's Bazaar*, May 2017]

Edward Berthelot/Getty Images

Advertisements and commercials often try to link their products to popular social and political movements. For example, during the late 1960s and early 1970s, tobacco companies tried to associate their products with the new wave of feminism by telling women smokers "You've Come a Long Way, Baby!" Numerous "green" products today hope to persuade consumers that their brands conscientiously support the environment. Identifying an advertised product with a favorable social cause is a form of cultural appropriation that sociologists and economists have termed co-option. Many cultural critics and activists oppose this tactic of commercializing a political cause or marketing a serious social movement in order to sell products. Through co-option, a non–profit-seeking socially conscious cause can be used to serve corporate purposes.

Advertisements for the Dior T-shirt pictured here began appearing in luxury women's magazines like Harper's Bazaar *in 2017. The ads had no text or captions — but the message was clearly conveyed by the T-shirt: "We should all be feminists." A number of Web sites selling shirts with the same message promoted them this way: "No matter if you're male or female, this shirt shows that we should all be feminists. Grab this shirt as a gift for your mom, dad, brother, sister, girlfriend or boyfriend and show the world your feminist pride."*

POINTS TO CONSIDER

1. What do you think the image is intended to represent? Aside from the T-shirt's message, what fashion statement do you think Dior hopes to convey?
2. This photo shows someone attending Paris Fashion Week in the shirt. Why, do you think, would a person choose to wear it to a high-profile event?
3. Consider the message "We Should All Be Feminists." How do you interpret it? Do you think it represents the commercialization of a serious social and political movement, a form of "co-option" as defined above? Why or why not? Could the message be construed as "We Should All Be Feminists — Even Me"?

Suzanna Danuta Walters

Why Can't We Hate Men?

[*The Washington Post*, June 8, 2018]

One of the most provocative opinion essays published in 2018 appeared in the Washington Post. *"Why Can't We Hate Men?," by sociology professor Suzanna Danuta Walters, received an outpouring of responses. A reaction at first to the abusive behavior of several male celebrities then in the news, the essay goes on to the larger issue of male domination in general. Walters does not mince her words: Given what we see in the world around us, "it seems logical to hate men." "I can't lie," she continues, "I've always had a soft spot for the radical feminist smackdown, for naming the problem in no uncertain terms."*

Suzanna Danuta Walters is a sociology professor and the director of the Women's, Gender, and Sexuality Studies Program at Northeastern University. She is also the editor of Signs, *a gender studies journal.*

BEFORE YOU READ

Why might women, as a group, be angry with men? Do you think women are taught not to be angry with (or hate) men?

WORDS TO LEARN

prerogative (para. 1): a privilege unique to an individual or to a particular group (noun)
obfuscation (para. 2): the act of muddling something to the point of confusion (noun)
decry (para. 3): to express disapproval of (verb)
permeate (para. 5): to pass through (verb)
inequities (para. 6): injustices (noun)
endemic (para. 7): particular to an area (adjective)
succor (para. 8): help; aid (noun)

It's not that Eric Schneiderman (the now-former New York attorney general accused of abuse by multiple women) pushed me over the edge. My edge has been crossed for a long time, before President Trump, before Harvey Weinstein, before "mansplaining" and "incels." Before live-streaming sexual assaults and red pill men's groups and rape camps as a tool of war and the deadening banality of male prerogative. 1

Seen in this indisputably true context, it seems logical to hate men. I can't lie, I've always had a soft spot for the radical feminist smackdown, for naming the problem in no uncertain terms. I've rankled at the "but we don't hate men" protestations of generations of would-be feminists and found the "men are not the problem, this system is" obfuscation too precious by half. 2

But, of course, the criticisms of this blanket condemnation of men — from transnational feminists who decry such glib universalism to U.S. women of color who demand an intersectional perspective — are mostly on the mark. These critics rightly insist on an analysis of male power as institutional, not narrowly personal or individual or biologically based in male bodies. Growing movements to challenge a masculinity built on domination and violence and to engage boys and men in feminism are both gratifying and necessary. Please continue. 3

But this recognition of the complexity of male domination (how different it can be in different parts of the world, how racism shapes it) should not — must not — mean we forget some universal facts. 4

Pretty much everywhere in the world, this is true: Women experience sexual violence, and the threat of that violence permeates our choices big and small. In addition, male violence is not restricted to intimate-partner attacks or sexual assault but plagues us in the form of terrorism and mass gun violence. Women are underrepresented in higher-wage jobs, local and federal government, business, educational leadership, etc.; wage inequality continues to permeate every economy and almost every industry; women continue to provide far higher rates of unpaid labor in the home (e.g., child care, elder care, care for disabled individuals, housework and food provision); women have less access to education, particularly at the higher levels; women have lower rates of property ownership. 5

The list goes on. It varies by country, but these global realities — of women's economic, political, social and sexual vulnerabilities — are, well, real. Indeed, the nations in which these inequities have been radically minimized (e.g., Iceland) are those in which deliberate effort has been made to both own up to gender disparities and to address them directly and concretely. 6

So, in this moment, here in the land of legislatively legitimated toxic masculinity, is it really so illogical to hate men? For all the power of #MeToo and #TimesUp and the women's marches, only a relatively few men have been called to task, and I've yet to see a mass wave of prosecutions or even serious recognition of wrongdoing. On the contrary, cries of "witch hunt" and the plotted resurrection of celebrity offenders came quick on the heels of the outcry over endemic sexual harassment and 7 violence. But we're not supposed to hate them because . . . #NotAllMen. I love Michelle Obama as much as the next woman, but when they have gone low for all of human history, maybe it's time for us to go all Thelma and Louise and Foxy Brown on their collective butts.

The world has little place for feminist anger. Women are supposed 8
to support, not condemn, offer succor not dismissal. We're supposed to feel more empathy for your fear of being called a harasser than we are for the women harassed. We are told he's with us and #NotHim. But, truly, if he were with us, wouldn't this all have ended a long time ago? If he really were with us, wouldn't he reckon that one good way to change structural violence and inequity would be to refuse the power that comes with it?

But, truly, if he were with us, wouldn't this all have ended a long time ago?

So men, if you really are #WithUs and would like us to not hate you 9
for all the millennia of woe you have produced and benefited from, start with this: Lean out so we can actually just stand up without being beaten down. Pledge to vote for feminist women only. Don't run for office. Don't be in charge of anything. Step away from the power. We got this. And please know that your crocodile tears won't be wiped away by us anymore. We have every right to hate you. You have done us wrong. #BecausePatriarchy. It is long past time to play hard for Team Feminism. And win.

VOCABULARY/USING A DICTIONARY

1. How do you define the terms "mansplaining" and "incels" (para. 1)?
2. What part of speech is *banality* (para. 1)? How would you respond to something *banal*?
3. If someone is known to be *glib* (para. 3), what kind of words might he or she speak?

RESPONDING TO WORDS IN CONTEXT

1. Note how Walters uses the word *violence* in paragraph 5. What is her purpose in saying that "male violence is not restricted to intimate-partner attacks or sexual assault"?
2. Look at the word *intersectional* (para. 3) in the context of its sentence. What do you think an *intersectional perspective* might consist of?
3. Walters uses the phrase "masculinity built on *domination* and violence" (para. 3). How might you define *domination* based on your understanding of its cognates and/or its pairing with the word *violence*?

DISCUSSING MAIN POINT AND MEANING

1. What are the "universal facts" Walters refers to in her fourth paragraph?
2. What case does Walters make for women's anger in paragraph 8?
3. Who is Walters speaking to in this essay? What does her title question assume? Who says women can't hate men?

EXAMINING SENTENCES, PARAGRAPHS, AND ORGANIZATION

1. Note the essay's title: Why do you think Walters phrased it as a question?
2. Identify a sentence, or at most three sentences, that answer Walters's question as to "why we can't hate men."
3. What is the tone or diction of phrases like "wouldn't he reckon" (para. 8) and "we got this" (para. 9)? Are they effective in Walters's essay?

THINKING CRITICALLY

1. What point do you think Walters establishes in paragraph 3? Why does she introduce criticism of a "blanket condemnation of men" since that is what she is doing in the essay? In what sense are the criticisms she mentions "mostly on the mark"? Do you think she undermines her argument by introducing these criticisms?
2. Why do you think Walters addresses men directly in her final paragraph? What is she asking men to do? Do you think men will be persuaded? Explain why or why not.
3. **Connect:** Walters describes being "pushed . . . over the edge" by various affronts and injustices done to women. Do you think the affront or injustice presented in Nelson's essay ("Barbie Is Exploiting Frida Kahlo's Legacy," p. 284) would also push Walters over the edge? How do you think she'd respond to the introduction of the Kahlo Barbie, the subject of Nelson's article?

WRITING ACTIVITIES

1. The term "mansplaining" was coined by Rebecca Solnit in her book *Men Explain Things to Me*. Either research the book and read the excerpt that was published in *Guernica* magazine in 2008, or research Solnit and the response to her essay and book. Write a brief essay that compares Solnit's message and tone to Walters's message and tone. Quote (and cite) from any source you use to illustrate your comparison.
2. Do you think that Walters's list of women's inequities in paragraph 5 are appropriate examples of violence? Argue for or against these examples as valid illustrations of violence against women. You may want to revisit question 1 in "Responding to Words in Context" and reflect on Walters's definition.

3. Walters's last paragraph is written directly to her male readers. First, change the paragraph so that the ideas are the same sentence to sentence, but make it an address to women about what men should do to avoid being hated. Then go back to the original and try to rewrite it so that it's *not* a direct address (so it's more of a third-person objective paragraph) but still discusses the same ideas. Do not change the ideas — just the perspective and the direction of the address!

Roxanne Roberts

In the Middle

[*The Washington Post Magazine*, October 21, 2018]

If we take the previous selection literally, does that mean that women in pursuit of gender equality should hate husbands, fathers, grandfathers, uncles, nephews, and even their own sons? That involves quite a lot of hating within just a family alone. Although she agreed with much of what Walters wrote, Roxanne Roberts — writing also for the Washington Post *— does not consider her twenty-five-year-old son an enemy but rather a potential solution to the problems the #MeToo movement has identified. In her essay "In the Middle," Roberts makes a case for women "who are grateful for Me Too but worry that a movement intended to protect and elevate women can be contemptuous of, and indifferent to, what happens to men — in the same way that men have been contemptuous of, and indifferent to, the fate of women."*

Roxanne Roberts is a feature writer and columnist for the Washington Post. *Note that the following selection is the opening section of a much longer essay.*

BEFORE YOU READ

How much do you know about the wave of feminism that took place before #MeToo? Should mothers of the young adults growing up during the #MeToo movement play a role in the direction of that movement?

WORDS TO LEARN

consensual (para. 7): existing by agreement (adjective)

torrent (para. 8): a rushing stream (noun)

contemptuous (para. 8): scornful (adjective)

inherently (para. 13): innately (adverb)

emphatically (para. 16): insistently or expressively (adverb)

Mom. My 25-year-old son looked up from his phone. "Have you seen this Aziz Ansari story?" It was a Sunday morning on a holiday weekend, which meant pancakes instead of headlines, a rare chance to spend the day untethered to the news. "No," I said. "What's up?" 1

In an online article, "Grace," a New York photographer, described meeting the "Master of None" star at a 2017 Emmy Awards after-party — a glamorous moment of flirting that led to dinner at a restaurant near his New York apartment a week later. Afterward, they walked back to his place, where things escalated quickly: one kiss, two naked bodies and then oral sex. 2

There followed a series of moves that were, according to Grace, not at all sexy. There was more oral sex, but no intercourse because she told him she wasn't ready. So they put on their clothes and watched an episode of "Seinfeld." Ansari kissed her again, and that's when Grace, 22, decided this was a horrible date. "You guys are all the same," she told him in frustration. She sobbed the whole ride home. 3

Ansari texted Grace the next day, saying it was fun meeting her. She responded that he had ignored her nonverbal cues and made her cry. "I'm so sad to hear this," he wrote back. "Clearly, I misread things in the moment and I'm truly sorry." 4

My son stopped reading. "What do you think?" he asked me. 5

The two of us have been talking about sex — and love, girls, kindness, responsibility and smart choices — for years. I thought about what it was like to be a 22-year-old woman on a first date, with a celebrity no less. I remembered that emotional roller coaster of dating — the hope, awkwardness and then realization that this person was not Mr. Right or even Mr. Right Now. "I think," I answered carefully, "that I would have said, 'I'm not comfortable with this' and gone home." But that's not what Grace did. After talking to friends, she concluded that Ansari had sexually assaulted her. She then shared her anger and hurt in an explicit, 3,000-word article that went viral. 6

In the midst of the Me Too revolution, Grace's story created a firestorm. Supporters backed her with the fury of avenging angels, citing the selfishness and entitlement of men. Detractors questioned whether Ansari, who maintained that the encounter was consensual, really deserved a public execution. 7

In the torrent of words, there were few voices of women in the middle. Women who know what harassment, humiliation and obnoxious dates feel like because they've lived through that and much worse. But women who are also mothers — or sisters, wives and daughters — who believe 8 that what happened between Grace and Ansari was a bad date, not a sexual assault. Women who are grateful for Me Too but worry that a movement intended to protect and elevate women can be contemptuous of, and indifferent to, what happens to men — in the same way that men have been contemptuous of, and indifferent to, the fate of women. I'm a woman; I'm the mother of a son. Why does it feel like I have to choose?

In the torrent of words, there were few voices of women in the middle.

During the past year, I've found myself on the sidelines of a war where the battles are played out with anger and tears and accusations, with cries for justice and due process. I've watched women and men belittle each other, all convinced they're right. I've listened with hope and despair, and I've found myself agreeing with both sides for different reasons. 9

Through it all, I've come to believe that mothers of sons may be in a unique position in the Me Too revolution: We have experienced the injustices of living in the world as women. We also see our sons as individuals who deserve to be judged on their merits and actions, not merely on their gender. 10

Yet if mothers of sons are the tuning forks of this cultural moment, then the pitch is badly off. In the cases of Harvey Weinstein, Matt Lauer, Les Moonves, Kevin Spacey and Charlie Rose, justice was swift, decisive and, by most accounts, richly deserved. But what about someone like former senator Al Franken of Minnesota, who was pressured to resign before any investigation was conducted? Or the bitter fight over newly confirmed Supreme Court Justice Brett Kavanaugh, where the truth was unknowable? And what are we to think of the millions of men — young, old and everything in between — who are afraid to say or do the wrong thing, even when they're not exactly sure what that means anymore? 11

Like most women, I view Me Too as a huge, overdue win for equality. The right to pursue a career without gender discrimination, the right to receive equal pay for equal work, the right to call out unwelcome and inappropriate sexual overtures, the fact that women feel able to openly talk about these issues without fear of retaliation — all this is groundbreaking and important, a gift to the next generation, both our daughters and our sons. 12

But over the past year, amid all the justifiable anger and solidarity, I find myself unsettled by the undercurrent of intolerance and resistance to anything that doesn't neatly fit narratives of men exploiting their privilege and power. That women are always victims and men always 13 oppressors. That women are universally to be believed and men are inherently untrustworthy. That feelings are more important than facts.

“I’ve had conversations with women who say, ‘Okay, maybe he’s innocent. But they did it to us so we’re going to do it to them,’” says Anne-Marie Slaughter, president of the New America Foundation. “And I’m like, ‘No. *No*.’ That’s not how I raised my children. Two wrongs don’t make a right.” 14

Slaughter rocketed to fame with her 2012 essay for the *Atlantic*, “Why Women Still Can’t Have It All,” about the difficulty of juggling her high-powered career, marriage and two teenage boys. She’s watching them, now college-aged, in this Me Too moment — keenly aware of both its strengths and its weaknesses. 15

“There are institutional structures of power, and I’m very attentive to them,” she told me. “But our goal has to be real equality for men and women. And that means procedures that do not presume either side is innocent or guilty.” As women, she and I emphatically agree, we want to be treated fairly. As mothers, we want our daughters and sons to be treated fairly. Whether that’s possible is the question that keeps us awake at night. 16

VOCABULARY/USING A DICTIONARY

1. What part of speech is *belittle* (para. 9)?
2. What is a *pendulum* (para. 32)?

RESPONDING TO WORDS IN CONTEXT

1. What does Roberts mean when she says “Grace’s” article *went viral* (para. 6)? What is the usual meaning of *viral*?
2. What is the meaning of *overdue* in paragraph 12? What other meanings does that word have in other contexts?
3. What does it mean in paragraph 19 for a student to be *reinstated* in the university? Can you give a definition of *instated*?

DISCUSSING MAIN POINT AND MEANING

1. Is it important for readers to know Roberts’s son’s age? What difference does it make?
2. Explain the author’s dilemma in this selection. In what sort of “middle” does she find herself?
3. What does the author like about the #MeToo movement? What does she find unsettling about it? How does she think the movement can be improved?

EXAMINING SENTENCES, PARAGRAPHS, AND ORGANIZATION

1. Consider Roberts's opening. Why do you think she begins with this particular conversation with her son? How does it set the stage for her remarks about the #MeToo movement?
2. Late in the article (which does not appear in the excerpt as printed in this book), Roberts includes the sentence: "Every woman I know has a story; every man wonders whether he ever crossed an invisible line." How does Roberts feel about the #MeToo movement? Can you discuss her position using this sentence as a guide?
3. Identify the quotations used in this argument. How many belong to supporters of #MeToo? How many belong to those who oppose or have doubts about the movement?

THINKING CRITICALLY

1. **Connect:** How do you think Roberts would respond to the Walters essay, "Why Can't We Hate Men?" (p. 275)?
2. Is it possible for women just not to raise rapists? Do you think men who assault women or just behave badly have their lives ruined by being held accountable? Discuss the black-or-white thinking that Roberts includes on both sides of the #MeToo question.

WRITING ACTIVITIES

1. Look up the word *feminist* in the dictionary. To whom does that word apply? Does it apply to you? Identify a well-known *feminist*, through research, common knowledge, or another way. Write a short paper discussing the beliefs, characteristics, and actions of the person you have chosen.
2. Research the Aziz Ansari story referenced in this article. Based on your research, does Roberts tell the whole story? Write a brief report on how her account of the story reflects what you've learned or how it leaves out certain elements (speculate on why this may be so).
3. Choose a current event or social issue that has meaning to you. Using Roberts's writing as a model, begin an article that examines this event or social issue with a personal anecdote that connects to the topic. In class, go over the introductions and ask if students feel they are more interested in hearing more or reading about this particular topic because of the personal narrative. Do they have any reservations about papers on such subjects that start off with a personal story, or is it an effective technique?

Amanda Nelson (student essay)

Barbie Is Exploiting Frida Kahlo's Legacy

[*PCC Courier*, July 16, 2018]

The following selection by Pasadena City College student Amanda Nelson picks up on the issue highlighted in the "In Brief" feature of this chapter: the commercial co-option of social and political movements. In the essay "Barbie Is Exploiting Frida Kahlo's Legacy," Nelson takes on the giant toy manufacturer Mattel, the Fortune 500 company that introduced its world-famous Barbie doll in 1959. Barbie had long been an object of feminist opposition mainly because the doll appeared to promote for young girls an extreme and unrealistic body type. When Mattel unveiled in the spring of 2018 a new doll representing the renowned Mexican artist and political activist Frida Kahlo as part of its "Inspiring Women" collection, it was too much for Nelson, who concludes her essay on Kahlo that she "deserves far more than to be commodified by the very capitalist institutions she scorned."

BEFORE YOU READ

What do you know about the artist Frida Kahlo and her work? Based on your knowledge of her, do you think Kahlo's a good candidate on which to model a Barbie? Why or why not?

WORDS TO LEARN

controversial (para. 2): given to controversy or dispute (adjective)
iconic (para. 3): widely recognized (adjective)
emblematic (para. 4): representative (adjective)
defiance (para. 4): combativeness (noun)
subversion (para. 4): the act of overthrowing something (noun)
biopic (para. 5): a biographical show (noun)
commodifies (para. 7): turns something into a commodity (verb)
fervently (para. 7): with warmth (adverb)

Her portrait adorns socks, purses, T-shirts, jewelry and even a distasteful tequila line. Now, the latest tarnish on the legacy of Frida Kahlo comes in the form of a Barbie doll. 1

Last week [March 6, 2018], Mattel released the controversial new doll bearing the late artist's name and likeness as part of their "Inspiring 2

Women" collection. Setting aside the claims from Kahlo's family that the corporation doesn't have the rights to use her image, the Frida doll does not represent the woman Kahlo was or the values she held.

Kahlo is an inspiration but it's difficult to believe that Mattel truly 3
has an interest in empowering young girls given their long history of belittling them. It is expected that the Frida doll has the typical extremely unrealistic body proportions of a Barbie. But, Mattel went even further in changing Kahlo's appearance by minimizing her iconic unibrow and completely omitting her upper lip hair.

Kahlo's embrace of her natural facial hair is emblematic of her defi- 4
ance against the status quo. Her independent spirit and unwillingness to relent to the oppressive standards of others are central tenets of how she lived her life. This subversion of western beauty ideals that she embodied also explains why so many women have been inspired by her.

As actress Salma Hayek, who portrayed Kahlo in the Academy 5
Award–nominated biopic *Frida,* stated in an Instagram post, "Frida Kahlo never tried to be or look like anyone else. She celebrated her uniqueness. How could they turn her into a Barbie?"

Mattel altered her image to make it 6
more palatable for the masses, something Kahlo never would have done. In doing so, they've both sent a message out that there was something wrong with how she naturally looked and also effectively ignored one of the reasons Kahlo is worthy of being included in groups of "Inspiring Women" in the first place. A Barbie with her true appearance may have inspired young girls to be unapologetically themselves as she was. Instead, Mattel's weak attempts at feminism still encourage them to comply with outdated and unreasonable physical standards.

> **Mattel altered her image to make it more palatable for the masses, something Kahlo never would have done.**

The Frida Barbie also further commodifies Kahlo's legacy and 7
reduces her to a cheap trend. Given the sea of material goods profiting off of her image, few are aware that Kahlo was a member of the Mexican Communist Party and fervently against consumerism. Attempts to honor her through sold merchandise contradict the beliefs she held.

She was a proud Mexican woman who detested colonialism and 8
wasn't very fond of American culture and how it's dominated by capitalism. She was even quoted as saying, "I don't like the gringos at all," after a visit to San Francisco. Mattel, an American company whose corporate leadership consists entirely of white people, has joined the succession of companies exploiting her image with little acknowledgment of her convictions.

Yes, her image is striking and beautiful but beyond Kahlo's portraits lies a complex, intelligent, strong woman. Reducing her to only a face ignores the deeper meanings in her artwork. The popularity of her image has risen greatly but attempts to truly understand what she stood for have stagnated. Her legacy should be expanded instead of merely serving as a trend for consumers. She deserves far more than to be commodified by the very capitalist institutions she scorned. 9

VOCABULARY/USING A DICTIONARY

1. What does it mean if there is a *tarnish* (para. 1) on something?
2. How do you define *unibrow* (para. 3)? What might be a clue to the definition?
3. What language is *status quo* (para. 4)? How do you define it?

RESPONDING TO WORDS IN CONTEXT

1. Paragraph 3 begins: "Kahlo is an inspiration but it's difficult to believe that Mattel truly has an interest in *empowering* young girls given their long history of *belittling* them." How do you define *empowering* and *belittling*? Are they antonyms?
2. "The popularity of her image has risen greatly but attempts to truly understand what she stood for have *stagnated*" (para. 9). In the context of this sentence, how would you define *stagnated*?
3. If Mattel altered Frida Barbie's appearance to make it more *palatable* (para. 6), but the real Kahlo never would have, what do you think Mattel is doing to it?

DISCUSSING MAIN POINT AND MEANING

1. What do you think Nelson means by Frida Kahlo's "legacy" (para. 9)?
2. In what way was Mattel attempting to advance feminist causes with its Barbie?
3. Why is Nelson upset about what Mattel has done to Kahlo's legacy?

EXAMINING SENTENCES, PARAGRAPHS, AND ORGANIZATION

1. Flip paragraphs 2 and 1 and read the essay that way. What is the effect of starting with paragraph 2 and how does it compare with the effect achieved by starting with paragraph 1? Why might Nelson have chosen paragraph 1 for her introduction?
2. Nelson writes, "Kahlo is an inspiration but it's difficult to believe that Mattel truly has an interest in empowering young girls given their long history

of belittling them" (para. 3) and "The popularity of her image has risen" greatly but attempts to truly understand what she stood for have stagnated (para. 9). Describe and discuss the structure of these sentences and why Nelson puts them together in this way.

THINKING CRITICALLY

1. What does Nelson mean by "Mattel's weak attempts at feminism" (para 6)? Do you think the doll hurts or helps feminism?
2. Where does Nelson touch on race and ethnicity in this article? Do you agree that they play a role in how this doll is problematic?
3. **Connect:** Consider this article in the light of Roberts's essay ("In the Middle," p. 279) about the #MeToo movement. Do you think Nelson would be sympathetic to Roberts? Do you think Nelson would align herself with #MeToo? What in her article leads you to think so?

WRITING ACTIVITIES

1. In writing, discuss Nelson's primary objections to the Frida Barbie. Do you think if Mattel had made a Barbie that more closely resembled Frida Kahlo the author would be in favor of it?
2. Do some research on Kahlo and her paintings. Find a painting that particularly interests you, and write a response to the artwork.
3. Nelson writes, "Yes, her image is striking and beautiful but beyond Kahlo's portraits lies a complex, intelligent, strong woman" (para. 9). She also talks about Mattel's conception of beauty. In a short assignment, write your thoughts on beauty and how they are similar to or different from those of Nelson (about Kahlo) or of Mattel.

LOOKING CLOSELY

Effective Persuasion: Expressing an Opinion Clearly and Emphatically

Although we should try to arrive at our opinions by openly exposing ourselves to conflicting or opposing opinions, that does not mean that once we have formed an opinion we cannot express it forcefully and passionately. Often, as many writers, activists, and political leaders know, persuasion may require a direct, personal, and unambiguous declaration of where we stand on an issue.

Note how Pasadena City College student Amanda Nelson opens her essay on the recent release of a Barbie doll based on one of the most famous feminist artists of the twentieth century. Nelson clearly finds the doll an outrageous form of exploitation and the opening of her essay clearly establishes her attitude. Note, too, that she accomplishes this without using the first person "I" or saying "I think" or "In my opinion." How might that enhance the emphasis?

1 *Establishes exploitation*

(1) Her portrait adorns socks, purses, T-shirts, jewelry, and even a distasteful tequila line. Now, the latest tarnish on the legacy of Frida Kahlo comes in the form of a Barbie doll.

2 *What inspired her essay*

(2) Last week [March 6, 2018], Mattel released the controversial new doll bearing the late artist's name and likeness as part of their "Inspiring Women" collection.

3 *Emphatically expresses her opinion*

(3) Setting aside the claims from Kahlo's family that the corporation doesn't have the rights to use her image, the Frida doll does not represent the woman Kahlo was or the values she held.

SPOTLIGHT ON DATA AND RESEARCH

Elizabeth Aura McClintock

The Psychology of Mansplaining

[*Psychology Today*, March 31, 2016]

In 2008, noted author and activist Rebecca Solnit published a now-classic essay, "Men Explain Things to Me." In her 2014 book of that title, she recalls that after the essay appeared, a "website named 'Academic Men Explain Things to Me' arose, and hundreds of university women shared their stories of being patronized, belittled, talked over, and more." She goes on to say that the term mansplaining *was coined soon after, but she "had nothing to do with its actual creation," though her essay "apparently inspired" the coinage. In the following study from* Psychology Today, *University of Notre Dame professor and gender researcher Elizabeth Aura McClintock takes a close look at the new word and the not-so-new behavior it describes.*

In a recent episode of *Jimmy Kimmel Live*, Kimmel "mansplains" the art of political speech to Hillary Clinton. He begins by mansplaining the concept of mansplaining: 1

JK: Are you familiar with mansplaining? You know what that is?

HC: That's when a man explains something to a woman in a patronizing way.

JK: Actually, it's when a man explains something to a woman in a condescending way. But you were close.

Kimmel goes on to interrupt Clinton frequently, offering contradictory and sexist advice. Of course, he and Clinton were intentionally parodying the phenomenon of mansplaining, but it reminded me of a conversation I'd actually had the day before:

Man: How do you calculate the area of a rectangle?

Me: Length times width.

Man: No, base times height.

In retrospect, my answer *should* have been that of course I know that — I've taken several advanced calculus courses and I teach statistics — and who is he to quiz my basic geometry knowledge anyway? 2

Taken together, the Kimmel-Clinton skit and my own experience piqued my interest in mansplaining more generally. The term has only been around since 2008 (Rothman, 2012) but it has attracted a great deal of popular attention, making the long list as a contender for Oxford's word of the year (Steinmetz, 2014) and the short list in the American Dialect Society's "Most Creative" category (Zimmer, 2013). According to the *Oxford English Dictionary* editors, mansplaining is "to explain something to someone, typically a man to woman, in a manner regarded as condescending or patronizing" (Steinmetz, 2014). The American Dialect Society defines it as "when a man condescendingly explains something to female listeners" (Zimmer, 2013). Lily Rothman, in her "Cultural History of Mansplaining," elaborates it as "explaining without regard to the fact that the explainee knows more than the explainer, often done by a man to a woman." 3

Mansplaining as a portmanteau may be new, but the behavior has been around for centuries (Rothman, 2012). The scholarly literature has long documented gendered power differences in verbal interaction: Men are more likely to interrupt, particularly in an intrusive manner (Anderson and Leaper, 1998). Compared to men, women are more likely to *be* interrupted, both by men and by other women (Hancock and Rubin, 2015). Perhaps in part because they are accustomed to it, women also respond more amenably to interruption than men do, being 4 more likely to smile, nod, agree, laugh, or otherwise facilitate the conversation (Farley et al., 2010).

Interruptions matter: They are linked to social power — in dyadic 5
interactions, the more *powerful* partner is more likely to interrupt (Kollock et al., 1985). Unfortunately, researchers have tended to focus on easily quantifiable *aspects* of speech, rather than the *content* of speech. More research is needed to ascertain the extent to which the condescension mansplaining posits is indeed common and gendered (directed disproportionately by men toward women).

Mansplaining is problematic because the behavior itself reinforces 6
gender inequality. When a man explains something to a woman in a patronizing or condescending way, he reinforces gender stereotypes about women's presumed lesser knowledge and intellectual ability. This is especially true when the woman is in fact *more* knowledgeable on the subject. This aspect of mansplaining was central to the Kimmel-Clinton parody — clearly, Clinton has the greater expertise giving political speeches. It is also evident in Rebecca Solnit's tale of a man trying to explain her *own* book to her, despite not having read it himself. It was her essay, "Men Explain Things to Me," and the subsequent book that many credit for sparking the dialogue that ultimately generated the term *mansplaining*. (To my knowledge, Solnit herself did not use the word.) Having had numerous men explain *gender* to me — both in a general sense and as relates to my own research — I can sympathize with Solnit.

But mansplaining is also problematic in the gender-stereotypic 7
assumptions it makes about *men* (see Cookman, 2015). Misandry doesn't promote equality, nor does it undermine misogyny. Yes, mansplaining is sexist and boorish, but the term isn't fair to the many men who support gender equality (and don't mansplain). Moreover, men don't have a monopoly on arrogance or condescension — women are quite capable of both.

Mansplaining has caught the popular imagination because it pro- 8
vides a label for a common and offensive social reality: Women are often assumed to be ignorant and unintelligent, at least compared to men. Having a label for something is useful in that it makes it more visible, potentially working to erode both the behavior and the sexist assumptions that drive it. But it risks becoming a means of trivializing mansplaining as not worthy of real outrage and of degrading men generally (Cookman, 2015).

References

Anderson and Leaper. 1998. "Meta-Analysis of Gender Effects on Conversational Interruption: Who, What, When, Where, and Why." *Sex Roles* 39(3–4): 225–252.

Cookman. 2015. "Allow Me to Explain Why We Don't Need Words Like 'Mansplain.'" *The Guardian.*

Farley, Ashcroft, Stasson, and Nusbaum. 2010. "Nonverbal Reactions to Conversational Interruptions: A Test of Complementary Theory and Status/Gender Parallel." *Journal of Nonverbal Behavior* 34(4): 193–206.

Hancock and Rubin. 2015. "Influence of Communication Partner's Gender on Language." *Journal of Language and Social Psychology* 34(1): 46–64.

Jimmy Kimmel Live, March 24, 2016.

Kollock, Blumstein, and Schwartz. 1985. "Sex and Power in Interaction: Conversational Privileges and Duties." *American Sociological Review* 50(1): 34–46.

Rothman. 2012. "A Cultural History of Mansplaining." *The Atlantic.*

Solnit. 2008. "Men Explain Things to Me." *LA Times.*

Steinmetz. 2014. "Clickbait, Normcore, Mansplain: Runners-Up for Oxford's Word of the Year." *Time.*

Zimmer. 2013. "Tag, You're It! 'Hashtag' Wins as 2012 Word of the Year." *Visual Thesaurus.*

DRAWING CONCLUSIONS

1. Does McClintock establish that mansplaining is a real social problem? Do you believe that the examples she gives prove the issue exists? Do you believe in mansplaining? Why or why not?

2. Besides mansplaining, what imbalances do you perceive in the ways men and women communicate? Do men use communication to establish power dynamics? If so, how?

3. McClintock points out that research has focused on the quantifiable aspects of speech, not its content, in studying mansplaining. How would you propose scientifically studying the content of speech to quantify mansplaining, or for that matter "womansplaining," "whitesplaining," and so on? Imagine an experiment you might design.

Will McPhail

Mansplaining

[*The New Yorker*]

"I said, 'I wonder what it means,' not 'Tell me what it means.'"

Will McPhail/The Cartoon Bank/Conde Nast Publications

AMERICA THEN . . . 1972

Judy Brady

I Want a Wife

[*Ms.*, 1972]

If you were a college student taking composition in the 1970s, you would almost certainly have been assigned Judy Brady's "I Want a Wife." The short essay appeared in practically every composition anthology available. Published when the contemporary feminist movement was in its early stages and gaining members rapidly (it was then often referred to as "women's liberation" or, in a sometimes heckling tone, "women's lib"), the essay appropriately first appeared in the premier issue of what became the movement's leading magazine, Ms. *Although the essay is no longer anthologized to the extent it once was, some books still include it. Nearly fifty years later, with the goals and principles of feminism far more established across the nation, it is interesting to see what this now-classic essay means to today's college generation.*

Before the legendary essay appeared in Ms.*, "I Want a Wife" was delivered aloud for the first time in San Francisco in 1970 at a rally celebrating the fiftieth anniversary of women's right to vote in the United States. Brady (1937–2017) was an activist for women's causes and the environment.*

BEFORE YOU READ

Think about the terms *husband* and *wife*. Would you define them very differently? Have husband and wife stereotypes changed at all since 1972?

WORDS TO LEARN

incidentally (para. 1): by the way (adverb)

sympathize (para. 4): to express sympathy with (verb)

adherence (para. 7): attachment (noun)

liberty (para. 8): freedom (noun)

I belong to that classification of people known as wives. I am A Wife. And, not altogether incidentally, I am a mother. 1

Not too long ago a male friend of mine appeared on the scene fresh from a recent divorce. He had one child, who is, of course, with his ex-wife. He is looking for another wife. As I thought about him while I was ironing one evening, it suddenly occurred to me that I, too, would like to have a wife. Why do I want a wife? 2

I would like to go back to school so that I can become economically independent, support myself, and, if need be, support those dependent upon me. I want a wife who will work and send me to school. And while I am going to school I want a wife to take care of my children. I want a wife to keep track of the children's doctor and dentist appointments. And to keep track of mine, too. I want a wife to make sure my children eat properly and are kept clean. I want a wife who will wash the children's clothes and keep them mended. I want a wife who is a good nurturant attendant to my children, who arranges for their schooling, makes sure that they have an adequate social life with their peers, takes them to the park, the zoo, etc. I want a wife who takes care of the children when they are sick, a wife who arranges to be around when the children need special care, because, of course, I cannot miss classes at school. My wife 3 must arrange to lose time at work and not lose the job. It may mean a small cut in my wife's income from time to time, but I guess I can tolerate that. Needless to say, my wife will arrange and pay for the care of the children while my wife is working.

I want a wife who will take care of my physical needs. I want a wife who will keep my house clean. A wife who will pick up after my children, a wife who will pick up after me. I want a wife who will keep my clothes clean, ironed, mended, replaced when need be, and who will see to it that my personal things are kept in their proper place so that I can find what I need the minute I need it. I want a wife who cooks the meals, a wife who is a *good* cook. I want a wife who will plan the menus, do the necessary grocery shopping, prepare the meals, serve them pleasantly, and then do the cleaning up while I do my studying. I want a wife who will care for me when I am sick and sympathize with my pain and loss of time from school. I want a wife to go along when our family takes vacation so that someone can continue to care for me and my children when I need a rest and change of scene. 4

I want a wife who will not bother me with rambling complaints about a wife's duties. But I want a wife who will listen to me when I feel the need to explain a rather difficult point I have come across in my course of studies. And I want a wife who will type my papers for me when I have written them. 5

I want a wife who will take care of the details of my social life. When my wife and I are invited out by my friends, I want a wife who will take care of the babysitting arrangements. When I meet people at school that I like and want to entertain, I want a wife who will have the house clean, will prepare a special meal, serve it to me and my friends, and not interrupt when I talk about things that interest me and my friends. I want a wife who will have arranged that the children are fed and ready for bed before my guests arrive so that the children do not bother us. I want a wife who takes care of the needs of my guests so that they feel comfortable, who makes sure that they have an ashtray, that they are passed the hors d'oeuvres, that they are offered a second helping of the food, that their wine glasses are replenished when necessary, that their coffee is served to them as they like it. And I want a wife who knows that sometimes I need a night out by myself. 6

I want a wife who is sensitive to my sexual needs, a wife who makes love passionately and eagerly when I feel like it, a wife who makes sure that I am satisfied. And, of course, I want a wife who will not demand sexual attention when I am not in the mood for it. I want a wife who assumes the complete responsibility for birth control, because I do not want more children. I want a wife who will remain sexually faithful to 7 me so that I do not have to clutter up my intellectual life with jealousies. And I want a wife who understands that my sexual needs may entail more than strict adherence to monogamy. I must, after all, be able to relate to people as fully as possible.

If, by chance, I find another person more suitable as a wife than the wife I already have, I want the liberty to replace my present wife with another one. Naturally, I will expect a fresh, new life; my wife will take the children and be solely responsible for them so that I am left free. 8

When I am through with school and have a job, I want my wife to quit working and remain at home so that my wife can more fully and completely take care of a wife's duties. 9

My God, who *wouldn't* want a wife? 10

VOCABULARY/USING A DICTIONARY

1. How do you define *classification* (para. 1)?
2. What is the definition of *hors d'oeuvres* (para. 6) and from what language is it borrowed?
3. What is *monogamy* (para. 7)?

RESPONDING TO WORDS IN CONTEXT

1. What does it mean to be *economically independent* (para. 3)?
2. What's another way to say "I want a wife who is a *nurturant attendant*" (para. 3)?
3. If a wife is *solely responsible* (para. 8) for the children, does she share the responsibility?

DISCUSSING MAIN POINT AND MEANING

1. Why is Brady thinking about wanting a wife?
2. If Brady's wife were to write a job description for what she does, what would she say?
3. What is the value of a wife's job, according to Brady? What in the text supports your answer?

EXAMINING SENTENCES, PARAGRAPHS, AND ORGANIZATION

1. Note how often Brady starts her sentences with "I want a wife." That repetition is clearly the dominant stylistic element of the essay. Why do you think she repeats the words so often, and what effect do you think it is intended to have on a reader?

2. Writers often use humor to make a serious point. In what ways does humor contribute to the point of Brady's essay?

3. The first paragraph is three sentences long: "I belong to that classification of people known as wives. I am A Wife. And, not altogether incidentally, I am a mother." Why do you think Brady starts this way? Why do you think the "not altogether incidentally" indication that she is also a mother is included?

THINKING CRITICALLY

1. **Connect:** In your opinion, what stereotypes about husbands and wives does Brady rely on in her essay? Do you think she exaggerates? Do you think these stereotypes still apply to marriages today? How would Katha Pollitt ("Why Boys Don't Play with Dolls," p. 321) respond to these stereotypes in 1995? Would it be possible for Pollitt to substitute "wife" for "kid" in her statement: "That's why, if you look carefully, you'll find that for every ___ who fits a stereotype, there's another who's breaking one down"? Explain your answer.

2. In what ways do wife-hood and motherhood intersect? How is motherhood in 1972 different from fatherhood? Is it still so different?

3. Brady's essay leads to the question/realization: "My God, who *wouldn't* want a wife?" Why does everyone want one so much?

WRITING ACTIVITIES

1. Note that at the opening of her essay Brady wishes for a wife because she "would like to go back to school" (para. 3). How is this significant? What does it tell you about the era in which the essay was written? What does school have to do with Brady's main goal in the essay? How does her behavior toward her "wife" change once she imagines herself being in school? Write a brief response to these questions.

2. Write a short paper that begins each paragraph with a simple statement (it could be your thesis), or consider rewriting a paper you already have in process by implementing this technique. Do you think it's effective? Would it be more effective if it were repeated several times within a paragraph (the way Brady does it)? In small groups, discuss the effectiveness of this approach — where it is more and less effective.

3. Brady has given a good picture not only of what a wife is like but also of what a husband is like. In a brief essay, discuss what a husband is like, given Brady's text.

Discussing the Unit

SUGGESTED TOPIC FOR DISCUSSION

Have women and men achieved equality since the sexual revolution of the 1960s? If so, what has feminism achieved, and what has yet to be accomplished? What ideas are now (or still) affecting the future of feminism and its goals?

PREPARING FOR CLASS DISCUSSION

1. What does feminism mean, exactly? How would the authors included in this chapter define it?
2. How does the #MeToo movement intersect with feminism? Are we experiencing a backlash against feminism as the #MeToo movement grows? Do you think that backlash is fair or unfair, or are there elements of both fairness and unfairness? Is it all part of the struggle that continues from the movements in the 1960s and 1970s, or is it something separate? Explain your answers.

FROM DISCUSSION TO WRITING

1. Some writers in this chapter insist that not much has changed since the early days of the women's liberation movement. They say that women are still treated like second-class citizens despite advances in the workplace and at home. Find two authors who argue that women still have a long way to go in terms of pushing past discrimination in order to have the same rights and privileges as men, and compare their arguments.
2. How do men and women treat each other as "other"? Using examples from at least three essays in this chapter, analyze the ways in which men and women respond to each other differently.

TOPICS FOR CROSS-CULTURAL DISCUSSION

1. How does Brady describe having a wife? Have the roles changed at all over the last fifty years? How have they changed and how have they stayed the same? Find at least two other writers in this section whose ideas can be compared and contrasted with Brady's description. Do wives or women still fill the roles mentioned in Brady's essay?
2. Do you think the arguments being made by Roxanne Roberts or Elizabeth Aura McClintock come from a place of privilege, or are they representative of women across racial and socioeconomic lines? What might change about these arguments made by a person of color? Or made by someone from a different socioeconomic background? Would they remain the same? Why or why not?

9

Gender: What Are the Issues Today?

If you were a high school or college student in the 1950s, the term "gender" would have meant only one thing: If you studied Spanish, French, or other languages derived from Latin, you would need to know the *gender* of nouns for grammatical purposes. It had little to do with human sexuality — inanimate objects like ships, tables, books, knives all had (and still have) a linguistic gender, being either masculine or feminine. Back then, when people were asked on a form to identify as male or female, they were simply asked what sex they belonged to. But today, the term "gender" has taken on a social and cultural complexity that goes far beyond grammar, though as the opening selection to this chapter indicates, language still plays a role.

Many issues that involve feminist and gender studies overlap. For example, many research studies look at differences between males and females from a gender perspective; that is, they may examine how and why boys and girls tend to favor different kinds of toys and clothing or develop different patterns of behavior. One major concept behind such studies is that masculinity or femininity are learned behaviors that exert an enormous influence over people's lives. There is no reason that someone who may identify as biologically male must also identify as "masculine" (however the broader society and culture define that concept). The earlier stages of gender studies tended to focus more on gay and lesbian issues — on the

AIDS epidemic, discrimination, and the access to equal rights in such areas as marriage and adoption. More recently, the emphasis has turned to issues affecting the transgender community, which also faces discrimination, marginalization, and civil rights challenges.

In this chapter, we will take a close look at a variety of today's gender issues, ranging from the use of proper pronouns to sex-neutral parenting.

American Dialect Society

The Word of the Year Is Singular *They*

[*American Dialect Society*, January 8, 2016]

Gender, as mentioned earlier, is still linked with grammatical issues. In 2015, the American Dialect Society voted for the singular pronoun they *and, by extension,* them *and* their *(as in "Whoever is elected president will have their work cut out for them"), as its Word of the Year. Once considered grammatically incorrect, the use of* they *to replace* he or she *when the gender of the person spoken about is uncertain has gained acceptance. This chapter's "In Brief" feature highlights the vote, in which phrases like "on fleek" and "thanks, Obama" were runners-up that same year, and emphasizes the central role* they *now plays, particularly as "an identifier for someone who may identify as 'nonbinary' in gender terms."*

The American Dialect Society was founded in 1889. It describes itself on its Web site as "dedicated to the study of the English language in North America, and of other languages, or dialects of other languages, influencing it or influenced by it. Our members include academics and amateurs, professors and students, professionals and dilettantes, teachers and writers, undergraduates and graduates. Anyone can join the society!" Each year, the society invites its members to vote on a word or phrase they consider especially significant to American culture and society. In 2014, for example, the word of the year was #blacklivesmatter. *The following report announces the winner for 2015.*

In its 26th annual words of the year vote, the American Dialect Society voted for *they* used as a gender-neutral singular pronoun as the Word of the Year for 2015. *They* was recognized by the society for its emerging use as a pronoun to refer to a known person, often as a conscious choice by a person rejecting the traditional gender binary of *he* and *she*. 1

Presiding at the Jan. 8 voting session were ADS Executive Secretary Allan Metcalf of MacMurray College and Ben Zimmer, chair of the New Words Committee of the American Dialect Society. Zimmer is also executive editor of Vocabulary.com and language columnist for the *Wall Street Journal*. 2

The use of singular *they* builds on centuries of usage, appearing in the work of writers such as Chaucer, Shakespeare, and Jane Austen. In 3

2015, singular *they* was embraced by the *Washington Post* style guide. Bill Walsh, copy editor for the *Post*, described it as "the only sensible solution to English's lack of a gender-neutral third-person singular personal pronoun."

While editors have increasingly moved to accepting singular *they* when used in a generic fashion, voters in the Word of the Year proceedings singled out its newer usage as an identifier for someone who may identify as "nonbinary" in gender terms. 4

"In the past year, new expressions of gender identity have generated a deal of discussion, and singular *they* has become a particularly significant element of that conversation," Zimmer said. "While many novel gender-neutral pronouns have been proposed, *they* has the advantage of already being part of the language." 5

Word of the Year is interpreted in its broader sense as "vocabulary item" — not just words but phrases. The words or phrases do not have to be brand-new, but they have to be newly prominent or notable in the past year. 6

The vote is the longest-running such vote anywhere, the only one not tied to commercial interests, and *the* word-of-the-year event up to which all others lead. It is fully informed by the members' expertise in the study of words, but it is far from a solemn occasion. 7

Members in the 127-year-old organization include linguists, lexicographers, etymologists, grammarians, historians, researchers, writers, editors, students, and independent scholars. In conducting the vote, they act in fun and do not pretend to be officially inducting words into the English language. Instead, they are highlighting that language change is normal, ongoing, and entertaining. 8

In a companion vote, sibling organization the American Name Society voted "*Caitlyn Jenner*" as Name of the Year for 2015 in its eleventh annual name-of-the-year contest, to recognize issues relating to naming conventions in the transgender community. 9

POINTS TO CONSIDER

1. What would you pick as the Word of the Year for this year? Why?
2. Some people claim a grammatical reason for keeping *they* plural — good style, they assert, demands a distinction between singular and plural pronouns. What arguments can you see on their side? Do you agree? Why or why not?
3. Many activists claim that pronoun inclusivity needs to go further and that all people should be able to choose their own unique pronouns. What do you think? Are there limits to how specialized pronouns should be in order to make everyone feel comfortable? Why or why not?

Alex Myers

How #MeToo Taught Me I Can Never Be a Man

[*Them*, November 26, 2017]

The following essay illustrates some of the ways that gender and feminist issues intersect. In "How #MeToo Taught Me I Can Never Be a Man," Alex Myers, who grew up female but who identifies as male, writes about how his experiences as a girl and young woman have sensitized him to the everyday abuses — both physical and psychological — women continually face. Having had these experiences, he understands what the #MeToo movement is truly about. Although he identifies as male, he does not identify with male sexist behavior: "Though I might look like you, I refuse to talk like you," he writes. "I refuse to think and act like you. I refuse to easily accept the privilege that calling myself a man might confer."

A writer, teacher, and speaker, Alex Myers was the first openly transgender student at Phillips Exeter, where he currently teaches English, and Harvard University. He is the author of a novel, Revolutionary *(2014).*

BEFORE YOU READ

What does your gender say about you? Do you believe that your experiences are fundamentally different from those of someone who identifies as another gender?

WORDS TO LEARN

inescapably (para. 3): unavoidably (adverb)
compression (para. 4): to push into one area (verb)
enumerate (para. 8): to count, one by one (verb)
confer (para. 9): to consult (verb)
entail (para. 10): to involve or lead to (verb)

Since coming out in 1995, I've spoken to many audiences about being transgender in my role as an author and teacher. One common question on those occasions has always nagged at me: Given that people don't tend to read me as transgender, why do I insist on being so publicly out? My answer has shifted over the years, but the recent focus on the sexual harassment and assault that women face has given me my clearest answer. It's important that people know I grew up 1 as a girl and young woman because my experiences in that gender identity have shaped and still shape who I am today: someone who is not and will never be comfortable being called or considering myself a man.

I only lived 17 years as a girl and a young woman, and I grew up in a safe environment: a small Maine town with loving parents who raised me to speak up and be self-empowered. Though these factors do not shield one from sexual assault — nothing truly does — I am fortunate not to have suffered such abuse. 2

But as I read the #MeToo entries on social media sites and news outlets, they cast me back to my adolescent years. At 11, 12, 13, I was just outgrowing the category of tomboy that had granted me some self-explanation, and had given me a little room to maneuver in my childhood. I was just beginning to come into a body that, more and more, felt inescapably like a woman's. 3

I remember that body; how every woman I saw reminded me: I would grow up to look like them. I dreaded that future. Even more, my body suddenly became subject to public commentary, as if it were on display for others to evaluate. I remember hearing, "I wouldn't have thought you'd have bigger boobs than Ann," from one boy at school, as if my being a tomboy had any correlation to how large my chest would get. "You should wear a bra," I heard from a wide range of mothers and fathers of my friends. Eventually, I figured out a sort of proto-binder — at first a couple of undershirts, extra small, and later the kind of compression shirt worn when you've broken a rib — that I donned through the end of middle school and beyond. 4

When I went off to boarding school in ninth grade, it was an intense relief that most students didn't go to the dances, where I'd learned in middle school how much boys liked to press up against any girl they could; I was delighted that many of the girls in my dorm preferred to work on their history papers or watch *The Princess Bride* on a Saturday night. But I was having a hard time with math that year, and I remember telling an older student that I'd made an appointment to meet with my teacher. "Who do you have?" she asked me. I told her my teacher's name — let's just call him Mr. P. "Don't go by yourself," she warned. 5

I enlisted another girl from my dorm, I'll call her Donna, to come to tutoring with me, and the two of us sat side by side in the math classroom with Mr. P standing behind us. He put his hands on my shoulders and leaned his face between us as he commented on our work, occasionally touching Donna's arm and hand as she wrote out her solutions. He patted our backs and squeezed our shoulders as he told us about quadratic equations. I remember the two of us scurrying back to the dorm that night, giggling and chattering: *gross, weird, kind of nasty*. We 6 ran to the older girl, the one who had warned me about Mr. P, and she just rolled her eyes. "Come to me for help next time," she said, and then named a few other teachers we shouldn't go to alone.

7 And then there's the very impersonal. The catcalls and jeers. The comments shouted from passing cars or out of dorm room windows. The men on buses and subway cars who sat down too close, who couldn't seem to stay in their own seats or manage not to bump against me. There were so many, they all blur together. Sometimes I would jab back with an elbow. Sometimes I would cross to the other side of the street. Mostly, I walked quickly and tried to ignore it all.

8 This is incredibly mild. Milquetoast. I have had the easiest of times, both as a girl and as a boy. The experiences I have enumerated are barely enough to register on the Richter scale of harassment. And yet, these instances made some of the deepest impressions on me about what it means to be a girl and a woman in this world. This is what women are trained to expect as their due.

9 Now, I move through the world and pass as a man. I share offices and bus seats and locker rooms with men. I hear how men talk about women when they think there aren't any women present. And I never feel more like a woman than when I am alone with men. If the #metoo movement has, hopefully, given women the inspiration and power to speak up about their experiences, then it has given me — a transgender guy — the inspiration and power to speak up to the men around me and say, I am not one of you. Though I might look like you, I refuse to talk like you. I refuse to think and act like you. I refuse to easily accept the privilege that calling myself a man might confer.

When I consider that oft-asked question that nags me — Why not just live as a man? — this is why not.

10 When I consider that oft-asked question that nags me — Why not just live as a man? — this is why not. I cannot and will not just live as a man because I have lived as a woman, in a body that vexed and confused me, in a body I neither wanted nor understood, a body that carried all the baggage that being perceived as a woman entails. Because of this, I understand that we have to keep talking about gender; we have to recognize what our insistence on upholding the gender binary does to people. Each of us — cisgender and transgender — has to understand that gender is one of the primary ways we structure power in our society, and that society continues to see women as less than men. Because of this, and my early life as a girl, I will never subsume my identity under the mantle of manhood. Call me transgender, or even a guy, but I am not and will never be a man.

VOCABULARY/USING A DICTIONARY

1. What does it mean if someone is *transgender* (para. 1)?
2. What is the etymology of the word *maneuver* (para. 3)?
3. What clues in the word *subsume* (para. 10) lead you to its definition?

RESPONDING TO WORDS IN CONTEXT

1. Does being a tomboy have any *correlation* (para. 4) to how large one's chest becomes? How do you define *correlation* in this context?
2. If something is *donned* (para. 4), what is happening to it?
3. After reading Myers's story, how would you explain what it means to *uphold the gender binary* (para. 10)?

DISCUSSING MAIN POINT AND MEANING

1. What does being "subject to public commentary" (para. 4) have to do with being male or female, according to Myers?
2. What do Myers's boarding school experiences in paragraphs 5 and 6 have to do with the point he is making?
3. How has the #MeToo movement affected him?

EXAMINING SENTENCES, PARAGRAPHS, AND ORGANIZATION

1. Myers repeats the word *this* in paragraph 8. What do you think he means by "this"? Is it important that the pronoun is vague?
2. What is the effect of using quotations in paragraph 4? How would the effect be different if the information was integrated into the text and not presented as dialogue?
3. How would the piece be different if it ended on paragraph 9 instead of 10? What would the difference be?

THINKING CRITICALLY

1. Why essentially does Myers say "I am not and will never be a man" (para. 10)? What led him to this conclusion?
2. In paragraph 8, Myers acknowledges he had the "easiest of times, both as a girl and as a boy." Did you expect this? Why or why not?
3. Is it possible for Myers to be part of the #MeToo movement *and* an ally for women within it? How do you think Myers perceives gender?

WRITING ACTIVITIES

1. Do you think it's true that each of us has to understand the relationship between gender and power, whether transgender or cisgender? In a short

essay, say whether you agree with Myers's discussion, using examples from the text as you argue your position.

2. **Connect:** Pollitt ("Why Boys Don't Play with Dolls," p. 321) writes that adults impose their gender "agenda" on children, perpetuating certain stereotypes and gender experiences. How does Pollitt's idea about gender connect to similar ideas in Myers's essay? In a short writing assignment, examine what the gender binary does to people, comparing the arguments of Pollitt and Myers.
3. Critique Myers's essay. Which part(s) do you find most compelling? What area(s) is weakest in your opinion? Why? Is there anything Myers should have added, cut, or changed to make the argument more compelling?

Adison Eyring (student essay)

A Narrowing Definition of Gender Will Marginalize Trans, Intersex Communities

[*The Cougar*, October 29, 2018]

In October 2018, the U.S. Department of Health and Human Services issued a memo that proposed a stricter definition of "sex." As the New York Times *reported it, the department "is considering narrowly defining gender as a biological, immutable condition determined by genitalia at birth." The* Times *regarded this as "the most drastic move yet in a government wide effort to roll back recognition and protections of transgender people under federal civil rights laws to narrow the definition of gender." In "A Narrowing Definition of Gender Will Marginalize Trans, Intersex Communities," University of Houston student, Adison Eyring reports on this memo and the harm a redefinition of sex would mean to the communities affected. Offered in support of the argument is a succinct distinction between "sex" and "gender," which Eyring maintains are "separate concepts that are both more complicated than initially assumed."*

Adison Eyring is an opinion columnist for the Cougar *at the University of Houston and a sophomore majoring in political science.*

BEFORE YOU READ

Who gets to choose how people identify in terms of gender — the individual or the government? Why is defining gender problematic?

WORDS TO LEARN

designation (para. 2): something that indicates or names something (noun)
marginalized (para. 2): in a position of little power (adjective)
align (para. 3): to arrange into a line (verb)
irreversible (para. 4): not reversible (adjective)
valid (para. 4): legally sound (adjective)
warrant (para. 6): to authorize (verb)
disenfranchisement (para. 6): the act of depriving a people of something (noun)

The U.S. Department of Health and Human Services is considering a narrower definition of gender under Title IX, according to a memo. This change would not recognize or protect transgender individuals. 1

The definition of gender would be determined "on a biological basis that is clear (and) grounded in science," based on an individual's external sex characteristics at birth. Transgender and intersex individuals would not be able to change their legal gender designation under any circumstances. This decision implies that the U.S. government has the ability to define marginalized groups out of their rights. In addition to endangering thousands of transgender and intersex individuals, such a ruling would be a clear abandonment of science and individual liberty. 2

This decision to redefine gender is not grounded in science, despite the administration's statement. Two percent of people in the United States have "a reproductive or sexual anatomy" that doesn't align with the typical definitions of male or female, according to the Intersex Society of North America. This is approximately the same percentage of individuals in the United States with red hair. The intersex community, however, does not receive visibility or recognition. 3

The current common practice for intersex newborns — which make up about 1 in every 1,500–2,000 live births in the United States — is a swift and immediate sexual assignment surgery, or rather, infant genital mutilation. Parents are often pressured by doctors to agree to these irreversible and invasive surgeries out of fear for their child's health and safety, although there are very few intersex conditions that come with serious medical risks. The Trump administration's potential redefinition of gender would normalize and enforce these traumatic medical practices and further erase intersex people as a valid and protected community. 4

BEYOND BIOLOGY

The general consensus among researchers is that sex and gender are separate concepts that are both more complicated than initially assumed. Sex refers to biological sex characteristics but "gender goes beyond biology," 5 said Dr. Jason Rafferty, the lead author of the American Academy of Pediatrics' transgender policy. Gender may be impacted by genetic factors, but it primarily exists as an innate psychological state within the brain. By definition, transgender people are individuals whose gender identity does not match the sex they were assigned at birth.

Our government's manipulation of science and research does not come without precedence. The U.S. has a history of employing pseudoscience to warrant disenfranchisement and state violence. This should not undermine the severity of a potential redefinition. The erasure of a marginalized identity is one of the beginning steps of dehumanizing and eradicating a culture. 6

For a country that claims to value individual liberty, a policy that fails to account for the identities of transgender and intersex individuals would go against this philosophy. Just as when women fought for their right for birth control or when the LGBT community battled against anti-sodomy laws, individuals have a right to their own bodies. 7

Though the personal is inherently political for those in marginalized groups, identity and anatomy should not be further policed by government officials. The power of the executive branch can only reach so far — in this case, it would primarily only affect Title IX and the Affordable Care Act. 8

This redefinition would send the message to transgender and intersex individuals that their realities don't matter when in truth, they are a significant community that is entitled to equal protection of their rights. 9

VOCABULARY/USING A DICTIONARY

1. The word *traumatic* (para. 4) derives from the word *trauma*. What is trauma, and how would you define *traumatic*?
2. What is the opposite of *undermine* (para. 6)?
3. What is a *precedent*? What does it mean for something to have *precedence* (para. 6)?

RESPONDING TO WORDS IN CONTEXT

1. In paragraph 3, Eyring says, "The intersex community, however, does not receive visibility or recognition." What is the distinction being made between visibility and recognition?
2. Eyring quotes the phrase "gender goes beyond biology" (para. 5). Can you explain what that means by defining *gender* and *biology*?
3. If parents of intersex babies are *pressured* by doctors (para. 4) to agree to sexual assignment surgery, what are the doctors doing, and what are the parents experiencing?

DISCUSSING MAIN POINT AND MEANING

1. What is the problem with the new definition of gender proposed by the Department of Health and Human Services?

2. What is one of the problems that exists for intersex children if gender is determined "on a biological basis that is clear (and) grounded in science" (para. 2)?
3. In what ways does gender go "beyond biology," according to some researchers?

EXAMINING SENTENCES, PARAGRAPHS, AND ORGANIZATION

1. What analogy is brought in to highlight the prevalence of intersex people and also to show how they are unrecognized? Where does it fall in the argument?
2. What is the purpose of this article? To inform? To argue? To clarify? Explain your answer.
3. Consider paragraph 4: "The current common practice for intersex newborns — which make up about 1 in every 1,500–2,000 live births in the United States — is a swift and immediate sexual assignment surgery, or rather, infant genital mutilation." What is the effect of the em dashes in this sentence? Why are they used here?

THINKING CRITICALLY

1. **Connect:** Think about the argument about gender in Compton's essay (p. 315). How does the parents' decision in that essay speak to and/or affirm Eyring's position on the narrower definition of gender being proposed? What issues does Eyring introduce that are *not* necessarily part of the Compton essay?
2. Should the government have the ability to define gender? Why is gender open to interpretation by the government?
3. Does the government have an obligation to support and defend the rights of what Eyring calls "marginalized groups" (para. 2)? Why or why not?

WRITING ACTIVITIES

1. Eyring states, "For a country that claims to value individual liberty, a policy that fails to account for the identities of transgender and intersex individuals would go against this philosophy" (para. 7). If you agree, write a short response to this quotation explaining why this particular liberty is important. If you disagree, write a response that explains what transcends that group's liberty and why you think as you do.
2. Explain in writing how this argument connects to women's fight for the right to birth control (para. 7). Research that history if you are unfamiliar with it.
3. Think about other things that the government (executive, legislative, judicial) defines for us — whether personal or non-personal. Write a paragraph or two about something else the government defines or wants to define, and then conclude with your position on that act of definition and the government's power to impose that definition.

LOOKING CLOSELY

Making Distinctions

Effective opinion writing often consists of making distinctions between closely related concepts. In fact, such distinctions also play a large role in the essay in general; many essays have been written that draw out important distinctions between envy and jealousy, sports and games, freedom and liberty, money and wealth, or fame and celebrity, to name a few closely related terms that most people may not recognize possess important differences. To make her case about the impact that any governmental redefinition of "sex" may have on transgender individuals, Adison Eyring relies on the importance of distinguishing "sex" and "gender." Although these terms can be used interchangeably, their differences can be significant. In "A Narrowing Definition of Gender Will Marginalize Trans, Intersex Communities," Eyring argues that it is scientifically important to differentiate between the two concepts. To further bolster her case, Eyring cites a pediatric medical expert who authorizes the distinction.

1
States a scientific distinction

2
Cites an authority supporting the distinction

(1) The general consensus among researchers is that sex and gender are separate concepts that are both more complicated than initially assumed. (2) Sex refers to biological sex characteristics but "gender goes beyond biology," said Dr. Jason Rafferty, the lead author of the American Academy of Pediatrics' transgender policy.

STUDENT WRITER AT WORK

Adison Eyring

Courtesy of Adison Eyring

R.A. What inspired you to write your essay? And publish it?

A.E. In our current political climate, it feels like there's twenty big news stories every day. It's very easy for us to get desensitized or only pay attention to high-level political controversy. I didn't want the implications of this issue to get immediately swept aside, and I recognized the platform (no matter how small) I had as a student writer to make sure that wouldn't happen.

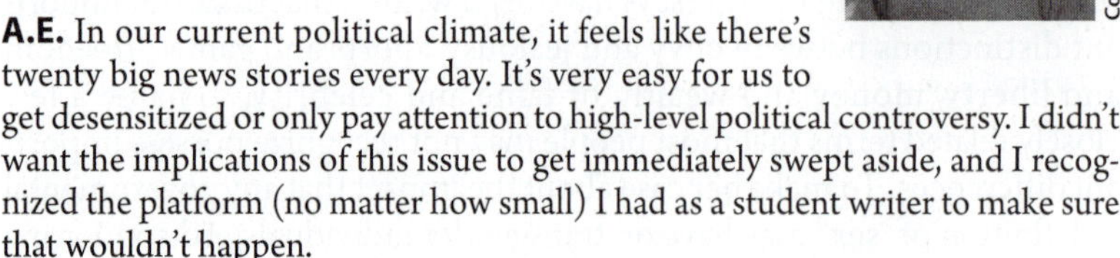

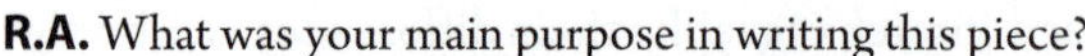

R.A. What was your main purpose in writing this piece?

A.E. With my school having such a huge and diverse student body, I knew that there would be trans, nonbinary, and intersex students who would be directly harmed by the Title IX definition change I write about, as well as students who agree with the decision and students who have no clue what any of it means. My goal was to write something that anyone, regardless of their preconceived stance on LGBTQ+ and intersex issues, could learn something from without feeling alienated or condescended to. I feel there's a long way to go in terms of fully recognizing and protecting transgender and gender nonconforming individuals.

R.A. Who was your prime audience?

A.E. One of the best pieces of writing advice I've received is that your audience is typically going to be a reflection of yourself, and I find this to be especially true for student journalism, no matter the size or demographics of your school. The audience we write for is comprised of our fellow students: young, sometimes ignorant, but willing to learn. In my experience, writing for student audiences is all about broaching important issues in an accessible and personal way.

R.A. Do you generally show your writing to friends before submitting it? Do you collaborate or bounce your ideas off others? To what extent did discussion with others help you develop your point of view on the topic you wrote about?

A.E. I wrote this piece in isolation, but my point of view was absolutely shaped through discourse (sometimes one-sided) with friends and strangers. As a cisgender woman with the privilege to not be directly harmed by the issue I wrote about, I definitely tried to find as many trans, nonbinary, and intersex people speaking on their own behalf about the harm a change in definition would pose.

R.A. What do you like to read?

A.E. I adore pieces that take a large issue like immigration or gender-based oppression and add a personal narrative. Even though it's vital that they get reported and we should all read the news, humans aren't really able to conceptualize huge global disasters. Our brains just aren't made for that. I think putting faces and personal stories to massive, seemingly abstract issues is the best way to make people really pause and consider the magnitude and individual cost of social conflicts.

R.A. What advice do you have for other student writers?

A.E. It's always better to have something terrible written than nothing written at all, surround yourself with harsh editors, and you're never too smart or accomplished to refresh on your basic comma rules.

SPOTLIGHT ON DATA AND RESEARCH

Aamer Madhani

Poll: Approval of Same-Sex Marriage in U.S. Reaches New High

[*USA Today*, May 23, 2018]

For years, one of the leading issues in debates over gender and civil rights was same-sex marriage. When the Supreme Court in 2015 made such marriages legal in all fifty states it resolved the constitutional issue, though it remained to be seen how the decision would be played out over time: How would the American public respond? In his news item, "Poll: Approval of Same-Sex Marriage in U.S. Reaches New High," reporter Aamer Madhani summarizes a 2018 Gallup poll that shows 67 percent of Americans now support same-sex marriage. Only 27 percent said they did when Gallup began polling on the issue in 1996. The numbers mark, Madhani writes, "the highest level of support . . . recorded in the more than 20 years [Gallup] has been querying Americans on the issue."

Aamer Madhani has been on the staff of USA Today *since 2008, having worked out of Baghdad, Washington (as a White House correspondent), and Chicago, where he currently reports on issues involving policing, cities, and Midwest politics.*

More than two-thirds of Americans say they support same-sex marriage, according to a new Gallup poll published Wednesday. 1

With 67% of Americans expressing their approval, it marks the highest level of support that the research firm has recorded in the more 2 than 20 years it has been querying Americans on the issue. Gallup said it has tallied 3 percentage point increases in support for each of its last three national surveys on the topic.

When Gallup first queried Americans on the issue in 1996, 27% said they supported gay marriage. 3

In the latest poll, 83% of respondents who identified as Democrats said they support legal recognition of same-sex marriage, while 44% of Republican respondents and 71% of independents expressed support. 4

The increased acceptance of same-same marriage — which a 2015 Supreme Court decision made legal in all 50 states — comes as greater numbers of lesbian, gay, bisexual and transgender adults are getting married in the U.S. More than 10.4% of LGBT adults are married to a same-sex spouse, according to daily tracking on the issue in 2017. 5

Gallup found the percentage of American adults identifying as lesbian, gay, bisexual or transgender (LGBT) increased to 4.5% in 2017, up from 4.1% in 2016 and 3.5% in 2012 when Gallup began tracking the measure. The latest estimate is based on over 340,000 interviews conducted as part of Gallup's daily tracking poll in 2017. 6

The increase in Americans identifying as LGBT was driven primarily by millennials — defined in the poll as those born between 1980 and 1999. The percentage of millennials who identify as LGBT expanded from 7.3% to 8.1% from 2016 to 2017, and is up from 5.8% in 2012. 7

The data on attitudes on same-sex marriage were collected as part of Gallup's annual Values and Morals poll, conducted May 1–10 of 1,024 adults. The poll's margin of error is ±4 percentage points. 8

POINTS TO CONSIDER

1. At one point, a majority of Americans disapproved of same-sex marriage. In what ways might the 2015 Supreme Court decision have altered opposition and changed people's minds? What would this suggest about the social importance of the Supreme Court?
2. The poll also indicated that the percentage of American adults identifying as LGBTQ+ has been increasing steadily since 2012 (para. 6). What connection would this have with same-sex marriage and its growing approval numbers?
3. According to the report, the increase in the number of Americans identifying as LGBTQ+ "was driven primarily by millennials" (para. 7). Why do you think millennials (defined as those born between 1980 and 1999) would account for this increase?

Julie Compton

Boy or Girl? Parents Raising "Theybies" Let Kids Decide

[*NBCnews* (features), July 19, 2018]

With a growing number of people beginning to think that traditional male/female gender roles can be personally and socially harmful, there has been increasing attention to how we either consciously or unconsciously inculcate and reinforce such binary roles. Some see a harmful polarization of gender instilled from infancy and early childhood and wish to find a more neutral way to raise children. In "Boy or Girl? Parents Raising 'Theybies' Let Kids Decide," Julie Compton visits a Massachusetts couple to observe firsthand how two toddlers, nonidentical twins Zyler and Kadyn, are being raised without the usual props of conventional gender distinctions. A large part of the method is making sure that no one — not even the children — knows what sex any child is. "If no one knows a child's sex," Compton writes, "these parents theorize the child can't be pigeonholed into gender stereotypes."

Julie Compton is a Brooklyn-based freelance journalist.

BEFORE YOU READ

Are there benefits to growing up without an assigned gender? What difficulties might "theybies" encounter as they face a gendered world?

WORDS TO LEARN

enclave (para. 4): an enclosed group (noun)
associate (para. 4): to form a connection with in the mind (verb)
binary (para. 5): based on two parts (noun)
conventional (para. 7): ordinary (adjective)
anatomy (para. 13): a body's structure or parts (noun)
foster (para. 18): to encourage (verb)
genitalia (para. 20): reproductive organs (noun)
spectrum (para. 23): a broad range or array (noun)
innate (para. 25): inherent (adjective)
aggressiveness (para. 27): assertiveness, marked by a tendency to go too far/become violent (noun)

Three-year-old twins Zyler and Kadyn Sharpe scurried around the boys and girls clothing racks of a narrow consignment store filled with toys. Zyler, wearing rainbow leggings, scrutinized a pair of hot-pink-and-purple sneakers. Kadyn, in a T-Rex shirt, fixated 1 on a musical cube that flashed colorful lights. At a glance, the only discernible difference between these fraternal twins is their hair — Zyler's is brown and Kadyn's is blond.

Is Zyler a boy or a girl? How about Kadyn? That's a question their 2
parents, Nate and Julia Sharpe, say only the twins can decide. The Cambridge, Mass., couple represent a small group of parents raising "theybies" — children being brought up without gender designation from birth. A Facebook community for these parents currently claims about 220 members across the U.S.

"A theyby is, I think, different things to different people," Nate 3
Sharpe told NBC News. "For us, it means raising our kids with gender-neutral pronouns — so, 'they,' 'them,' 'their,' rather than assigning 'he,' 'she,' 'him,' 'her' from birth based on their anatomy."

Parents in the U.S. are increasingly raising children outside tradi- 4
tional gender norms — allowing boys and girls to play with the same toys and wear the same clothes — though experts say this is happening mostly in progressive, well-to-do enclaves. But what makes this "gender-open" style of parenting stand out, and even controversial in some circles, is that the parents do not reveal the sex of their children to anyone. Even the children, who are aware of their own body parts and how they may differ from others, are not taught to associate those body parts with being a boy or girl. If no one knows a child's sex, these parents theorize, the child can't be pigeonholed into gender stereotypes.

This type of parenting received widespread attention in 2011, when 5
a Toronto couple announced that they were raising their child, Storm, without gender designation, sparking a media frenzy. Progressive parents, who see their child's gender as fluid rather than binary, took notice. A Brooklyn couple runs a blog featuring their 2-year-old, Zoomer, and offering advice on how to navigate the world while raising a "theyby." Others have taken to Instagram to share photos and support.

Some developmental experts see gender-open parenting as a noble 6
goal, but they also wonder how it will hold up once kids enter a gendered world that can be hostile to those who don't fit clearly into categories. Gender-nonconforming children are more likely to be bullied. Last year, 10 states considered "bathroom bills" requiring people to use bathrooms aligned with the gender assigned to them at birth (none passed).

"Once your child meets the outer world, which may be day care, or 7
preschool, or grandparents — it's pretty much impossible to maintain a gender-free state," Lise Eliot, professor of neuroscience at the Chicago Medical School and author of "Pink Brain, Blue Brain," said in an email. "And depending on how conventional your community is, you could be setting your child up for bullying or exclusion."

Parents like the Sharpes understand these realities — but they're 8
determined to shield their children from them for as long as possible.

DECIDING TO RAISE A "THEYBY"

The Sharpes, both mechanical engineers in their early 30s, say their 9
decision to raise their twins without designated genders evolved from a mix of research and personal experience. When Julia found out she was pregnant, she felt conflicted about learning the sex of the twins. As a female engineer in a male-dominated profession, she understood the constraints of gender expectations firsthand.

"It's taken a lot of work for me to feel confident in my designs and 10
my suggestions, and to really stand up for myself," she said.

At first, Nate didn't understand why Julia wanted to wait to find out 11
the babies' sex. But after the couple began researching how stereotypes affect a child's development, he changed his mind.

"We read about how from when they're 20-week fetuses, they're 12
already starting to be gendered, and people are calling the little girls 'princesses,' and buying certain things for different children," Julia said. "We wanted to prevent that, so that's how it started. And then about a couple weeks before they were born, Nate just said, 'What if we didn't tell people ever?'"

When the Sharpe arrived at the hospi- 13
tal for the delivery, they asked the staff not to announce the twins' sex. Even after the newborns were put in their arms, their anatomy remained a mystery for several hours.

Even after the newborns were put in their arms, their anatomy remained a mystery for several hours.

"It just wasn't something that was 14
interesting," Julia said. "It was all about meeting the children and interacting with them, and just not something that we focused on at all."

Now toddlers, Zyler and Kadyn aren't focused on it either. On a 15
recent morning, they were busy playing with large cardboard blocks. They constructed a tower, then a robot.

"Look how tall it is!" Kadyn declared. 16

"If you put one more block on it, it will be taller than you!" Zyler 17
squealed. "We can get it up to the ceiling!"

Their Cambridge home is littered with toys that come from both 18
the girls' and the boys' aisles — a dollhouse, a play gym, a bedroom full of stuffed animals, a basket of dolls. Their parents want to foster an environment of openness where the twins feel loved whether they grow up

to identify as LGBTQ or not. That means learning to see their children simply as "kids" rather than as "boys" or "girls," and encouraging others to do the same.

That's not always easy, or comfortable, in a gendered world. Family, friends and day care workers struggle with they/them pronouns, and not everyone understands the Sharpes' decision to keep the children's sex private. 19

"We definitely got more pushback from co-workers, who were like: 'Wait, you're not going to tell me what you're having? You're not going to tell me what your kids are?'" Julia said. "I'm like, 'I'm telling you they're children.' But they got really, really frustrated that we wouldn't tell them what their genitalia was, which is kind of a weird thing when you think about it." 20

Kadyn and Zyler still have little understanding of gender, according to their parents, but have started to pick up on it. One day recently, Zyler asked Julia what "she" and "he" mean. 21

"Since we've tried to avoid really getting into gender until they're old enough to understand it, I answered that 'he' and 'she' are pronouns and you use them to make sentences simpler, so instead of saying someone's name over and over in the sentence, you'll say 'he' or 'she' or 'they' instead," she said, "and Zyler got distracted after that and moved on." 22

IS GENDER HARD-WIRED?

At birth, reproductive organs reveal a baby's assigned sex. Gender, however, comes later, around age 4, when children begin to identify as masculine, feminine or somewhere along that spectrum, experts say. 23

People tend to think that this gender identity is hard-wired, because most people identify with the gender that matches their sex at birth. But large-scale research suggests gender is largely influenced by a child's environment, said Christia Spears Brown, a developmental psychologist and author of *Parenting Beyond Pink and Blue: How to Raise Your Kids Free of Gender Stereotypes.* 24

When boys and girls are born, their brains are virtually indistinguishable; while boys have slightly bigger brains on average, they also have bigger bodies. Studies suggest there are some minor observable differences in behavior early on. For instance, baby girls seem slightly better at regulating their impulses and attention than boys, according to a 2006 study from the University of Wisconsin–Madison. Experts agree that girls tend to speak a few months earlier than boys, though it's not understood why. "But in general," Brown said, "the differences get larger as kids get older, which really suggests that it's society and culture that are shaping the differences that we see — not innate differences from birth." 25

From the day they're born, baby boys and girls are ushered into blue and pink worlds where they are dressed in different clothes and given different toys. As they get older, they begin to pay attention to gender-based marketing: Recent research shows that when a girl is given a toy that is pink, she is more likely to play with it, but when the same toy is blue, she's less likely to. 26

Experts say the way parents interact with their children also shapes them from a young age. For example, parents are more likely to explain numbers to sons and use emotion-based words with daughters, according to *The Handbook of Parenting*, an authoritative collection of research on parenting. Parents also tend to encourage aggressiveness in boys and emotions in girls, the handbook says. 27

Parents raising their children without designated genders aim to block these biases, allowing kids to explore and determine where they fall in their own time. 28

VOCABULARY/USING A DICTIONARY

1. What does it mean for something to be *pigeonholed* (para. 4)? What is a pigeonhole?
2. How do you understand the word *theyby*? How do you think the name originated?
3. What is a *bias* (para. 28)? What is an antonym for *bias*?

RESPONDING TO WORDS IN CONTEXT

1. If the only *discernible* (para. 1) difference between the Sharpe twins is their hair, how would you describe the difference being referred to?
2. The Sharpe twins are *fraternal* (para. 1) twins. What is the other type of twin? What does *fraternal* mean in this context and what is the literal dictionary definition?
3. How would you define a *constraint* (para. 9)? What are the *constraints* of gender pronouns?

DISCUSSING MAIN POINT AND MEANING

1. What does Compton acknowledge are the benefits of raising children without gender awareness? What does she acknowledge could be the disadvantages?
2. Why did the Sharpes make the decision to parent their twins this way?
3. Why might the claim be made that society and environment create gender differences?

EXAMINING SENTENCES, PARAGRAPHS, AND ORGANIZATION

1. Why do you think Compton begins her report on "theybies" by looking closely at a particular set of twins and their parents? How else might she have begun? How effective do you find this method of introducing her topic?
2. The paragraphs of this article are very short, sometimes only one or two sentences long. What effect does that have on the reader? How would that effect change if the paragraphs were longer, not broken where they are now?
3. Why do you think Compton included so much dialogue in this essay, both from the Sharpes and from different authors and experts?

THINKING CRITICALLY

1. The report makes it appear that raising "theybies" is a growing trend in the United States today. Yet Compton points out that a "Facebook community" for such parents claims "about 220 members across the U.S." (para. 2). Do you think she wants readers to accept that number as large or small? How do you interpret that number?
2. Why are people around the Sharpes frustrated by their decision to keep their children's gender private? Do you think you would find this frustrating as well? Why or why not?
3. **Connect:** How would Myers ("How #MeToo Taught Me I Can Never Be a Man," p. 303) respond to this essay? Do you think he would be in favor of how the twins are being raised, or would he suggest something else? Do Compton and Myers agree on the difficulties of maintaining a gender-free state? With Myers in mind, what will change for the Sharpe twins once they make decisions about their own gender?

WRITING ACTIVITIES

1. Why does Compton point out that raising "theybies" is, according to experts, "happening mostly in progressive, well-to-do enclaves" (para. 4)? Cambridge, Massachusetts, is one such enclave. In a short writing assignment, discuss this trend, considering Compton's comment. What is your opinion about why this might be the case?
2. Take a passage from any text—story, article, essay—and rewrite it with nonbinary pronouns (use "they" or another nonbinary pronoun of your choice, instead of "he" or "she"). Does the substitution have an effect? Explain. Write down your experience of the text and how it differs—or is the same—as your first reading.
3. Find an advertisement with humans pictured in it. Write about the target audience for the ad. Who's being sold to? Men? Women? Is the ad directed toward a nonbinary audience? How can you tell? What messages about gender are sent in the ad?

AMERICA THEN . . . 1995

Katha Pollitt

Why Boys Don't Play with Dolls

[*The New York Times Magazine*, 1995]

Katha Pollitt, a rare writer who is both a poet and a journalist, published the following essay in 1995. At the time, she was surprised that so many years after the founding of the National Organization for Women (NOW) in 1966 "boys still like trucks and girls still like dolls." In reading this now, some twenty-five years after her essay was published, we may ask ourselves if nothing has changed. Surely, if you visit sites to purchase toys online you will see many of the same gender stereotypes she addresses in "Why Boys Don't Play with Dolls." As Pollitt examines the conflicting theories and explanations of sex roles in our society (she never once uses the word gender*), she pessimistically sees how difficult it will be to change our conventional habits rooted in traditional male and female differences. At the same time, however, she optimistically sees feminism as "the ideology of flexible and converging sex roles" that will ensure "our children's future." Has time proven her correct, or do we still have far to go?*

Katha Pollitt is a columnist at The Nation *where she writes frequently on political and feminist issues. Besides two volumes of poetry, she has published most recently* Pro: Reclaiming Abortion Rights *(2014).*

BEFORE YOU READ

Where do messages come from about what it means to be a man or what it means to be a woman? Do we have control over the messages we receive?

WORDS TO LEARN

prenatal (para. 1): prior to birth (adjective)
innate (para. 4): inborn (adjective)
transmit (para. 6): to spread (verb)
ambivalently (para. 7): with mixed feelings (adverb)
obnoxious (para. 8): offensive (adjective)
bliss (para. 10): great happiness (noun)
dominant (para. 11): main or ruling (adjective)
psychic (para. 11): having to do with mind or soul (adjective)
chafe (para. 12): to irritate (verb)
paradox (para. 13): a contradictory but possible situation (noun)
hierarchical (para. 13): having to do with a ranking system (adjective)
ideological (para. 14): relating to a belief system (adjective)
inculcate (para. 16): to impress by repeated teaching (verb)

It's twenty-eight years since the founding of NOW,[1] and boys still 1
like trucks and girls still like dolls. Increasingly, we are told that the source of these robust preferences must lie outside society—in prenatal hormonal influences, brain chemistry, genes—and that feminism has reached its natural limits. What else could possibly explain the love of preschool girls for party dresses or the desire of toddler boys to own more guns than Mark from Michigan?[2]

True, recent studies claim to show 2
small cognitive differences between the sexes: he gets around by orienting himself in space, she does it by remembering landmarks. Time will tell if any deserve the hoopla with which each is invariably greeted, over the protests of the researchers themselves. But even if the results hold up (and the history of such research is not encouraging), we don't need studies of sex-differentiated brain activity in reading, say, to understand why boys and girls still seem so unalike.

The feminist movement has done much for some women, and something for every woman, but it has hardly turned America into a playground free of sex roles.

The feminist movement has done much for some women, and 3
something for every woman, but it has hardly turned America into a playground free of sex roles. It hasn't even got women to stop dieting or men to stop interrupting them.

Instead of looking at kids to "prove" that differences in behavior 4
by sex are innate, we can look at the ways we raise kids as an index to how unfinished the feminist revolution really is, and how tentatively it is embraced even by adults who fully expect their daughters to enter previously male-dominated professions and their sons to change diapers.

I'm at a children's birthday party. "I'm sorry," one mom silently 5
mouths to the mother of the birthday girl, who has just torn open her present — Tropical Splash Barbie. Now, you can love Barbie or you can hate Barbie, and there are feminists in both camps. But *apologize* for Barbie? Inflict Barbie, against your own convictions, on the child of a friend you know will be none too pleased?

Every mother in that room had spent years becoming a per- 6
son who had to be taken seriously, not least by herself. Even the most

---

[1] NOW (para. 1): The National Organization for Women was founded in 1966. — Eds.

[2] Mark from Michigan (para. 1): Mark Koernke, a former right-wing talk-show host who supports the militia movement's resistance to federal government. — Eds.

attractive, I'm willing to bet, had suffered over her body's failure to fit the impossible American ideal. Given all that, it seems crazy to transmit Barbie to the next generation. Yet to reject her is to say that what Barbie represents — being sexy, thin, stylish — is unimportant, which is obviously not true, and children know it's not true.

Women's looks matter terribly in this society, and so Barbie, however ambivalently, must be passed along. After all, there are worse toys. The Cut and Style Barbie styling head, for example, a grotesque object intended to encourage "hair play." The grown-ups who give that probably apologize, too. 7

How happy would most parents be to have a child who flouted sex conventions? I know a lot of women, feminists, who complain in a comical, eyeball-rolling way about their sons' passion for sports: the ruined weekends, obnoxious coaches, macho values. But they would not think of discouraging their sons from participating in this activity they find so foolish. Or do they? Their husbands are sports fans, too, and they like their husbands a lot. 8

Could it be that even sports-resistant moms see athletics as part of manliness? That if their sons wanted to spend the weekend writing up their diaries, or reading, or baking, they'd find it disturbing? Too antisocial? Too lonely? Too gay? 9

Theories of innate differences in behavior are appealing. They let parents off the hook — no small recommendation in a culture that holds moms, and sometimes even dads, responsible for their children's every misstep on the road to bliss and success. 10

They allow grown-ups to take the path of least resistance to the dominant culture, which always requires less psychic effort, even if it means more actual work: just ask the working mother who comes home exhausted and nonetheless finds it easier to pick up her son's socks than make him do it himself. They let families buy for their children, without *too* much guilt, the unbelievably sexist junk that the kids, who have been watching commercials since birth, understandably crave. 11

But the thing that theories do most of all is tell adults that the *adult* world — in which moms and dads still play by many of the old rules even as they question and fidget and chafe against them — is the way it's supposed to be. A girl with a doll and a boy with a truck "explain" why men are from Mars and women are from Venus, why wives do housework and husbands just don't understand. 12

The paradox is that the world of rigid and hierarchical sex roles evoked by determinist theories is already passing away. Three-year-olds may indeed insist that doctors are male and nurses female, even if their own mother is a physician. Six-year-olds know better. These days, something like half of all medical students are female, and male applications 13 to nursing school are inching upward. When tomorrow's three-year-olds play doctor, who's to say how they'll assign the roles?

14 With sex roles, as in every area of life, people aspire to what is possible, and conform to what is necessary. But these are not fixed, especially today. Biological determinism may reassure some adults about their present, but it is feminism, the ideology of flexible and converging sex roles, that fits our children's future. And the kids, somehow, know this.

15 That's why, if you look carefully, you'll find that for every kid who fits a stereotype, there's another who's breaking one down. Sometimes it's the same kid — the boy who skateboards *and* takes cooking in his afterschool program; the girl who collects stuffed animals *and* A-pluses in science.

16 Feminists are often accused of imposing their "agenda" on children. Isn't that what adults always do, consciously and unconsciously? Kids aren't born religious, or polite, or kind, or able to remember where they put their sneakers. Inculcating these behaviors, and the values behind them, is a tremendous amount of work, involving many adults. We don't have a choice, really, about *whether* we should give our children messages about what it means to be male and female — they're bombarded with them from morning till night.

17 The question, as always, is what do we want those messages to be?

VOCABULARY/USING A DICTIONARY

1. If someone or something is *robust* (para. 1), like a person or a flavor, how else might it be described?
2. How might an action be done if it is done *tentatively* (para. 4)?
3. What type of action is *flouting* (para. 8)?

RESPONDING TO WORDS IN CONTEXT

1. Given Pollitt's description, how might *feminism* (para. 1) be defined?
2. What might *cognitive differences* (para. 2) refer to? What might be an example of one?
3. How might *manliness* (para. 9) be defined in the context of this essay?

DISCUSSING MAIN POINT AND MEANING

1. Where has feminism failed, according to Pollitt?
2. Why does rejecting Barbie not work?
3. What rebuttal is offered to the criticism that feminists who challenge gender stereotypes are imposing their particular ideas on children?

EXAMINING SENTENCES, PARAGRAPHS, AND ORGANIZATION

1. Outline Pollitt's essay, paragraph by paragraph. Offer one main idea she hits in each paragraph and notice the transitions between them. What do you notice about the organization of her argument?

2. Paragraph 9 is made up entirely of questions. Try writing the paragraph with the questions rephrased as statements. What is the effect of questions over statements?
3. Pollitt starts out with the balanced statement that "boys still like trucks and girls still like dolls," but Barbie gets a good deal of the spotlight in her essay. Is her focus (on traditional girls' toys over boys' toys) unbalanced? Why do you think Barbie gets so much space?

THINKING CRITICALLY

1. Do you agree with Pollitt's assessment of media messages and how they shape the way kids play with toys? Can you think of other examples that support her position today? Do you think things have changed since this essay was written? Explain.
2. How do you respond to Pollitt's suggestion in paragraph 16? Where do *your* messages come from? How much did parents or adults in your life have to do with shaping how you see the world and yourself?
3. **Connect:** Pollitt notes in her opening paragraph, "It's twenty-eight years since the founding of NOW, and boys still like trucks and girls still like dolls." Consider how Compton's essay ("Boy or Girl? Parents Raising 'Theybies' Let Kids Decide," p. 315) responds to that statement. Would Pollitt be in favor of the Sharpes' experiment, raising their twins as "theybies"? Explain.

WRITING ACTIVITIES

1. As you reread the essay, consider carefully the role of the media in upholding the status quo with regard to differentiated roles for girls and boys. Drawing on Pollitt's essay and on your own experience, identify — and discuss — the specific social responsibilities you would like to see America's mass media take more seriously.
2. Look through toy advertising. Where do you note gender stereotypes? Keep a tally of those with blatant gender stereotypes and those with suspected stereotypes. Did you find anything that surprised you? In a short paper, discuss your findings using specific examples from your research.
3. In paragraph 15, Pollitt writes: "That's why, if you look carefully, you'll find that for every kid who fits a stereotype, there's another who's breaking one down." In a brief personal essay, write about someone you know who either (a) fits all stereotypes and doesn't deviate from them in any way in their lives or (b) breaks stereotypes down. You must know the person well enough to create a written portrait of sorts. You may include how they have affected your life and any choices you have made because of them. Be sure you have this person's permission to write about them, and respect their privacy.

Discussing the Unit

SUGGESTED TOPIC FOR DISCUSSION

Many of the characteristics presumed of someone who is "male" or "female" continue to stereotype gender. Women still struggle for equality, and some insist that the binary leaves them powerless in the most fundamental ways. But beyond the gulf between "men" and "women," gender identity, once limited to categories of "male" or "female," is now seen by many as more fluid. The embrace of the word *they* as a generic singular pronoun is evidence of a growing rejection of a traditional gender binary, and some families are trying to raise their children without gender in an attempt to escape stereotype and conditioning. Discuss other examples you've noticed of American culture accepting a more fluid experience of gender.

PREPARING FOR CLASS DISCUSSION

1. When you think about gender, what traits do you think are particularly male? What traits are particularly female? Do you prefer not to think of gender in terms of the binary at all?
2. Are there traits that you would consider "gender neutral"? If so, what are they? Is the erasure of gender identity a way to erase bias?

FROM DISCUSSION TO WRITING

1. Which of the essays in this chapter advocate for gender equality, and which state that divisions between men and women simply exist? Write a short comparison of how the authors in these essays view gender.
2. Do you think Pollitt would understand the arguments that Compton and Eyring are making? Write an essay that compares their main points about gender and the problems that come with gender identification.

TOPICS FOR CROSS-CULTURAL DISCUSSION

1. Do the differences that were once so pronounced between men and women still exist today? If not, what happened to them? What about the concept of gender on a spectrum (rather than fixed binary)? Are men and women still treated differently?
2. When it comes to your gender, how do you think of yourself? Would it bother you if someone referred to you as "he" instead of "she," or "they" or "she" instead of "he" or "they," depending on your gender identification? Using two essays from this chapter, write an essay in which you consider your gender identification and explore how these essays support your perception of gender.

10

The News Media: How Well Does It Serve the Public?

By now, nearly all Americans are familiar with the notion of "fake news." But what does the term mean exactly? Is it news that is overly subjective or biased? News that is primarily opinion disguised as fact? News with a propagandistic agenda? News that is deliberately false and misleading? News that is erroneous, though not deliberately? News that is entirely fabricated or intended as a hoax? News that has been purposely paid for or that is actually an advertisement? All of these categories, it seems, get into the mix whenever someone complains about the news media's misinformation or inaccuracy. One of the chief complainers is President Trump, who has made "fake news" a household term.

Trump did not invent "fake news." As we will see at the end of this chapter, "fake news" has a long history in print and broadcast media. In the 1830s, newspapers routinely fostered lies and exaggerations to sell papers, and the practice continues today with sensationalist headlines, innuendoes that may not be supported by any facts, and doctored photography. But by the mid-twentieth century — with new standards of journalism in place — newspapers, which were the main source of news before radio and television, had gradually cleaned up their act, though as late as the 1980s and early 1990s popular columnists were still relying on invented or composite characters for their "true" stories — a once common device that is no longer permitted by most media outlets.

But by the twenty-first century, four major influences changed the way news is delivered to the American people: the Federal Communications Commission's elimination of the Fairness Doctrine in 1987, the growth of highly competitive cable news programs, the rise of social media, and the development of new artificial intelligence (AI) technologies that could make the fake indistinguishable from the real. The first led to a biased, single-opinion news presentation, the next two led to the decline of newspapers and other print journalism, and have contributed to the escalation of polarized political positions and skepticism toward journalistic objectivity. The fourth has recently increased public skepticism and trust and is seen today as an imminent political danger.

This chapter examines the nature of news today. It will consider such questions as "What is fake news?" "Can we distinguish between fact and opinion?" "Can advocacy journalism be objective?" "Should we reinstate the Fairness Doctrine?" "Can fake news result in mass delusion?"

The International Federation of Library Associations (IFLA)

How to Spot Fake News

[The International Federation of Library Associations, 2016]

After Oxford Dictionaries called post-truth *their Word of the Year in 2016, the International Federation of Library Associations decided that "action is needed to educate and advocate for critical thinking — a crucial skill when navigating the information society." The federation based the following infographic on an article published in November 2016 by FactCheck.org that systematically set out eight ways for people to develop better skills for evaluating and understanding what they see and hear in the news media (https://www.factcheck.org/2016/11/how-to-spot-fake-news/). IFLA says that it "made this infographic with eight simple steps . . . to discover the verifiability of a given news-piece in front of you."*

The International Federation of Library Associations describes itself as "the leading international body representing the interests of library and information services and their users. It is the global voice of the library and information profession."

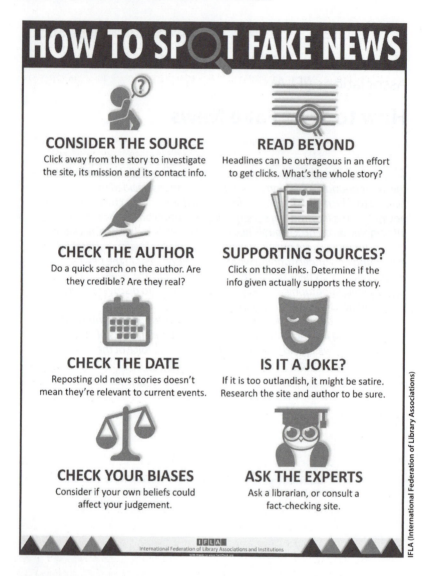

HOW TO SPOT FAKE NEWS

CONSIDER THE SOURCE

Click away from the story to investigate the site, its mission and its contact info.

READ BEYOND

Headlines can be outrageous in an effort to get clicks. What's the whole story?

CHECK THE AUTHOR

Do a quick search on the author. Are they credible? Are they real?

SUPPORTING SOURCES?

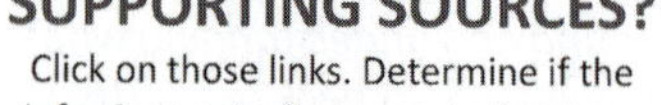

Click on those links. Determine if the info given actually supports the story.

CHECK THE DATE

Reposting old news stories doesn't mean they're relevant to current events.

IS IT A JOKE?

If it is too outlandish, it might be satire. Research the site and author to be sure.

CHECK YOUR BIASES

Consider if your own beliefs could affect your judgement.

ASK THE EXPERTS

Ask a librarian, or consult a fact-checking site.

IFLA
International Federation of Library Associations and Institutions

IFLA (International Federation of Library Associations)

POINTS TO CONSIDER

1. Judging by this infographic, what seem to be the leading sources of fake news? What words in the captions help point to these sources?
2. Why do you think the topic of fake news has gained such importance recently? What changes in the news media may have caused an interest in discerning "fake" stories from true and accurate ones? What motives can you think of for spreading bogus and untrue stories?

3. The IFLA describes the infographic as offering "eight simple steps" to help you better evaluate the truth and falsity of any news items you encounter. In your opinion, how "simple" are these steps? How likely would you be to follow these steps each time you received a piece of news information that seems not credible? Explain your answer.

SPOTLIGHT ON DATA AND RESEARCH

American Dialect Society

Word of the Year: Fake News

[*American Dialect Society*, January 6, 2018]

With the election of Donald Trump in 2016, the idea of "fake news" gained momentum and would become one of the major political issues of recent years. It came as no surprise, then, when the American Dialect Society in January 2018 voted for "fake news" as the 2017 Word of the Year. In the following press release, the Society briefly defines fake news and explains why the term was selected "as best representing the public discourse and preoccupations of the past year." Trump didn't invent the term but, as one reporter maintains, "latched on to" it and put it to his own political purposes.

For more on the American Dialect Society, see "The Word of the Year Is Singular They,*" p. 301.*

Grand America Hotel, Salt Lake City, Utah — Jan. 5 — In its 28th annual words of the year vote, the American Dialect Society voted for *fake news* as the Word of the Year for 2017. Defined in two ways, "disinformation or falsehoods presented as real news" and "actual news that is claimed to be untrue," *fake news* was selected as best representing the public discourse and preoccupations of the past year. 1

Presiding at the Jan. 5 voting session were Grant Barrett, vice president of the American Dialect Society and co-host of the public radio show "A Way With Words," and Jane Solomon, lexicographer for Dictionary.com and member of the American Dialect Society's New Words Committee. 2

Fake news was first considered by the American Dialect Society a year ago in the voting for the 2016 Word of the Year, but at the time its meaning was restricted to fictional or embellished stories presented as authentic news, disseminated for financial gain or for propagandistic purposes. 3

In 2017, however, the meaning of *fake news* shifted and expanded, in large part due to its repeated use by President Donald Trump.

4 "When President Trump latched on to *fake news* early in 2017, he often used it as a rhetorical bludgeon to disparage any news report that he happened to disagree with," said Ben Zimmer, chair of the American Dialect Society's New Words Committee and language columnist for the *Wall Street Journal*. "That obscured the earlier use of *fake news* for misinformation or disinformation spread online, as was seen on social media during the 2016 presidential campaign."

5 "Trump's version of *fake news* became a catchphrase among the president's supporters, seeking to expose biases in mainstream media," Zimmer continued. "But it also developed more ironic uses, and it spread to speakers of all ages as a sarcastic putdown." *Fake news* was nominated by the sixth-grade class of Academy I Middle School in Jersey City, NJ, and voters at the Word of the Year event agreed with their choice.

6 Word of the Year is interpreted in its broader sense as "vocabulary item" — not just words but phrases. The words or phrases do not have to be brand-new, but they have to be newly prominent or notable in the past year.

7 The vote is the longest-running such vote anywhere, the only one not tied to commercial interests, and *the* word-of-the-year event up to which all others lead. It is fully informed by the members' expertise in the study of words, but it is far from a solemn occasion.

8 Members in the 129-year-old organization include linguists, lexicographers, etymologists, grammarians, historians, researchers, writers, editors, students, and independent scholars. In conducting the vote, they act in fun and do not pretend to be officially inducting words into the English language. Instead, they are highlighting that language change is normal, ongoing, and entertaining.

9 In a companion vote, sibling organization the American Name Society voted "*Rohingya*" as Name of the Year for 2017 in its thirteenth annual name-of-the-year contest.

POINTS TO CONSIDER

1. How did the meaning of fake news change between 2016 and 2017? What was the original definition?
2. How did Donald Trump alter the definition of "fake news"? What did he add to the original meaning?
3. In selecting the term "fake news" as Word of the Year, is the American Dialect Society honoring Donald Trump's linguistic prowess? Explain why or why not.

Charles Carr

Reinstate the Fairness Doctrine!

[*Times Advocate* (Escondido, California), December 28, 2018]

A little known fact in the history of contemporary American media has had enormous consequences. In 1987, broadcasters throughout the nation persuaded the Federal Communications Commission (FCC) to eliminate a rule that had been in effect since 1949 — the Fairness Doctrine. This rule stipulated — as journalist Charles Carr aptly summarizes it — that all broadcasters "would be required to present controversial issues of public importance in a manner that was, in the FCC's language, 'honest, equitable, and balanced.'" In "Reinstate the Fairness Doctrine!," Carr offers a succinct account of how this decision led to the spate of the "junk news" we receive hourly and how reversing it can ensure "a true diversity of opinion" that will eventually heal our divisive polarization.

Charles Carr is an award-winning journalist who writes and edits for many publications. He recently won a San Diego Press Club award.

BEFORE YOU READ

Do you think the news you are presented is balanced and fair? Should news be regulated in some way to prevent presenting biased reporting as truth?

WORDS TO LEARN

buffet (para. 2): a meal laid out so that people can help themselves (noun)
repeal (para. 3): to formally withdraw (verb)
pulverize (para. 3): to crush (verb)
cynically (para. 4): pessimistically (adverb)
aggregators (para. 8): people who have combined forces (noun)
intervention (para. 9): interference (noun)
divinely (para. 9): heavenly (adverb)

Like most people, there are certain things over which I have precisely zero will power. Junk food, for example. If it's anywhere in the house, I'll sniff it out like a Mangalitsa pig rooting truffles. Nearly three-quarters of a century ago some very wise lawmakers realized that America had something of a junk food problem of its own: the fact that people tend to believe that the opinions they already hold are correct and will not go far out of their way to subject them to scrutiny. It's only human nature. 1

To deal with it, just after WWII in 1949, our nation implemented a 2
Federal Communications Commission (FCC) rule called the Fairness Doctrine. The Fairness Doctrine stated that all holders of broadcast licenses would be required to present controversial issues of public importance in a manner that was, in the FCC's language, "honest, equitable, and balanced." Older readers may remember watching local news broadcasts in which editorial segments were immediately followed by a spokesperson presenting an "opposing viewpoint" — almost unthinkable in today's largely all-junk-news-all-the-time buffet.

They did it, but they sure didn't like it and in 1987 pressured the 3
FCC to eliminate it. It didn't take the ad boys and girls in TV and radio land to realize that its repeal could provide a massive revenue windfall. And those are pretty much the only two dots you need to connect to create the picture we've got today: 1) repeal the Fairness Doctrine 2) start capitalizing on people's basest instincts. Don't believe me? Here are just a few of the terms I pulled off of supposedly balanced political websites TODAY: smack-down, eviscerates, destroys, annihilates, slaughters, pulverizes, murders, and on and on . . . I only get a thousand words here.

In the three decades since its repeal, there have been many attempts 4
to reinstate the doctrine, so far without success. And, not coincidentally, over pretty much that exact period the severe ideological polarization in which America currently finds itself has increased dramatically. A recent Gallup poll revealed that, "Polarization in presidential approval ratings began to expand under Reagan and has accelerated with each president since Clinton." It has vaulted from a record 70 point gap under Barack Obama to 77 points under Donald Trump. News as sport. Opinion unfettered by correction. And dump trucks of bucks from a viewership kept too het up to risk turning away from the screen — a legislatively determinative number of people which has cocooned itself within a false reality so deep, so convincing, so perfectly — if cynically — crafted that they are unable to see what they believe to be a perfect window into the world is, in fact, a mirror.

Keep your biases if you want, but only after someone with a different way of looking at the issue has had a shot at making their best pitch to you.

Reinstating the Fairness Doctrine, 5
or something much like it, would again require that opposing views be presented at the key moment viewers are being asked to make a decision. Keep your biases if you want, but only

after someone with a different way of looking at the issue has had a shot at making their best pitch to you. Sort of like the nutrition label on that candy bar. You don't have to read it, but it's there. No wonder the food industry is always trying to get them removed.

Reinstatement of the Fairness Doctrine would deliver a 9.9 shock directly to the tender bits of the news-as-sport industry and go a long ways to returning us to the days of Murrow, Cronkite, Sevareid, and the like — a world almost everyone purports to miss but hasn't the slightest idea how to get back to. A world where the word "news" would no longer be what it has become in many quarters today — a four-letter word. 6

It would be fair to ask, if the Fairness Doctrine couldn't survive way back in 1987 when the nation was far less polarized than it is now, what are the odds that it could ever be reimplemented in the hyper-partisan environment in which we currently find ourselves? Not great, I'll concede. But perhaps we can at least begin the conversation. Perhaps, as our nation continues toward 100% polarization, conversation will turn to action. Perhaps. 7

In the meantime, there's a lot we can do individually to create our own personal Fairness Doctrines of a sort. Modern online news aggregators have developed the uncanny ability to tailor web results to our exact tastes and opinions. We can show their smart-alecky AI we're not so easy to peg by going out of our way to visit a wider range of news and opinion sites than we have in the past. Before long, their algorithms will begin to have a more diverse range of choices. And let's face(book) it, the way social networks have been shown time and time again to value profit over the welfare of their users, these sites are not our friends. Refusing to click on faux news stories, political ads, and divisive news stories will quickly make the pages unprofitable for the scammers who own them. Better yet, we can flag them as offensive, just as we would porn. In key ways, they are. 8

When it comes to our junk news addiction, America needs an intervention. Let's return to the Fairness Doctrine and a true diversity of opinion. It will be like tasting some divinely fresh food after a long diet of nothing but junk food. 9

That's all he wrote — for this year. See you in 2019. Got to go now; I think I figured out where my wife hid that Christmas box of Harry and David chocolate truffles! 10

VOCABULARY/USING A DICTIONARY

1. Do you know what it means to *scrutinize* something? What is *scrutiny* (para. 1)? What part of speech is it?

2. What is the difference between *equitable* (para. 2) and *equal*?
3. What part of speech is *ideological* (para. 4)? How do you define *ideology*?

RESPONDING TO WORDS IN CONTEXT

1. How might you restate the phrase *massive revenue windfall* (para. 3)?
2. Write down some words that share the root of *eviscerates* (para. 3). How would you define *eviscerates* based on the other words in that sentence from paragraph 3?
3. In paragraph 4, Carr describes the presidential approval rating in this way: "It has *vaulted* from a record 70 point gap under Barack Obama to 77 points under Donald Trump." One traditionally hears of *vaulting* in gymnastics. Does the word have the same meaning here?

DISCUSSING MAIN POINT AND MEANING

1. What was the purpose of the Fairness Doctrine?
2. Why was the Fairness Doctrine repealed?
3. What does Carr mean when he writes about instituting a "personal Fairness Doctrine" (para. 8)?

EXAMINING SENTENCES, PARAGRAPHS, AND ORGANIZATION

1. Had you ever heard the phrase *het up* (para. 4)? Does it fit in the sentence in which you find it? Explain.
2. How does Carr set up an analogy of the nutrition label on the candy bar in paragraph 5 to explain the Fairness Doctrine? Does it explain the importance of it to you?
3. Consider the food trope that runs through the essay. Is it effective? Why or why not?

THINKING CRITICALLY

1. **Connect:** Read Ryan Fawwaz's essay about journalistic advocacy ("Seeking Truth Is Intertwined with Journalistic Advocacy," p. 337). How do his ideas fit in with Carr's urging to return to the Fairness Doctrine? Consider how the two would respond to the other's argument and where they might agree. Are their opinions in opposition?
2. Why have attempts to reinstate the Fairness Doctrine been unsuccessful? What do you think that reveals about our society?
3. Does America have a junk news addiction? Why or why not? Explain your answer.

WRITING ACTIVITIES

1. Carr's essay, beginning with the title, is a call to action. Think about issues you feel strongly about and write your own call to action. Model your essay on Carr's. Define your terms, or describe a scenario for your reader who may or may not be familiar with it, and move on from there to argue your position.
2. Take a look at the news — find a station and a news broadcast on some particular topic. Does it fit the description of "honest, equitable, and balanced" (para. 2) reporting? Analyze the broadcast and explain your answer in writing.
3. Look carefully at paragraph 7. Carr writes, "It would be fair to ask, if the Fairness Doctrine couldn't survive way back in 1987 when the nation was far less polarized than it is now, what are the odds that it could ever be reimplemented in the hyper-partisan environment in which we currently find ourselves? Not great, I'll concede. But perhaps we can at least begin the conversation." In a brief writing assignment, summarize the conversation he refers to. Also, provide your own answer to his question about the odds of the Fairness Doctrine being reimplemented now.

Ryan Fawwaz (student essay)

Seeking Truth Is Intertwined with Journalistic Advocacy

[*The Daily Trojan* (University of Southern California), May 16, 2018]

One of the journalistic issues closely related to the difference between fact and opinion (see previous selection) is the distinction between objectivity and advocacy. If a reporter takes a stand and actively supports a particular cause or political perspective, is the resulting news story biased and flawed? Can advocacy journalism also be responsible journalism? In "Seeking Truth Is Intertwined with Journalistic Advocacy," University of Southern California student Ryan Fawwaz addresses the problem of objectivity and activism in news reporting. Reminding us of the illustrious history of investigative journalism, he concludes that "being an active, responsible journalist means confronting faults and inherent biases and overcoming them with the public's best interests in mind."

Ryan Fawwaz is a journalism student at the University of Southern California.

BEFORE YOU READ

What is the difference between "fake news" and "active, responsible" reporting? Should journalists have opinions and advocate for causes in their reporting?

WORDS TO LEARN

objectivity (para. 3): state of being unbiased (adjective)
advocacy (para. 3): act of supporting something (noun)
unadulterated (para. 3): pure (adjective)
encyclopedia (para. 5): books on various topics covering all branches of knowledge (noun)
chaotic (para. 5): disordered (adjective)
ubiquitous (para. 6): being everywhere (adjective)
progressive (para. 9): favoring progress or reform (adjective)
inherent (para. 9): essential to something (adjective)

Last Friday, media mogul Oprah Winfrey delivered a commencement speech to graduates of the USC Annenberg School for Communication and Journalism. In her 23-minute-long speech, Winfrey dished out several familiar, commencement-style blanket statements as she encouraged the crowd of Annenberg graduates to make the world a "better place." 1

But she also posed a challenging question: "What are you willing to stand for?" 2

In the world of journalism, many have asked this question and many have refused to answer. To reporters who have been trained to approach stories with complete objectivity, the idea of "taking a stand" — of advocating for a certain cause — is nothing more than a disruption to their search for absolute, unadulterated truth. But we need to realize that, in many ways, exposing the truth is in fact a form of advocacy. And it's not a bad thing. It's journalism. 3

Reporters have had a long history of stepping outside the boundaries of objectivity and pushing for what they saw as positive change to society. During the late 19th and early 20th centuries, people who took on this role were known as "muckrakers": Investigative journalist Ida B. Wells, for example, was a leading figure in the anti-lynching movement. In 1968, renowned television news anchor and "most trusted man in America" Walter Cronkite famously opposed U.S. involvement in the Vietnam War during a special CBS News broadcast — which, in turn, shifted the attitudes of a public that was becoming increasingly distrustful of the government. 4

Today, as the label of "fake news" looms over the industry like a dark cloud, many reporters have shied away from the idea that their work should have a specific purpose. In an increasingly digital environment where encyclopedias of information can be accessed with a few finger taps, many of journalists' duties have been determined by their 5 responsibilities to take the most pertinent stories and present them in a manner the public can understand — to make sense of a chaotic amount of information.

This concept represents a shift in perceptions of what Winfrey 6
referred to as the "editorial gatekeeper": Whereas journalists were once able to control what information the public can access, the rise of social media platforms and "citizen journalism" has made that information ubiquitous and, at times, uncontrollable. But while they may not always take an overt stand like Wells or Cronkite, the reporters disseminating and repackaging content are inherently active players in their stories as well.

Journalists have long debated whether 7
they should write *for* or *about* a community. But, as previously mentioned, the two options are often inextricably linked — intentional or not. We must realize that although many journalists may execute an objective reporting technique — resembling an uninvolved yet informed bystander — they contribute to the values and beliefs of the community they are writing about. The choices they make in including and excluding certain perspectives all contribute to the general message readers take away from a story.

Journalists have long debated whether they should write *for* or *about* a community.

Therefore, considering that they have a powerful and far-reaching 8
platform at their disposal, journalists have an obligation to speak both their voices as well as those of populations who remain unheard. As Oprah mentioned in her speech, graduating from college is a privilege not everyone has access to. Becoming a journalist is a privilege not everyone has access to. We live in a world where, as USC Annenberg Dean Willow Bay said, "so many people are shouting to be heard." Journalists, then, must also learn to listen. They cannot make the public understand a story if they do not first understand it themselves.

But truth will not encourage progressive activism if readers cannot 9
tell whether or not that truth is, well, true. Now more than ever, journalists must work for the public's trust. Much of the difference between advocacy journalism and propaganda lies in transparency, which entails not only informing readers of where and how they got information, but also remaining accountable when that information isn't correct. Being an active, responsible journalist means confronting faults and inherent biases and overcoming them with the public's best interests in mind. It also means encouraging an active, responsible readership — one that

checks the facts and ethics behind articles and contributes to discussions in the comments sections.

10 As our world continues to evolve and as perspectives continue to diversify, the platforms communicating that diversity will shift as well. Indeed, it goes without saying that our society — the values and ideas that constitute the modern Zeitgeist — is changing at an unprecedented pace. But we need to realize that journalists, too, will be a part of that change. They always have.

VOCABULARY/USING A DICTIONARY

1. What is a *media mogul* (para. 1)?
2. Where does the phrase *dish out* (para. 1) originate? What has it come to mean?
3. How do you define *zeitgeist* (para. 10)? From what language is that word borrowed?

RESPONDING TO WORDS IN CONTEXT

1. Can you give an example of a journalist *taking a stand* (para. 3) in recent or past times (other than the examples that Fawwaz provides)?
2. What does Fawwaz mean by *transparency* in journalism? How is it different from *propaganda* (para. 9)?
3. Fawwaz says society is changing at an *unprecedented* pace (para. 10). What might that adjective mean?

DISCUSSING MAIN POINT AND MEANING

1. What journalistic conflict does Fawwaz introduce in para. 3. What is his stance on the relationship between "exposing the truth" and "advocacy"?
2. According to Fawwaz in paragraphs 4–6, how has the role of journalists changed? What has primarily caused this change?
3. How does Fawwaz characterize a good ("active, responsible") journalist (para. 9)? What makes a good journalist different from any other?

EXAMINING SENTENCES, PARAGRAPHS, AND ORGANIZATION

1. Look at how Fawwaz opens his essay. What approach is he using to get to his thesis? Do you find his introductory remarks effective? Why or why not?
2. Why do you think Fawwaz includes the information about Ida Wells and Walter Cronkite in the essay? Is there a reason it is placed where it is?
3. In paragraph 10, Fawwaz gives a definition of sorts of "our society." Do you think the definition is needed? Does it add anything to the sentence or paragraph? Explain.

THINKING CRITICALLY

1. How do you understand the distinction — or lack of it — between writing *for* or *about* a community (para. 7)? Is Fawwaz's explanation effective? If so, how so? If not, how could it be made more effective?
2. In the modern world of easily accessed information, everyone is "shouting to be heard" (para. 8). Do you think everyone should be heard? Why or why not?

WRITING ACTIVITIES

1. Consider Fawwaz's point in paragraph 7. Write a description of an "objective reporting technique" in response to that paragraph. Does Fawwaz think today's journalists should abandon that technique? What is his position on "objective" reporting?
2. What is Fawwaz's position on "advocacy journalism" — is he for it or against it? How does he clarify his position in paragraph 9? Write a short paper that explains his stance and explores the following questions: How can advocacy journalism avoid turning into propaganda? And, in your opinion, how does Fawwaz's own journalism as demonstrated in this selection reflect the principles he advocates?
3. Go to an event in your school or community and listen to a speaker give a talk on a subject. Take notes during the event and/or include any reactions to the talk or to the question-and-answer period with the audience. Write a short article about the event as if you were writing up a brief for a newspaper or community Web site. What were the speaker's main points? What background information did the speaker bring in and do you need to introduce any information for context? What was your final takeaway from the event?

LOOKING CLOSELY

Supporting Opinions with Specific Examples

In the book's introduction we saw that the use of specific examples was one of the most effective ways of supporting an opinion (see p. 15). If you wanted to argue that television commercials were now targeting a more diverse range of consumers, you would want to support that observation with concrete examples to persuade your readers. Without examples, your observation would sound like an empty impression with no basis.

Notice how University of Southern California student Ryan Fawwaz uses two well-chosen examples to establish his general point that reporters have long gone outside of objectivity to benefit society. He introduces two major individuals as examples of this tendency and provides a brief description of what they did. Note also that his examples are more persuasive because of the specific historical events he associates them with.

1
States general point

(1) Reporters have had a long history of stepping outside the boundaries of objectivity and pushing for what they saw as positive change to society.

2
Provides first example

(2) During the late 19th and early 20th centuries, people who took on this role were known as "muckrakers": Investigative journalist Ida B. Wells, for example, was a leading figure in the anti-lynching movement.

3
Provides second example

(3) In 1968, renowned television news anchor and "most trusted man in America" Walter Cronkite famously opposed U.S. involvement in the Vietnam War during a special CBS News broadcast — which, in turn, shifted the attitudes of a public that was becoming increasingly distrustful of the government.

AMERICA THEN . . . 1938

Dorothy Thompson

Mr. Welles and Mass Delusion

[*The New York Herald Tribune*, November 2, 1938]

On the night before Halloween in 1938, the American public witnessed what would become one of the greatest media hoaxes of modern history. It was brought to radio by the film director and actor Orson Welles and his Mercury Theater group who performed an adaptation of H. G. Wells's (no relation) classic science fiction novel about a Martian invasion of the earth, War of the Worlds *(1898). Welles's show took the form of a news broadcast with intermittent bulletins that pretended to interrupt a program already in progress. Although the performance was announced as fiction, many listeners were alarmed and some panicked. Newspaper reports the next day exaggerated the extent of panic, thus compounding "fake news" with more fake news.*

One major reporter, however, Dorothy Thompson, wrote a compelling account of what happened. Although she believed the news reports of mass hysteria, she saw the incident as an illustration of how easily the public can be deceived. Writing within the context of an expanding Nazi Germany, she praised Welles for providing "the perfect demonstration that the danger is not from Mars but from the theatrical demagogue."

Dorothy Thompson (1893–1961) was a distinguished syndicated columnist who had covered the early women's movement and then the European political scene in the 1920s with special attention to the rise of Nazi Germany. In 1939, Time *magazine considered her and Eleanor Roosevelt the two most influential women in America.*

BEFORE YOU READ

When you run across information on the Internet or hear something on the radio, do you automatically believe it to be true if it's presented convincingly? Do you ever respond to things emotionally before you take the time to sort out a logical response?

WORDS TO LEARN

proposition (para. 1): plan (noun)
potently (para. 2): powerfully (adverb)
appalling (para. 2): causing dismay (adjective)
demoralization (para. 11): destruction of morale (noun)
credible (para. 13): believable (noun)
verisimilitude (para. 13): the appearance of truth (noun)
fallacy (para. 17): a deception (noun)
incite (para. 21): to provoke (verb)
monopoly (para. 22): exclusive control of something (noun)
subservience (para. 28): submissiveness (noun)
jubilation (para. 31): an expression of joy (noun)

All unwittingly Mr. Orson Welles and the Mercury Theater on the Air have made one of the most fascinating and important demonstrations of all time. They have proved that a few effective voices, accompanied by sound effects, can so convince masses of people of a totally unreasonable, completely fantastic proposition as to create nation-wide panic. 1

They have demonstrated more potently than any argument, demonstrated beyond question of a doubt, the appalling dangers and enormous effectiveness of popular and theatrical demagoguery. 2

They have cast a brilliant and cruel light upon the failure of popular education. 3

Average net paid circulation for September exceeded
Daily---1,800,000
Sunday-3,150,000

DAILY NEWS

Copyright 1938 by News Syndicate Co., Inc. Reg. U. S. Pat. Off. NEW YORK'S PICTURE NEWSPAPER Entered as 2nd class matter, Post Office, New York, N. Y.

FINAL

Vol. 20. No. 109 New York, Monday, October 31, 1938★ 48 Pages 2 Cents IN CITY LIMITS | 3 CENTS Elsewhere

FAKE RADIO 'WAR' STIRS TERROR THROUGH U.S.

—Story on Page 2

(NEWS foto)

"War" Victim

Caroline Cantlon, WPA actress, listening to this radio in West 49th St., heard announcement of "smoke in Times Square." Running to street, she fell, broke her arm.

(By Associated Press)

"I Didn't Know". Orson Welles, after broadcast expresses amazement at public reaction. He adapted H. G. Wells' "War of the Worlds" for radio and played principal role. Left: a machine conceived for another H. G. Wells story. Dramatic description of landing of weird "machine from Mars" started last night's panic.

—Story on page 2.

4 They have shown up the incredible stupidity, lack of nerve and ignorance of thousands.

5 They have proved how easy it is to start a mass delusion.

6 They have uncovered the primeval fears lying under the thinnest surface of the so-called civilized man.

7 They have shown that man, when the victim of his own gullibility, turns to the government to protect him against his own errors of judgment.

8 The newspapers are correct in playing up this story over every other news event in the world. It is the story of the century.

9 And far from blaming Mr. Orson Welles, he ought to be given a Congressional medal and a national prize for having made the most amazing and important contribution to the social sciences. For Mr. Orson Welles and his theater have made a greater contribution to an understanding of Hitlerism, Mussolinism, Stalinism, anti-Semitism and all the other terrorisms of our times than all the words about them that have been written by reasonable men. They have made the reductio ad absurdum of mass manias. They have thrown more light on recent events in Europe leading to the Munich pact than everything that has been said on the subject by all the journalists and commentators.

10 Hitler managed to scare all Europe to its knees a month ago, but he at least had an army and an air force to back up his shrieking words.

11 But Mr. Welles scared thousands into demoralization with nothing at all.

12 That historic hour on the air was an act of unconscious genius, performed by the very innocence of intelligence.

13 Nothing whatever about the dramatization of the "War of the Worlds" was in the least credible, no matter at what point the hearer might have tuned in. The entire verisimilitude was the names of a few specific places. Monsters were depicted of a type that nobody has ever seen, equipped with "rays" entirely fantastic; they were described as "straddling the Pulaski Skyway" and throughout the broadcast they were referred to as Martians, men from another planet.

14 A twist of the dial would have established for anybody that the national catastrophe was not being noted on any other station. A second of logic would have dispelled any terror. A notice that the broadcast came from a non-existent agency would have awakened skepticism.

A second of logic would have dispelled any terror.

15 A reference to the radio program would have established that the "War of the Worlds" was announced in advance.

16 The time element was obviously lunatic.

Listeners were told that "within two hours three million people have 17
moved out of New York" — an obvious impossibility for the most disciplined army moving exactly as planned, and a double fallacy because only a few minutes before, the news of the arrival of the monster had been announced.

And of course it was not even a planned hoax. Nobody was more 18
surprised at the result than Mr. Welles. The public was told at the beginning, at the end and during the course of the drama that it *was* a drama.

But eyewitnesses presented themselves; the report became second 19
hand, third hand, fourth hand, and became more and more credible, so that nurses and doctors and National Guardsmen rushed to defense.

When the truth became known the reaction was also significant. 20
The deceived were furious and of course demanded that the state protect them, demonstrating that they were incapable of relying on their own judgment.

Again there was a complete failure of logic. For if the deceived had 21
thought about it they would realize that the greatest organizers of mass hysterias and mass delusions today are states using the radio to excite terrors, incite hatreds, inflame masses, win mass support for policies, create idolatries, abolish reason and maintain themselves in power.

The immediate moral is apparent if the whole incident is viewed in 22
reason: no political body must ever, under any circumstances, obtain a monopoly of radio.

The second moral is that our popular and universal education is fail- 23
ing to train reason and logic, even in the educated.

The third is that the popularization of science has led to gullibility 24
and new superstitions, rather than to skepticism and the really scientific attitude of mind.

The fourth is that the power of mass suggestion is the most potent 25
force today and that the political demogogue is more powerful than all the economic forces.

For, mind you, Mr. Welles was managing an obscure program, com- 26
peting with one of the most popular entertainments on the air!

The conclusion is that the radio must not be used to create mass 27
prejudices and mass divisions and schisms, either by private individuals or by government or its agencies, or its officials, or its opponents.

If people can be frightened out of their wits by mythical men from 28
Mars, they can be frightened into fanaticism by the fear of Reds, or convinced that America is in the hands of sixty families, or aroused to revenge against any minority, or terrorized into subservience to leadership because of any imaginable menace.

The technique of modern mass politics calling itself democracy is to create a fear — a fear of economic royalists, or of Reds, or of Jews, or of starvation, or of an outside enemy — an exploit that fear into obtaining subservience in return for protection. 29

I wrote in this column a short time ago that the new warfare was waged by propaganda, the outcome depending on which side could first frighten the other to death. 30

The British people were frightened into obedience to a policy a few weeks ago by a radio speech and by digging a few trenches in Hyde Park, and afterward led to hysterical jubilation over a catastrophic defeat for their democracy. 31

But Mr. Welles went all the politicians one better. He made the scare to end scares, the menace to end menaces the unreason to end unreason, the perfect demonstration that the danger is not from Mars but from the theatrical demagogue. 32

VOCABULARY/USING A DICTIONARY

1. What is *demagoguery* (para. 2)? What is a demagogue?
2. What is the etymology of the word *primeval* (para. 6)?
3. How would you define a *menace* (para. 32)? Can you give an example of one?

RESPONDING TO WORDS IN CONTEXT

1. **Connect:** How is the situation Thompson is speaking of an example of *mass delusion* (para. 5)? How does this idea connect to Taschka's ("What's Wrong with Hitler Comparisons?" p. 64) discussion of comparisons with Hitler — and the effect of creating false equivalencies?
2. If the Orson Welles scenario showed people falling victim to their own *gullibility* (para. 7), how might you define *gullibility*? Explain.
3. How does the fact that Welles's program was *obscure* (para. 26) strengthen the argument that the populace's reaction was out of proportion?

DISCUSSING MAIN POINT AND MEANING

1. What does Thompson suggest as an antidote to the hysteria caused by Welles's broadcast, in the moments when it was happening?
2. What is the first moral, or lesson, of the incident that Thompson stresses?
3. What conclusion is reached by Thompson? Try phrasing it as an "if . . . then" statement: "If people can be so frightened by a radio broadcast, then ____________."

EXAMINING SENTENCES, PARAGRAPHS, AND ORGANIZATION

1. Why does Thompson choose to create one-sentence paragraphs at various points in the essay? What effect is she creating by doing so? Is it the same effect each time?
2. Thompson calls attention to herself once in this essay. Where and how does she do this?
3. Thompson calls Welles's broadcast the "scare to end scares, the menace to end menaces, the unreason to end unreason" (para. 32). What kind of language is this? How would you discuss it in terms of style, in this particular instance and in terms of the essay overall?

THINKING CRITICALLY

1. Why does Thompson insist that this story is "the story of the century" (para. 8)? Do you agree or disagree with that position? Why?
2. How does Thompson connect Orson Welles's story and people's reaction to political fanaticism and propaganda? Do you think the links are clearly there? What other forces are at work? Is what happened in response to Welles's broadcast avoidable?
3. Do you think Orson Welles should be blamed for what happened as a result of his broadcast? Do you think your reaction would have been the same as his audience's or not? Even if you're not as trusting as Welles's listeners, have you ever believed information you've received digitally, through social media or other sources, without questioning or investigating the source if you're not familiar with it?

WRITING ACTIVITIES

1. Have you ever been so afraid of something that you weren't able to think logically? When was that, and what was at stake? Write a narrative essay that explores a time when you were swept away by something you heard or read even though there was no particular reason to believe it. Consider your reactions to information you find online, news stories, family lore, or podcasts.
2. Think about things and people that scare others. How much does fear come from those things and people themselves? How much has to do with what's going on inside the person who is fearful? Where do messages that make us fearful of others and of situations come from? Should we challenge those messages? Does Thompson give any advice on how to challenge them? Write your responses to these questions and formulate a thesis statement from what you've written.

3. Read accounts of Welles's broadcast. Find audio of the broadcast itself online. After listening and reading different perspectives on what happened, write your own interpretation of the events that transpired. As you write, discuss the power of radio broadcast and draw parallels to television news and online stories that people consume today.

Discussing the Unit

SUGGESTED TOPIC FOR DISCUSSION

Historically, the American public has relied on established media sources for information. Much of that information was streamlined through major newspapers, radio stations, or television broadcasts. But how do we evaluate media today? What is fact and what is fiction, and how do we know the difference?

PREPARING FOR CLASS DISCUSSION

1. Do journalists observe the distinction between fact and opinion? Has that distinction always been part of news reporting? Where or when does the line between the two get fuzzy?
2. Are there ways in which the public's trust or distrust of the media is extreme? Why do we trust or distrust our news sources?

FROM DISCUSSION TO WRITING

1. What is "fake" news? Do sources matter? How do we make decisions about "good" or "bad" reporting? Choose three of the essays in this chapter and discuss each writer's position on the place of fact and opinion in journalism and the veracity of news sources.
2. Student writer Fawwaz ("Seeking Truth Is Intertwined with Journalistic Advocacy," p. 337) quotes media mogul Oprah Winfrey who posed a question to a group of journalism graduates: "What are you willing to stand for?" (para. 2). He writes, "Exposing the truth is . . . a form of advocacy. . . . It's journalism" (para. 3). How does Fawwaz's idea that connects advocacy and journalism compare to other descriptions of journalism, good or bad, in this chapter? Pair Fawwaz with another writer and compare and contrast their ideas about journalism. How are their definitions of journalism similar or different?

TOPICS FOR CROSS-CULTURAL DISCUSSION

1. Consider our response to news broadcasts today in the light of Thompson's essay ("Mr. Welles and Mass Delusion," p. 342). Do people consider their sources or are media consumers discriminating about where their news comes from? Are their reactions to and belief of news stories a product of knowledge and reason or something else? What makes people believe the news stories they are told?
2. What do political leanings or particular backgrounds have to do with how we take in news stories today? Is there a news outlet that supports whatever political position you hold, or that comes from a particular cultural bent? How does the public make choices about news — separating what is "valid" from what is "fake" — or is all news suspect?

11

Patriotism: Is It Obsolete?

Throughout the nation's history, especially during times of war or domestic turmoil, Americans have considered patriotism to be a sentiment required of all citizens. In the 1960s, for example, during the Vietnam era, anyone who protested the war or resisted the draft was often branded as unpatriotic, especially by a large percentage of the nation who equated dissent with hatred of one's country. Some believe that to engage in dissent and to resist unfair laws or injustices is what it means to be truly American; to want their nation to be best for everyone is for them a patriotic duty. Yet, others feel that true patriotism involves such a deep-rooted, passionate, and unswerving love of country that to criticize and protest its actions is to be un-American.

What are the differences between patriotism and nationalism? What is xenophobia? Is patriotism in decline? Is it obsolete in an increasingly global economy and culture? Is protesting the national anthem unpatriotic? How patriotic should minorities or marginalized groups feel? Who should decide the answers to these questions? In this chapter, we will explore these questions and look at how the enduring national tension between what's American and what's un-American is playing out today.

Jen Sorensen

Patriotism vs. Nationalism

[*The Progressive*, January 2018]

Is there a significant difference between patriotism and nationalism, between one's feeling patriotic and another's feeling nationalistic? In the following brief comic strip, the progressive illustrator Jen Sorensen tries to capture the distinction between a patriot and a nationalist in just four paired panels. It is not hard to see which she prefers.

A nationally published political cartoonist, Jen Sorensen received the 2014 Herblock Prize and a 2013 Robert F. Kennedy Journalism Award. Her work appears regularly in such publications as The Progressive, The Nation, Daily Kos, *and* Politico.

POINTS TO CONSIDER

1. In what ways do the paired cartoons differ? What do you think the cartoonist believes is the fundamental distinction between patriotism and nationalism?
2. Sorensen defines nationalism in one panel as "pride in who you aren't." What do you think this means? Try putting that definition into your own words to explain it.
3. Note that patriots are partly defined as having "fought Nazis." Americans have served in many wars. How would the definition be changed if Sorensen used a different enemy?

José Azel

Patriotism vs. Nationalism

[*PanAm Post*, November 1, 2018]

In José Azel's "Patriotism vs. Nationalism," we examine in more depth the distinction highlighted in the cartoon above. In Sorensen's cartoon, the distinctions seem bold and binary, but Azel — though he finds the distinctions to be highly significant — acknowledges that the terms are often used as synonyms and sees that the concepts can be overlapping, especially in countries where the term "nationalism" has no derogatory sense and is even used in naming political parties. In the United States, Azel adds, "while nationalism can unite us, it often unites us against other people."

José Azel is a Senior Scholar at the Institute for Cuban and Cuban-American Studies (ICCAS) at the University of Miami. He is the author of Mañana in Cuba: The Legacy of Castroism and Transitional Challenges for Cuba *(2010) and* Reflections on Freedom *(2017).*

BEFORE YOU READ

When do you feel patriotic? Have you ever felt nationalistic? Are the two terms ever interchangeable?

WORDS TO LEARN

somber (para. 1): gloomy (adjective)
intone (para. 2): to utter with a particular tone (verb)
problematic (para. 3): questionable or uncertain (adjective)
synonym (para. 3): word that means the same thing as another word (noun)
coherent (para. 3): making logical sense (adjective)
abiding (para. 4): enduring (adjective)
prestige (para. 4): reputation or importance (noun)
exalt (para. 5): to elevate (verb)

Patriotism is that majestic feeling that brings tears to our eyes. I have felt it, while placing flags at gravesides in Arlington National Cemetery, as a bugler played Taps. I have felt it, walking in somber gratitude, at the Normandy American Cemetery in France, which honors American troops who died in Europe during World War II. I have felt it, in Independence Day rodeos in Montana, where a young woman carries the American flag around the arena, on horseback at full gallop, while the US national anthem is played. I have felt it, reciting the Pledge of Allegiance. 1

I have felt it, in ceremonies standing at military attention with the aging Cuban heroes of the Brigade 2506 — who carried out the 1961 Bay of Pigs invasion landing in Cuba — as we struggle singing the lyrics of The Star-Spangled Banner. And then, as we effortlessly intone the words of the Cuban national anthem memorized in our youth. I have felt it, reading in English Thomas Jefferson's beautiful prose in the Declaration of Independence and, reading in Spanish, José Marti's Versos Sencillos (Simple Verses). 2

Patriotism is best defined as love and devotion to a homeland, and a sense of alliance with other citizens who share the same values. It is a love and devotion I feel for both: my place of birth, and the country that, nearly six decades ago, welcomed me as a 13-year-old political exile. But, patriotism is related to, and shares ideals with, a more problematic concept: nationalism. The two words are often used as synonyms. They are not. George Orwell, in his forceful essay "Notes on Nationalism," offers a coherent distinction: 3

Patriotism is best defined as love and devotion to a homeland, and a sense of alliance with other citizens who share the same values.

"Nationalism is not to be confused with patriotism . . . By 'patriotism' I mean devotion to a particular place and a particular way of life, which one believes to be the best in the world but has no wish to force upon other people. Patriotism is by its nature defensive, both militarily and culturally. Nationalism, on the other hand, is inseparable from the desire for power. The abiding purpose of every nationalist is to secure more power and more prestige, not for himself, but for the nation or other unit in which he has chosen to sink his own individuality." 4

In other words, patriotism is primarily a feeling. Nationalism goes beyond; it exalts one nation above all others, and seeks power and prestige by projecting a national identity based on shared social characteristics, such as culture, language, religion, or political beliefs. But, nationalism takes a nasty turn when it takes the chauvinistic form of 5 believing that a state should be reserved only for those sharing those sociopolitical and ethnic characteristics. As such, jingoistic nationalism transforms patriotism into a posture of superiority and aggression toward other nations. For example, that kind of nationalism was central to Hitler's philosophy, and also led to the Japanese invasion of China in 1937. Today, in the Ukrainian conflict, Russian President Vladimir Putin is a nationalist imperialist, and the Ukrainian protesters are patriots.

Patriotism is essential to liberty, because pride in our nation, 6
and the willingness to defend it, form the basis of national self-determination. In tandem with patriotism, nationalism has the virtue of being a strong force for unity, particularly in wartime. But, it must be added that, while nationalism can unite us, it often unites us against other people. Patriotism flows from the individual, nationalism focuses on the state.

Patriotism is connected with admirable ideas such as bravery, valor, 7
or duty, while nationalism is often associated with unsavory sociopolitical movements such as white supremacy or anti-Semitism. Nationalism can mean different things to different people and, in the United States we seldom apply that label to ourselves. Instead, we adopt the much more benign form of "American exceptionalism." However, in other countries the term "nationalist" is favored, and often included, in some form, in the names of political parties.

Finally, I will borrow the colloquial expression used by U.S. Supreme 8
Court Justice Potter Stewart to acknowledge the problem of defining pornography: Patriotism or nationalism, "I know it when I see it."

VOCABULARY/USING A DICTIONARY

1. What is an *alliance* (para. 3)?
2. If something is *separable*, what can happen to it? What does *inseparable* (para. 4) mean?
3. What part of speech is *jingoistic* (para. 5)? How do you define it?

RESPONDING TO WORDS IN CONTEXT

1. What do you think Azel means when he writes, "Patriotism is by its nature *defensive*" (para. 4)?
2. When Azel refers to a *posture* in paragraph 5, what does he mean?
3. In what other context may you have heard the word *tandem* (para. 6)? If nationalism is *in tandem* with patriotism, how are they situated in relation to each other?

DISCUSSING MAIN POINT AND MEANING

1. In his first two paragraphs, how does Azel describe patriotism? How is it associated with emotional experiences? What do the experiences have mostly in common?
2. How, according to Azel, does nationalism take a "nasty turn" (para. 5)?
3. How does George Orwell's distinction between patriotism and nationalism, explained within the article (para. 4), inform Azel's views? How would you summarize Orwell's distinction?

EXAMINING SENTENCES, PARAGRAPHS, AND ORGANIZATION

1. What rhetorical device does Azel lean on heavily during the first half of the essay? Do you find it effective?
2. The essay is about patriotism and nationalism. How long does it take Azel to get to the second idea in his essay? How would the essay be different if he'd mentioned it sooner or simultaneously with patriotism?
3. When does it come to light that Azel is a citizen not only of America? Is that information important? How is the information presented?

THINKING CRITICALLY

1. How is Azel's patriotism different from that of many American citizens? How have his life experiences affected what he feels about patriotism?
2. Discuss the point of Azel's final paragraph when he cites a former U.S. Supreme Court justice? Is he saying the terms "patriotism" and "nationalism" cannot be defined? What has "pornography" to do with the argument?
3. **Connect:** How do you think Azel would answer the question: "Is Patriotism Obsolete?" (p. 357)? Would Jonette Christian agree or disagree with the points Azel makes? Which ones would Christian respond to, and why?

WRITING ACTIVITIES

1. As Orwell sees it, can nationalism ever be benign or virtuous? In a few brief paragraphs, explain Orwell's characterization of nationalism.
2. In a brief personal narrative, offer a description of when you've felt patriotic or nationalistic, or show the contrast between the two (how your feelings are specifically one and not the other).
3. Write an essay that offers examples of citizens' behavior that one might term nationalistic rather than patriotic. Find specific historic examples of this behavior. The nation you identify can be the United States or another country. Provide a Works Cited page for the research of the period and events you've chosen.

Jonette Christian

Is Patriotism Obsolete?

[*Portland Press Herald*, December 30, 2017]

In an increasingly globalized culture and society, is patriotism doomed? Are Americans growing more interested in a global perspective and less interested in taking pride in their own country? Jonette Christian ponders these questions and others in the following essay, "Is Patriotism Obsolete?" For Christian, patriotism "is the emotional glue that holds us together." It is not about singing the anthem or supporting the military: "Pride in America is the reason we care about each other, about poverty, injustice and trash in our streets."

Jonette Christian is a licensed clinical professional counselor and a contributor to the Bangor Daily News *and the* Portland Press Herald.

BEFORE YOU READ

Is patriotism something that brings us together? Should we be proud of who we are because that pride is important to who we are?

WORDS TO LEARN

documentary (para. 3): a filmed version of a re-created event (or a film that informs the audience about a real event) (noun)
obligation (para. 4): duty (noun)
forged (para. 4): moved forward steadily; formed (usually out of metal) (verb)
adapt (para. 9): adjust or modify (verb)
heritage (para. 10): something handed down (noun)

During the Vietnam War, I decided that patriotism was useless. It clouds rational thinking and drives nations into foolish conflict, I thought. Fifty years later, I've completely changed my mind. 1

It was a gradual realization that patriotism is the emotional glue that holds us together. It's not just singing the national anthem at football games or whipping ourselves into war fury. Pride in America is the reason we care about each other, about poverty, injustice and trash in our streets. 2

But Ken Burns' documentaries on America were what moved me from an intellectual understanding of patriotism to a heartfelt recognition of my own. Watching the "Civil War" series, I felt connected to both sides. And I realized: These are my people and our story, and we share both their shame and their triumph. 3

4 And with their story, I've inherited a huge obligation to those who built America, who forged the bonds of union with their blood and sweat, and stayed focused on the ideal, that all men are created equal. We are a remarkable nation, with a remarkable story.

5 I don't know how long before immigrants would share these feelings, but I wouldn't expect them to feel it immediately. If we decide that patriotism is obsolete, then it probably doesn't matter if anyone feels it. I think it does.

6 A while ago, our Chilean exchange student returned from a party with other foreign students, and asked me an astonishing question: "Why do Americans teach their children to hate America?" The foreign students were struck by the extreme negativity, even contempt, toward America from their classmates. I explained: "We set high standards. Self-criticism is good for us." Her response: "No. All our nations have made mistakes. But we love our country, and we're proud of who we are."

7 Pride in who we are? Is that something we should teach our children?

8 Many educated elites today are hostile to patriotism. They would argue that we need a global, more inclusive perspective, that our planet is increasingly connected, and that teaching our children to appreciate foreign cultures and foreign peoples is much more important than teaching them pride in America.

9 Their vision for the future is a borderless world, where individuals freely move about, adapt to new cultures and languages, seeking out the best employment opportunities, ridding themselves of small-minded national loyalties. Which raises the question: If we are free of national loyalty, then where do our obligations lie? Do we turn ourselves into self-interested units, calling ourselves "world citizens"? Or might we spread ourselves a bit thin with that one, disguising the fact that we end up with no deep obligation to anyone in particular? Citizenship is a responsibility that demands time, money and sacrifice; it's not a "feeling for all mankind."

> **If we are free of national loyalty, then where do our obligations lie?**

10 Contrary to the globalist view, as described by social psychologist Jonathan Haidt, my vision of a world that works is one where groups of people with common values, language and heritage — we might call them "national families" — collectively work together. I cannot see that a borderless world of disconnected, migrating individuals, everyone out for himself, "free" of national loyalties, will lead to anything but chaos. But apparently, many of our educated citizens are intoxicated with the moral beauty of the globalist vision, and quite contemptuous of those who feel patriotism, like people who voted for Donald Trump.

We need to decide: Do we remain a national family with borders, united by patriotism, making the employment and improvement of our own citizens our first priority, or do we turn ourselves into a borderless economic region, based on "migrant rights" and global governance, as articulated by the U.N. Compact on Migration? 11

If we give up on patriotism and borders, then ancient group identities may emerge. People will identify with one group or another. We could fracture along competing ethnic, racial and class lines. The idea that all men are created equal has united a nation of many cultures for two centuries. But it's not clear that any ideal, no matter how lofty and inclusive, will override deeper claims of blood, race and religion in a borderless, multicultural world. The bonds of our union are fragile. 12

Final thoughts from our exchange student. At the end the year, I asked how she had changed. "I go home with a new feeling of appreciation for my own country. Compared to America, we are small and insignificant, just trying to help our people. We have nothing to prove," she said. "Nothing to prove"? What a strange observation from a 17-year-old. 13

VOCABULARY/USING A DICTIONARY

1. What does it mean if something is *obsolete* (para. 5 and title)?
2. What is the opposite of *inclusive* (para. 8)?
3. If someone is part of an *elite* (para. 8) group, where would they fall in a social hierarchy?

RESPONDING TO WORDS IN CONTEXT

1. What is the opposite of *borderless* (para. 9)? What might describe the opposite to the *borderless world* that Christian says many people envision?
2. Christian says, "If . . . patriotism is *obsolete*, then it probably doesn't matter if anyone feels it" (para. 5). What does it mean for something to be *obsolete*?
3. If people were to *fracture along . . . ethnic, racial and class lines* (para. 12), what would happen?

DISCUSSING MAIN POINT AND MEANING

1. The article begins with some historical reflection. What is some of the history Christian reflects upon as she considers the value of patriotism?
2. Why does Christian introduce the comments of her exchange student in para. 6? Does the exchange student's point support or challenge Christian's argument?
3. In para. 12, Christian issues a warning: What does she think is likely to happen if we "give up on patriotism and borders"?

EXAMINING SENTENCES, PARAGRAPHS, AND ORGANIZATION

1. What is the effect of bringing in the Vietnam War in the first paragraph? Why does Christian begin in this way?
2. In paragraph 2, Christian writes, "Patriotism is the emotional glue that holds us together." What kind of language is she using in that sentence?
3. In paragraph 10, Christian writes that elites are "intoxicated" with the idea of a borderless world and "contemptuous" of those who are patriotic. How would you describe the adjectives chosen in this sentence?

THINKING CRITICALLY

1. Who might the "educated elites" referred to in paragraphs 8 and 9 be? What is Christian's attitude toward them? Do you think she summarizes their position fairly?
2. **Connect:** What kind of entity does Christian suggest would counter the elite's idea of "world citizen"? Compare her comments in paragraph 10 to the points made in the Sorensen comic ("Patriotism vs. Nationalism") (p. 352). Do you think Christian would agree with the distinction Sorensen makes between the terms "nationalism" and "patriotism"?
3. What is behind Christian's question (regardless of whether patriotism is obsolete)? What about U.S. citizens' responses to their own country makes her think that it is?

WRITING ACTIVITIES

1. Are there any benefits to being a "borderless economic region" (para. 11)? Look to a real-life model — the formation of the European Union and the various responses to Brexit — as you consider this question further. Write a short report that discusses some of the problems that led to the British vote to pull out of the European Union. Also discuss the reactions of those who feel Brexit is a bad decision. What do you discover in your research, and does it put you more in agreement or disagreement with Christian's stance on patriotism?
2. How do you interpret the final paragraph? In writing, reflect on why Christian thinks the exchange student's remark of "nothing to prove" is a "strange observation from a 17-year-old." What do you think she means by that and why does she end on that note?
3. Watch a Ken Burns documentary on the Civil War or a documentary about the Vietnam War. How does the film make you feel? Patriotic or against patriotism? Depending on which war you are watching in film, your answer may differ. Write an explanation for why the documentary you've chosen evokes the feelings it does. Analyze the different approaches used and why the documentaries are built the way they are.

Tom Jacobs

Patriotic Americans Are Pro-Immigration

[*Pacific Standard*, July 24, 2018]

Recent data shows that the concern in Christian's essay ("Is Patriotism Obsolete?" on p. 357) about Americans growing less patriotic overall may be accurate. Around every Fourth of July, pollsters like to inquire into the patriotic sentiments of Americans, and a 2018 Gallup poll showed that patriotic feelings fell to a "new low": People who say they are "extremely proud" to be an American has dropped to 47 percent. It had in the years right after 9/11 (2001–2003) reached 70 percent.

But as journalist Tom Jacobs points out in the following feature, pollsters interested in attitudes toward the country have also tried to measure "levels of patriotism, nationalism, and xenophobia — distinct concepts with definitions that sometimes get muddled in the public discourse." In "Patriotic Americans Are Pro-Immigration," he summarizes a study that indicates, perhaps surprisingly, that "for most Americans, there is no contradiction between love of country and a welcoming attitude toward those who wish to move here."

A veteran journalist, Tom Jacobs is a senior staff writer at Pacific Standard, *where he specializes in social science, culture, and learning.*

Given the prominence and volume of those voices expressing fear and dislike of immigrants — especially of the undocumented variety — it's easy to forget that theirs is a minority opinion. A Gallup poll released earlier this year found 75 percent of Americans think immigration is "generally a good thing" for the country. 1

A new analysis of public views on the politically charged topic provides a nuanced look at public opinion on this topic — and comes to some fascinating conclusions. For one: More patriotic Americans also tend to be more pro-immigration. 2

Daniel K. Pryce of North Carolina Central University analyzed data from the 2014 General Social Survey to try to pin down which mindsets are linked to pro- and anti-immigrant sentiments. His paper, published in the *Social Science Quarterly,* is based on answers provided by 1,274 Americans who took the survey that year. 3

Attitudes toward immigration were measured by responses to two statements: "Immigrants are generally good for America's economy" and "Immigrants make America more open to new ideas and cultures." Participants responded using a scale of one (strongly agree) to five (strongly disagree). 4

Other questionnaires were designed to measure participants' levels of patriotism, nationalism, and xenophobia — distinct concepts with definitions that sometimes get muddied in the public discourse. "Patriotism," Pryce writes, is "a state of mind that makes a citizen proud of his or her country." 5

In contrast, nationalism "may be understood as elevating America above all other nations." And xenophobia consists of hostility toward people seen as outsiders or foreigners, who are seen as threatening the health of the culture and/or the economy. 6

Patriotism was measured by asking participants how proud they were of America "in the way its democracy works," "in the way its social security system works," and "in its fair and equal treatment of all groups in society." They responded to each on a scale of one (very proud) to four (not proud at all). 7

Nationalism was measured by their level of agreement (on a five-point scale) with three statements: "Generally speaking, people should support America even if the country is in the wrong"; "Generally speaking, America is a better country than most other countries"; and "The world would be a better place if people from other countries were more like Americans." 8

Participants similarly responded to three statements reflecting xenophobia: "Immigrants increase crime rates"; "American culture is generally undermined by immigrants"; and "Immigrants take jobs away from people who were born in America." Finally, they responded to a statement reflecting a very different attitude: "I feel more like a citizen of the world than of any other country." 9

Confirming prior research, Pryce found younger Americans and women were more pro-immigration than older Americans and men. To no one's surprise, "the greater U.S. citizens' xenophobic sentiments, the less likely they were to hold pro-immigration attitudes." Conversely, the more they identified as "citizens of the world," the more likely they were to welcome immigrants. 10

More strikingly, he found higher levels of patriotism were associated with a stronger pro-immigrant stance. Pryce notes that one can feel strongly attached to your group (in this case, fellow countrymen) but still have respect for those considered outsiders. This "may translate into greater willingness to welcome immigrants," he writes. 11

OK, but surely nationalism — the belief that America is superior to all other nations — is associated with hatred of immigrants, right? Actually, no. Pryce found no statistically significant relationship 12 between this mindset and sentiments toward immigration. Perhaps a good number of America-first types are pleased to see outsiders wanting to move here, given that it validates their world view.

The interesting question now, Pryce notes, is whether President Donald Trump's loud and persistent opposition to immigration (of both the legal and illegal variety) will change public opinion. He notes that, traditionally, political leaders have "tapped into patriotism to stir emotions of unity, loyalty, and civic responsibility in the nation's citizens." 13

Given that the current administration is effectively equating patriotism with exclusionary attitudes, it's conceivable the attitudes captured here could shift over the next few years, in one direction or another. 14

But this research shows that, for most Americans, there is no contradiction between love of country and a welcoming attitude toward those who wish to move here. The idea that we are "a nation of immigrants" has deep roots, and it won't be undone easily. 15

POINTS TO CONSIDER

1. How does the survey's definitions of patriotism and nationalism compare to the definitions we've seen in the previous selections? How does adding the concept of xenophobia clarify the differences?
2. Jacobs's summary of the survey shows that "higher levels of patriotism were associated with a stronger pro-immigrant stance" (para. 11). But he does not clarify whether the survey distinguished between "legal" and "undocumented" immigrants. How might this distinction affect the results?
3. How does Jacobs explain the survey's showing that even nationalism did not change feelings toward immigration? Can you think of other reasons?

Roshae Hemmings (student essay)

Burning Shoes to #BoycottNike Won't Change That Fact That Kaepernick and His Kneeling Aren't Going Anywhere

[*The Maneater* (Missouri University), September 10, 2018]

As quarterback for the San Francisco 49ers, Colin Kaepernick refused to stand for the national anthem during the 2016 preseason as a form of protest against racial injustice. As the regular season began, he kneeled instead when the anthem was played and eventually many players throughout the league started to take a knee to join his protest. In September 2017, President Trump criticized the protests and thought the NFL should fire all players who refused to stand for the anthem. After the 2017 season, Kaepernick, who is biracial, went unsigned and as a free agent sued the NFL for colluding to keep him out of football. In February 2019, the case was settled for an undisclosed amount.

Kaepernick's case caused quite a controversy at the time, not only within the sports community but also with the entire public. The controversy eventually died down but, as the following essay by Missouri University student Roshae Hemmings explains, was "reignited" when in September 2018 Nike decided to make Kaepernick a key figure in its "Just Do It" advertising campaign, a decision that at first had many opponents burning Nike gear in protest. But the protests backfired and Nike's profits soared. In "Burning Shoes to #BoycottNike Won't Change That Fact That Kaepernick and His Kneeling Aren't Going Anywhere," Hemmings supports Kaepernick's activism and Nike's involvement. "Without this type of comradery and partnership," she concludes, "the change that this country needs to see will never happen."

Roshae Hemmings is a journalism major at Missouri University and an opinion columnist who covers civil rights at the Maneater.

BEFORE YOU READ

What do you know about Colin Kaepernick's protest and the Nike ad that features him? Why are people threatening to burn their shoes?

WORDS TO LEARN

inception (para. 1): start (noun)
collaboration (para. 5): the process of working together (noun)
desecrate (para. 9): to defile (verb)
enact (para. 10): to make into law (verb)
solidarity (para. 12): unity (noun)
marginalized (para. 13): in a position of little importance (adjective)
comradery (para. 13): community (noun)

I am not going to stand up to show pride in a flag for a country that oppresses black people and people of color. To me, this is bigger than football and it would be selfish on my part to look the other way. There are bodies in the street and people getting paid leave and getting away with murder." Those words expressed by Colin Kaepernick marked the inception of the now infamous kneeling protest that has garnered both support and persistent opposition. The protests, having begun during the 49ers' preseason, continued throughout 2017 and gained intense, polarizing media coverage. However, as of late the controversy surrounding Kaepernick and the protests has been somewhat quiet. That is, until now. 1

I rarely ever click on links to news stories that I see on my Twitter feed. Typically, my Twitter scrolls are done senselessly, in order to pass the time that I have between classes or to absolve my boredom. When news of Kaepernick's part in Nike's 30th anniversary of their "Just Do It" slogan broke on Sept. 3, my reaction was more or less the same; give it a thoughtless like and move on. However, my interest wasn't piqued until talks of cutting off swooshes and burning Nike gear came up on my timeline. 2

Despite the work Kaepernick continued to do for the movement after the hype was gone, Nike helped to direct conversation back to a question that dates back to 2016: to kneel or not to kneel? The athletic brand's choice to highlight the shunned quarterback not only reignites important conversations, but gives Kaepernick the support that the NFL wouldn't. 3

From Kaepernick's initial protests back in 2016, to his work with Nike now, those in opposition to his protests have only one leg to stand on when it comes to their argument: the military. After Monday's announcement, many copycat posts were made replacing the tightly cropped black and white photo of Kaepernick with photos of vets while the original text, "Believe in something, even if it means sacrificing everything," remained. The problem with this response is twofold. 4

Firstly, the origin of the infamous kneeling protest is not one rooted in disrespect for the National Anthem, American flag or military, but rather the opposite. In fact, the gesture was created in collaboration with former football player and U.S Army veteran Nate Boyer. 5

"We sorta came to a middle ground where he would take a knee alongside his teammates," Boyer said. "Soldiers take a knee in front of a fallen brother's grave, you know, to show respect. When we're on a patrol, you know, and we go into a security halt, we take a knee, and we pull security." 6

Despite this, many still view this action as a sign of disrespect, including President Donald Trump. 7

"The issue of kneeling has nothing to do with race. It is about respect for our Country, Flag and National Anthem. NFL must respect this!" Trump said in 2017. 8

This then brings me to my second point; the willingness to cry disrespect is not only a cop-out and trivializing Kaepernick's motives, but it is branding the military as something that it is not. To use the lives and sacrifices of former and active veterans as a guise to support racial injustices desecrates the military more than getting down on a knee ever could. 9

Those who fight for our nation do so in order to uphold the liberty, justice, freedom, and equality that all are supposed to be granted here in America. Unfortunately, with the police brutality in our streets, mass shootings in our schools and abandoned children at our borders, these 10 promises and values have not been upheld. The kneeling that Kaepernick and many others in support of him have done is a call to action for politicians and policymakers to enact change in a political climate that consistently chooses to turn a blind eye.

For Nike to get behind this is genius, mainly because they are doing something the NFL refused to. In response to collective backlash, the NFL announced that all players on the field must stand during the national anthem or stay in the locker room until it is finished or else a fine will be issued. "Protests created a false perception among many that thousands of NFL players were unpatriotic," said the league in a statement. 11

This response is a less than satisfactory one, especially considering that the racial makeup of the NFL is 70 percent black. Instead of offering support and solidarity to its players and primary money makers, the NFL chose to silence individuals whose communities and peers are directly affected by the injustices in this country. 12

Nike's involvement is an example of what needs to be done when the oppressed and marginalized speak out. Those in positions of power, and therefore unaffected by systematic oppression, need to share their platforms so that there is an opportunity for the silenced to speak. Without this type of comradery and partnership, the change that this country needs to see will never happen. 13

VOCABULARY/USING A DICTIONARY

1. If something is *polarizing* (para. 1), how does it affect people?
2. Have you heard the word *absolve* (para. 2) before? If so, in what context?
3. How might you guess the meaning of *infamous* (para. 5) without a dictionary?

RESPONDING TO WORDS IN CONTEXT

1. What does it mean that Kaepernick's kneeling has "*garnered* both support and persistent opposition" (para. 1)?
2. What is *hype* (para. 3)? What is the hype around Kaepernick's kneeling? Around the Nike ad?
3. Given the context of the word *shunned* in paragraph 3 ("shunned quarterback"), what connotations would you attribute to the word?

DISCUSSING MAIN POINT AND MEANING

1. What does Kaepernick's protest have to do with race? What is he protesting?
2. Is Kaepernick's action disrespectful? To whom? Why does Hemmings say someone might assume that to be true?
3. What was the NFL's response to Kaepernick and other players' protest?

EXAMINING SENTENCES, PARAGRAPHS, AND ORGANIZATION

1. Why does Hemmings quote Nate Boyer in paragraph 6? What is the effect of that insertion?
2. Describe the transitions Hemmings uses to move from Kaepernick to Nike. How does the transition succeed or fail?
3. Why does Hemmings put herself in the essay in paragraph 2? Do you think that inclusion is important to the essay? Why?

THINKING CRITICALLY

1. Why is Nike's text "Believe in something, even if it means sacrificing everything" such an important message? Why is it problematic?
2. According to Hemmings, why is it important that a corporation like Nike has turned the spotlight on Kaepernick's stance?
3. Why does Hemmings call Nike's public support of Kaepernick "genius" (para. 11)?

WRITING ACTIVITIES

1. What is your understanding of Kaepernick's protest and the reaction to the Nike ad? Write a short essay that outlines the events as you remember them or as Hemmings writes of them here. What do you think of what Kaepernick did? What significance does it hold? Were you affected in some way by his actions or by the Nike ad? Explain your reaction.
2. Look at the advertising on Nike.com. To whom are their products geared? How can you tell? Analyze what you see and try to determine who they are marketing to.
3. **Connect:** In his essay "Patriotism vs. Nationalism" (p. 352), Azel writes, "Patriotism flows from the individual, nationalism focuses on the state." In her article, Hemmings writes, "The kneeling that Kaepernick and many others in support of him have done is a call to action for politicians and policymakers to enact change in a political climate that consistently chooses to turn a blind eye" (para. 10). Respond to these sentences, and consider whether Kaepernick's action can be called *patriotic* and backlash against kneeling can be called *nationalism*.

LOOKING CLOSELY

Using Quotations Effectively

As we have seen in the introduction to this book (p. 7), opinion writing can be usefully viewed as an extension of discussion, as a way we can ourselves publicly respond to the ideas and opinions of others. Clearly, one of the most effective ways of entering into public discussion in our writing is by quoting the statements of others, usually those who represent some authority or expertise in the topic under discussion. Writers will usually employ quotations (1) to bolster or support their own opinions, (2) to defend the opinions of others, or (3) to refute or oppose the opinions of others.

Note how Missouri University student Roshae Hemmings effectively uses quotations in "Burning Shoes to #BoycottNike Won't Change That Fact That Kaepernick and His Kneeling Aren't Going Anywhere." She opens with a direct quotation from Kaepernick himself to establish the controversy with which he is associated. She then supports her point that his protests were not against the military by citing an army veteran and former NFL player. To oppose President Trump's criticism and the NFL's position, she provides direct quotations from each.

1
Opens with direct quotation about protest

(1) "I am not going to stand up to show pride in a flag for a country that oppresses black people and people of color. To me, this is bigger than football and it would be selfish on my part to look the other way. There are bodies in the street and people getting paid leave and getting away with murder."

2
Quotation shows military supported protest

(2) "We sorta came to a middle ground where he would take a knee alongside his teammates," Boyer said. "Soldiers take a knee in front of a fallen brother's grave, you know, to show respect. When we're on a patrol, you know, and we go into a security halt, we take a knee, and we pull security."

3
Quotation to oppose Trump's criticism

(3) "The issue of kneeling has nothing to do with race. It is about respect for our Country, Flag and National Anthem. NFL must respect this!" Trump said in 2017.

4
Quotation to oppose NFL's position

(4) "Protests created a false perception among many that thousands of NFL players were unpatriotic," said the league in a statement.

STUDENT WRITER AT WORK

Roshae Hemmings

Roshae Hemmings

R.A. What inspired you to write your essay? And publish it?

R.H. When the Kaepernick Nike ad came out, it was a hot topic on social media. There was a variety of people pleased with the ad, as well as those upset or confused. Seeing the juxtaposition of views made me realize that there is a lack of education among many about the issue. Because of the confusion and misconceptions, I wanted to write something that would explain the motives behind Kaepernick's controversial means of protest, and why the Nike ad matters.

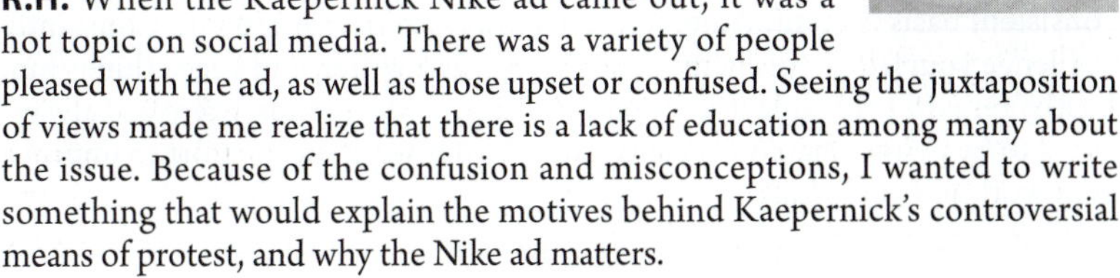

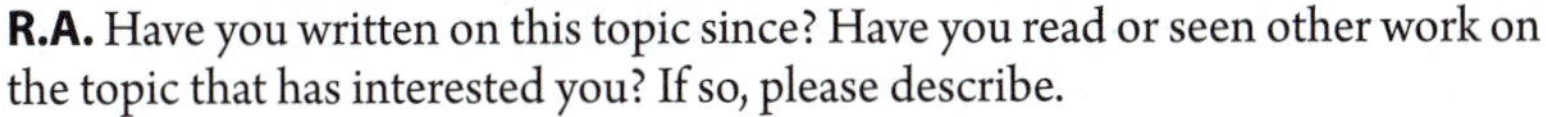

R.A. Have you written on this topic since? Have you read or seen other work on the topic that has interested you? If so, please describe.

R.H. I've written about similar topics. The majority of the pieces I write address social justice and activism, with an emphasis on issues that pertain to/affect the Black community. Although I have not written about Kaepernick since this piece, I did write about the tasteless Serena Williams cartoon that came out in September 2018, which is commentary on racism and misogyny within sports.

R.A. How long did it take for you to write this piece? Did you revise your work? What were your goals as you revised?

R.H. I would say that the process for writing this piece as a whole took anywhere from five to seven days. This includes doing research, pitching the idea, writing, editing, and it going to print. Writing this piece, specifically, took about three hours. When revising my work, I try to address the comments left by my editor, as well as ensuring that I am as concise and clear about my stance, while also providing adequate reasoning to support my argument. I also focus on organization, the language that is used, sentence structure, etc.

R.A. What topics most interest you as a writer?

R.H. I'm really interested in social justice issues, especially those that are specific to Black women, because that is the lens through which I view the world. I also enjoy writing about my take on people and topics within the sphere of pop culture.

R.A. Are you pursuing a career in which writing will be a component?

R.H. I am, yes. I am majoring in journalism. As of writing this, I haven't chosen an interest area, but I am thinking about magazine writing as well as convergence journalism. My goal is to write for a larger print publication such as the *New York Times* or the *Washington Post*, but I'm not sure yet. Luckily, I still have some time to figure that out.

R.A. What advice do you have for other student writers?

R.H. First, write on a consistent basis; this is the only way that you'll get better at your craft. Second, read the type of stuff you want to write. I've always heard that if you want to be a better writer, you've got to read more, and I agree. Take it further by reading publications and authors that closely align with where and who you want to be as a writer. Third, play around with what you write and how you write it. While writing in a certain form or about a certain topic on a consistent basis is comforting, it doesn't always allow for growth. Constantly challenge yourself — this helps diversify you as a writer, and keeps things fun. Lastly, remain teachable and open to critique. As a writer, there are always going to be people that look at and critique your work, in an effort to improve your work and your skills.

AMERICA THEN . . . 1852

Frederick Douglass

From "What to the Slave Is the Fourth of July?"

One of America's greatest public figures, Frederick Douglass (1817–1895), was born into slavery in Maryland and worked as a field hand and servant until he managed to escape to New York City in 1838 at the age of twenty-one. Self-educated (he taught himself to read and write) and fiercely determined, Douglass transformed himself into one of the nation's most formidable intellectuals and writers of his time. He served in a number of government positions, published his own periodicals, and was known as an outstanding orator and eloquent civil rights advocate. His life and career became a model for such powerful African American leaders as W. E. B. Du Bois and Martin Luther King Jr. Besides a large number of famous speeches (such as his 1852 Fourth of July oration), Douglass is also the author of the enduring American memoir The Life and Times of Frederick Douglass, *which first appeared in 1881.*

Douglass delivered his best-known speech on July 5, 1852, in Rochester, New York, where he was invited to help celebrate the nation's seventy-sixth birthday. The speech is very long and, for those interested, the full text can easily be found online. Early in the speech, Douglass makes his position clear when he famously says: "This Fourth of July is yours, not mine. You may rejoice, I must mourn." It must be remembered that the address was delivered in an era when slavery not only was still widely practiced in America but also had many defenders. Although abolitionism — the movement to abolish slavery — was gaining ground in northern states, the Civil War and Lincoln's Emancipation Proclamation were years away. In the following excerpt, which demonstrates the intricate art of persuasion, Douglass passionately argues not about the evils of slavery but about why arguments to abolish it are needed at all.

BEFORE YOU READ

What do you know about Frederick Douglass and the time in which he lived? Why might he be particularly impassioned when discussing slavery and the Fourth of July?

WORDS TO LEARN

tumultuous (para. 1): turbulent (adjective)
grievous (para. 1): causing grief (adjective)
jubilee (para. 1): celebration or festivity (noun)
denounce (para. 1): to accuse (verb)
equivocate (para. 1): to be ambiguous (verb)
severest (para. 1): most severe (adjective)
relatively (para. 4): in comparison with other similar things (adverb)
sunder (para. 5): to break into two parts (verb)
rebuke (para. 6): reprimand (noun)
hypocrisy (para. 6): pretending to be something you're not or believe something you don't (noun)
denunciation (para. 7): censure (noun)
bombast (para. 7): pretentious speech (noun)
impiety (para. 7): lack of reverence (noun)
barbarity (para. 8): cruelty (noun)
reign (para. 8): to rule (verb)
rival (para. 8): competitor (noun)

Fellow-citizens; above your national, tumultuous joy, I hear the mournful wail of millions! whose chains, heavy and grievous yesterday, are, today, rendered more intolerable by the jubilee shouts that reach them. If I do forget, if I do not faithfully remember those bleeding children of sorrow this day, "may my right hand forget her cunning, and may my tongue cleave to the roof of my mouth!"[1] To forget them, to pass lightly over their wrongs, and to chime in with the popular theme, would be treason most scandalous and shocking, and would make me a reproach before God and the world. My subject, then, fellow-citizens, is AMERICAN SLAVERY. I shall see, this day, and its popular characteristics, from the slave's point of view. Standing, there, identified with the American bondman, making his wrongs mine, I do not hesitate to declare, with all my soul, that the character and conduct of this nation 1

[1] Biblical quotation, from Psalm 137.

never looked blacker to me than on this 4th of July! Whether we turn to the declarations of the past, or to the professions of the present, the conduct of the nation seems equally hideous and revolting. America is false to the past, false to the present, and solemnly binds herself to be false to the future. Standing with God and the crushed and bleeding slave on this occasion, I will, in the name of humanity which is outraged, in the name of liberty which is fettered, in the name of the constitution and the Bible, which are disregarded and trampled upon, dare to call in question and to denounce, with all the emphasis I can command, everything that serves to perpetuate slavery — the great sin and shame of America! "I will not equivocate; I will not excuse;"[2] I will use the severest language I can command; and yet not one word shall escape me that any man, whose judgment is not blinded by prejudice, or who is not at heart a slaveholder, shall not confess to be right and just.

But I fancy I hear some one of my audience say, it is just in this circumstance that you and your brother abolitionists fail to make a favorable impression on the public mind. Would you argue more, and denounce less, would you persuade more, and rebuke less, your cause would be much more likely to succeed. But, I submit, where all is plain there is nothing to be argued. What point in the anti-slavery creed would you have me argue? On what branch of the subject do the people of this country need light? Must I undertake to prove that the slave is a man? That point is conceded already. Nobody doubts it. The slaveholders themselves acknowledge it in the enactment of laws for their government. They acknowledge it when they punish disobedience on the part of the slave. There are seventy-two crimes in the State of Virginia, which, if committed by a black man, (no matter how ignorant he be), subject him to the punishment of death; while only two of the same crimes will subject a white man to the like punishment. What is this but the acknowledgment that the slave is a moral, intellectual and responsible being? The manhood of the slave is conceded. It is admitted in the fact that Southern statute books are covered with enactments forbidding, under severe fines and penalties, the teaching of the slave to read or to write. When you can point to any such laws, in reference to the beasts of the field, then I may consent to argue the manhood of the slave. When the dogs in your streets, when the fowls of the air, when the cattle on your hills, when the fish of the sea, and the reptiles that crawl, shall be unable to distinguish the slave from a brute, *then* will I argue with you that the slave is a man! 2

For the present, it is enough to affirm the equal manhood of the Negro race. Is it not astonishing that, while we are ploughing, planting and reaping, using all kinds of mechanical tools, erecting houses, constructing 3

---

[2] Douglass quotes noted abolitionist William Lloyd Garrison (1805–1879).

bridges, building ships, working in metals of brass, iron, copper, silver and gold; that, while we are reading, writing and cyphering, acting as clerks, merchants and secretaries, having among us lawyers, doctors, ministers, poets, authors, editors, orators and teachers; that, while we are engaged in all manner of enterprises common to other men, digging gold in California, capturing the whale in the Pacific, feeding sheep and cattle on the hill-side, living, moving, acting, thinking, planning, living in families as husbands, wives and children, and, above all, confessing and worshipping the Christian's God, and looking hopefully for life and immortality beyond the grave, we are called upon to prove that we are men!

Would you have me argue that man is entitled to liberty? that he is the 4
rightful owner of his own body? You have already declared it. Must I argue the wrongfulness of slavery? Is that a question for Republicans?[3] Is it to be settled by the rules of logic and argumentation, as a matter beset with great difficulty, involving a doubtful application of the principle of justice, hard to be understood? How should I look to-day, in the presence of Americans, dividing, and subdividing a discourse, to show that men have a natural right to freedom? speaking of it relatively, and positively, negatively, and affirmatively. To do so, would be to make myself ridiculous, and to offer an insult to your understanding. — There is not a man beneath the canopy of heaven that does not know that slavery is wrong *for him.*

What, am I to argue that it is wrong to make men brutes, to rob them 5
of their liberty, to work them without wages, to keep them ignorant of their relations to their fellow men, to beat them with sticks, to flay their flesh with the lash, to load their limbs with irons, to hunt them with dogs, to sell them at auction, to sunder their families, to knock out their teeth, to burn their flesh, to starve them into obedience and submission to their masters? Must I argue that a system thus marked with blood, and stained with pollution, is *wrong*? No! I will not. I have better employments for my time and strength than such arguments would imply. What, then, remains to be argued? Is it that slavery is not divine; that God did not establish it; that our doctors of divinity are mistaken? There is blasphemy in the thought. That which is inhuman, cannot be divine! Who can reason on such a proposition? They that can, may; I cannot. The time for such argument is passed.

At a time like this, scorching irony, not convincing argument, is 6
needed. O! had I the ability, and could I reach the nation's ear, I would, today, pour out a fiery stream of biting ridicule, blasting reproach, withering sarcasm, and stern rebuke. For it is not light that is needed, but fire; it is not the gentle shower, but thunder. We need the storm, the whirlwind, and the earthquake. The feeling of the nation must be quickened; the conscience of the nation must be roused; the propriety of the nation

---

[3] He means citizens of a republic, not the political party that Lincoln belonged to.

must be startled; the hypocrisy of the nation must be exposed; and its crimes against God and man must be proclaimed and denounced.

7 What, to the American slave, is your Fourth of July? I answer: a day that reveals to him, more than all other days in the year, the gross injustice and cruelty to which he is the constant victim. To him, your celebration is a sham; your boasted liberty, an unholy license; your national greatness, swelling vanity; your sounds of rejoicing are empty and heartless; your denunciations of tyrants, brass fronted impudence; your shouts of liberty and equality, hollow mockery; your prayers and hymns, your sermons and thanksgivings, with all your religious parade, and solemnity, are, to him, mere bombast, fraud, deception, impiety, and hypocrisy — a thin veil to cover up crimes which would disgrace a nation of savages. There is not a nation on the earth guilty of practices, more shocking and bloody, than are the people of the United States, at this very hour.

8 Go where you may, search where you will, roam through all the monarchies and despotisms of the old world, travel through South America, search out every abuse, and when you have found the last, lay your facts by the side of the everyday practices of this nation, and you will say with me, that, for revolting barbarity and shameless hypocrisy, America reigns without a rival.

VOCABULARY/USING A DICTIONARY

1. What is *bondman* (para. 1) another word for?
2. What does it mean to *abolish* something? What is an *abolitionist* (para. 2) in this context?
3. What is the opposite of *affirm* (para. 3)?

RESPONDING TO WORDS IN CONTEXT

1. What is *treason* (para. 1)? Is it surprising that it's connected with the Fourth of July celebrations?
2. Douglass writes, "It is admitted in the fact that Southern statute books are covered with *enactments* forbidding, under severe fines and penalties, the teaching of the slave to read or to write" (para. 2). What is he referring to? What is an *enactment* in this case?
3. What might a *doctor of divinity* (para. 5) be, given the context?

DISCUSSING MAIN POINT AND MEANING

1. Who are the millions that Douglass hears wailing in the opening paragraph?
2. What does Douglass imagine the audience wants him to do, to make a better case about abolitionism and slavery? Why does he object?

3. In paragraph 7, Douglass asks the question, "What, to the American slave, is your Fourth of July?" How does he answer that question?

EXAMINING SENTENCES, PARAGRAPHS, AND ORGANIZATION

1. Douglass includes rhetorical questions throughout the essay. Identify one of them. Why do you think he uses them? What effect do they have on the reader?
2. Who is Douglass's audience? Who in particular do you think he is addressing when he refers to "you"?
3. Look closely at paragraph 3. Why do you think it is structured the way that it is? What can you say about the language Douglass is using? How is this paragraph different from the others, if it is different?

THINKING CRITICALLY

1. Did all who heard Douglass's words consider African American slaves men? What points does he make about why they are or must be considered men? What in the essay indicates that they were not considered men?
2. Why would slaves react strongly to the celebration of the Fourth of July?
3. **Connect:** Would Douglass agree with Gordon-Reed's ("America's Original Sin: Slavery and the Legacy of White Supremacy," p. 217) assessment of U.S. history? How would Gordon-Reed interpret Douglass's sentence: "America is false to the past, false to the present, and solemnly binds herself to be false to the future" (para. 1)? With this statement as a guide, has any progress on that front been made in the United States?

WRITING ACTIVITIES

1. Write a persuasive essay or speech in Douglass's style. Use as many as possible of the literary devices Douglass uses (rhetorical questions, repetition, listing, and so on). Share your work in small groups. How do these devices work to persuade?
2. Write a brief reflective essay on patriotism with Douglass's speech in mind. Why might one person feel patriotic and another not? What fuels patriotism in a person? Is it citizenship? The rights of a citizen? What else makes one feel patriotic, and what might we take for granted when we talk about patriotism?
3. Write a response, well over a hundred years later, to Douglass's speech. Begin with his line "Go where you may, search where you will, roam through all the monarchies and despotisms of the old world, travel through South America, search out every abuse, and when you have found the last, lay your facts by the side of the everyday practices of this nation, and you will

say with me, that, for revolting barbarity and shameless hypocrisy, America reigns without a rival." Speak to Douglass, as you write, about whether you believe this statement to be true, and why you hold the opinion you do. Feel free to respond to other parts of his speech as well.

Discussing the Unit

SUGGESTED TOPIC FOR DISCUSSION

America began as a land of "patriots" and, over its history, having and expressing feelings of patriotism was seen as part of being American. How has showing patriotism become something to question, or become associated with blind fervor? What does it mean to be a patriotic American? What does it mean to be someone who promotes nationalism over patriotism — or who promotes both?

PREPARING FOR CLASS DISCUSSION

1. Do immigrants and citizens feel patriotism differently? How do you define "patriotism"? Does the word have positive or negative connotations for you? Explain.
2. How do you understand the meaning of "nationalism"? Is it important for citizens of a nation to feel nationalistic?

FROM DISCUSSION TO WRITING

1. Do you think our country is experiencing a unique time of patriotism or nationalism? Explain your answer using three of the texts in this chapter (including the Jen Sorensen cartoon) for support of your answer.
2. Can you tell which of the writers of these essays consider themselves patriotic? Why or why not? Draw specific examples from the essays to support your answer. Is it possible to tell? Why do you think so?

TOPICS FOR CROSS-CULTURAL DISCUSSION

1. What do religion and race have to do with American identity? Do people hold different opinions on this issue? If one group thinks only people who believe in a certain god can be patriotic Americans, or only one group can be truly patriotic, explain (using details from any of these texts) why this attitude exists. What about those who believe the opposite, or believe that people of any race or religion can be patriotic Americans? Contrast these two ideas.
2. Frederick Douglass wrote his speech in 1852. How might some people, especially those Americans who are descendants of former slaves, respond to his speech today? How might race shape one's experience of American patriotism?

12

Political Polarization: How Disunited Is the United States?

As we saw in "The American Political Spectrum: A Brief Survey" (p. 16), the nation's political life is largely divided between two parties: Democrats and Republicans, or, as the members of those parties are customarily termed, liberals and conservatives. Within these two parties, however, we find plenty of disagreement, as each party itself consists of a further spectrum of opinion. For example, the Democrats have recently experienced an undeniable surge of energy from progressives who prefer to see the party adopt more liberal views. In fact, a number of progressive and socialist intellectuals often remain extremely critical of the mainstream Democratic Party, which they consider neoliberal and too accepting of corporate capitalism. This divide can be seen in the enormous popularity of the independent Vermont senator and presidential candidate, Bernie Sanders, who identifies as a Democratic Socialist. Although the term "socialism" has been tossed around a great deal in the media since the 2018 midterm elections, genuine members of the Socialist Party regard most American "socialists" as basically political "reformers," activists who strive for a more equitable society but do not ultimately want the state to control all forms of production. Republicans, however, though not so divided ideologically (the party does not embrace socialist views whatsoever) have their own internal battles over many issues, including immigration, drugs, trade and tariffs, and foreign diplomacy.

To cover the complexity of America's current political conflicts would, of course, require several books. In this chapter, we will examine a few recent topics that have attracted much political commentary: the fear that civil discussion and bipartisan collaboration are no longer viable political options, and a widespread concern that our polarization has grown so vast that we are on the verge of another civil war. For example, a June 2019 Pew Research poll found that 85 percent of Americans say that in recent years "the tone and nature of political debate in the U.S. has become more negative." In this chapter, we will also examine some of the reasons why so many Americans seem distressed over our fractious political discourse.

Thomas J. Donohue

Putting the "Civil" Back into Civil Society

[*The Weekly Standard*, July 9/16, 2018]

The following opinion advertisement (or "op ad," see Introduction pp. 40–44) appeared in the conservative journal the Weekly Standard, *which ceased publication at the end of 2018. Written by Thomas J. Donohue, the president and CEO of the U.S. Chamber of Commerce, the ad promotes both civility and the writer's pro-business organization. It criticizes "a growing faction of people who are no longer content to argue the merits of their ideas with their opponents," but who instead prefer to "silence their voices and shut them out of the debate." Donohue considers such behavior "un-American" and timed the ad to appear around the Fourth of July.*

Thomas J. Donohue has been president of the U.S. Chamber of Commerce since 1997. "Through Mr. Donohue's efforts," the New York Times *reported, "the Chamber has become the most visible and effective business lobby in the country."*

Winston Churchill once said: "Some people's idea of free speech is that they are free to say what they like, but if anyone says anything back, that is an outrage." 1

There's no shortage of outrage in America today. Coarse language, entrenched political beliefs, efforts to silence those you disagree with, and a 24/7/365 media prone to sensationalism are eroding an essential ingredient of democracy and progress — civility. 2

It's tough to make progress in a 50-50 nation, especially when the two sides prefer shouting over sharing and making a point over making a law. The result is a less civil, more bombastic political conversation that frankly disgusts many Americans and prevents our government from solving problems. 3

In this environment, there's a growing faction of people who are no longer content to argue the merits of their ideas with their opponents — they simply want to silence their voices and shut them out of the debate. I can't think of anything more un-American — or more 4 dangerous — than a frontal attack on free speech, the bedrock of our democracy.

Restoring civility is something we all need to take personally 5
and work on every day. We try to set an example at the U.S. Chamber of Commerce by ensuring that all of our employees are respected in the workplace. We insist that our employees demonstrate good manners and high integrity. We work with any credible group to advance issues we agree on or help bridge differences of opinion to achieve a policy that will benefit all sides. We focus on policies, not personalities.

We believe that our right to speak carries with it the responsibility 6
to listen, give others a fair hearing, and be open to different points of view. You can be tough without being a jerk, or trying to run those you disagree with right out of the public square.

Restoring civility to our public dia- 7
logue is a challenge, but let's not wax nostalgic about the past. Thomas Jefferson once called Alexander Hamilton the son of a whore, and Hamilton publicly exposed Jefferson's affair with his slave. During the debate over the abolition of slavery, one senator nearly caned his colleague to death on the Senate floor. And our nation did, after all, endure a bloody Civil War.

Restoring civility to our public dialogue is a challenge, but let's not wax nostalgic about the past.

As Mahatma Gandhi once advised us: "Be the change that you wish 8
to see in the world." Civility starts with each of us. Wouldn't engaging in a respectful dialogue with someone you disagree with be a great way to honor the founding of our country on the Fourth of July?

POINTS TO CONSIDER

1. Donohue doesn't specifically name any faction of political party as being guilty of incivility. Why do you think he doesn't point a finger at anyone? Do you think he does have particular groups in mind?
2. Why would the Chamber of Commerce take out this ad? Of what connection is the political topic of "civility" to that organization? How might the Chamber of Commerce benefit from the ad?
3. Note that in paragraph 7, Donohue mentions a few historical incidents. Why does he introduce these? What is his point? Do you think they strengthen or weaken his case?

Livia Gershon

Should Politics Be Civil?

[*JSTOR Daily*, July 9, 2018]

As columnist Livia Gershon observes in the following selection, "Recent coverage of U.S politics has been unusually focused on the topic of civility." She goes on in "Should Politics Be Civil?" to acknowledge the work of several philosophers who have studied the concept of civility in the political sphere. According to one political philosopher she cites, "Standards for appropriate political speech are often based on elite norms, making it easy to dismiss members of marginalized groups who use different styles of communication." The demand for civility may actually be a way to "stifle dissent" or maintain the status quo.

Livia Gershon describes herself as "a freelance writer in Nashua, New Hampshire," who is "interested in the intersections of economics, politics and everyday life." Her work appears in Aeon, Huffington Post, Longreads, Vice, *and many other periodicals that focus on contemporary political issues.*

BEFORE YOU READ

Is civility in the political realm important? What is the relationship of civility to deeper political issues, if there is one?

WORDS TO LEARN

civility (para. 1): common courtesy (noun)
convey (para. 3): to communicate (verb)
bludgeon (para. 5): a heavy club with a thick end (noun)
civilly (para. 7): politely (adverb)
fundamental (para. 7): essential (adjective)

From President Trump's name-calling and obscene language, to incidents where members of his administration have been shouted at or denied service at restaurants, recent coverage of U.S. politics has been unusually focused on the topic of civility. In 2013, philosopher Christopher F. Zurn explored the question of how seriously we should take civility in politics. 1

Zurn was writing three years before Trump's election, with a different set of uncivil behaviors in mind. In 2009, a member of Congress had shouted "you lie" at President Obama during a speech. Even more 2 dramatically, in 2011, U.S. Representative Gabrielle Giffords was shot, not long after her name had appeared on a "target list" of politicians, with their districts marked by crosshairs.

Drawing on the work of Cheshire Calhoun, a philosopher who 3
has analyzed civility in the personal sphere, Zurn writes that civility is always tied to social convention — rules that are based in a particular time and place — but following those rules conveys "the equal respect owed universally to all persons as moral agents."

Another view on civility comes from John Rawls, who argued 4
that — given the variety of moral doctrines we bring to politics — civil political discourse means grounding our political arguments in the areas where our beliefs overlap. Otherwise, Zurn writes, our arguments can only be convincing to people who share our particular religious or philosophical background.

Others suggest that arguments about 5
civility are a distraction from the real political issues. If politics is essentially a battleground for armies with opposing, non-negotiable fundamental principles, those calling for civility are either asking for "a mild consensus and a bland unanimity" or cynically using the idea of civil discourse as a bludgeon against their opponents. In some cases, according to Zurn, social pressure to behave civilly in politics may stifle dissent or "be strategically deployed to distract from deep racial injustice of chattel slavery or racial segregation."

Others suggest that arguments about civility are a distraction from the real political issues.

Zurn also points out that standards for appropriate political speech 6
are often based on elite norms, making it easy to dismiss members of marginalized groups who use different styles of communication. In the 1980s, rhetoric of "civilized discussion" helped exclude conversations about sexual orientation and the rights of LGBTQ people from the political stage.

Ultimately, Zurn concludes, civility must be balanced with other 7
political virtues. "I would be much more worried, for instance, about the systemic denial of voting rights to some citizens than I would be at the prospect of vituperative and denigrating campaigns, if somehow I were forced to choose," he writes. He also notes that simply speaking more civilly can't fix the structural problems in our political system that have led to gridlock in Washington, or address fundamental differences in values.

VOCABULARY/USING A DICTIONARY

1. What is the opposite of *obscene* (para. 1)?
2. When does one use *crosshairs* (para. 2)?
3. What is the etymology of the word *vituperative* (para. 7)?

RESPONDING TO WORDS IN CONTEXT

1. If a group is offering *consensus* and *unanimity,* what is its position? What about when you add the adjectives *mild* and *bland* (para. 5)?
2. What is meant by the term *political stage* (para. 6)?
3. How would you describe a *systemic* denial (para. 7) of something like voting rights (as opposed to just a denial of voting rights)?

DISCUSSING MAIN POINT AND MEANING

1. What outcomes of civility or incivility are drawn out in this article? How are they of dire importance to the state of the Union?
2. How would you summarize the point being made in paragraph 4?
3. Does the concluding paragraph shed light on the importance of civility? What is Zurn's position at the end?

EXAMINING SENTENCES, PARAGRAPHS, AND ORGANIZATION

1. Of what importance is it for Gershon to note in paragraph 2 that the Zurn article she cites appeared "three years before Trump's election" and also refers to events five and seven years before that election?
2. How would this article be different if Gershon included her personal opinions? Does the essay feel different when Zurn is quoted in first person in the conclusion? Explain.
3. Look at the structure of the sentence in paragraph 3 (which is the entire paragraph). Is it hard to tease apart whose ideas are being examined in this article? Do you need more information about Cheshire Calhoun to be satisfied with why his words are important or relevant (or about John Rawls in paragraph 4)? Why or why not?

THINKING CRITICALLY

1. What is Zurn's point in paragraph 5? Do you agree that politics is a "battleground" of "opposing, non-negotiable" principles? If that is the case, how can "civility" be used as a political strategy?
2. Do you think a renewed focus on civility in politics would be beneficial now, even though Zurn was commenting on pre-Trump politics? Do you think Zurn was aware of a change in the political climate?
3. Is there any value to civility? Even if you don't find that value in politics, where is the expression and experience of civility important and why?

WRITING ACTIVITIES

1. Given Gershon's summary of Zurn's position, how would you answer the question her title poses? "Yes" or No"? Write a response to the question that draws support from or responds to Gershon's argument.
2. **Connect:** Gershon's article is organized around an examination of Christopher F. Zurn's exploration of the importance of civility in politics. Try structuring a short essay that also examines a larger question through close scrutiny and explanation of another's writing on that question. Use either Gordon-Reed's ideas ("America's Original Sin: Slavery and the Legacy of White Supremacy," p. 217) to explore the question "Can we avoid racism in America?" or use Williams and Ceci's ideas ("There Are No Good Alternatives to Free Speech on Campus," p. 79) to explore the question "Should there be limits to free speech on college campuses?" You should model your essay closely on Gershon's for this assignment.
3. Choose a specific example of incivility that Gershon mentions in the text. Write up that incivility in a report (as if you are writing a news brief). Include any relevant information about the incident, but also include any reactions of the people involved or the witnesses and bystanders to the event. As you conclude your report, address the importance of the event as you understand it — what does it say or reflect about other political attitudes or issues, if anything at all?

Avi Tuschman

Political Evolution: Why Do Young Voters Lean Left? It's in the Genes

[*Bloomberg Businessweek*, April 17, 2014]

There's an old saying with many variations that usually goes something like this: "If you are not a liberal at 25, you have no heart. If you are not a conservative at 35, you have no brain." Is there any truth to this adage? Do people grow more conservative as they grow older? In the following essay, biologist Avi Tuschman opens with his variation of the old saying and argues that the conventional wisdom appears to be true from an evolutionary standpoint. Tuschman in fact believes that political stances may be in our genes — at least in part. Examining a wide survey of studies and societies, Tuschman surmises that young people tend to be more liberal because evolution rewards them for open-mindedness. The image of a hard-edged conservative elder is, moreover, more than a cliché according to

Tuschman: As we have families and settle down, we all become more concerned about dangers lurking around corners. "Political Evolution" connects these trends in our cognitive development to the traditional left–right split of American politics. "Despite generational idiosyncrasies," Tuschman concludes, "the universal stages of life do influence our political orientations." Recent research polls on age differences in politics have confirmed Tuschman's analysis.

Avi Tuschman is a former adviser to the president of Peru and the author of the book Our Political Nature: The Evolutionary Origins of What Divides Us. *His research has been covered in numerous publications, including the* New York Times, *the* Economist, MSNBC, Politico, *the* Atlantic, Bloomberg Businessweek, *and* Forbes.

BEFORE YOU READ

Why do we form ties with one political party or another? Are there times in our life when these allegiances are more likely to change?

WORDS TO LEARN

variation (para. 1): modification (noun)
conscientiousness (para. 2): meticulousness (noun)
cohort (para. 6): group of individuals (noun)
actuaries (para. 10): clerks (noun)
stratify (para. 11): to arrange (verb)
correspond (para. 11): to be in agreement with (verb)

If you're not a liberal when you're 20, you have no heart. If you're not a conservative by the time you're 30, you have no brain." Variations of this saying have been attributed to Benjamin Disraeli, Otto von Bismarck, George Bernard Shaw, Woodrow Wilson, Theodore Roosevelt, Aristide Briand, and Winston Churchill. The thought first came, in fact, from a French statesman, François Guizot (1787–1874). Regardless of its origin, the adage raises a fascinating question: Do the young really lean left because of passions and idealism? And as people age, do they incline toward the right because they become more realistic or cynical? 1

For the past 10 years, I've studied political divisions through the lenses of evolutionary anthropology, genetics, and neuroscience. Research reveals that during their 20s people around the world experience significant shifts in the traits biologists use to describe the human personality. Specifically, "openness" declines and "conscientiousness" increases. Higher openness is associated with intellectual curiosity, a preference for variety, and voting for the left; higher conscientiousness, 2 characterized by self-discipline and dutifulness, predicts support for more conservative politics.

This rightward shift in political personality is fairly universal, and so is the timing. A 2004 study by psychologists Robert McCrae and Jüri Allik in the *Journal of Cross Cultural Psychology* of 36 cultures across Africa, Europe, and Asia discovered that openness and conscientiousness differ between 18- to 22-year-olds and older adults. If an individual's political personality hasn't changed by the time of his or her 30th birthday, however, it's not likely to differ all that much at 40, 50, or 60. This isn't to say that all teenagers are liberal and all older people are conservative. In any age group, people are distributed along the left-right spectrum on a bell curve. The entire curve, however, moves somewhat to the right during the mid-20s. 3

A common explanation for this personality change in young adulthood was voiced during the politically turbulent 1960s in the U.S. At the time, the young leftist counterculture claimed that its ideological enemies could be found on the far side of Guizot's magic number, 30. This belief implied that people older than that became more conservative because they were more likely to own a house, to earn a higher salary, and to have too much at stake to back a revolutionary call to destroy the existing order. 4

Contrary to popular belief, paying taxes, accumulating wealth, and being in the 1 percent or the 99 percent are extremely poor predictors of left-right political orientation. According to American National Election Studies, an academically run survey project, the correlation between family income and party identification for U.S. voters in the 2012 presidential election was a mere 0.13. This weak statistical relationship is typical of past elections. 5

There is one life event, though, that greatly accelerates a person's shift to the right.

There is one life event, though, that greatly accelerates a person's shift to the right, and it often occurs in the 30s: parenthood. Its political impact is easy to see among a cohort of Canadian college students studied by psychologist Robert Altemeyer. Their scores on an ideology test at age 22 grew more conservative by an average of 5.4 percent when they were retested at 30. But among those 30-year-olds who'd had children, conservatism increased by 9.4 percent. 6

Why did having kids push people to the right? Parents stay on the lookout for possible sources of danger that nonparents can ignore. This shift in perception is so strong it creates an illusory sense of risk; new parents tend to believe that crime rates have increased since they had 7 children even when actual crime has dropped dramatically. Because "dangerous world" thinking is associated with political conservatism, parenthood pushes people to the right, and more so when they have daughters.

Experts on personality, such as McCrae, a psychologist at the National Institute on Aging, say people's personalities may also be hardwired to shift over time. As we age, changes in gene expression may subtly alter openness, conscientiousness, and other traits. These traits and the personality shifts that unfold between late adolescence and early adulthood are moderately heritable between generations. 8

To understand why both nature and the environment tug at our personalities at certain times, we must trace these subtle changes in our personality to activity in the brain. Neuroscientists once assumed that the brain, along with the rest of the body, finishes dramatic development after puberty. But we now know that it doesn't reach full maturity until at least age 25. Consider the prefrontal cortex, which lies directly behind the forehead. It's responsible for regulating emotions, controlling impulses, and making complex cost-benefit judgments that weigh immediate incentives against future consequences. Unlike most regions of the brain, the prefrontal cortex continues to grow, and its cautionary functions go on developing well into the mid-20s. 9

Much earlier, in adolescence, a part of the brain called the limbic system, which plays a central role in sexual arousal and pleasure, kicks into action, stimulating thrill-seeking and risk-taking. Actuaries who work for car insurance companies have long deemed people younger than 25 risky. Why would nature permit this tempestuous gap between the flaring up of teenage passions and the onset of mental maturity 10 years later? These personality changes are probably evolutionary adaptations to different phases of the life cycle. High levels of openness encourage the young to wander the world and find a mate. Conscientiousness is crucial when raising a family. 10

Political pollsters are well aware of these life cycle personality changes, which is why they pay so much attention to age. When youth turn out to vote in higher numbers, as they do in presidential elections, analysts can stratify their samples to look for trends by age brackets that correspond roughly to before and after the brain developments that happen in the mid-20s: That is, they analyze the 18- to 24-year-old group separately from the 25- to 29-year-old group. In midterm elections, when the youth vote is underrepresented, pollsters often lump them all into one demographic group, 18 to 29. 11

In this era of big data, political pros of course have other tools at their disposal that make analysis of these large groups less relevant. As Chief Executive Officer Jim Walsh of the political ad network 12

DSPolitical points out, it's now easy to microtarget individuals of any age and according to dozens of other demographic and consumer categories. Nevertheless, public opinion experts still keep tabs on age groups to study their impressionability to the changing flow of history, culture, and economic cycles. In some cases, current events trump life cycle stages, altering the collective attitudes of a cohort in surprising ways. In 1984, 18- to 24-year-olds voted for Ronald Reagan over Walter Mondale by a 22-percentage-point margin — the same margin as 50- to 64-year-olds. This youth vote may have been anomalously conservative, because Reagan had presided over a strong recovery from recession and Mondale was perceived to be a weak candidate. Young Republican voters in 1984 may also have been expressing their feeling of disconnect with the liberal social movements of the 1960s and 1970s.

Today's young voter adheres more closely to the personality pattern shaped by evolution, though environmental variables such as the social media revolution have left a mark as well. As expected, millennials lean substantially to the left on most social issues, but slightly less so on economic issues. These "digital natives," who grew up steeped in social media, have also been dubbed the Selfie Generation. And Selfie may be a more apt description: The age group is characterized by individualism across the board. According to the Pew Research Center, millennials are far less affiliated with traditional political, religious, and cultural institutions and less likely to be married than previous generations were. Some commentators have accused the Selfie Generation of having a sense of entitlement, interpreting their individualism as a kind of Facebook (FB)-induced narcissism. Other observers have argued that millennials measure higher in cynicism and singleness — and more often live with their parents — because they face worse economic prospects than did the previous two generations. 13

Whichever perspective one takes, our changing economic and technological environments have surely left an impression on millennials and molded their political behavior in various unforeseen ways. Still, like most 18- to 29-year-old cohorts, their vote is markedly more liberal than average. Despite generational idiosyncrasies, the universal stages of life do influence our political orientations, true to Guizot's words. And like many other facets of our political nature, these life cycle shifts have deep evolutionary roots. 14

VOCABULARY/USING A DICTIONARY

1. What is an *adage* (para. 1)?
2. What is the *limbic system* (para. 10)?
3. What part of speech is *apt* (para. 13)? What does it mean?

RESPONDING TO WORDS IN CONTEXT

1. When Tuschman suggests that the 1960s were *turbulent* (para. 4), what does that indicate about the time period?
2. If something is altered *subtly* (para. 8), how is it altered?
3. If the fact that young people preferred Reagan over Mondale suggests they were *anomalously* conservative (para. 12), what does that mean about that group?

DISCUSSING MAIN POINT AND MEANING

1. What does research reveal about the brains of people in their twenties?
2. What does that change in the twenties suggest will happen to their preferences politically?
3. What other life event does Tuschman suggest pushes young people, usually in their thirties, from left to right?

EXAMINING SENTENCES, PARAGRAPHS, AND ORGANIZATION

1. Is Tuschman's opening effective? How does he begin his essay?
2. How does Tuschman identify himself as an expert on his topic from the outset of his essay?
3. Does Tuschman argue from a place of certainty, or does he leave room for doubt and reconsideration?

THINKING CRITICALLY

1. Why do you think having children might push someone to the right, politically? What does it offer that a parent might appreciate?
2. Do you think younger people are always more idealistic than older people? Explain your answer.
3. How are millennials different from or similar to the young people of the 1960s?

WRITING ACTIVITIES

1. "Don't trust anyone over thirty." Consider this famous slogan from the 1960s, and write a short report about the difference between younger and older people in the 1960s.
2. How are your political leanings different, if they are, from those of the person or people who raised you? In a brief personal essay, explain how their political ideology may have influenced you, if at all. Respect the privacy of anyone you write about in this essay, and obtain their permission to do so.
3. Tuschman explains the political evolution from one's twenties to one's thirties. What shifts might take place from childhood and adolescence to one's twenties? What about from one's thirties to forties and beyond? Speculate on what this political evolution might look like in areas Tuschman hasn't explored.

Angel Diaz (student essay)

How the Overton Window Theory Explains Today's Extreme Political Rhetoric

[*The Reporter*, Miami Dade College, February 22, 2019]

No one doubts that today's political discourse is especially nasty and divisive. The extreme rhetoric can be seen and heard everywhere: on TV news, talk radio, blogs and websites, the daily papers, and especially all over social media. But why is this happening and why does it appear to be getting progressively worse? In "How the Overton Window Theory Explains Today's Extreme Political Rhetoric," Miami Dade student columnist Angel Diaz suggests that a popular theory of media and discourse can explain how a generally accepted political attitude can shift to an extreme position. "What should be considered absurd," she argues, "is now viewed as normal."

Angel Diaz is a student attending Miami Dade College in Florida.

BEFORE YOU READ

Diaz asks the question, "How is it that campaigns have turned into dogfights and extreme rhetoric has become acceptable?" Do you agree with this perception of American politics, and do you have an answer?

WORDS TO LEARN

partisan (para. 2): partial to a particular group or party (adjective)
infamous (para. 3): known for a very bad reputation (adjective)
methodology (para. 4): set of guiding principles (noun)
nuances (para. 5): subtle variations (noun)
reversible (para. 10): capable of changing direction (adjective)
reform (para. 11): to change the state of something (verb)

The American political system was created in 1789 after the establishment of the United States Constitution. Since then, the political game has devolved into a whirlwind of conspiracy theories and foul play. 1

Early political campaigns were mostly divided along partisan lines with debates on which ways the government should be conducted. However, we now find ourselves in the 21st century, when party ideas and norms mean almost nothing in politics. What should be considered 2 absurd is now viewed as normal. How is it that campaigns have turned into dogfights and extreme rhetoric has become acceptable?

Because of Donald J. Trump and Hillary Clinton's presidential cam- 3
paigns, 2016 has gone down in history as an infamous election year. Not because of the astounding policy debates, but because of the overabundance of hearsay and the promotion of scandals and conspiracy theories that circulated around both candidates.

It is important to note that both candidates were not subjected 4
to these scandals and theories by the media, but rather by each other. Now-President Trump's radical methodology enables him to present his extreme decisions in what proves to be an effective manner. More telling than his constant misconduct and banter with other politicians is the fact that he has made the impossible possible when it comes to the norms of political campaigns.

The 2016 election was an enormous spectacle of child's play. With 5
widespread media coverage that only fueled the egos of Trump and Clinton's campaigns, both candidates in their debates departed from conventional professionalism. Both individuals were found to go over time, speaking overturn, uttering to spite the other, and figuratively clawing at each other.

With the formality established in early American history gone, 6
these campaigns have become a boxing ring of words where purposeful declarations and action plans are absolute.

From calling former Secretary of State Hillary Clinton's email scandal 7
"worse than Watergate" to demanding a paid-off version of the Great Wall of China on the southern border of the U.S., Trump's actions would have been considered immoral and disrespectful in earlier stages of American politics. Now it has become normal. Why is this now normal and why did the public and the debate moderators allow this conduct to continue?

In political science there is a theory that explains how the shifting 8
of what the public considers normal is possible. The Overton window theory[1] states that there is a window, an imaginary box, set in the middle of the left and right wings that establishes what the public views as normal and is willing to accept.

The theory suggests that in order to make the far left or far right 9
seem normal, one would have to start by making every extreme seem normal. President Trump has used this theory to paint his more radical notions as normal by demanding unthinkable legislation. Throughout his presidency, the Overton window has only moved farther and farther

---

[1] A theory developed by Joseph P. Overton (1960–2003) to explain how the boundaries of political discourse are established. [Ed.]

to the right, making everything to the far right seem less radical. This expansion of the political spectrum could also be seen when former President Barack Obama declared support for same-sex marriage and helped make the concept more acceptable to an American public that disapproved of it just years before.[2]

The media has now fostered a problem that might not be reversible. By reporting what was once radical as usual and what was once normal as radical, the media has moved the window farther to the right. This might mean that the Democratic party will in turn be considered radical and unthinkable. 10

It seems that President Trump aims to make things easier for the Republican Party as they move forward. This is not wrong in any way. But it does, however, make things more difficult for those who seek to reform the country. 11

With the 2020 elections looming over the nation, the Overton window finds itself situated in the middle of the right wing. Of course, the upcoming catfights will pull the window toward a favored party, but if Trump wins the presidency again, what incredible views will become the next normal? 12

VOCABULARY/USING A DICTIONARY

1. What is a *conspiracy*?
2. What is a *norm*? Is it a different word or the same as *normal*?
3. How would you define the word *hearsay*, based on the definitions of the two words that make it up?

RESPONDING TO WORDS IN CONTEXT

1. What is an example of *extreme rhetoric*? How might the author define *extreme rhetoric*?
2. How does media coverage *fuel the ego*? What is another way to say that?
3. If the Overton window under Obama made same-sex marriage more *plausible*, what was the general consensus on gay marriage at that time?

DISCUSSING MAIN POINT AND MEANING

1. Who, according to Diaz, is responsible for the scandals and conspiracy theories around the Trump and Clinton campaigns?
2. What is the Overton window? Explain it in your own words.

---

[2] For how public acceptance of same-sex marriage has evolved over the years, see Aamer Madhani's "Poll: Approval of Same-Sex Marriage in U.S. Reaches New High" on p. 313. [Ed.]

3. Where does Diaz place Trump on the political spectrum? How does this affect the Overton window?

EXAMINING SENTENCES, PARAGRAPHS, AND ORGANIZATION

1. What is the effect of Diaz's metaphors and figurative language on the reader's understanding of the argument—campaigns that turn into *dogfights* or campaigns that are a *boxing ring*? Do these uses work in the context of the essay? Can you find other examples?
2. Do you like the effect of ending an essay on a question? Why or why not? What do you like/dislike about Diaz's choice?
3. Why does Diaz begin with mention of the U.S. Constitution in paragraph 1? Why not just start with paragraph 2?

THINKING CRITICALLY

1. Did you watch the Clinton/Trump debates? Do you agree with Diaz's observation that both candidates "were found to go over time, speaking overturn, uttering nuances to spite the other, and figuratively clawing at each other"? Does Diaz provide support for this claim?
2. **Connect:** Why does Diaz call Trump's comments and actions "immoral and disrespectful" in light of earlier political norms? How would Gershon respond to this claim?
3. Is this article biased or unbiased? On what examples do you base your answer? Does Diaz bring in examples from both parties to explain the Overton window and the American public's experience of extreme rhetoric?

WRITING ACTIVITIES

1. Election debates always come under scrutiny: Who won? Why? What was the effect of each candidate on the viewers, and how did they answer their questions? Ask students to analyze another presidential debate (one that received a lot of press attention at the time was the John F. Kennedy/Richard Nixon debate). Have them consider the approach and medium of a particular debate with a summary of the candidates and the time period. Diaz says of Clinton and Trump, "Both individuals were found to go over time, speaking overturn, uttering nuances to spite the other, and figuratively clawing at each other." What do they notice about the rhetoric of the debate they've chosen?
2. The claim is made in this article that the "incredible" and the "immoral" is becoming the norm under Trump, with the Democratic Party becoming "unthinkable." What do you think of these descriptions of the norm in politics? Do they ring true—or not? Why? In a short essay, explain why you agree or disagree with this take on current American politics.

3. Research "Overton window" on the Web and draw a diagram that shows how it works with a specific example. What do people believe and say about climate change, for example, or health care? Try to find a hot-button topic and diagram how the window is working. Write as many "acceptable" or "normal" ideas and reactions to policy on these topics as you can. In class, try to find someone who has chosen the same topic or a similar one to yours and discuss your findings. Present these to the class.

LOOKING CLOSELY

The Art of Argument: Using a Theory to Make Your Point

In the Introduction, the section "How to Support Opinions" (p. 15) covers some of the ways writers use various forms of evidence and examples to bolster their arguments. One way to back up our contentions or observations about an issue is to show that they can be explained by a credible theory. For instance, a writer may explain certain kinds of behavior by citing various standard psychoanalytic, cognitive, or developmental theories. In Angel Diaz's "How the Overton Window Theory Explains Today's Extreme Political Rhetoric," the Miami Dade student columnist suggests that a well-known theory can help explain why recent political discussion and debate has become so abnormally extreme.

Note that Diaz does not begin with the theory, but builds up to it by citing various examples of extreme discourse. After a sufficient number of examples and questions, Diaz then introduces the main point: the Overton window theory helps explain what has caused the recent outbursts of extreme rhetoric in our political discourse.

1
Cites today's excesses

(1) How is it that campaigns have turned into dogfights and extreme rhetoric has become acceptable?

2
Asks why this is now normal

(2) Why is this now normal and why did the public and the debate moderators allow this conduct to continue?

3
A theory explains it

(3) In political science there is a theory that explains how the shifting of what the public considers normal is possible.

The Hidden Tribes of America

America's Seven Political Tribes

[The Hidden Tribes of America Project, October 2018]

Most recent polls and research studies confirm America's growing polarization. In fact, a June 2018 Rasmussen poll indicated such a level of polarization that 31 percent of voters thought a second Civil War was likely in the next five years. But one recent survey, though it did find a deeply divided nation, concluded that America is not as hopelessly split apart as many people believe. The Hidden Tribes of America project surveyed in depth more than 8,000 citizens to measure the extent of the nation's polarization. The report is too long for this chapter, but the most salient information appears in the following excerpt. According to the survey, the data tells a "very different story than the tale of a deeply polarized America, split into two camps locked in a fight, determined to crush each other."

According to its Web site, The Hidden Tribes of America "is a year-long project launched by More in Common [in late 2018] to better understand the forces that drive political polarization and tribalism in the United States today, and to galvanize efforts to address them. The Hidden Tribes of America study forms the initial phase of the project."

POLARIZATION

America has never felt so divided. Bitter debates that were once confined to Congressional hearings and cable TV have now found their way into every part of our lives, from our Facebook feeds to the family dinner table. But most Americans are tired of this "us-versus-them" mindset and are eager to find common ground. This is the message we've heard from more than 8,000 Americans in one of our country's largest-ever studies of polarization: We hold dissimilar views on many issues. However, more than three in four Americans also believe that our differences aren't so great that we can't work together. 1

A NATION DIVIDED

Our research concludes that we have become a set of tribes, with different codes, values, and even facts. In our public debates, it seems that we no longer just disagree. We reject each other's premises and doubt each other's motives. We question each other's character. We block our 2 ears to diverse perspectives. At home, polarization is souring personal relationships, ruining Thanksgiving dinners, and driving families apart.

3 We are experiencing these divisions in our workplaces, neighborhood groups, even our places of worship. In the media, pundits score points, mock opponents, and talk over each other. On the Internet, social media has become a hotbed of outrage, takedowns, and cruelty — often targeting total strangers.

4 But this can change. A majority of Americans, whom we've called the "**Exhausted Majority**," are fed up by America's polarization. They know we have more in common than that which divides us: our belief in freedom, equality, and the pursuit of the American dream. They share a deep sense of gratitude that they are citizens of the United States. They want to move past our differences.

5 Turning the tide of tribalism is possible — but it won't be easy. Americans have real differences and real disagreements with each other. We must be able to listen to each other to understand those differences and find common ground. That's the focus of the Hidden Tribes project: to understand better what is pulling us apart, and find what can bring us back together.

HOW WE GOT HERE

6 Today's polarization reflects a perfect storm: Unsettling changes in our economy and society have left many Americans feeling like strangers in their own land. Old certainties are gone. The secure job, the growing wage, and the safety of neighborhood life where everyone knew each other — these all feel like relics of a bygone era. It feels as though hard work is no longer rewarded, and the gap between rich and poor widens every year.

7 Many Americans wonder who and what they can still trust. The institutions that once bound us are disappearing, and we no longer seem to have each other's backs. Everyone appears to have a varying version of world events, and it feels harder than ever to sort fact from fiction. Our news feeds seem to just echo our own views, and when people post

Which of the following statements do you agree with more?

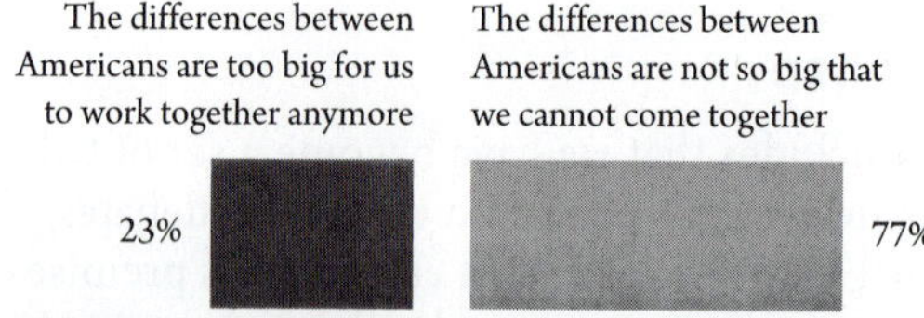
The differences between Americans are too big for us to work together anymore
The differences between Americans are not so big that we cannot come together
23%
77%

Hidden Tribes, More in Common (2018)

alternative opinions they are often attacked by angry mobs. We don't seem to disagree anymore without perceiving another person's views as stupid, wrong or even evil. We're being played off each other; and told to see each other as threats and enemies, not Americans just like us but with separate experiences and views. The loudest and most extreme voices get heard, and others just feel like tuning out altogether.

Nobody wants simply to turn the clocks back, because there was a 8
lot that wasn't right about the world of the past. Today, we seem more fractured and fragmented than anyone can remember. Instead of helping us find solutions to move us all forward, politics is driving us apart.

When people don't understand each other, they can't converse or 9
find common ground. Yet somehow, if we could only press a "reset" button, it feels like things could be different and we could move forward together as a country.

AMERICA'S HIDDEN TRIBES

America is not split into two tribes, as we're sometimes told. In fact, 10
we've identified seven distinct groups of Americans. These are our Hidden Tribes of America: distinguished not by who they are or what they look like, but what they believe.

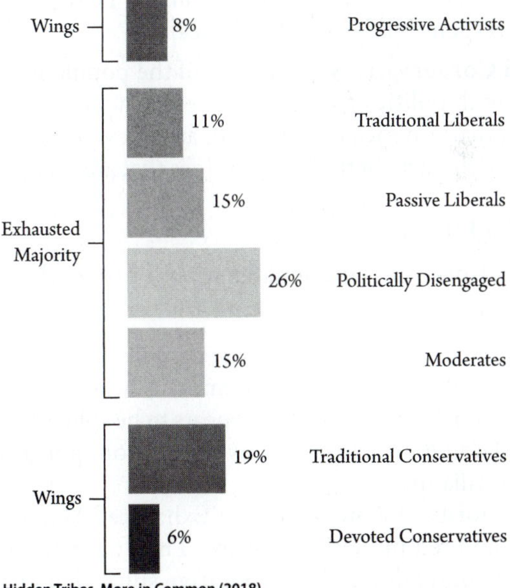

Hidden Tribes, More in Common (2018)

Here's a quick snapshot of each group: 11

Progressive Activists (8 percent of the population) are deeply concerned with issues concerning equity, fairness, and America's direction today. They tend to be more secular, cosmopolitan, and highly engaged with social media.

Traditional Liberals (11 percent of the population) tend to be cautious, rational, and idealistic. They value tolerance and compromise. They place great faith in institutions.

Passive Liberals (15 percent of the population) tend to feel isolated from their communities. They are insecure in their beliefs and try to avoid political conversations. They have a fatalistic view of politics and feel that the circumstances of their lives are beyond their control.

The Politically Disengaged (26 percent of the population) are untrusting, suspicious about external threats, conspiratorially minded, and pessimistic about progress. They tend to be patriotic yet detached from politics.

Moderates (15 percent of the population) are engaged in their communities, well informed, and civic-minded. Their faith is often an important part of their lives. They shy away from extremism of any sort.

Traditional Conservatives (19 percent of the population) tend to be religious, patriotic, and highly moralistic. They believe deeply in personal responsibility and self-reliance.

Devoted Conservatives (6 percent of the population) are deeply engaged with politics and hold strident, uncompromising views. They feel that America is embattled, and they perceive themselves as the last defenders of traditional values that are under threat.

OUR SHARED FUTURE

The Hidden Tribes study illuminates several new findings regarding America's past, present, and future. 12

- The American electorate is more complex than the oversimplified story of polarization would make us believe.
- The reason American society appears to be split 50/50 is that the loudest and most extreme viewpoints monopolize airtime and social media space.
- The majority of Americans, the Exhausted Majority, are frustrated and fed up with tribalism. They want to return to the mutual good faith and collaborative spirit that characterize a healthy democracy.

- Being able to discuss our genuine disagreements remains important. At the root of those disagreements are differences in **core beliefs** — the underlying psychological architecture that governs what we value and how we see the world.
- While our differences are often rooted in divergent views, that does not mean we cannot find common ground.
- By acknowledging and respecting the values that animate our beliefs, we can begin to restore a sense of respect and unity.
- The vast majority of Americans — three out of four — believe our differences are not so great that we cannot come together. Let's make that a reality.

POINTS TO CONSIDER

1. How would you describe the central purpose of the Hidden Tribes of America project? What is the project intended to disclose about the nation?
2. Why do you think they term most Americans the "Exhausted Majority"? What do these Americans have in common?
3. In paragraph 7, the report says, "We're being played off each other, and told to see each other as threats and enemies, not Americans just like us but with separate experiences and views." The report doesn't say, but who do you think is playing us off each other? Why do you think the report doesn't blame anyone or any group in particular for the polarization?
4. Although the report seems to take a politically neutral stance, do you think — based on your previous knowledge and the readings in this chapter — that it would appeal more to liberal or conservative-minded individuals? Explain why, using specific points and language from the report.

AMERICA THEN . . . 1787

Benjamin Franklin

I Agree to This Constitution, with All Its Faults

On May 25, 1787, a large group of Americans assembled in Philadelphia to create a form of government that would guide a brand-new nation into its very uncertain future. On September 17, they met to sign the document that would become the Constitution of the United States. It is amazing that in an age without a single modern convenience, without any of the technology we depend on today, when the primary implement of communication was a quill pen and most travel depended on horses and favorable winds, that the final draft of the most important political document in modern world history was produced in under seventeen weeks. But it wasn't produced easily or without bitter discussion and some hard-fought compromises that still cause partisan dissension. That the framers themselves were well aware of these issues can be seen in the following speech the feeble, eighty-one-year-old Benjamin Franklin asked a colleague to read just before the delegates signed the document he publicly acknowledged was far from perfect.

One of the nation's iconic figures, Benjamin Franklin (1706–1790) was an ingenious inventor, a prolific essayist, an astute entrepreneur, and a farsighted statesman. He was also one of the nation's first humorists; when signing the Declaration of Independence, he apparently quipped, realizing the terrible risk his inadequate colonies took in revolting against England: "We must, indeed, all hang together, or assuredly we shall all hang separately." Thomas Jefferson claimed that Franklin was asked only to help draft the Constitution because if he had written the entire document, he could not have resisted adding a few jokes. Born into a large, impoverished Boston family, Franklin left for Philadelphia as a teenager to make his fortune, and he became one of the earliest examples of the classic American rags-to-riches story, a persistent national myth he helped create. For many reasons, he is often considered the "first American."

BEFORE YOU READ

Do you think the signers of the Constitution should have signed off on it if they thought it was flawed? What do you make of Franklin's argument if he were signing off on an important and lasting document today?

WORDS TO LEARN

sect (para. 2): a group or faction under a particular leader (noun)
dispute (para. 2): argument or debate (noun)
despotic (para. 2): relating to a despot (oppressor) (adjective)
salutary (para. 4): healthful (adjective)
posterity (para. 4): the people who will follow the current generation (noun)
endeavor (para. 4): strivings (noun)

MR. PRESIDENT

I confess that there are several parts of this constitution which I do not at present approve, but I am not sure I shall never approve them: For having lived long, I have experienced many instances of being obliged by better information, or fuller consideration, to change 1 opinions even on important subjects, which I once thought right, but found to be otherwise. It is therefore that the older I grow, the more apt I am to doubt my own judgment, and to pay more respect to the judgment of others. Most men indeed as well as most sects in Religion, think themselves in possession of all truth, and that wherever others differ from them it is so far error. Steele[1] a Protestant in a Dedication tells the Pope, that the only difference between our Churches in their opinions of the certainty of their doctrines is, the Church of Rome is infallible and the Church of England is never in the wrong. But though many private persons think almost as highly of their own infallibility as of that of their sect, few express it so naturally as a certain french lady, who in a dispute with her sister, said "I don't know how it happens, Sister but I meet with no body but myself, that's always in the right — *Il n'y a que moi qui a toujours raison.*"

In these sentiments, Sir, I agree to this Constitution with all its faults, if they are such; because I think a general Government necessary for us, and there is no form of Government but what may be a blessing to the people if well administered, and believe farther that this is likely to be well administered for a course of years, and can only end in Despotism, as other forms have done before it, when the people shall become so corrupted as to need despotic Government, being incapable of any other. 2

I doubt too whether any other Convention we can obtain, may be able to make a better Constitution. For when you assemble a number of men to have the advantage of their joint wisdom, you inevitably assemble with those men, all their prejudices, their passions, their errors of opinion, their local interests, and their selfish views. From such an assembly can a perfect production be expected? It therefore astonishes me, Sir, to find this system approaching so near to perfection as it does; and I think it will astonish our enemies, who are waiting with confidence to hear that our councils are confounded like those of the Builders of Babel; and that our States are on the point of separation, only to meet hereafter for the purpose of cutting one another's throats. 3

Thus I consent, Sir, to this Constitution because I expect no better, and because I am not sure, that it is not the best. The opinions I have had of its errors, I sacrifice to the public good. I have never whispered a syllable of them abroad. Within these walls they were born, and here they shall die. If every one of us in returning to our Constituents were to report the objections he has had to it, and endeavor to gain partizans 4

[1] Richard Steele (1672–1729), Irish political figure who also was one of England's most esteemed essayists.

in support of them, we might prevent its being generally received, and thereby lose all the salutary effects & great advantages resulting naturally in our favor among foreign Nations as well as among ourselves, from our real or apparent unanimity. Much of the strength & efficiency of any Government in procuring and securing happiness to the people, depends, on opinion, on the general opinion of the goodness of the Government, as well as of the wisdom and integrity of its Governors. I hope therefore that for our own sakes as a part of the people, and for the sake of posterity, we shall act heartily and unanimously in recommending this Constitution (if approved by Congress & confirmed by the Conventions) wherever our influence may extend, and turn our future thoughts & endeavors to the means of having it well administered.

On the whole, Sir, I can not help expressing a wish that every mem- 5
ber of the Convention who may still have objections to it, would with me, on this occasion doubt a little of his own infallibility, and to make manifest our unanimity, put his name to the instrument.

VOCABULARY/USING A DICTIONARY

1. What does it mean to be *fallible*? What about *infallible* (para. 1)?
2. How would you define *procuring* (para. 4)? What does it mean to *procure* something?
3. What is the difference between *unanimity* (para. 4) and *unanimously* (para. 4)?

RESPONDING TO WORDS IN CONTEXT

1. What is the difference between *infallible* (para. 1) and *infallibility* (para. 1)? What parts of speech are they?
2. What does Franklin mean when he says "in these *sentiments*" (para. 2)? How would you define *sentiments*? Is there another definition of *sentiment*? Are there other words that share this root?
3. What is the meaning of *confounded* (para. 3) in this text?

DISCUSSING MAIN POINT AND MEANING

1. Why does Franklin agree to the Constitution, even if he feels it's flawed?
2. What surprises him about the Constitution as it stands, and why?
3. What does Franklin ask of the others who must ratify the Constitution?

EXAMINING SENTENCES, PARAGRAPHS, AND ORGANIZATION

1. What makes Franklin's opening sentences unusual? Did they surprise you? Why?

2. Why might Franklin's discussion of the church be important in a document such as this in this particular time period?
3. How would you describe the movement of Franklin's thinking from the beginning to the end of his letter to the president? What is the focus of the beginning? What is the focus of the ending?

THINKING CRITICALLY

1. Does Franklin believe that the men assembled at the Constitutional Convention are wise men? Explain your answer.
2. In his opening paragraph, Franklin cites the Protestant British essayist Richard Steele, who says in a dedication to the Catholic pope that "the only difference between our Churches in their opinions of the certainty of their doctrines is, the Church of Rome is infallible and the Church of England is never in the wrong." What do you think Steele meant by this statement? Try putting it in your own words. What is Franklin's purpose in citing it?
3. Franklin writes to the president: "For having lived long, I have experienced many instances of being obliged by better information, or fuller consideration, to change opinions even on important subjects, which I once thought right, but found to be otherwise. It is therefore that the older I grow, the more apt I am to doubt my own judgment, and to pay more respect to the judgment of others" (para. 1). Why do you think Franklin begins this way? What purpose does it serve? In what ways are these remarks both humorous and serious?

WRITING ACTIVITIES

1. Write a letter to the president. In it, address a policy that you think is made by flawed people presenting the best idea possible. Or address a policy that is made by people who know best and are infallible, and explain why the policy should be rethought, with other opinions entertained.
2. Research this period in history. Write a short report on the discussions had by the framers of the Constitution, with a focus on Benjamin Franklin's position. What were some of the difficulties they faced? How did they approach the Constitution? What was at stake for the signers?
3. Read the U.S. Constitution and write a summary of what you find there. Also discuss the purpose of the document and include a paragraph of your opinion of it.

Discussing the Unit

SUGGESTED TOPIC FOR DISCUSSION

In American politics, is "partisan" a bad word? How do Americans conduct themselves politically, and is their partisanship becoming more or less common?

PREPARING FOR CLASS DISCUSSION

1. Why do we respond as we do to political issues? What would it take to change our opinions about an issue? What is meant by "partisan politics"?
2. What difficulties does partisanship create in our country? What would it mean to be nonpartisan? Are there any descriptions or examples of nonpartisan behavior or politics in any of the essays in this unit?

FROM DISCUSSION TO WRITING

1. What are some of the issues facing the country today, and would you describe them as partisan? Consider two or three of the texts in this chapter and explain how the writers view partisanship and the American political system.
2. Do you think your politicians do their jobs well? Are they civil in their dealings with each other and the world? Are their decisions based in partisanship or in something else? Why or why not? Which authors in this chapter would agree with you?

TOPICS FOR CROSS-CULTURAL DISCUSSION

1. Avi Tuschman begins his essay by quoting a famous saying: "If you're not a liberal when you're 20, you have no heart. If you're not a conservative by the time you're 30, you have no brain." He goes on to say that the statement has been attributed to many people; the names he mentions are all Americans or Europeans. Do you think the saying can be applied to people all over the globe — that it would be true of young people no matter what nation or culture they belong to?
2. Has partisanship changed since this country's inception? Since the Civil War? Since Civil Rights and the Sexual Revolution? Explain your answer using two or more of the texts in this chapter to support your answer.

Continued from page ii

William C. Anderson. "Solidarity Abolishes Borders." Truthout, November 17, 2018. https://truthout.org/articles/solidarity-abolishes-borders/. Reprinted by permission.

José Azel. "Patriotism vs. Nationalism." *PanAm Post*, November 1, 2018. Reprinted by permission.

Rosalind Bentley. "Southerners Less Supportive of Confederate Flag, New Poll Finds." From *The Atlanta Journal-Constitution*, December 18, 2018. Copyright © 2018 The Atlanta Journal-Constitution. All rights reserved. Used under license.

Judy Brady. "I Want a Wife." *Ms.* magazine, 1972. Copyright © 1970 by Judy Syfers. Reprinted by permission of the author.

Megan Brenan. "Ten Takeaways about Americans' View of Guns." Republished with permission of Gallup Press, from Gallup, May 2, 2018. Copyright © 2018 Gallup, Inc.; permission conveyed through Copyright Clearance Center, Inc.

Jonah Engel Bromwich. "Tell Us What to Call the Generation after Millennials (Please)." From *The New York Times*, January 23, 2018. Copyright © 2018 The New York Times. All rights reserved. Used under license.

Danny Bugingo. "A Need for Safe Spaces." *The University of Idaho Argonaut*, December 4, 2017. Reprinted by permission.

Matthew Bulger. "What Makes an American?" *Humanist*, July 2, 2015. Reprinted by permission.

Charles Carr. "Reinstate the Fairness Doctrine!" *Times Advocate* (Escondido, California), December 28, 2018. Reprinted by permission of the author.

Mona Charen. "No Names." *Townhall*, February 15, 2018. By permission of Mona Charen and Creators Syndicate.

Brittney Christ. "We Should Be Allowed to Protect Ourselves." *State Hornet*, June 25, 2015. Copyright © 2015 by Brittney Christ. Reprinted by permission of the author.

Jonette Christian. "Is Patriotism Obsolete?" Pressherald.com, December 20, 2017. Reprinted by permission of the author.

Julie Compton. "'Boy or Girl?' Parents Raising 'Theybies' Let Their Kids Decide." NBCnews (features), July 19, 2018. Reprinted by permission of NBCUniversal News Group, a division of NBCUniversal Media, LLC.

Michele de Cuneo. "Violence in the Virgin Islands." Excerpted from Michele de Cuneo's "Letter on the Second Voyage [of Christopher Columbus]," October 28, 1495, translated by Elissa Weaver. Copyright © 1999. Reprinted by permission of Elissa Weaver.

Robin DiAngelo. "White America's Racial Illiteracy: Why Our National Conversation Is Poisoned from the Start" (original title: "White Fragility: Why It's So Hard to Talk to White People about Racism"). *The Good Men Project*, April 9, 2015. Copyright © 2015 by Robin DiAngelo, PhD.

Angel Diaz. "How the Overton Window Theory Explains Today's Extreme Political Rhetoric." Originally published as "Extreme Rhetoric Normalizes Intense Policies," *The Reporter* (the student newspaper at Miami Dade College), February 22, 2019. Reprinted by permission of Angel Diaz.

Francie Diep. "Why Did We Ever Call Undocumented Immigrants 'Aliens'?" *Pacific Standard*, August 12, 2015. Copyright © 2015 The Social Justice Foundation. Reprinted by permission.

Thomas J. Donohue. "Putting the 'Civil' Back into Civil Society." *The Weekly Standard*, July 9/16, 2018. Reprinted by permission of Weekly Standard LLC.

Sarah Elliott. "Women: Stop Apologizing, Be Confident." *The Graphic*, October 28, 2015. Copyright © 2015. Reprinted by permission of *The Graphic*, the student newspaper of Pepperdine University.

Adison Eyring. "A Narrowing Definition of Gender Marginalizes Trans, Intersex Communities." *The Daily Cougar*, October 29, 2018. Reprinted by permission.

Saadia Faruqi. "Cut from the Same Cloth." *The Texas Observer*, June 2017. Reprinted by permission.

Ryan Fawwaz. "Seeking Truth Is Intertwined with Journalistic Advocacy." *The Daily Trojan*, May 16, 2018. Reprinted by permission.

Suzanne Fields. "Submerged in a Din of Identity Politics." *Townhall*, July 27, 2018. By permission of Suzanne Fields and Creators Syndicate.

Eric Foner. "Birthright Citizenship Is the Good Kind of American Exceptionalism." From *The Nation*, September 14–21, 2015. Copyright © 2015 The Nation Company. All rights reserved. Used under license.

John A. Fry. "Allowing More Guns Won't Make Campuses Safer." *Philadelphia Inquirer*, October 19, 2015. Copyright © 2015. Reprinted by permission of the author.

Ernest B. Furgurson. "The End of History?" Reprinted from *The American Scholar*, Vol. 84, No. 4, Autumn 2015. Copyright © 2015 by the author. Reprinted by permission.

Paul Fussell. "A Well-Regulated Militia." From *Thank God for the Atom Bomb and Other Essays* by Paul Fussell (Summit Books, 1988). Reprinted by permission.

Livia Gershon. "Should Politics Be Civil?" *Daily Jstor*, July 9, 2018. Reprinted by permission of the author.

Dahleen Glanton. "Stop Saying We Can't Do Anything to Stop Mass Shootings. We Can." From *Chicago Tribune*, February 19, 2018. Copyright © 2018 Chicago Tribune. All rights reserved. Used under license.

Annette Gordon-Reed. "America's Original Sin: Slavery and the Legacy of White Supremacy." Republished with permission of the Council on Foreign Relations from *Foreign Affairs*, January/February 2018. Copyright © 2018 Council on Foreign Relations; permission conveyed through Copyright Clearance Center, Inc.

Roshae Hemmings. "Burning Shoes to #BoycottNike Won't Change That Fact That Kaepernick and His Kneeling Aren't Going Anywhere." *The Maneater* (Missouri University), September 10, 2018. Reprinted by permission.

Langston Hughes. "That Word *Black*." From *The Return of Simple* by Langston Hughes, edited by Akiba Sullivan Harper. Copyright © 1994 by Ramona Bass and Arnold Rampersad. Reprinted by permission of Hill and Wang, a division of Farrar, Straus & Giroux.

Tom Jacobs. "Patriotic Americans Are Pro-Immigration." *Pacific Standard*, July 24, 2018. Copyright © 2018 The Social Justice Foundation. Reprinted by permission.

Gish Jen. "Identity 101." *Washington Post Magazine*, October 29, 2017. Copyright © 2017 by Gish Jen. Reprinted by permission of The Friedrich Agency.

Wendy Kaminer. "A Civic Duty to Annoy." First published in the *Atlantic* (September 1997). Copyright © 1997 by Wendy Kaminer. Reprinted by permission of the author.

Knight Foundation. "Eight Ways College Student Views on Free Speech Are Evolving." Medium.com, March 12, 2018. Reprinted by permission of the Knight Foundation.

Laila Lalami. "Blending In." From *The New York Times Magazine*, August 6, 2017. Copyright © 2017 The New York Times. All rights reserved. Used under license.

Aamer Madhani. "Poll: Approval of Same-Sex Marriage in U.S. Reaches New High." From *USA Today*, May 23, 2018. Copyright © 2018 Gannett-USA Today. All rights reserved. Used under license.

Dawn Lundy Martin. "Weary Oracle." *Harper's Magazine*, March 2016. Copyright © 2016 by Dawn Lundy Martin. Reprinted by permission of the author.

Elizabeth Aura McClintock. "The Psychology of Mansplaining." *Psychology Today*, March 31, 2016. Copyright © 2016 by Elizabeth Aura McClintock. Reprinted by permission of the author.

Dasia Moore. "When Does Renaming a Building Make Sense?" From *The Nation*, February 17, 2017. Copyright © 2017 The Nation Company. All rights reserved. Used under license.

More in Common. From "The Hidden Tribes of America, America's Seven Political Tribes." https://hiddentribes.us. Reprinted by permission of More in Common.

Alex Myers. "How #MeToo Taught Me I Can Never Be a Man." *Them*, November 26, 2017. Copyright © Conde Nast. Reprinted by permission.

Amanda Nelson. "Barbie Is Exploiting Frida Kahlo's Legacy." *Pasadena City College Courier*, March 27, 2018. Reprinted by permission of the author.

New York Times Editorial Board. "End the Gun Epidemic in America." From *The New York Times*, December 5, 2015. Copyright © 2015 The New York Times. All rights reserved. Used under license.

Michael I. Niman. "As Confederate Flags Fall, Columbus Statues Stand Tall." *The Public*, September 16, 2015. Copyright © 2015 Michael Niman. Reprinted by permission of the author.

Katha Pollitt. "Why Boys Don't Play with Dolls." *New York Times Magazine*, October 8, 1995. Reprinted by permission of the author.

Susan Power. "Native in the Twenty-First Century." *World Literature Today*, August 2017. Reprinted by permission of the author.

Princeton University James Madison Program in American Ideals and Institutions. "Think for Yourself: Some Thoughts and Advice for Our Students and All Students." https://jmp.princeton.edu/announcements/some-thoughts-and-advice-our-students-and-all-students. Reprinted by permission of the Princeton University James Madison Program in American Ideals and Institutions.

Claudia Rankine. "You and your partner go to see the film *The House We Live In* . . ." From *Citizen: An American Lyric*. Copyright © 2014 by Claudia Rankine. Reprinted with the permission of The Permissions Company, Inc., on behalf of Graywolf Press, Minneapolis, Minnesota, www.graywolfpress.org.

Scott Rasmussen. "The Immigration Mess." *Townhall*, June 28, 2018. By permission of Scott Rasmussen and Creators Syndicate.

Roxanne Roberts. "In the Middle." From *The Washington Post*, October 21, 2018. Copyright © 2018 The Washington Post. All rights reserved. Used under license.

Brent Staples. "Just Walk On By: Black Men and Public Spaces." Copyright © 1986 by Brent Staples. Reprinted by permission of the author.

Sravya Tadepalli. "My Name." Originally published on oregonhumanities.org, November 2018. Reprinted by permission.

Sylvia Taschka. "Trump-Hitler Comparisons Too Easy and Ignore the Murderous History." theconversation.com, March 12, 2018. Reprinted by permission of the author.

Jane Vincent Taylor. "New Law Makes Local Poet Nervous." *This Land*, Vol. 4, No. 3 (February 1, 2013). Copyright © 2013 by Jane Vincent Taylor. Reprinted by permission of the author.

Dorothy Thompson. "Mr. Welles and Mass Delusion." From *The New York Herald Tribune*, November 2, 1938. Copyright © 1938 The New York Times. All rights reserved. Used under license.

Avi Tuschman. "Political Evolution: Why Do Young Voters Lean Left? It's in the Genes." *Bloomberg Businessweek*, April 17, 2014. Reprinted by permission.

Tadeu Velloso. "Brown." *Portland Magazine*, Summer 2014. Copyright © 2014. Reprinted by permission of the author.

Suzanna Danuta Walters. "Why Can't We Hate Men?" *Washington Post*, June 8, 2018. Reprinted by permission of the author.

Chandra D. L. Waring. "Black and Biracial Americans Wouldn't Need to Code-Switch If We Lived in a Post-Racial Society." *The Conversation*, August 17, 2018. This article includes quotes from Chandra D. L. Waring, "'It's Like We Have an "In" Already': The Racial Capital of Black/White Biracial Americans," *DuBois Review*, Vol. 14, No. 1, Spring 2017. Reprinted by permission of the author.

Gene Weingarten. "Don't Use Your Words." From *The Washington Post*, October 29, 2017. Copyright © 2017 The Washington Post. All rights reserved. Used under license.

Wendy M. Williams and Stephen J. Ceci. "There Are No Good Alternatives to Free Speech on Campus." *Inside Higher Ed*, May 2, 2018. Reprinted by permission of the author.

Index of Authors and Titles